THE
ASTROLOGY
OF
YOU
AND
ME

ARIES
March 21–April 20

TAURUS
April 21–May 21

GEMINI
May 22–June 21

CANCER
June 22–July 22

LEO
July 23–August 23

VIRGO
August 24–
September 22

LIBRA
September 23–
October 22

SCORPIO
October 23–
November 21

SAGITTARIUS
November 22–
December 21

CAPRICORN
December 22–
January 20

AQUARIUS
January 21–
February 19

PISCES
February 20–
March 20

THE ASTROLOGY OF YOU AND ME

HOW TO UNDERSTAND AND IMPROVE EVERY RELATIONSHIP IN YOUR LIFE

GARY GOLDSCHNEIDER

Best-selling author of *The Secret Language of Birthdays*

QUIRK BOOKS
PHILADELPHIA

Copyright © 2009, 2018 by Gary Goldschneider

All rights reserved. No part of this book may be reproduced in any form without written permission from the publisher.

Library of Congress Cataloging in Publication Number: 2017951343

ISBN: 978-1-68369-042-9
Printed in the United States of America
Typeset in Brandon Grotesque, Berkeley, and Baskerville

Designed by Andie Reid
Illustrations by Camille Chew
Production management by John J. McGurk
Photograph on page 10 © 2009 by Louise Whelan

20   19   18   17   16

Quirk Books
215 Church Street
Philadelphia, PA 19106
quirkbooks.com

This book is dedicated to my seven children—
Andrew, Aron, Isak, Sara, Anton, Ariana,
and Isadora—who gave me my first real-life
lessons in psychology

TABLE OF CONTENTS

INTRODUCTION

One rainy afternoon in October 2007, I found myself once again in my hometown of Philadelphia and gave David Borgenicht, president and publisher of Quirk Books, a quick call to say I was in town. He immediately invited me over, and soon I was treading on the familiar cobblestone streets of Old City, ringing the doorbell of this unusual publishing house. Ushered in by a receptionist, I waited for David and was immediately attracted by the awards his Worst-Case Scenario books had won, which were framed and prominently displayed on the wall. David and I had never met, but we had been introduced through a mutual friend, Rick Lightstone, of the American Book Center in Amsterdam, where Rick and I both live. I was impressed by the cordial yet relaxed work atmosphere at Quirk. David welcomed me in and offered me a seat at a

Gary Goldschneider
Born: May 22
Sign: Gemini

long table in his conference room, across from library shelves containing a selection of books that included my own *Secret Language of Birthdays*.

Rick had suggested cooking up a new book project with David. As if reading my mind, David immediately encouraged me to share any ideas for my next full-length work. I mentioned a few that had been running around in my head, and after carefully noting them down, David jumped right in:

"I have an idea for a new book. It would be an astrology book about the other guy."

"The other guy?" I asked, puzzled.

"Yes," he replied. "You know, in the nineties it was all me-me-me. People were crazy about books that told them about themselves, and your *Secret Language of Birthdays* really locked into that trend. What I have in mind is a kind of astrological handbook that tells you how to approach other people by their astrological sign, essentially how to handle a Capricorn, Leo, Gemini, etc., in almost any area of life."

Six months later, in April 2008, David stopped to see me in Amsterdam on his way to the London Book Fair. Seated across from me at a table in Café Luxembourg on the Spui, he outlined the major sections of the book that he and his staff had fleshed out: Work, Love, and Friends and Family. Under each category were subheads like Libra Boss, Aquarius Lover, and Gemini Friend, and underneath each of those were another six subsections addressing such issues as Asking the Libra Boss for a Raise, Sex and the Aquarius Lover, and Borrowing Money from the Gemini Friend. The total number of words this project would entail—around 170,000 to 180,000—was daunting, but since each of the three Secret Language books had totaled about half a million words, we both knew I could do it.

I found—and still find—David's original idea a brilliant one. People today *are* more interested in the other person, and maybe just a tad less interested in themselves. Only later would I realize that this was the book I had always wanted to write and, in fact, had presented to publishers as my sun sign book. I felt it was time, at last, for another important book in this genre, one that had been curiously absent in this popular field since the 1960s and Linda Goodman's groundbreaking book *Sun Signs*. This dovetailing of our mutual ideas and interests has been a satisfying stimulus to writing this volume. I thank David and the entire staff at Quirk who have made our mutual creation such a wonderful experience. I do not think I have ever enjoyed writing a book as much as I have this one.

Gary Goldschneider
Amsterdam
November 2008

Aries

BIRTHDATE **MARCH 21–APRIL 20**

Aries is the first sign of the zodiac, representing cardinal fire and symbolizing the pure and highly intuitive energies of the sign. Since Mars is their ruling planet, Aries individuals tend to be forceful, aggressive, and insistent on getting their way and winning. Although often childlike and open, they can also be hard to reach emotionally and find it difficult to express their complex feelings. They dislike being analyzed and take the attitude "what you see is what you get" with regard to themselves.

Work

ARIES
March 21–April 20

The Aries Boss

Aries bosses are born leaders, so there will be little doubt as to their wishes concerning the direction the group should take. Explicit, clear, and demanding, these fiery individuals will ask for every ounce of commitment and energy their employees can muster, and then some. Because they are so comfortable in this role, they are eager to make decisions and see them implemented. True individuals, they naturally respect individuality in others and are surprisingly open to and even expectant of their employees acting on their own, once they understand what is expected of them.

Asking the Aries Boss for a Raise

Aries bosses will probably already have anticipated you in this regard. Most likely they will offer you a raise (if you deserve it) on their own without your even asking. However, this also implies that if you need to ask for a raise you will probably be turned down. Aries bosses enjoy being magnanimous, but only if it is warranted. They are particularly impressed by the dramatic deal you may have pulled off, one that gives new spark and direction to the group. Less impressed by steady or plodding behavior, they may overlook the faithful employee who has served without attracting notice.

Breaking Bad News to the Aries Boss

Make sure you wear your crash helmet. Aries bosses are likely to fly off the handle (don't rule out yelling, screaming, or throwing nearby objects) after an initial ominous silence. A deepening red complexion may be the second warning sign. Seismic outbursts are likely to last a few minutes but are usually gone, like summer storms, rather quickly. One alternative is simply to hand the Aries boss the disturbing report in writing and then make a quick retreat.

Arranging Travel and/or Entertainment for the Aries Boss

Aries bosses are very pleased when you arrange things exactly as they would have themselves and much less than pleased when you do not. Thus, getting to know their special desires and wishes is essential to your success. Since organization is not usually their strong suit, they may depend on you entirely to have things perfectly worked out. Keep

STRENGTHS

Inspiring
Dynamic
Trailblazing

WEAKNESSES

Unheeding
Stressed
Unaware

INTERACTIVE STYLE

Confrontational
Commanding
Blunt

in mind that they love the grand gesture and will spare no expense to make themselves look good. Particularly observant of that little touch that indicates your sensitivity to their preferences, Aries bosses would look favorably upon those who go the extra mile, so you would do well to alert the restaurant, hotel, or travel agent of your boss's preferences beforehand.

Decision-Making and the Aries Boss

Aries bosses naturally make all important decisions themselves, and usually without asking for your advice. That said, they like you to be decisive when it comes to your own decision-making—just hold your breath when they are faced with what you have done. Constantly in the act of making decisions and giving orders, Aries bosses will not tolerate insubordination or misunderstanding. Nor do they change their minds often. As a result, when faced with difficulties or failures, they are likely to pin the blame on you, pointing to what they perceive as your flexibility or weakness. Better to courageously implement their doctrines and gently remind them of their original orders when the going gets rough.

Impressing and/or Motivating the Aries Boss

The first step is getting your Aries boss's attention. This will be best accomplished not by periodic gentle memos but by a terse, well-thought-out plan that can quickly penetrate the Aries armor. This should be delivered when the two of you are alone, since taking the chance of embarrassing your Aries boss in front of coworkers is not advised. Do not try to butter up Aries bosses or deliver your spiel in a roundabout or subtle fashion; this will only make them more impatient. Once you have hurled your thunderbolt, it is best to leave them alone for a while, since they will get back to you when ready.

Making Proposals and/or Giving Presentations to the Aries Boss

With Aries bosses, it's best to keep it short and sweet. State your points/results at the beginning rather than saving them until the end. Itemize your main points in a list of no more than five items. Do not be afraid to state the problems inherent in your plan and do not minimize the expense and effort involved. Aries bosses are attracted by challenge, and it is often the improbable or even impossible that rouses their fighting energies. Make sure that plenty of room is left for their personal involvement, without which the proposal could not succeed. Since their irritation factor is often high, try to dress in muted or neutral colors and styles.

The Aries Employee

Despite their strong independent streak, Aries employees are very good at following rules and taking direction from their superiors. At the same time, they will spot the mistakes of their superiors immediately and also see the shortcomings and loopholes in their plans. Usually they keep quiet about such matters until one day, perhaps provoked or unjustly accused of making a mistake, they will trot out the full list of unfair and incorrect demands that have been placed on them. Expect that Aries employees will come up with suggestions to change things, but usually only if they feel the group or boss is open to them.

Interviewing and/or Hiring the Aries Employee

The Aries interviewee is looking for a clear, well-defined task to perform, without ambiguities or overly imaginative demands. Interviewing and hiring an Aries will be most successful if it is done in a straightforward fashion. It is particularly important to hold back on the sauces and salad dressing, since false or misleading promises will not be forgotten. Do not mistake the Aries matter-of-fact attitude for lack of enthusiasm; new Aries employees are more than ready to lend their prodigious energies to the tasks at hand. Cheerful, upbeat settings are most effective to bring out the best in them.

Breaking Bad News to or Firing the Aries Employee

This can be a tough one to deal with because when Aries think they have been doing a good job it may be very hard to confront them with their failures. For many Aries, failure is the most difficult element of life to deal with. Furthermore, Aries employees often lack objectivity about themselves and their work, seeing only what they want or need to see. They should be prepared for bad news or firing gradually over a few weeks, if possible, to give them time to adjust and let the warning signs sink in. By all means, avoid taking sudden action against them since they may display equally sudden and tempestuous reactions, making things most unpleasant for all concerned.

Traveling with and Entertaining the Aries Employee

Although highly capable of living out of their suitcases on the road, most Aries employees do their best work in a secure, familiar setting. Although they are dynamic individuals in general, they can have difficulty adjusting to new, constantly changing situations, and they may become confused when traveling for prolonged periods, thus limiting their effectiveness. In matters of entertainment, Aries employees can be excellent organizers, setting up dinners, celebrations, and nights out on the town for colleagues, clients, and bosses. They are also particularly good at knowing what others like and, therefore, make excellent gift givers.

Assigning Tasks to the Aries Employee

As long as the task is well defined, there is usually no problem. Aries employees are very good at knowing what they don't like and letting you know about it beforehand. Therefore, they should be encouraged to tell you up front whether they feel they can carry out a given assignment without undue worry or stress. There are cases, however, in which Aries employees can be prodded or encouraged to accept a less-than-desirable task if their leader or boss is

STRENGTHS

Hard working

Energetic

Helpful

WEAKNESSES

Rebellious

Touchy

Unforgiving

INTERACTIVE STYLE

Honest

Faithful

Outspoken

sure they will like it once they get their feet wet. Such assignments are best given on a trial basis, where the Aries employee has the option to back out gracefully without blame attached.

Motivating or Impressing the Aries Employee

Money can be a strong motivating factor for the average Aries employee, who believes that if you are serious, you will put your money where your mouth is. Bonuses can be a strong incentive for motivating Aries employees. Due to their often prodigious energies, Aries employees do not mind working overtime to earn a little extra. Care must be taken, however, to ensure that they do not overstress themselves by being unrealistic about their capabilities. Although you may impress Aries employees and they may accept and work hard on a given assignment, be careful to guard against a breakdown due to their over-estimation of their own powers.

Managing, Directing, or Criticizing the Aries Employee

Aries employees are extremely sensitive to criticism. They can handle it if you take the time to fully explain what you mean, but they may be particularly touchy and deeply wounded by an offhand, thoughtless remark. They also cannot handle the kind of nagging criticism that goes on day after day, usually lacking the tough skin to let such negativity bounce off. Getting them to laugh, or at least smile, at their own shortcomings, or at anything amusing or ridiculous in a tense situation, can be a huge help in getting through to them. Generally speaking, Aries employees are easy to manage and direct as long as you are honest with them and not guilty of subterfuge or making misleading guarantees.

The Aries Coworker

Aries coworkers can generally be expected to hold up their end of shared responsibilities and to have a positive attitude on the job. However, because they are easily discouraged (often leading to discontent or outright depression), they need to be reassured by their colleagues of their worth to the group. Feeling essential to what is going on, even being at the center of it, is an important need that should be satisfied for Aries coworkers. Not all Aries need to be stars and stand out from the group; just being valued for the role they play is usually enough.

Approaching the Aries Coworker for Advice

Most Aries coworkers will be flattered that you chose to consult them and will do their best to help. However, because of their direct and highly opinionated approach, their advice should be heeded but not necessarily followed literally. Since Aries coworkers will follow up to see if you followed their advice, you should be prepared for a second or even third discussion. If you are not prepared for this, then you should not approach them in the first place, since they take such matters quite seriously. Giving offhand or casual advice is not their specialty.

Approaching the Aries Coworker for Help

Aries like to be approached for help and will generally do whatever they can to assist you, no matter how demanding the work involved. Remember that the Aries coworker is driven by challenge and also needs to feel important and valued. Having a strong Aries as a help-mate can definitely be an advantage. You must be careful though not to call on them too often or make them feel taken advantage of. Thus, it is best to hold their help in reserve for occasional emergency situations rather than relying on it on a daily or weekly basis.

Traveling with and Entertaining the Aries Coworker

Because of their individuality and strict values, it is best not to leave Aries coworkers in total control of making travel or party plans. They usually function well as part of a group as long as their task is well defined. Aries colleagues love to have fun, particularly when they find they are actually enjoying a task they were not particularly looking forward to. Laughter and joking will be important to keep them in a good mood and their energy flowing easily. They love colorful displays and enjoy customizing arrangements to the special tastes of colleagues and bosses.

The Aries Coworker Cooperating with Others

Aries coworkers have very strong likes and dislikes, particularly when it comes to people. They will generally give the other person a first chance, but rarely a second or third if they feel let down or betrayed. Do not expect them to be particularly cooperative with those they dislike personally. They can work with such people, but will not obviously warm to them or go out of their way to be overly helpful. Nor should you expect them to take the first steps toward reconciliation. For best results, make them part of a group that they feel comfortable in.

Impressing and Motivating the Aries Coworker

Most impressed by honesty and directness, Aries coworkers need to know that you are leveling with them and never jerking them around. They are particularly suspicious of manipulative, sneaky, or underhanded behavior, even if it is a subtle attempt on your part to grease a squeaky wheel. They are strongly motivated by challenge, even to the point of needing to accomplish seemingly impossible tasks. Here you must guard them and the group against their own hubris, seeking realistic rather than extraordinary methods, particularly on a day-to-day basis. Give Aries coworkers smaller, doable tasks and build their self-confidence gradually.

Persuading and/or Criticizing the Aries Coworker

Aries are difficult to persuade, particularly when your point of view is diametrically opposed to theirs. They will meet seductive or flattering approaches with suspicion and overly aggressive approaches with stiff resistance. The best way to persuade Aries colleagues is to show them by example that a certain approach can succeed, keeping arguments as pragmatic and unemotional as possible. Because of their great sensitivity to criticism, keep it short and sweet, and hear them out if they state objections to your point of view or offer an explanation in their defense.

(The Aries Coworker)

STRENGTHS

Involved

Contributing

Energetic

WEAKNESSES

Discouraged

Self-critical

Depressed

INTERACTIVE STYLE

Positive

Friendly

Helpful

The Aries Client

STRENGTHS

Self-assured

Unambiguous

Forthright

WEAKNESSES

Overly demanding

Unforgiving

Impatient

INTERACTIVE STYLE

Results-oriented

Tempestuous

Difficult

Satisfying Aries clients is not difficult as long as you listen to them carefully and give them what they require. The problem is that they may feel they have been very clear in their wishes, when in fact certain important facts were not thoroughly defined. In other words, Aries clients will often assume you understand them because they feel their thoughts are so clear and unambiguous that no one could possibly misunderstand them. Imagine their surprise when you ask for further clarification. They might assume you are a bit slow or outright mentally deficient. Use your intuition and try to get it right the first time.

Impressing the Aries Client

Aries clients expect you to be alert, intelligent, and totally tuned in to what they have to say. They can become bewildered by complexities, problems, and uncertainties you raise, as well as highly impatient. Once you have demonstrated your understanding and willingness to satisfy their wishes on time, feel free to impress them with your knowledge of their favorite subject, which you hopefully have researched in advance. Never mind if you didn't—they will probably let you know what it is anyway, particularly if you ask or guess what they like.

Selling to the Aries Client

Forget it. Aries clients are not interested in being sold. Either they have heard it all before or they will simply mistrust your motives and brush off your spiel mid-sell. They are the important ones, not you, and they want their demands met. Compromise is not really in their dictionary. Should you still try to convince them of the value of a new product or service, bring it up once you have agreed to their demands and in a subtle, seductive, non-serious manner, to best succeed in getting their attention.

Your Appearance and the Aries Client

Keeping in mind that the Aries client is the more important of you two, do not try to upstage an Aries with your beautiful clothes or a dynamite hairstyle. Your appearance should be muted, confident, and quiet. That said, the Aries client will be gratified that you found the meeting important enough to appear your best for it. Thus, keep your appearance orderly and your manner businesslike. Above all, do not indulge in idle chatter or try too hard to be amusing. Your well-prepared leadoff joke or witticism will probably fall flat or just receive a token snicker anyway, thus setting you back a light-year from the start.

Keeping the Aries Client's Interest

The Aries client will be most impressed by results. This does not mean making promises, but rather emphasizing your past track record, particularly if you have done good work for a competitor. Just the mention of the main competition will bring a reaction and a renewed interest in what you have to say. Emphasize with Aries clients why you prefer to be working for them, which they will lap up like a cat with milk. Once they know you have worked for others in their field, they will try to do everything they can to please you.

Breaking Bad News to the Aries Client

Would you willingly walk into a hurricane? How about challenging a tornado? Aries clients do not want bad news. They are paying you to provide good news. So give it. If you run out of good news, present the bad news in a good light, stressing that it could have been a lot worse. Do not stress how you did your best or how it was just plain bad luck; such explanations will only have a negative effect. Be prepared with a fallback position through which you can rescue the whole project and still satisfy the Aries client's wishes—explain that you can get the job done with a bit more time, and offer to work for a bit less.

Entertaining the Aries Client

Do some investigating beforehand to determine the Aries client's preference in dining—food, service, ambience, presentation—and concentrate on the details. Secretaries and office scuttlebutt are prime sources. Also, when it comes to entertainment, it will probably be common knowledge what kind of music or club atmosphere the Aries client prefers. Generally speaking, Aries like to eat and also drink, so you may have a problem keeping their alcohol consumption under control. Don't worry—they are more likely to agree with you if they are having a great time. Make sure the mode of transportation you provide is quick and easy.

The Aries Business Partner

Aries partners can lend prodigious energies to any endeavor. Their often frenetic and one-track approach can prove to be a problem, however, if they are heading off in the wrong direction, which can spell great loss of time and money. Therefore, it is recommended that things be fully discussed and planned out before the implementation stage and that you keep an eye on their progress. They will dislike making weekly reports to you or the group, so this should be done in a discreet fashion. Aries partners like to work on their own, providing their own fuel for their motor.

Setting Up the Business Partnership with Aries

The role of your Aries partner should be well defined from the start; otherwise Aries may tend to put a finger in too many pies. Also, their motives for wanting you as a partner are important to review. Why would such an independent person need or want a partner, and why you? Full legal safeguards in writing for both partners are recommended, meaning having a single lawyer who can take into consideration the wishes of both of you. Spelling out possible future difficulties in detail will make your Aries partner impatient, but it is necessary should things go awry.

Tasking with the Aries Business Partner

Aries partners may think they are multitaskers capable of accomplishing almost any herculean feat, but the partnership will work best on a day-to-day basis if their jobs are limited and clearly defined. This can be determined on a per-project basis, but their true

STRENGTHS
Loyal
Positive
Honest

WEAKNESSES
Detached
Forgetful
Insensitive

INTERACTIVE STYLE
Aggressive
One-track
Ambitious

strengths (whether marketing, public relations, sales, research and development, etc.) will become quickly apparent. Aries partners may encounter the problem that what they like to do best is not necessarily what they do best or what the company needs. They can be very stubborn in hanging on to their favorite tasks, despite negative outcomes or performance.

Traveling with and Entertaining the Aries Business Partner

Aries partners generally enjoy both travel and work-related entertainment but are not necessarily the best ones to make arrangements. Be sure that you or your assistant keeps an eye on the plans your Aries partner makes, since the Aries partner can be forgetful and overlook important details in their haste and impatience to get things organized. Aries partners often make good representatives for the partnership on the road or at home, being positive, forthright, and ambitious. Be sure they put the interests of the group before their own when dealing with clients. Too often self-centered, they may sacrifice the good of the group for their own enjoyment.

Managing and Directing the Aries Business Partner

Generally speaking, Aries partners are not manageable. You will have to rely on their intuition and judgment in most situations. Also, taking direction is not their forte since they feel they always know best, particularly when crises arise. Because their intuitive powers are high, particularly when they detect scams and con artists, the company will often benefit from such abilities. Try to make your wishes clear to them, drop a few broad hints, and then leave the implementation up to them.

Relating to the Aries Business Partner in the Long Run

The Aries partner is remarkably faithful and, once committed, is in it for the long haul. However, problems of a long-standing nature will no doubt arise, and these can undermine the relationship. All personal matters should be kept out of the business partnership whenever possible. Aries are very touchy on certain subjects, which, when raised, can elicit explosive responses. Remember that objectivity rather than deep feeling is their forte and that things are best left without getting too involved personally. Even when your Aries partner is blunt, remain tactful, patient, and firm, if possible.

Parting Ways with the Aries Business Partner

Dissolving a partnership with an Aries after years of working closely can be accomplished as long as things are done in a mutually advantageous, pragmatic, and practical manner. Because of their honesty, Aries partners will rarely ask for anything they do not feel entitled to. It is not so much their interest in you personally, but rather their innate sense of fairness that keeps them from taking advantage of you. Appeal can always be made to ethical behavior, which they will rarely care to transgress. Their disappointment in having to acknowledge failure will be acute, but their independence will motivate them to move on.

The Aries Competitor

Aries competitors can be quite ferocious and intimidating when confronted directly. At the very least, their approach can threaten to overwhelm their opponents with surges of energy, infusions of capital, and dedicated, persistent campaigns that cannot be ignored. Encounters with such opponents can come to resemble battles, and the entire struggle for consumers and clients that is likely to ensue will be an all-out war. Winning out over the Aries competitor will involve a thorough study of their tactics and, just as in war, an intimate knowledge of the terrain and present circumstances of the market. Simply ignoring the Aries competitor, going about your business, and hoping that he/she will fail or just go away usually does not work.

STRENGTHS

Persistent

Combative

Overwhelming

WEAKNESSES

Overconfident

Blind

Unreasoning

INTERACTIVE STYLE

Dynamic

Resilient

Challenging

Countering the Aries Competitor

As in boxing, the most effective strategy against the Aries competitor is to counter-punch. Letting Aries make the first move is not difficult of course, but having the patience and self-control to hold back, look for weak spots, and only then to dive in to attack may be hard, but it is essential if victory is to be achieved. Aries competitors can cause their own downfall if you let them wear themselves out and make mistakes, which you can then capitalize on. You may even consider occasionally rousing them to a frenzy through taunts and challenges.

Out-Planning the Aries Competitor

The Aries plan is generally a simple one, employing a one-track attack strategy. Create a long-range plan that allows the initial attack to spend its force while weaving a complex net of containment that creates small obstacles and problems that will wear down your opponent. Keep your plan versatile and tuned in to the competitor's most recent thrusts. Also be ready to merge forces with other competitors in the field and to give way and compromise when necessary. A flexible, rather than rigid, defensive plan is best. By refusing to present a fixed objective, you frustrate the enemy's need to attack.

Impressing the Aries Competitor in Person

Your Aries competitor will no doubt refuse to be impressed by you in person. Better to just be yourself and not even try. By ignoring their need to impress you with how unimpressed they are, you will emerge on top. It's best to maintain eye contact when challenged and respond to their provocative statements with subtle, somewhat ironic replies. Being nebulous and sarcastic can arouse their fury. Smiling or laughing at their remarks can be like pouring gasoline on the Aries fire. Speak slowly, clearly, and allow silence to work in your favor.

Undercutting and Outbidding the Aries Competitor

Rather than adopting the aggressive approach of Aries, accomplish your objectives quietly and efficiently, dealing more with details than with employing the grand gesture. If the Aries competitor is in the lead marketwise, eat away at their dominance and profit margin bit by bit, undercutting and outbidding him/her gradually, allowing time to be on your side. On the other hand, if you are the dominant force in the market and Aries is the challenger, build a tough skin and sail on serenely, refusing to let their pointed barbs or bullets penetrate. Retain your confidence but at the same time look out for real threats to your dominance and counter these promptly, without fuss.

Public Relations Wars with the Aries Competitor

The Aries approach to public relations will probably be an extreme blitz, so it is best for you to counter with a more conservative, wise approach. While building the reliability factor for your company, show the faults in your opponent's thinking, making fun of their simplistic ads and embarrassing them with their naïveté. Issuing challenges to Aries opponents by advertising the superiority of your product or service will elicit high-spending responses that can drain them financially. This can drive them to adopt desperate, costly measures to counter your provocative charges.

The Aries Competitor and the Personal Approach

This can prove to be the weak spot in the impressive Aries arsenal. Not usually so strong on defense, Aries opponents cannot handle personal elements surfacing in business dealings. Keep in mind that you do not necessarily have to sting or hurt them, either. By adopting an understanding, kind, ethical, and pragmatic approach, you may earn their respect, perhaps even resulting in future mutually cooperative endeavors. Nothing will take the wind out of the sails of an Aries attack more than agreeing with him/her and showing how the two of you working together toward a single objective might turn out better than an all-out war.

Love

ARIES
March 21–April 20

The Aries First Date

Prepare to be charmed, dazzled, swept off your feet, whatever! Whether filled with pizzazz or quiet self-confidence, this person will leave little doubt as to his or her wishes, preferences, or the direction he/she feels events should take. Unlikely to send mixed messages or be ambiguous, the Aries will take the lead on the first date. Should you decide to preempt this role, Aries will no doubt allow you to do so, but at any sign of faltering or incertitude an Aries date is likely to take over command, mercifully, rather than watch you flounder. Once Aries begins making decisions for both of you, he/she is unlikely to stop.

Wooing and Picking Up the Aries First Date

Catching the eye of an attractive Aries is not usually difficult. Once an Aries sees you are interested, he/she may ignore you completely whether the attraction is mutual or not. Because of this tactic, it may be difficult to determine if Aries is in fact interested in you. Approaching Aries directly can lead either to him/her walking away or to a sharp verbal thrust. If you are not put off by this response and proceed to advance, Aries is likely to confront and ultimately accept your invitation to talk, walk, or have the customary drink. Since Aries crave attention, you should follow up the initial meeting within a few hours or a day or two with a phone call, email, or both.

Suggested Activities for the Aries First Date

Aries is fond of bright lights, action, films, and all sorts of entertainment, and your first evening together will be unforgettable, as long as you please their strong tastes and preferences. Likely to sulk over your lack of attention or yawn at your dull demeanor, the Aries first date will expect a lot of you. Yet Aries has an independent streak and strong leadership qualities that may require you to follow along and hang on for dear life while you try to keep up. You may get the idea that your Aries date is less interested in you than in putting on a performance for your benefit.

STRENGTHS

Impressive
Self-confident
Decisive

WEAKNESSES

Didactic
Opinionated
Dominant

INTERACTIVE STYLE

Convincing
Determined
Direct

Turn-Ons and Turn-Offs for the Aries First Date

Aries are averse to anyone who tries to dampen their spirits, calm them down, or act possessively toward them. Light affection, such as early touching, casually putting an arm around him/her, or taking his or her arm, is not recommended. Remain as aloof as possible without showing your emotions, positive or negative. Aries often becomes bewildered and turned off by premature displays of feeling. Find out which subjects interest your date and keep the conversation moving in that direction. Remember that satisfying your needs and wants is only important to them as it reflects on their success in pleasing you. Avoid suddenly falling silent; keep things going.

Making "the Move" with the Aries First Date

Aries like to make the first move. It will happen very suddenly—probably before either of you is aware of it—and can disappear as quickly as lightning. Even if it should continue through the wee hours it is unlikely that either of you will remember a whole lot about what happened. To the Aries, it is all about being carried away by the experience, not your presence, personality, or, God forbid, problems. Aries want what they want when they want it—and that's it. Do not expect displays of affection or empathy, because you won't get them.

Impressing the Aries First Date

Just being able to survive a first date with an Aries is impressive. Do not seek to show off your talents or good qualities. Aries will be truly impressed only by your abilities to stand up to their intensity and understand their wishes and desires. Highly opinionated, Aries dates do not expect you or anyone else to agree with them, but will nonetheless never give up trying to convince you of how right they are. Don't avoid arguments, since Aries enjoys interactions ranging from rapier-quick repartee to out-and-out knock-down dragouts. Prove a worthy adversary.

Brushing Off the Aries First Date

Generally speaking, under that coating of Aries bravado and self-confidence is a tiny child who hates and fears rejection above all things. If you wish to avoid the unpleasantness of either continued unwanted intentions from your Aries date or a violent reaction to being rebuffed, you must play it smarter. Give a broad hint about dumping your Aries date (perhaps adding that this is customary with you) and he/she will no doubt leap in to turn the tables and be the one who does the rejecting first. Winning and losing are very important matters to most Aries. Losing is not their style.

The Aries Romantic Partner

Aries romantic partners can be counted on for their honesty and desire to maintain a close involvement. However, their dynamism is so great that you may not be able to meet their constant demands on your energies. Although they are extremely independent—and most likely will encourage you to be also—they will want to have daily contact with you, whether virtual, auditory, or physical. They would hate being called needy, since their self-image is one of total independence, but they are very dependent on their romantic partner, at the very least to listen to them, take their advice seriously, and obey their commands.

Having a Discussion with the Aries Romantic Partner

Too often, having a discussion with your Aries romantic partner will mean quietly listening to what they have to say. Basically, Aries is interested not in discussions but in actions. You will soon get the idea that the main purpose of a discussion is to correct an improper action on your part, and therefore when Aries says "we need to talk," expect the worst. Admonishment, blame, guilt trips, moralizing—all are possible. Yet, when in the mood, Aries can sparkle and shine verbally, being witty and charming to the extreme. Aries also enjoy jokes, stories, and wordplay—just keep it short.

Arguments with the Aries Romantic Partner

For your own sake, avoid arguments with Aries as much as possible. Aries are the cardinal fire signs and have nasty tempers. Too often an argument with your Aries Romantic Partner can result in him/her abruptly slamming the phone or stomping out of the room. Usually, arguing with an Aries will not get you anywhere. It merely allows your Aries partner to express their resentments and a chance to voice their objections to your behavior. Since Aries partners hold so much inside, this in and of itself can become one of the truly positive results of an argument with them.

Traveling with the Aries Romantic Partner

Traveling with Aries partners can be truly exciting as long as you do not try to cramp their style. They think of themselves as extremely healthy and expect you to be that way too. That means you should never try to slow them down by complaining about or demonstrating a physical difficulty. They will most often be less than sympathetic to your plight and urge you to get back to normal as soon as possible. Furthermore, you will feel the stress of keeping up with their prodigious energies.

Sex with the Aries Romantic Partner

Aries are not much for delayed gratification. They usually push for what they want immediately, and when they don't get it they become very unhappy, quiet, and often depressed. Aries want what they want when they want it, and they usually get it. Although they can be top performers, somehow you never really find out much about how they feel about you or the experience. Don't try asking, either, since they figure you should already know how wonderful it was or they were. Headstrong and impulsive publicly, Aries can be very tender and sweet in private. However, they may not always want to wait until the surroundings are more comfortable or private to express their more passionate feelings.

Affection and the Aries Romantic Partner

Most Aries do not seem like cuddly types. Certainly you should not expect affection in social situations, where they will most often remain cool. Yet in private, they can

STRENGTHS

Independent

Honest

Energetic

WEAKNESSES

Self-unaware

Demanding

Pushy

INTERACTIVE STYLE

Purposeful

Focused

Dynamic

be extremely affectionate, and they enjoy being on both the giving and receiving ends. Quiet times together will reveal a tender side to them that you never knew existed, as long as you can find the time to pin them down for a few calm hours. In fact, what Aries really needs, and even unconsciously wants most, is to find a person with whom they can be comfortable and trusting enough to let down their guard.

Humor and the Aries Romantic Partner

An Aries in a relationship loves to be silly and have fun, but often has difficulty doing so because of their serious and self-conscious demeanor. When they truly let their hair down, they enjoy playing word and board games, telling jokes, and playing like the true children they are. Best to let them give the signal that they are ready to play, and then you can gently encourage them until a general state of hilarity is reached. Don't let things go too far, however, since their fire could get out of control and prove destructive. Beware of their tendency to play practical jokes.

The Aries Spouse

The Aries spouse demands honesty above all things. Of course, should your Aries spouse stray once or twice in the course of a marriage, they would expect to be forgiven—that is, if you ever found out. On a day-to-day basis, Aries spouses are there to get the job done, but often their priorities will fall on the side of their profession rather than their family. As their mate, you will be expected to hold down the fort, ensuring that things run smoothly at home. Aries generally are not dedicated cleaners, so keeping things orderly will probably fall on your shoulders.

Wedding and Honeymoon with the Aries Spouse

Although generally not big on ceremonies and public displays of feeling, Aries will put out 100 percent for the wedding in terms of enthusiasm and cooperation. Aries tend to spend far beyond their means, so you may find yourself strapped for cash in your early married days, after the prodigious cash outlays of the wedding and honeymoon splurges. Expect full attention from Aries in the bedroom; you may feel worn out and in need of a true vacation after your honeymoon. It will probably be your job to get your place of residence in shape while your Aries spouse is trying to scrounge up some cash.

Home and Day-to-Day Married Life with the Aries Spouse

Flamboyant Aries are usually too taken up with themselves, their ideas, and their careers to make a steady contribution to more mundane domestic matters. It would be a good idea to create and structure their responsibilities from the get-go, rather than allowing them to sink into a steady pattern of domestic neglect or, worse, expectations of you doing all the work. They are actually quite good on a day-to-day basis as long as their tasks are well defined and you keep a watchful eye on their activities. Praise and reward are essential to keep their spirits high.

Finances and the Aries Spouse

Overspending is a big problem for Aries and, therefore, for their mate as well. Not only do they often spend heedlessly to get what they need, maxing out the credit cards and spending money they do not have, but they often go so far as to put themselves in debt for sums they could never muster. Again, it will be you, the spouse, who is expected to come to the rescue. Somehow Aries always seems to muddle through financially, however, often avoiding complete disaster at the last moment. Strangely, their unconcern about such matters seems to bring them luck and work in their favor.

Infidelity and the Aries Spouse

Yours is not tolerated, but theirs is. This would create an impossible double standard were it not for the fact that Aries tends to be faithful, straying only occasionally. Furthermore, their extramarital involvements do not generally last long and, although intense, do not go deep emotionally. If you can, ignore their attractions and flirtations since they won't amount to much or pose a real threat to your marriage. A lot of what happens goes on in your spouse's active imaginary world anyway. In such states, Aries finds it difficult to distinguish fantasy from reality.

Children and the Aries Spouse

Aries can make excellent parents but do not particularly like to do the dirty work. Excellent counselors, teachers, and advisors to their children, they readily lend their energies to encouraging their offspring in sports, academics, and making friends. The main problem is that they will not be around most of the time, so taken up are they with their careers and personal involvements, leaving "guess who" to deal with the nitty-gritty. The Aries parent will be there when emergencies arise but will definitely not specialize in solving the little problems that arise every day, tending to either blow them out of proportion or simply ignore them.

Divorce and the Aries Spouse

Since Aries is allergic to admitting failure, there are only two possibilities when it comes to marital problems: staying together no matter what, or getting you to admit it was all your fault. Beware when the Aries spouse promises to make a new start and swear to avoid past mistakes. Although well intentioned, Aries tends to have a low reality factor when it comes to themselves. Promises are made with every good intention but somehow do not reach fulfillment, for the most part. If divorce is inevitable, it is best if you coolly work out all legal, custodial, and financial issues on paper and get your Aries spouse to agree without blame or anger.

The Aries Lover

Ardent and intense, the Aries lover will give all for love. Yet sometimes you wonder whether all that energy is being directed toward you or an ideal of love—one so perfect it can never be realized. Thus, despite its intensity, Aries love is often decidedly non-

Dedicated

Ardent

Intense

WEAKNESSES

Unrealistic

Overly demanding

Blind

INTERACTIVE STYLE

Committed

Idealistic

Positive

physical in its belief and expression. At times, the Aries lover appears to be a priest or priestess in love's hallowed halls, revering love like a religion. Being put up on a pedestal can only make it more challenging for you, since it will be difficult if not impossible to live up to expectations, despite their extreme need to believe in you.

Meeting the Aries Lover

Aries lovers are likely to be motivated to seek you out through their unhappiness or dissatisfaction with an existing relationship. You will therefore not have to do anything in order to meet them. It will probably occur at a party or by chance in a public place. The look on Aries's face and accompanying demeanor will tell you immediately what they are after and why. Be careful with an involvement, since you are likely to be elevated by the same idealism they attached to their previous or current relationship. Enjoy the beginning of the affair, when you can do no wrong and their passions run high.

Location and the Aries Lover

The Aries lover is likely to meet you at your place, since they are likely already married or living with someone else. This location can become a sanctuary for them, one that they visit with regularity and look forward to as a home away from home. This puts you in control of certain aspects of the situation but also at the mercy of others, notably being number two in line. When they start wanting to sleep over, you must decide whether this enjoyable liaison is something you want more permanently. Think carefully before making this decision but don't avoid it for too long.

Sex and the Aries Lover

The Aries lover will be focused on you and give their all sexually. The problem is that somewhere in that welter of passion may be anger or resentment that is being expressed toward a previous or current partner, thus in a way diminishing your importance except as a substitute. You, of course, want to be loved for yourself and not compared to someone else. Often the greater the resentment, the stronger the sexual expression toward you, which can make things even worse, despite the extreme physical pleasure involved. A discussion of this point may be necessary, but the Aries fire may subsequently cool.

Holding On to the Aries Lover

Normally this should not be a problem, since the Aries lover is totally absorbed in their love for you. If you want to keep your Aries as long as possible, you may have to studiously avoid discussions about their motives, intentions, and other involvement(s). Aries will probably bring them up sooner or later and then you must be ready to listen with an understanding ear. However, make it clear that despite your fondness or love, you will not sacrifice your self-esteem or self-respect at the altar of the Aries ego. You have needs and wants as well, and the Aries lover must recognize that. Be tactful.

Entertaining the Aries Lover

Aries loves to go out and have a good time. Appearances at clubs, movies, and parties are things they enjoy. Problem number one is meeting one of their friends, colleagues, or family members who don't know of your existence. You may have to be prepared to either lie or bend the truth a bit in such a brief encounter, letting Aries do the talking. Quiet dinners for two or a casual drink after work are also agreeable to most Aries and can guarantee you a bit more privacy within a social setting. Keep an eye on Aries's alcohol intake, which can spiral out of control rapidly, particularly if they are enjoying themselves.

Breaking Up with the Aries Lover

Breaking up will be very difficult for Aries lovers if they are still in the idealistic stage of the affair. The rejection they feel will be unbearable to them, and they will think of a million reasons to continue and find it almost impossible not to text, call, email, or knock on your door. However, once you have made up your mind to part, you must be strong and adamant in your refusal to see them in person. Temper this with understanding but firm communications that allow the breakup to develop without a single abrupt shock if you want to avoid extremes of unpleasantness, fury, and hurt.

The Aries Ex

The anger and resentment of an Aries ex are unlikely to disappear very quickly after the breakup. Because of the blame Aries will have no doubt loaded on your shoulders, they may continue to be aggressive and refuse to seek reasonable accommodation to your needs and wants. Your Aries ex's whole attitude will center on what they feel entitled to because of your past mistakes. Thus, in seeking retribution for your wrongdoing, they may insist, even for years afterward, that you pay for such behavior. Should you refuse to acknowledge wrongdoing, your Aries ex is unlikely to forgive you or let up in laying guilt trips.

Establishing a Friendship with the Aries Ex

The first step toward establishing a friendship with your Aries ex will have to be admitting your past mistakes and asking to be forgiven. Once your ex has accepted this, however begrudgingly, you can move forward. Do not seek to demand the same thing from them. Surprisingly, your Aries ex may offer it later, on their own terms. Fast friendships are possible with an Aries ex and usually last once made. Aries exes can be quite magnanimous as long as they do not feel pushed but instead feel free to give. Furthermore, they can be counted on in situations where you really need help, and they will be there for you in emergencies.

Issues of Getting Back Together with the Aries Ex

A great deal depends on which of you is pushing for a reunion. If your ex really wants this, then the decision is yours. If you are the one who is most interested, things become a bit more complicated. The Aries ex will have to be wooed just as if you were getting married or even going out for the first time. Do not expect long involved conversations on this subject. Remember that the Aries way is one of action, and that these actions can be

STRENGTHS
Strong
Intent
Unceasing

WEAKNESSES
Unforgiving
Blaming
Angry

INTERACTIVE STYLE
Confrontational
Belligerent
Demanding

based on snap decisions made after long periods of either avoiding the issue completely or endlessly mulling it over.

Discussing Past Issues with the Aries Ex

With the Aries ex, discussions are likely to become monologues in which surprisingly few words are uttered. The Aries ex is likely to become restless with you speaking on the subject for even a couple of minutes. His or her continual interruptions may put an end to any real communication between you two. It is unlikely that the Aries ex can deal objectively with the past without the customary blame and anger breaking through. Try to defuse emotional matters and keep level-headed, refusing to let Aries push your buttons with accusations. It may be helpful to meet in a quiet and private yet social setting, where Aries is more likely to remain calm.

Expressing Affection to the Aries Ex

The Aries ex will be very suspicious of your affection, so it is best to strictly avoid such expressions and keep things more objective. After two years or so, an occasional touch on the arm or pat on the back can develop into a brief hug. Although Aries often feels affection, they have trouble expressing or accepting it, preferring the extremes of cutting out physical contact completely or engaging in it without reserve. Wait for small signs of affection, usually understated, and respond in kind.

Defining the Present Relationship with the Aries Ex

Such definitions will have to be de facto and improvised for the most part, since the Aries ex is usually loath to make verbal or written agreements. Thus, you will have to be ultra-sensitive to Aries's wishes and never remind them of what you thought you had agreed on. Aries exes should never be pushed to express their feelings or make assessments, since they are usually unwilling or unable to do either (or both). Allow the new relationship with your Aries ex to quietly evolve on its own without planning it out.

Sharing Custody with the Aries Ex

An Aries ex may see your common offspring as living proof of your past mistakes, particularly emphasizing the problems that the kids face due to your perceived neglect. It may be difficult to have the Aries ex concentrate on the present situation since they are still so tied up with the past. As time goes by, an Aries ex should be gently encouraged to think of what is best for the child(ren) rather than dwelling on their own damaged ego. You must insist that your ex obey court decisions. Keep up your end of the deal and insist that your ex do the same. Do not expect deep understanding of emotional problems.

Friends and Family

The Aries Friend

Over the years, Aries friends can be counted on to remain faithful, even if they do not contact you often. A phone call or visit twice or three times a year will show that you are still on your Aries friend's mind and in their heart. Usually, their schedule is jam-packed anyway, almost guaranteeing they will have little time to spend with friends. However, as Aries's best or oldest friend, you may very well find yourself included in family celebrations, underlining your being considered at least as close as a brother or sister. Having friends in common will guarantee the need to pass along the latest news or gossip to each other, usually by telephone.

Asking for Help from the Aries Friend

The first problem here is getting ahold of Aries friends, since they are usually moving at the speed of light. Once you have left a message for Aries friends, they are sure to get back in touch with you within a week. By this time, your problem may have been solved. Once the fact registers that you really need them, Aries friends will help, but within the time constraints of their busy schedule. More often than not, Aries will choose to make valuable suggestions or give recommendations rather than turning up in person. It's best to keep your requests for help infrequent rather than regular.

Communication and Keeping in Touch with the Aries Friend

Aries friends do not specialize in either communication or keeping in touch. Since your interactions will probably be infrequent, you will do best to text or email them rather than expect the relaxed luxury of a messenger or phone conversation. Leaving short messages will keep Aries up-to-date on your activities and also give your friend the opportunity to respond occasionally on the run or during a brief breathing space. Do not hold your breath for a response, however. Aries's usually breathless lifestyle sends the clear message: Catch me—if you can!

Borrowing Money from the Aries Friend

This will be difficult. They are usually stretched to the limit. Maxing out credit cards and pushing checking accounts into overdraft are Aries specialties, leaving few extra funds to

STRENGTHS

Constant

Caring

Thoughtful

WEAKNESSES

Scattered

Gossipy

Unfocused

INTERACTIVE STYLE

Busy

Chatty

Close

lend to friends. That said, they will help when they can and often are extremely generous. Their attitudes toward money are not terribly serious, for they are idealists, usually taken up with issues much more important to them than financial return or remuneration. This true unconcern is reflected in an attitude often conveyed in their manner, which says: I give money if I have it. If it is returned, then it was a loan.

Asking for Advice from the Aries Friend

Aries friends are always ready to give advice, whether you ask for it or not. They may offer to play a leading role in your problem, either as your representative or behind the scenes as your advisor. Being asked for advice makes them feel needed and important, and their eagerness to take the lead in any endeavor is apparent. You may come to regret asking them in the first place after a while since their input may turn dominant, indicating that they now regard the problem as their responsibility (perhaps implying your helplessness or outright incompetence). Thus, be careful before you ask, or keep your initial request casual.

Visiting the Aries Friend

Aries friends do not easily make themselves available at home, since they are either absent or, if they are there, it's precisely to escape from the world. What they prefer is meeting you between a couple of their appointments, perhaps for lunch or a drink. An hour is usually all their frenetic pace will allow. During your time together they will usually give you their undivided attention. Make sure you suggest they turn off their mobile phone, otherwise interruptions can be expected. Be ready to pay or not, since they will probably either grab the bill on their way out or dash off and leave you holding the tab.

Celebrations/Entertainment with the Aries Friend

Aries friends love to celebrate birthdays, particularly their own. It may get tiring year after year to attend the same party with the same people and the same conversations, but this is what Aries enjoys most. A present should be selected carefully, since your Aries friend is likely a very good gift-giver and expects something well chosen in return. When an Aries throws a party for friends and family, it is usually done in lavish style. They expend so much energy that it will be difficult for you to easily refuse their invitation. If you cannot make the occasion, spend time thinking up a really good excuse. Remember your previous excuse and that your family member of choice can die only once!

The Aries Roommate

Aries roommates may find it difficult to get along with those they live with on a day-to-day basis—and vice versa. Not really cut out for performing mundane tasks, highly idealistic Aries roommates may trip over their own possessions while having their mind on a more important goal. Furthermore, their interesting thoughts, ideas, and feelings must be noticed and discussed—never ignored—by those they live with. Their frustration level has a low threshold, and they are likely to express their hurt with a brooding, menacing quiet that either erupts as irritation and angry outbursts or settles into periodic depressions. Usually one look at their face will tell the whole story. Keep them happy.

Sharing Financial Responsibilities with the Aries Roommate

Aries roommates will fulfill their financial responsibilities as long as they are carefully laid out—not only the amount they contribute but when and how it will be paid. Putting important matters out of their mind is an Aries specialty, so you may be faced with the chore of reminding them tactfully at the end of the month that the rent is coming up. In general, you should avoid discussions of money, particularly theirs. It may be necessary to have a fall-back plan for the eventuality that your Aries roommate cannot make food, rent, or utility payments on time.

Cleaning and the Aries Roommate

Although Aries roommates have the energy for cleaning, they most often lack the motivation and inclination. Here a structured, unemotional approach works best. Draw up a weekly list of chores, even being specific to the day, so that they know what is expected of them. Arguments can easily arise when they ignore such a list and give the invariable excuse that they will get to it later. Even worse, they may just disappear for a few days. Leaving their mess as it is and cleaning only your own space will not work since they are likely to ignore their own stuff anyway. Giving perks for their neatness will help, as will a system of small rewards and expressions of appreciation.

Houseguests and the Aries Roommate

If the friends are mutual, a great time can be had by all. However, if they are just your friends and the Aries roommate finds them irritating or troublesome—look out! Aries has a very short fuse, and their honesty and frequent lack of self-control will guarantee conflict. Confronted later, they are likely to deny the whole thing or say that it was your friends(s) who started it. Often it is more tactful to invite new friends or old ones incompatible with Aries when your roommate is scheduled to be busy elsewhere.

Parties and the Aries Roommate

Aries roommates can be great fun when the party is held on home territory. They will prove generous in their outlays of cash and time, as well as coming up with ways to amuse and please your guests. (Such a party may also serve as an incentive for them to clean, at least in preparation.) Should you take your Aries roommate with you to a cross-town party, do not expect them to sit quietly or gradually get comfortable. The Aries way is most often to dive right in, thus dividing the guests into two camps—one that enjoys the Aries show and the other that does not. Either way, your Aries roommate is bound to be the center of attention, sooner or later.

Privacy and the Aries Roommate

Aries roommates can be surprisingly private people; they need their own room to retreat to. Never breach this privacy by walking right in, but always knock and be prepared with something to say. It is best to leave them alone when they are angry or depressed;

STRENGTHS
Interesting
Idealistic
High-minded

WEAKNESSES
Unaware
Irritated
Depressed

INTERACTIVE STYLE
Involved
Goal-oriented
Energetic

FRIENDS AND FAMILY

otherwise you risk a most fiery and decidedly unpleasant confrontation. Make sure they also know that you expect them to observe your privacy, for they can be very casual about that, particularly borrowing things when you are absent. If each of you has your own room, things will work out best. If one of you or another roommate sleeps on a couch in the common living room, there could be problems.

Discussing Problems with the Aries Roommate

Discussing your problems is always a possibility with your Aries roommate, but discussing theirs generally is not. Aries is unable to easily discuss their own feelings or to explain why certain things are bothering them. On the other hand they can be quite open to hearing you talk about yourself and frequently offer surprisingly helpful suggestions. However, their penchant for giving unsolicited advice is equally strong, so they are likely to put in their two cents whether asked or not. Should the problem deal with their avoidance of household chores, payment of rent or food money, or forgetfulness about telephone calls or messages, be prepared for a rough ride. Always look for the right moment to bring up such subjects.

The Aries Parent

Aries parents are involved with their offspring—sometimes too much. No matter how far out they are, they usually try hard to keep their kids on the straight and narrow. Aries parents have strong ethical beliefs and will not tolerate transgressions to their ideas of right and wrong. Punishment and reward can figure prominently in their approach to raising a child. For the most part, they will agree with the norms of the society in which they live but will urge their children to be strong individuals with their own unique way of handling things. However, they must remember to back off and truly let their children make mistakes and decide for themselves.

Discipline Style of the Aries Parent

Aries parents generally believe in discipline, which they do not hesitate to impose on their children, certain that it will help them later in life. Their idea is that discipline builds character and gives structure to an otherwise chaotic situation. Getting physical is not really their style, although occasionally their fiery fury may overflow in volcanic proportions, usually passing quickly. More often they will impose strict limitations on their kids and ground them if transgressed. Although tending to be strict and unyielding, they have surprisingly soft hearts and will frequently forgive mistakes, particularly those made unknowingly. Their children should avoid directly challenging their authority.

Affection Level and the Aries Parent

Aries parents are very affectionate toward their children a good deal of the time. Their frequently strict and forbidding demeanor usually belies a soft heart. Aries parents love to have fun with their kids, constantly thinking up all sorts of entertainment possibilities for mutual enjoyment. Watching them play with their children, you may frequently wonder which of them is the child! It is not at all uncommon for Aries parents to treat their own children more like brothers and sisters so wholeheartedly that they would get down in the sandbox with them. Yet when their kids act up or directly defy their wishes and beliefs, this affection can be instantly withdrawn.

Money Issues and the Aries Parent

Most Aries parents will give their kids a weekly allowance but will also keep an eye on how it is spent. Should a child need money for a special event or project, they should approach the Aries parent directly and speak their case clearly. Chances are good that the cash outlay will be approved. In many cases, the Aries parent will not ask for it back, particularly if the investment the child makes is something that furthers their self-development. Once Aries parents make the promise for a cash outlay, they will come through, but the child should make it absolutely clear how and when the money should be paid.

Crises and the Aries Parent

Aries parents are easily aroused. Once the alarm bells start ringing, they are likely to spring into immediate action. Unfortunately, this does not work positively in all cases since, in their rush to act, they sometimes move too hastily in the wrong direction. However, they are also capable of putting on the brakes, stopping on a dime, and changing course. Generally speaking, their instincts are good and their involvement total, so they can be true lifesavers. They savor the role of hero, so they will probably totally enjoy the experience, no matter how hair-raising. Do not alarm them unnecessarily.

Holidays/Family Gatherings and the Aries Parent

Traditionalists at heart, Aries parents enjoy family gatherings and taking the customary vacation. Particularly fond of natural settings, they are likely to especially enjoy picnics, cookouts, and camping trips. Keep in mind that the Aries parent is really a big kid just waiting to rediscover their childhood. Make sure to include the Aries parent in all activities, never assuming that being an adult means not being interested in kids' games and fun. They can be counted on for buying the necessary equipment or paying travel and lodging expenses with warmhearted generosity. Aries parents love spending money on things, people, and activities they like. They will worry about the bills only later.

Caring for the Aging Aries Parent

An aging Aries parent will be difficult to deal with. Aries do not always appreciate being helped, particularly with things they are convinced, however wrongly, they can do themselves. An aging Aries's perception of reality is not always accurate and, as a result, they will not easily accept their inabilities to take care of things unaided. Aries parents are fiercely independent, yet when they are able at last to meekly accept help, they tend to reveal a side you never knew existed. Regressing to a childlike state is often their fate, so do not hesitate to patiently take the lead, play the parent, and have things all studiously worked out, eliminating uncertainty and replacing it with structure.

The Aries Sibling

Aries siblings will want to take the lead among their brothers and sisters, particularly if they are the oldest. A younger or middle Aries sibling, on the other hand, may expect to be protected, often burying themselves in the peace and security of the family bosom. In the case of dysfunctional or unstable families, the Aries sibling can be a bulwark or mainstay in a chaotic situation, even substituting for the parents and helping to raise brother(s) or sister(s). An older Aries sibling can also be quite dictatorial, assuming the role of a generalissimo whose orders must be obeyed without question. Such tyranny, however, can prove reassuring to the younger ones, since Aries's strict discipline lends a feeling of stability.

Rivalry/Closeness with the Aries Sibling

As far as the Aries sibling is concerned there is no problem with rivalry, since they are the undisputed boss. Although Aries siblings can show affection to siblings, and frequently care for them in the absence of parents, in most matters they will not tolerate challenges to their authority. Other siblings who try to contest this authority or attempt to quash it in a younger Aries sibling are in for a rough time. The Aries sibling may express affection to the others and feel close from time to time, but generally their strict attitude will rarely let up for very long.

Past Issues and the Aries Sibling

Aries siblings do not easily forgive or forget. Any slights, persecutions, or other confrontations will linger long into adult life, as will their patterns of dominance over other siblings. Thus their need to carry childhood roles and issues into adulthood frequently get in the way of establishing normal relationships with their brothers and sisters. It is not so much a refusal to let go of these matters as it is a genuine inability to do so. Patience and understanding on the part of others are needed for time to do its healing work, bringing acceptance in its wake.

Dealing with the Estranged Aries Sibling

The estranged Aries sibling is extremely difficult to bring back into the family fold. Once an Aries sibling has made the break, either through feeling rejected or misunderstood, or simply having lost interest, he or she will stubbornly avoid others' attempts to get in touch or otherwise communicate. Generally, the most effective way to make contact would be through the one sibling or parent who was closest to them in childhood. In the meantime, the others should stay away, since any attempts on their part usually only make things more difficult. It is also possible to effect reconciliations through your estranged sibling's spouse or a mutual friend.

Money Issues (Borrowing Money, Wills, Etc.) and the Aries Sibling

Aries siblings are usually generous with what they have. However, when it comes to wills and inheritances, they usually dig in their heels and refuse to budge. This is generally not because of money or property, per se, but because of what it symbolizes, namely what they perceive as the love, affection, or caring expressed by the deceased parent. Thus, being cut out of a will or being inadequately remembered will appear as total rejection and, therefore, an expression of the feeling that the Aries sibling was truly unimportant to the parent in life.

Holidays/Celebrations/Reunions and the Aries Sibling

Usually Aries siblings can be counted on to make a significant contribution to family reunions and other celebrations. However, they may prefer to do so monetarily since their busy schedule does not allow them to contribute their time. Hopefully they will show up, but this is not guaranteed. If they do, they may depart just as quickly and unexpectedly as they arrived. Wise siblings will be careful about bringing up touchy subjects, since the inflammability may easily ignite if Aries is teased or needled. Pushing their buttons is all too easy and should be avoided.

Vacationing with the Aries Sibling

Unless the Aries sibling is allowed to take the lead and his or her authority is accepted in most matters, it will be difficult to share an enjoyable vacation together. The problem frequently arises because of Aries's disinterest in arranging practical matters. As soon as the other sibling(s) discovers this and attempts to rectify matters to avoid disaster, the Aries sibling may take this as criticism of how they handled (or forgot to handle) important arrangements. Further, Aries siblings will see such efforts as challenges to their authority. Once the vacation is successfully under way, the Aries sibling can add positive energy, dynamism, and a pioneering spirit to most activities.

The Aries Child

Since Aries is the sign of the child, symbolically representing the beginning of the grand cycle of life, the Aries child should feel right at home at a young age. This is why it is particularly sad to find one who has had an unhappy childhood. In a way, the Aries child demands more from this period of life than those born under other signs. All Aries children really need is to be left alone in a secure setting to fully express themselves without undue censure, punishment, or constriction. The biggest mistake that a parent can make is to load heavy responsibilities, especially adolescent and adult ones, on and Aries child. Allowed to play, learn, and grow naturally, the Aries child enjoys youth more than most.

STRENGTHS

Playful

Natural

Happy

WEAKNESSES

Constricted

Criticized

Sad

INTERACTIVE STYLE

Open

Fun

Energetic

Personality Development and the Aries Child

Rather than attempting to mold the Aries child, you should allow their personality to unfold naturally. Constant disapproval will stunt their growth by undermining natural self-confidence. Aries kids love to play (sometimes in an overly exuberant fashion), but putting a heavy damper on their energies is not the answer. Gently guide them to see things from other points of view and to learn that what they enjoy doing may not always be enjoyable for their playmates. There is always the problem of what to do with the excess energy that the Aries child generates. Fun but constructive tasks will channel such energies and pay rich rewards developmentally.

Hobbies/Interests/Career Paths for the Aries Child

Aries children are action- rather than study-oriented. Although they enjoy reading, they most like putting their ideas into practice rather than just thinking about them. If an Aries child is convinced that a hole dug deep enough will come out on the other side of the world, you may one day discover them excavating a huge cavity in your back-yard. Aries children love hobbies and leisure-time activities, often ones of their own making. Whatever they discover instantly becomes theirs. They lead a big interior life often peopled with their favorite fantasy characters. In choosing a career path, an adult Aries who becomes most successful is likely to be one who can successfully incorporate this element of play and innovation into their profession.

Discipline and the Aries Child

Aries children need discipline, which can provide the structure needed to channel their prodigious energies, but rules must make sense to them and never manifest as needless, harping criticism. Such negativity is likely to extinguish their essential fire or reduce it to a dull glow. Thus a good balance must be found between the equally undesirable extremes of their chaotic, frenetic behavior on the one hand and your repressive and excessively limiting conditions on the other. Normally, a wise, sensitive parent will find the right way to treat the Aries child, balancing permissiveness and firm guidance in an intelligent fashion.

Affection Level and the Aries Child

Aries children desperately crave affection, but as adults they may have trouble expressing it. Although hugs are welcome occasionally, it is a smile, a kind word, or a loving gesture that touches their hearts the most. For the Aries child, affection is simply kindness expressed in an easy manner. Aries children are most mistrustful of the grand gesture on an adult's part, having an unerring instinct for what is real and what is fake in the realm of feelings. They seek to read affection in people's eyes and voices, and they are tough customers to fool.

Dealing with the Aries Child and Interactions with Siblings

Since Aries children tend to play a dominant role relative to siblings, parents may find themselves scolding them too often. Such behavior, particularly in front of the other child(ren), should be avoided. It is best to take the Aries child aside and calmly explain why the behavior was unacceptable. Should Aries be the oldest and prone to jealousy upon the birth of a sibling, their interest in neglecting or hurting the other child must be turned in a constructive direction, toward protecting and gently playing with their new sibling. This can normally be accomplished if the parent is patient and sensitive to the needs of both children.

Interacting with the Adult Aries Child

Should Aries children feel that they were deprived of a true childhood, it will be very difficult for parents to gain their approval and trust. Frequently, such Aries children are over-serious and studiously avoid or even deny their own essentially childlike nature. Parents are often successful in reestablishing tight bonds with their Aries children by finding common activities that they both enjoy, rather than attempting to talk things out or analyze them. Aries adults will generally shy away from psychological approaches on the part of their parents, but despite initial resistance to undergoing therapy, they will often seek it out when living on their own.

Taurus

BIRTHDATE **APRIL 21–MAY 21**

Taurus represents fixed earth in the zodiac cycle, underlining the stubbornness and sensuality inherent in those born under this sign. With Venus as their ruling planet, Tauruses are taken up with beauty and all types of physical expression, from sports to fashion and design. Although they can be quite active once they get going, Tauruses love relaxing and taking it easy, so much that they tend to procrastinate, preferring to remain comfortable right where they are rather than moving on.

Work

TAURUS
April 21–May 21

The Taurus Boss

Many people have described the Taurus personality as bossy. Indeed, the Taurus boss is comfortable in this role, but prefers to stay behind the scenes and let things run smoothly on their own. This, of course, assumes that employees have been well coached and know what to expect from a Taurus boss. Such assumptions are not always justified, although Taurus bosses usually take the time and trouble to spell out how they want their employees to proceed. Rules and regulations are usually kept to a minimum but are written in stone, at least as far as the Taurus boss is concerned.

Asking the Taurus Boss for a Raise

Thorough preparation is necessary when asking a Taurus boss for a raise. Schedule an appointment at least a week in advance, giving yourself enough time to state your case in writing, underlining your past achievements in order to make a strong presentation. Bring this document to the meeting and leave it with your Taurus boss when you exit. It is important not to rush during the meeting, nor to exert any pressure. Let the facts speak for themselves, but at the same time, voice your demands unequivocally. Unless you truly intend to do so, never threaten to leave the company if your request is not met. The Taurus boss will not take you seriously again unless you follow through on what you say you will do. Do not make idle threats to a Taurus boss.

Breaking Bad News to the Taurus Boss

Cushioning the blow by engaging in pleasant foreplay is advised. It is very important that you prepare your Taurus boss, making the atmosphere comfortable and relaxed. Avoid blurting out the news after an uncomfortable silence; rather, lead into it with background materials that explain the reasons for the failure or breakdown. Assuming responsibility will impress your Taurus boss. Under no circumstances should you try to shift the blame to your manager, the company, or a coworker. Work out a scenario ahead of time in response to your boss's inevitable query about damage control and what new direction to take.

STRENGTHS
Stable
Attentive
Careful

WEAKNESSES
Bossy
Inflexible
Insensitive

INTERACTIVE STYLE
Concerned
Instructive
Explicit

Arranging Travel and/or Entertainment for the Taurus Boss

True sensualists, Taurus bosses like comfort and pleasure. Thus you must pay attention to the details that will ensure their having a good time during a night out or an overnight stay on the road. For many, the fringe benefits of their jobs are almost as important as a good salary, and this certainly includes food, drink, entertainment, and the luxuries of business-class travel. Do not be wasteful with the company's funds, however, since the Taurus boss is keenly aware of what these things cost. Bargains that do not sacrifice quality will be appreciated, and you will earn points for your astute investigations.

Decision-Making and the Taurus Boss

Taurus bosses will be especially watchful and critical when evaluating your decisions. Few matters give them greater insight into your character and abilities. When it comes down to crunch time, they want to know they can count on your good judgment. Therefore, do not make impulsive or spur-of-the-moment decisions, but give yourself the time necessary to think out and then implement your plans thoroughly. Your Taurus boss may even (without your knowledge) set up a situation that is in fact a test case in which you are being assessed for promotion to an administrative post.

Impressing and/or Motivating the Taurus Boss

Taurus bosses are most impressed by dedication and hard work. Dependability also rates highly. It is not generally strokes of brilliance or lightning successes that carry the most weight for them, but rather the day-to-day smooth running of your department. Avoid being branded as a troublemaker or even as a mover and shaker. It's best to be the diplomat or peacemaker—the quiet, capable, effective employee. Pragmatic to the extreme, the Taurus boss will want to see solid achievements over a period of time when evaluating your work. This, above all else, will motivate your Taurus boss to offer you a raise or advancement.

Making Proposals and/or Giving Presentations to the Taurus Boss

Use tried-and-true methods. In group settings, make sure that you have copies of well-prepared written material for each person present. Keep presentations simple and don't feel the need to use high-tech communication. Drawings and computerized visuals on a single screen will be simple yet effective without drawing attention. The spotlight should be on your spoken and written words rather than on the means of presentation. Let your content speak for itself. Your Taurus boss will be most impressed with your data, well-thought-out ideas, and practical reasoning. Avoid wide-eyed idealism or unrealistic predictions.

The Taurus Employee

Taurus employees are decidedly work-oriented. However, they have their own way of accomplishing things, and it's usually in a relaxed fashion. This means that because their own personal comfort is so important to them, they are likely to proceed slowly and surely. Moreover, since they will never do today what they can put off until tomorrow, they may have trouble meeting deadlines. Terrible procrastinators, Taurus employees frequently put off things that they are not really in the mood to do, solely for the sake of their own personal pleasure. Their bosses and coworkers will get better results through cajoling and gentle prodding rather than sharply ordering them about.

Interviewing and/or Hiring the Taurus Employee

In general, Tauruses are interested in the security that a job has to offer. Although they will expect a decent salary, they are more captivated by benefits such as medical insurance, retirement, vacation leave, and profit-sharing or bonuses. Tauruses want to know what they are getting into before signing on the dotted line. You should thoroughly explain the philosophy and goals of the company, particularly stressing the role they will play in the organization. Nasty surprises are the bane of all Tauruses, so leave nothing out in your description of the job.

Breaking Bad News to or Firing the Taurus Employee

Tauruses can handle blunt behavior, so it is best to just come out and tell them without beating around the bush. Taurus employees are, generally speaking, not quitters, so it is unlikely that they will save you the trouble of firing them by leaving. Since they tend to hang on until the bitter end, you will have to deliver the coup de grâce yourself once you decide to get rid of a Taurus. Make the reasons for your decision clear, although Tauruses will probably stubbornly disagree with charges or allegations made against them.

Traveling with and Entertaining the Taurus Employee

True sensualists, Tauruses like to fully enjoy the physical comforts of whatever activity they are engaged in. You may have to put them on a fixed budget to keep them from overspending, since their weakness for food and comfortable accommodations can put your finances to the test. They dislike sharing a room or eating only part of a meal; what they have is theirs and to be enjoyed by them alone. Although capable of sharing, they generally do not really like to, except of course for the social aspects of enjoying a show, dance, or conference.

Assigning Tasks to the Taurus Employee

As long as a task is well defined and they believe they can accomplish it, Taurus employees will produce decent, if not excellent, results. However, if they do not understand your less-than-sterling presentation or have serious doubts that you choose to ignore, you can expect the worst. The secret to procuring good work from Taurus employees is making sure they are on track from the start. They are unlikely to take a detour or make a sudden about-face in the middle of a project. Keep in mind their pragmatic approach and do not expect or demand brilliance or even overly imaginative results.

STRENGTHS

Dedicated

Work-oriented

Slow and sure

WEAKNESSES

Procrastinating

Over-relaxed

Hedonistic

INTERACTIVE STYLE

Steady

Confident

Understated

Motivating or Impressing the Taurus Employee

Tauruses are very reward-oriented, so the carrot-on-the-stick approach usually works. The stick can be used sans carrot also, but only if it is to gently prod rather than flog. Taurus employees will be impressed most by wisdom and knowledge of the world, but also by your command of facts. Your persuasiveness and charm will be noticed but not necessarily succumbed to. Although what you have to say is generally more important than the way you say it, the average Taurus employee reacts well to a soft voice and a warm, human approach.

Managing, Directing, or Criticizing the Taurus Employee

Tauruses are capable of handling constructive criticism that is offered in the right spirit. Actually, they would much prefer to have an honest evaluation of their work (particularly one they can benefit from, even if negative) rather than false compliments and flattery. Taurus employees want to produce the best possible results, and if your criticism and direction can help them produce it, so much the better. They can be left to work on their own, but will occasionally want your input or approval to be sure they are heading in the right direction. Just have a quick look over their work every now and then.

The Taurus Coworker

STRENGTHS
Dedicated
Hard working
Dependable

WEAKNESSES
Resistant
Stubborn
Recalcitrant

INTERACTIVE STYLE
Well-directed
Helpful
Stable

Taurus coworkers can become the mainstays and workhorses of a department. Ultra-dependable, they should not be taken advantage of or pushed beyond reasonable bounds, because even they have a limit. This is not to imply a lack of intelligence on their part by any means. Generally, Taurus coworkers can be counted on, unless they are diametrically opposed to the direction things are taking. At that point, there may be only two alternatives left for them: either to slow their efforts to the point of civil disobedience or to outright quit or apply for a transfer.

Approaching the Taurus Coworker for Advice

If you are agitated and upset, a few minutes with a Taurus advisor may calm you down. Often possessed of life wisdom, Taurus coworkers will take the time and trouble to be truly helpful to you in a time of need. Although they may well offer you unsolicited advice, things usually go better when they are approached by others. They may ask for a period of time to mull things over to come up with a workable solution to your problem(s). If your situation demands confrontation, they will urge it but, whenever possible, may advocate a hands-off approach that lets things work themselves out.

Approaching the Taurus Coworker for Help

Taurus coworkers may decline getting involved in direct help or protest, preferring not to rock the boat. (However, should the bull see red, or feel like you are being unfairly treated, it will usually gallop to your defense.) Taureses are particularly sensitive about the mistreatment of those much younger or much older than they are, being quick to defend if they suspect these people are being taken advantage of. They will help financially when possible, but usually to a limited extent, being conservative in such matters. Tauruses will also share their space, transportation, or even clothing during emergency situations without question of repayment when they are in need.

Traveling with and Entertaining the Taurus Coworker

Basically, Taurus coworkers prefer to be at home. That said, they enjoy traveling once or twice a year to faraway places. They are very good about making travel reservations and plans for themselves as well as others. Entertaining is a Taurus specialty, although they are likely to want to take over the planning of office parties or celebrations. In such situations, try managing the Taurus dominant streak by assigning your coworker one specific task and urging them to stick to it. However, when needed to fill in at the last minute, they can always be called on.

The Taurus Coworker Cooperating with Others

It is easy for Taurus coworkers to cooperate with others as long as projects are running smoothly. But if problems emerge they can become very vocal in their dissatisfaction and often insist on taking most of the responsibilities on their own broad shoulders. Problems can arise when others see them as being too dominant, bossy, or stubborn. Taurus professionals are very demanding and above all hate shoddy or sloppy work and outright incompetence. Others who do not understand that a bad job is being done may very well resent the Taurus urge to set things right.

Impressing and Motivating the Taurus Coworker

Tauruses are best motivated by reward, although they will rarely demand it. Their inner motivation is usually just their desire to see a job finished well, with benefits accruing for all. Their own personal reward may thus simply be satisfaction, but motivating them through bonuses, a vacation, or a raise will be gratefully accepted and will urge them to work even harder. Taurus coworkers are always impressed by the gratefulness and thanks of others, although these are not required. Impressed by prestige, the Taurus coworker gratefully accepts personally delivered thanks or commendation from the highest levels of the organization.

Persuading and/or Criticizing the Taurus Coworker

Legendarily stubborn, Taurus coworkers can be difficult to convince initially and, once they have made up their minds, often impossible to change. Criticism is not usually a problem for Tauruses and they may even be grateful for such attitudes as long as the criticism proves helpful and is delivered the right way. They should be approached quietly and alone whenever possible, for they resent being called out or embarrassed in any way in front of the group. In a peaceful and neutral setting they will usually be happy to talk things out and listen. Once they have heard you, however, they will resent having to listen to you a second or third time.

The Taurus Client

STRENGTHS

Easygoing

Strong

Knowing

WEAKNESSES

Inflexible

Unamused

Unimaginative

INTERACTIVE STYLE

Fixed

Focused

Demanding

Although deceptively easygoing, Taurus clients will present their wishes and demands unequivocally. It is not a good idea to change the subject while they are speaking, propose alternatives, or in any way divert attention from the task at hand. Furthermore, in your initial planning and implementation of a program that will satisfy their desires, it is best to remain on track, focused on their primary wishes and objectives. However, all Tauruses love richness and fullness as well, so as things develop, your Taurus clients will be pleased with any and all kinds of goodies and extras that you attach to a product or service. They are most pleased when their customers respond positively to such bells and whistles.

Impressing the Taurus Client

Taurus clients will generally be impressed only with those who can keep their eyes on the ball. Very critical and short-tempered with those who flit superficially like butterflies from one subject to the next, these solid customers are difficult to charm and get around. They will also be very critical if you repeat something they have already said or give other indications that you are not listening carefully to them. Moreover, they will remind you of such lapses and be apt to chide you for this kind of behavior, even at your first meeting. Let them do most of the talking, but answer intelligently and succinctly when questioned.

Selling to the Taurus Client

Often a Taurus customer will reach a point in your first meeting where he or she comfortably leans back and gives you that look that says, simply, "Convince me." At this point, you must be fully prepared to muster every ounce of heavy artillery at your disposal, including facts, charts, graphs, and any appropriate visual material, since this client is very visually oriented. Should you pass this test, whenever it arrives, you will have gone a long way toward making your sale. You will often, but not always, be able to read your success or failure in the face of your Taurus client, although many such clients will studiously hide any reaction until they have had time later to consider and reconsider your presentation.

Your Appearance and the Taurus Client

Look good. Do not be afraid to wear stylish cuts, in rich colors and fabrics, and look your best in order to demonstrate the quality of the company you represent. Remember that to a Taurus client, all the material aspects of your presentation, including every single line of written, auditory, or visual material, must reek of quality. Conversely, any mistake you make will be seen as a reflection on the slipshod quality of your company's service or production. Thus, before your first meeting, make sure you are totally prepared for the most demanding scrutiny.

Keeping the Taurus Client's Interest

Although serious, Taurus clients also love to be pleased and entertained. They may be heavy in their demands, but as long as you have the facts at your fingertips and otherwise are impeccably prepared, you can turn on the charm from time to time. They are often fascinated by a light touch on your part, and occasional humor in the form of banter (rather than a joke that could bomb) is highly recommended. If you feel they are losing interest at any point, offer them refreshment or a break, change the subject, or ask them outright what they would like to know. Avoid long, uncomfortable silences. Maintain a calm but steady rhythm in your presentation.

Breaking Bad News to the Taurus Client

If the bad news is well presented, Taurus clients may surprise you by receiving it in a matter-of-fact way. This does not necessarily mean that they like it or even accept it, but rather than telling you so, Tauruses are instead more likely to go to your boss or board of directors. In presenting the bad news, do not attempt to disguise it, but treat it in an objective, albeit concerned, manner. At least then you will not be accused of misrepresenting the facts or lying. Should you feel exceptionally bad or responsible for what happened, you would be wise to express your feelings succinctly.

Entertaining the Taurus Client

Venus-ruled, Taurus clients love beauty, physical enjoyment, entertainment, food, drink, and pleasant surroundings. Thus, for example, in taking them out to dinner you will find that the ambiance, service, and presentation of the food will be just as important to them as its taste. Be prepared for them to expect a top restaurant and to order expensive items, since they are known to have lavish tastes. Once you see that they are thoroughly enjoying themselves, you can breathe a sigh of relief, knowing that you have a good chance of success in your business dealings. Keep the conversation amusing and do not raise business issues, allowing your Taurus client to make the first move on the subject.

The Taurus Business Partner

Generally speaking, Taurus business partners will feel they have a better understanding of what is going on than you do. Highly opinionated and a tad bossy, they are less concerned with taking the lead than with making the final decisions. In fact, that is what most interests this solid and committed individual. You may find your objections brushed aside or unheeded, creating some tension and frustration. However, even in cases where you think your Taurus partner is completely wrong, over time you may come to understand and even agree with their point of view. The Taurus partner can also be a good buffer against the more unpleasant aspects of business, providing security for you, the company, and everyone who works for and with you.

Setting Up the Business Partnership with Taurus

Rather than leave the setting up of the partnership to Taurus partners, you would be better off submitting your plans to them and allowing them to critically comment, edit, and add to them. Usually a good compromise can be reached through this simple method. It will usually not work, however, if you let a Taurus submit the first draft to you or work alongside you in writing the agreement, for Taurus partners will become

STRENGTHS

Protective

Solid

Committed

WEAKNESSES

Bossy

Unheeding

Opinionated

INTERACTIVE STYLE

Conclusive

Immovable

Formidable

discouraged if they constantly feel their input is requested and then rejected or, worse, ignored. Be sure to spell out their role in the partnership very clearly in the original proposal, being sure to assign them a good deal of the responsibility for the day-to-day running of things.

Tasking with the Taurus Business Partner

It is a mistake to think that this tough, pragmatic individual should be given only practical tasks. Taurus partners are also ideas people who understand the theoretical aspects of production, marketing, sales, and especially public relations. They can be a bit irresponsible with cash outlays, tending to spend freely when they feel an item is essential to their work, although a saving grace is that they usually seek out the best bargains, too. Be sure that your agreement is needed on cash outlays over a certain amount. Because of their strong physical presence, Tauruses can be impressive representatives for the firm.

Traveling with and Entertaining the Taurus Business Partner

Taurus partners can run up huge bills when they are doing the traveling and entertaining. The Taurus partner has an undeniably lavish streak that is motivated by a love of luxury and comfort. Strangely enough, when it comes to office parties and arranging trips or entertainment for others, this individual can often be counted on to do things economically but still well enough to delight all concerned. Taurus partners will have to be protected against their blind spots when it comes to cash outlays for themselves; this can be managed by you or your financial manager presenting them with a strict budget beforehand.

Managing and Directing the Taurus Business Partner

Although most Taurus partners want to be the boss in most situations, they can be managed and directed as long as you appeal to their practical side and acknowledge their skill at making things work out for the best. Once they agree with your basic idea, leave the implementation to them, if logistically possible. In outright confrontations they can be alternately passive and aggressive—on defense, resembling the immovable object, and on offense, the irresistible force—so it is best to avoid head-on collisions. If you are sensitive to their feelings or show you trust them, they will be quite open to considering your suggestions. Avoid giving them orders.

Relating to the Taurus Business Partner in the Long Run

Taurus partners are usually loyal and committed in their business relationships, being long-suffering types who hang in there for the duration. This does not imply that they are easy to relate to, however, since they can go along with things silently for only so long before making their true feelings known, usually in a blunt and forceful manner. Therefore, it helps to have regular meetings in which you encourage them to voice their complaints rather than burying resentments inside. Once they see that you are prepared to accept what they say and act on it, or even that you are open to hearing them out, they will be much easier to work with.

Parting Ways with the Taurus Business Partner

Taurus partners are highly possessive and usually will come to look on your business as largely their own. Thus it is very hard for them to give up the company, particularly one they feel they have nurtured, directed, and developed. If mutual legal representation by an arbiter can be agreed upon, that is the best scenario. However, stubborn Tauruses may seek their own personal legal representative or even represent their own interests. Be prepared to debate finances, real property, responsibilities, insurances, and even objects to which they have become attached. Often they will be interested in buying you out and continue the business on their own.

The Taurus Competitor

Tenacious and determined, Taurus competitors are not ones you can easily sweep out of the way, particularly if they have a long history in the field, for they will resist any attempt to oust them from their station, especially if they have been number one. Every ounce of their energy and that of their company will be put into resisting, undermining, and carefully attacking your product. Thinking them a bit stodgy or slow, you may seek to outwit or trick them, but they can be extremely canny and wary of swallowing the bait. Perhaps the best you can hope for is that each of your companies solidifies its own position and prospers alongside the other without undue damage to either.

Countering the Taurus Competitor

Seek to develop a share of the market that you can make your own. Avoid attacking Taurus competitors head-on, but instead seek another route around them. Once they see that you are not a threat to the main part of their domain, they are likely to let up a bit in their vigilance and be more accepting of your efforts. Also convince them that there is room for two excellent products. Seeking peaceful negotiations, embracing the status quo (at least for the time being), and being open to compromise will soothe their savage protectiveness. Above all, always treat them with respect and not a hint of ridicule.

Out-Planning the Taurus Competitor

If it must be all-out war or fierce competition, you will have to work hard to out-plan your Taurus foes. They are excellent defensively, and it is extremely difficult to tease them into reacting so you can find an opening in their armor. You will do best to psych them out, discovering by aboveboard means what their plans are and how they mean to attack you, if at all. Do not anticipate them in this effort, but proceed slowly and surely, doing the necessary research. Once you are sure of their intent, you can make your own battle plan, which perhaps will begin with a lightning strike or blitz on their weak spot.

Impressing the Taurus Competitor in Person

Remain cool, calm, and collected. Taurus competitors will be most impressed with the subjects discussed only if you show you have done extensive research and have all the facts at your fingertips. Your dress, style, and manner should be a bit on the conservative

STRENGTHS
Tenacious
Determined
Resisting

WEAKNESSES
Overly conservative
Unimaginative
Stuck

INTERACTIVE STYLE
Proud
Imperious
Unyielding

side so that they will take you seriously. Show that you respect them as a worthy opponent but also that your roles vis-à-vis each other can be more accepting and less adversarial. Although Taurus competitors can be long-winded and dominate the conversation, you should not seek to halt their verbal flow but rather undermine their position gradually with short, well-chosen remarks.

Undercutting and Outbidding the Taurus Competitor

Should you both be vying for the same client or seeking to promote the same or similar products, you will be forced to adopt an aggressive approach. This will necessarily involve not only making your product or service look good but also making theirs look bad. There is probably no need to make up faults or exaggerate existing ones since there are probably real drawbacks to their company's approach that are well known to everyone in the field. Home in on these weak spots and hammer them unmercifully. Then show how your company can succeed in these very areas and offer even more bonuses to the consumer and professional alike.

Public Relations Wars with the Taurus Competitor

Chances are that the Taurus public relations approach will attempt to be chic and stylish but also just a tad outmoded. Seek to mount a glitzy campaign, dazzling in its novel approach, and sweep your opponents off their feet. You will know that you have succeeded not only by rising sale figures and corresponding drops for your opponents but also by the silence emanating from the enemy camp, the surest compliment they are able to give. Concentrate on getting the media interested in your work so that you become news rather than plain-old paid advertising. Use your charm to obtain print and video coverage, particularly in landing interviews.

The Taurus Competitor and the Personal Approach

When dealing one-on-one with Taurus opponents, it is best to avoid the personal approach and instead deal with them in a strictly professional fashion. This may motivate them at some point in your dialogue or future interactions to cross the line and attempt to be a bit more informal or friendly; here you will be able to decide whether to accept this overture or not. Either way, you will be in the driver's seat. Should you both be addressing the same group or appearing at a customer's board meeting, be sure that your Taurus opponent speaks first. Pay particular attention to their approach and be prepared to reference their mistakes in your presentation, but keep your tone friendly and light.

Love

The Taurus First Date

Taurus first dates are usually slow movers. They want to have a look at you first, and in their own time they will decide whether they want to see you again or to define the nature of your relationship with them. Tauruses have a good sense of what clicks and what doesn't, but they are unlikely to be overly demonstrative on the first date; they are usually careful not to give away what they think or feel in this respect. Often physically appealing, they will make a strong impression with their looks, but also with their voices, which can be seductive and well modulated.

Wooing and Picking Up the Taurus First Date

Quite friendly, most Tauruses will be at least open to your initial advances. They will expect, however, that you not come on too strong, for these patient customers need time to make up their minds. Suggest going for a walk, or, if you are already walking, continue doing so. If you literally bump into each other or meet casually at a social event, you will do best in the initial moments to be quiet and listen to what the Taurus has to say, also giving them an opportunity to take a good look at you. If you can arouse a Taurus's curiosity with your silence, so much the better.

Suggested Activities for the Taurus First Date

Ruled by Venus, Tauruses will love activities of an aesthetic and sensual nature. When you are selecting a meeting point for coffee or a drink, a restaurant, or a film or show, keep in mind that quality is very important to them. Going for a walk in a beautiful environment is always a good idea for the nature-loving Taurus, provided that the weather is good. Walking around in the rain or cold is definitely not the Taurus's idea of a good time. Generally, Taurus first dates are full of warmth, comfort, and security.

Turn-Ons and Turn-Offs for the Taurus First Date

Taurus first dates are usually unimpressed or outright turned off by a big mouth. On the other hand, they are impressed by modesty and self-confidence. Most of all, they want to find something intriguing about you that will make them want to know you better. Never try to rush or pressure them, but allow them to proceed at their own pace.

STRENGTHS

Confident

Thoughtful

Good-looking

WEAKNESSES

Procrastinating

Unresponsive

Undemonstrative

INTERACTIVE STYLE

Balanced

Self-assured

Physical

By falling into their rhythm, you will be able to advance to the next step without sliding backward in your efforts. Their facial expressions and body language will let you know how you are doing.

Making "the Move" with the Taurus First Date

A typical situation with Taurus first dates: you make a casual move to put your arm around them, touch them, or take their hand, and you get a sharp look that seems to say, "Don't," and to silently add more softly, "I'll tell you when." Always remember that Venus-ruled Tauruses regard love as their province, resenting any and all intrusions into their world. Allow them to make their choices, and be responsive as often as possible, without them having to tell you. Show them silently that you are both on the same wavelength.

Impressing the Taurus First Date

Taurus first dates are less impressed with an aggressive attitude, verbal facility, or good looks than by an interesting nature and ability to understand them and their wishes. Thus, the best way to impress them is by establishing an easygoing atmosphere in which they feel free to either respond or not. Allow things to unfold naturally; gently guiding the date in a positive direction (yours) is probably the best way to proceed. Impress them along the way with your steady persistence and acceptance rather than a show-off attitude. Show your appreciation of their clothes, hairstyle, and general appearance if they have gone to some trouble in their preparation.

Brushing Off the Taurus First Date

Generally, it is the Taurus who will do the brushing off, and this can happen very quickly, in quite a brutal fashion. But Tauruses are not that easy to brush off because, if they like you, they will be very determined and persistent in their efforts. However, their pride and strong self-image will not tolerate much outright rejection, so if you want to get rid of them, just make it completely clear either that you are definitely not interested or that things are not working out. As long as you are not sending mixed messages, getting rid of them should not be a problem. With difficult cases, take the time to explain.

The Taurus Romantic Partner

Tauruses tend to be very possessive in matters of love. They will look at you as belonging to them as much as their home, their car, or their clothes, and they will consider this a great compliment to you. Problems arise, of course, if you do not entirely agree with them, insisting that you are your own person and have the freedom to do as you wish. They may even seem to agree with you, since doing so only reinforces their belief in their fairness and shows how secure their love for you really is. But, in fact, they will never want to share you or give you up when their feelings go deep enough.

Having a Discussion with the Taurus Romantic Partner

Tauruses can be patient listeners but are quite opinionated and tend to be judgmental. Generally, rather than being moral, their values reflect their pragmatic nature, which care more about whether something will work rather than whether it is right or wrong. Thus, they can be quite objective in their discussions with you, since they are open to listening and rarely will condemn you ethically. You would do well to listen to their advice because their judgment is often sound, but beware of their tendency to be dogmatic and fixed on certain ideas.

Arguments with the Taurus Romantic Partner

Tauruses will very stubbornly hold on to their well-entrenched position on most topics. Thus, arguments with them tend to be counterproductive because the more you try to attack or convince them, the more recalcitrant they will become. Often cool, calm, and collected, Tauruses will show great patience and even endure an occasional insult. But when they reach the breaking point it can be like waving the red flag in front of the proverbial bull. Their charge can be explosive and is best not ignited at all costs. Avoiding arguments with them altogether is often the best solution.

Traveling with the Taurus Romantic Partner

Although Tauruses can be good travelers and enjoy this pursuit thoroughly, they are also often happier to stay at home. Two problems with traveling with Tauruses are their love of luxury and their tendency to carry, or have you carry, half of their possessions at all times. Even worse, since they love to shop, their bags, backpacks, or suitcases may be almost unliftable by the time you are ready to head home. Of course, as the weight of your luggage goes up, the weight of your wallet goes down, for few astrological signs enjoy buying gifts, and in general spending money, as much as this one.

Sex with the Taurus Romantic Partner

Taurus romantic partners tend to be matter-of-fact and frank about sex. They are not at all shy about talking about it or, for that matter, initiating it. It is often truly carnal sex for its own sake that they are interested in, more or less satisfying their hunger for it as they would for food or sleep. Consequently, you may be less than satisfied with the lack of mystery or subtlety in their approach to the subject. Also, the act can be curiously impersonal, causing you to wonder if they really know, or even care, who you are.

Affection and the Taurus Romantic Partner

Venus-ruled Taurus romantic partners can be extremely affectionate. But do not forget that for them, affection is affection, sex is sex, love is love, and none of them is a satisfactory replacement for another. Their expressions of affection can be decidedly physical, including, but not limited to, a hug, caress, reassuring touch, or fond glance. Somehow they manage to convey ownership with any of these, however, which can make you decidedly uncomfortable, particularly in front of close friends. Rejecting their affectionate gestures is the worst thing you can do, however. Just grin and bear them.

(The Taurus Romantic Partner)

STRENGTHS
Loving
Caring
Involved

WEAKNESSES
Overpossessive
Controlling
Manipulative

INTERACTIVE STYLE
Forthright
Frank
Giving

Humor and the Taurus Romantic Partner

Tauruses are literalists, and therefore most jokes, puns, and wordplay do not generally get a big rise out of them. They hate being laughed at but occasionally can join in when they do not feel unduly threatened. The comedians they like are usually fine actors who so perfectly play their role that Taurus's admiration, enjoyment, and, hence, laughter are fully elicited. Always up for enjoying themselves and having a good time, Taurus will often prefer light humor in the form of films, plays, or the latest pulp fiction. Keep them in a good mood as much as possible to avoid problems.

The Taurus Spouse

Taurus spouses can be extremely devoted, stable, dependable, and caring. They will usually assume a dominant role in domestic and family matters, wanting to make the major decisions or, at the very least, playing an important role in implementing them. Although capable of procrastination on such matters for weeks or even years, once they make up their minds and begin to act, Tauruses cannot usually be stopped. Fond of the pleasures of bed and table, the Taurus spouse will want the home to be a comfortable and secure place where children, friends, and family can all feel at ease.

Wedding and Honeymoon with the Taurus Spouse

Although practical and able to find good bargains, Tauruses will usually want to spare no expense in providing an impressive ceremony and lavish reception for their wedding. Likewise, they will want the honeymoon to take place in an especially beautiful location, either natural or luxurious or both. The surroundings will also serve to put them at ease so that they can enjoy the honeymoon to the fullest. Taurus newlyweds are not interested in troublesome scenes, worried thoughts, or any form of negativity that will keep them or you from enjoying the experience of a lifetime.

Home and Day-to-Day Married Life with the Taurus Spouse

Not ones to be uncertain in their plans, Taurus newlyweds will have a very good idea what type of home they want to have. They want it to be comfortable and beautiful, with harmonious colors, chic fabrics, pleasing lines, and eye-catching settings and highlights. Once the home is set up, Taurus spouses are unlikely to want to change things and will have a decided resistance against your wishes to do so. Furthermore, they are convinced their taste is impeccable, so your objections are just evidence of your lack of it. Thus, you should leave the decorating to them whenever possible.

Finances and the Taurus Spouse

Tauruses are not always the most exciting people in the world, but they are among the more expensive. Their tastes tend toward the lavish, and they cannot keep themselves from spending money, particularly when it comes to a sale or bargain. Arguments about money and how it should be spent can be an ever-present issue with them, so whenever possible, they should spend their own money if they are working, or have their say within the limits of a fairly strict budget. Letting them make independent financial decisions will serve to diminish arguments.

Infidelity and the Taurus Spouse

Because of their generally amoral attitude toward sex, Tauruses will see nothing wrong with sharing intimacies with others, as long as such affairs can be shrugged off and do not threaten their marriage. Yet if truly happily married, they will rarely, if ever, cheat on their mates. Tauruses are drawn to physical beauty like a moth to a flame, however, so if they are very (or even a bit) unhappy or dissatisfied, they will find it difficult to resist an invitation to spend an occasional afternoon or night in the arms of a lover.

Children and the Taurus Spouse

Generally speaking, Tauruses make wonderful parents. True nurturers, they get enormous satisfaction out of giving to or caring for others. Moreover, they have a decided aversion to all forms of mistreatment of children and small animals, so their homes are often filled with hordes of both. Tauruses fully expect that their children's friends and pets will also be considered part of the family and therefore be present a good deal of the time. The only child of a Taurus parent may feel truly suffocated by the attention lavished on him or her, so having at least one brother or sister is best.

Divorce and the Taurus Spouse

Be prepared to be taken to the cleaners. Tauruses do not give up money or possessions very easily. Their true consolation in losing you may prove to be getting plenty of cash and most of the furniture and house. Generally not shy or deceitful about such matters, Tauruses will make their demands abundantly clear through a lawyer. Not ones to seek revenge, they will simply want to be adequately compensated for their years of selfless service, as they see it. They will be happy to talk things over in great detail in an unambiguous and unemotional fashion and to be as fair toward you as they possibly can.

The Taurus Lover

Don't be surprised when Taurus lovers expect you to return to your spouse or romantic partner after your first enjoyable rendezvous. Taurus lovers can be so matter-of-fact about their desires that they will often make it clear their feelings do not imply living together, sharing affection, or even spending the night together after the main reason for getting together has passed. However, once you really get under their skin, they will want to hold on to you and probably become your regular romantic or married partner. As in other areas, Tauruses become attached and very possessive over time.

Sexual

Expressive

Honest

Insensitive

Unsympathetic

Overly possessive

Frank

Unambiguous

Up-front

Meeting the Taurus Lover

Chances are that you will be introduced to Taurus lovers by a mutual friend. Indeed, friendship is often the keynote of such a liaison to begin with, rather than raging animal passion or even physical attraction. You will feel comfortable with them, able to share and talk about yourself, including, of course, your love life. Once they get the idea that this last item is less than satisfactory or absent, they will begin to think of themselves as prime candidates for the role of your lover. Remember, Tauruses are nurturers and instinctively react to anyone being hurt or unfairly treated.

Location and the Taurus Lover

Tauruses are more comfortable in their own place, preferring to meet there whenever possible. Even if they are living with someone they can arrange to be free for periods of time. Part of their seductive charm will be their desire for you to view their tasteful or valuable personal effects, on which they may be prepared to lecture you at length. Not ones for sudden sprawling on the floor or standing against a wall, the bed will probably be very comfortable and well suited to love-making. Be prepared for an enjoyable experience.

Sex and the Taurus Lover

Generally speaking, there are two types of people when it comes to sex: passionate and sensual. Taurus lovers belong to the second category. Not ones to let out their feelings suddenly or violently in explosive bursts, they tend to really enjoy their physical interactions while fully exploring all the sensual realms: taste, touch, smell, sight, sound. They also expect to be pleased in all of these areas for long, uninterrupted periods. Taurus lovers delight in all the carnal sensations that sex has to offer, preferably in an unhurried and uninhibited fashion. Pleasing you means pleasing them, but they also expect you to reciprocate in kind.

Holding On to the Taurus Lover

This is usually unnecessary and frequently impossible, since Tauruses are often the ones who do the holding on—that is, if they are interested. They tend to become more, rather than less, interested as time goes by if things really click. Taurus lovers just can't get enough of their love objects, and like the cornucopia (the proverbial horn of plenty) they never run out of new delights for you. The capacity of Taurus lovers to give is truly amazing, and whether or not you choose to share so much with them is irrelevant as long as they are getting what they want out of the relationship.

Entertaining the Taurus Lover

Taurus lovers usually prefer food above all other forms of entertainment, and thus dining out and eating delicious meals are much more than just amusements to them. Although they are willing to share their experience with you, it will become clear almost immediately that with or without you they would still indulge their appetites to the fullest. Having you along is therefore entertaining, but not essential. Hopefully you are an empathetic type who can appreciate their enjoyment vicariously. If you are able to savor your meal as well (and pay for it), it's an added bonus.

Breaking Up with the Taurus Lover

Taurus lovers will let you know when it is over. Yet they are capable of hanging in there for long periods of time, often absorbing a lot of punishment in the process. Chances are your Taurus lover will put up with a lot more from you than would another zodiac sign, as long as it is their choice. Remember that Taurus is a fixed sign; so just like their reluctance to leave the house, it may be difficult for Tauruses to leave you since they would have to start looking for a new lover all over again. Tauruses get comfortable in their relationships and do not give them up easily.

The Taurus Ex

Taurus exes are likely to pile their responsibilities onto you, particularly when children are involved. Even when going through difficult periods financially and emotionally, they can usually be counted on; in the event that they cannot meet a payment on time, they will certainly let you know beforehand. If the breakup or divorce was Taurus's idea, you may not expect a whole lot more from them than what is required by law.

Establishing a Friendship with the Taurus Ex

It is advisable to form friendships with Taurus exes but beware of their tendency to want to control the family after the breakup. Remember that the average Taurus is not only nurturing but also possessive, and after the marriage is over it is not easy for them to break certain well-developed patterns and attitudes. They will generally be the ones to set the terms of the friendship, and you will have to see whether it is possible for you to agree to these terms. Your Taurus ex will prefer to keep things harmonious between you whenever possible.

Issues of Getting Back Together with the Taurus Ex

Although reconciling may be a possibility in your mind, Taurus exes rarely share that view. For most, when that door closes it remains shut post-separation. However, it is quite possible to forge a new relationship with them, which, in certain respects, can be more successful and rewarding than the original one. The rocks on which the relationship foundered may cease to be obstacles, allowing for the calming of stormy seas. You are probably better off developing this new relationship than trying to return to one that failed—and might fail again for the very same reasons.

Discussing Past Issues with the Taurus Ex

Discussing past issues with a Taurus ex is possible but unlikely to produce significant results. Tauruses know full well why the relationship broke down, and they do not expect to get any new information about this from you. Furthermore, they are rarely interested in raking up old problems for examination or dissection. They do, however, tend toward sentimentality, so it may be nice to occasionally sit down and look at photos or videos and casually reminisce. Beware of letting it go further than that.

STRENGTHS

Responsible

Ethical

Reliable

WEAKNESSES

Controlling

Possessive

Closed

INTERACTIVE STYLE

Frank

Sensual

Honest

Expressing Affection to the Taurus Ex

Affection and sensuality come so naturally to Tauruses that it is difficult to banish these from any relationship with these exes. Tauruses will, of course, be hurt when affection is withheld, and unless they thoroughly hate you, they will be grateful for an occasional kind word or warm expression of feeling. But once a two-year healing period has passed, it will be rare for them to want any more than that. Also, the affection they allow you to express to them, and that they express to you, will be of a different type and on a different level than before—more objective and stylized and less heartfelt or emotional.

Defining the Present Relationship with the Taurus Ex

You will know exactly how Taurus exes feel about your present relationship with them without defining or discussing it. The tone of their voice and behavior patterns are usually a dead giveaway to their feelings about you. You must never state or even imply that they do not know their own minds in this respect or that they are unaware of a true love they feel but cannot express toward you. Tauruses know what they know about themselves, and what they may not know is of no interest to them. Denial and conflict are sure to follow any attempt you make to convince them otherwise.

Sharing Custody with the Taurus Ex

If you are not a responsible or capable parent in their eyes, Taurus exes are not likely to want to put the children in your care at all, instead fighting to retain complete control and custody. However, they are sensible and fair enough to know that children often need and want both parents, so they will generally agree to you seeing them on weekends or occasionally during vacations. Should you be given custody, expect that your Taurus ex will want to see the children frequently. Allow this privilege whenever possible.

Friends and Family

The Taurus Friend

Taurus friends will go out of their way for you, being there in your time of need. Faithful and dedicated to your friendship, the Taurus friend is truly involved in helping whenever possible. However, because of their fixed ideas, Tauruses may give the wrong kind of advice while being convinced that they are absolutely right, feeling that their counsel should be followed without question. They seem to view everything so clearly in black-and-white terms, but what they see is too often only what they want to see. Usually fun to be with, Taurus friends will enjoy entertainment, shopping, and short day trips. They will also want your respect in not taking advantage of their generous nature.

Asking for Help from the Taurus Friend

It is best to ask your Taurus friend for help only when you truly need it, for two reasons. First, you may not want to be told what to do or saddled with advice or an inflexible offer of assistance that you don't want to follow. Taurus friends may well take turning down such an offer, or refusal to follow their advice, as a personal rejection of them and their beliefs. Secondly, if you constantly beg for help, like the boy who cried wolf once too often, they will cease to take you seriously. Thus, asking a Taurus friend for help may prove not to be worth the aggravation in the long run.

Communication and Keeping in Touch with the Taurus Friend

Taurus friends like routine and are very much creatures of habit. Keeping in touch through daily email, messaging, text messaging, and calling are all possibilities. Early in the morning and late at night are their favorite times for getting in touch with you. Taurus friends have even been known to keep their cell phones on next to their beds in case you need them in the middle of the night for help or just a chat. Do not take advantage of this fact; try to contact them only during reasonable daytime hours and be considerate of the time they make available to you.

Borrowing Money from the Taurus Friend

Money matters are very important to Tauruses and should not be taken lightly. Money means security to them, and therefore a large loan or one that cannot be paid back in

STRENGTHS
Generous
Helpful
Convincing

WEAKNESSES
Overbearing
Controlling
Omnipotent

INTERACTIVE STYLE
Commanding
Self-assured
Giving

the near future may cause them anxiety and worry. For this reason, even though they may lend you money, it is often best to ask a non-Taurus friend because of the heavy responsibility involved with a Taurus. A casual loan of a small sum that is repaid in a few days is usually no problem for a Taurus friend to handle. Once you have proved yourself trustworthy in this regard you could even find yourself borrowing the same small sum regularly before the weekend and paying it back on Monday.

Asking for Advice from the Taurus Friend

Taurus friends love to give advice, often unsolicited, so you may be spared the trouble of asking them for it. Their bossy and opinionated nature guarantees they will have views on almost any subject. Not only will they expect you to listen to them, but they will also expect you to believe that what they say is true and to follow it without question. The truth in any given situation is so obvious to them that they are often bewildered by those who disagree. Advice given to them in return is appreciated, but not always followed. Tauruses are slow movers and difficult to manage. Besides, giving advice is usually good enough for them without your being expected to reciprocate.

Visiting the Taurus Friend

Taurus friends enjoy occasional visits but do not like you using their places as permanent hangouts or crash pads. They need privacy in order to get work done and also have a limit when it comes to socializing. It is best if you schedule visits in advance rather than dropping in. They would not be at all embarrassed to meet you at the door and replying "yes" to your question, "Am I catching you at a bad time?" Once you have gotten the idea, there is no need for such an event to take place again. Scheduled appointments with Taurus friends will be scrupulously kept and they are most often on time, or at least not usually more than 15 minutes late, which to them is the same thing.

Celebrations/Entertainment with the Taurus Friend

Taurus friends are usually up for a good time as long as others are available to help. Often the problem is that they need to do everything themselves, from cooking to making all the arrangements, including shopping and sending out invitations. Afterward, they are likely to be exhausted and a tad resentful. Therefore, they should be asked to help set things up only if they agree beforehand to share responsibilities with others. Even if they do, you must keep an eye on them since they feel they always know how to do things better and are likely to usurp the authority of others before they even realize they are doing it.

The Taurus Roommate

Because Tauruses are so possessive about their space and furniture, they may find it difficult to share with those they live with. Better off living alone or with a partner, Tauruses experience difficulties sharing space with others whose lives, professionally or privately, are independent of their own. You are probably better off if all concerned parties sit down and hammer out general guidelines and specific rules about what is and is not allowed in the day-to-day living situation in order to avoid problems later. Tauruses can be excellent cleaners, but can also, at times, be unconcerned about spreading their clothes around. Usually they will have to stubbornly do things their own way.

Sharing Financial Responsibilities with the Taurus Roommate

Generally, Taurus roommates are financially responsible, with two exceptions. First, they are likely to have difficulty getting the rent together at the end of the month, and second, they are often in financial debt. Both of these characteristics can make it difficult for them to easily discharge their financial responsibilities in the living situation. Basically, Tauruses are at the mercy of their own needs to spend money and, of course, to over-spend. They have great faith in money appearing out of the blue, which it frequently does for them, and they also do not mind working hard to get it if necessary, but stress will be felt by all from time to time.

Cleaning and the Taurus Roommate

Taurus roommates are good at cleaning once they are motivated to do so. However, they are slow-moving customers who can put up with disorder, particularly their own, as long as most. What really bothers them is your mess, which they will probably impatiently clean up before they do their own or allow you to do so. Because Taurus roommates can submit to schedules when it comes to cleaning, you would be wise to post the cleaning schedule prominently. Expect that they will postpone such responsibilities, since they tend to neglect them for a while and then finish them all off at once. Cleaning often puts them in a bad mood.

Houseguests and the Taurus Roommate

Taurus roommates have a very short fuse when it comes to other people using their stuff. They also get itchy when unfamiliar faces keep appearing with some regularity, and even itchier when familiar faces keep showing up. In short, Tauruses will do their best to put up with you, but not a whole menagerie of friends. Expect them to be blunt and downright impolite in an effort to get your guests to feel unwelcome enough to depart. The best way to handle this issue is for you both to agree that if the Taurus guests are welcome, then yours are too, and that at least acting in a pleasant manner will make things easier for all concerned.

Parties and the Taurus Roommate

If the party is Taurus's idea, you can expect them to follow through with all the necessary shopping, cooking, and cleaning, or at the very least doing a big share of the work. If the party is your idea, your Taurus roommate may make an appearance or not, depending on their mood. Tauruses sometimes have problems sharing common friends, so if you do the planning and inviting, they may bow out for the evening or play sick by holing up in their room. That said, Tauruses have a weak spot for food as well as attention, so they can often be lured out of their retreat with tempting offers of tasty treats and fun conversation.

(The Taurus Roommate)

STRENGTHS

Conscientious

Hard working

Responsible

WEAKNESSES

Difficult

Possessive

Sloppy

INTERACTIVE STYLE

Insistent

Demanding

Blunt

Privacy and the Taurus Roommate

Taurus roommates know how to relate to others when they choose to. Although quite adept socially, they may withdraw completely from time to time and refuse to see anyone, including you. Tauruses that are unable to maintain their strict privacy when they need it can be the unhappiest of campers. On the other hand, when something is preying on their mind or a sudden need surfaces, they are quite likely to walk right in on you and demand your attention. They usually see nothing wrong with this double standard, arguing that you will only benefit in the long (or short) term by their concerned, albeit tactless, intervention.

Discussing Problems with the Taurus Roommate

Tauruses are up for discussing problems, particularly yours. Moreover, they may not be at all shy about giving you advice on life in general and your personal problems in particular without being asked. Do not try to return the favor, since it is generally not appreciated. When you can see that Taurus roommates need to air their discontents and difficulties but are finding it difficult to do so, you can patiently encourage them to speak up over a period of time. They will never thank you for this, but clearly will appreciate your ability to open avenues of communication and allow them to express themselves.

The Taurus Parent

Being nurturers, Tauruses are in their true element as parents. Moreover, they have as much to give three or four children over the long haul as they do to one, and they are quite fond of large families. It is difficult, however, for them to give unconditionally. The conditions that must be met usually conform to their strong beliefs, and if their conditions are not met, Taurus parents are quite capable of not following through on a promise or even taking back what they have given. It is not surprising, then, that their children grow wary when Taurus parents are in a generous mood.

Discipline Style of the Taurus Parent

The discipline that Taurus parents enforce is not usually of a physical nature, except when they see red and lose their composure. For the most part, they choose to diminish or take away privileges. They are experts at insinuating that their children will be grounded, and this warning usually accomplishes its desired coercive purpose. Taurus parents know that continual outright threats will soon lose their power, however, and that they should be made only if there is intent behind them to follow through. Most likely a glance coupled with a restraining touch or hand gesture is enough to get the message across. When Taurus parents grow suddenly silent, it is best to leave them alone.

Affection Level and the Taurus Parent

Taurus parents are fond of cuddling. Extremely physical, they are intoxicated by the sight, touch, and smell of their infants (particularly the skin and scalp). Bringing an upset child into their beds at night to be soothed, or at the very least walking them and humming a favorite melody, is characteristic of their behavior. Although Tauruses are often criticized for letting their offspring be in control, it should be remembered that Taurus parents need a lot of sleep and so are likely to coax a child back to slumber as pleasantly as possible. As their kids grow into childhood, Taurus parents are always there to give a hug and a kind word, often without being asked.

Money Issues and the Taurus Parent

Teaching their children how to handle money is important to Tauruses. Usually they will encourage their children to save whenever possible, either adding coins to a piggy bank or eventually opening a bank account for them. Often, a Taurus parent will act as the bank, keeping scrupulous records and dispensing funds when needed. However, Tauruses will usually give strong advice on how their children's money should be spent. Seeing cash outlays as a chance to invest, they will encourage their kids to put their money into rewarding areas that can pay a return, if not financially, then educationally, rather than wasting it on candy or junk food.

Crises and the Taurus Parent

Although Taurus parents are generally there for their kids in times of crisis, through experience their children may learn to handle problems alone without involving their folks at all. This is because Taurus parents often overreact, take over the situation, and in the future adopt an overly protective or blaming attitude. Meting out punishment is also a reaction that favors secrecy in such matters. Often Taurus parents will even precipitate a crisis through their own behavior. In most cases, if they had been able to back off rather than provoke, the crisis would never have surfaced in the first place.

Holidays/Family Gatherings and the Taurus Parent

When it comes to holidays and family gatherings, Taurus parents usually have it all figured out. Unfortunately for their children, this includes strict guidelines for their kids' expected behavior, including details of assigned tasks. Attempting to wiggle out of such rigid expectations does not work, since the Taurus parent will see any excuse, including even a bona fide sickness, as evidence of malingering or outright rebellion. It is best to obey Taurus parents rather than oppose them in such situations, since the resulting unpleasantness is not usually worth the struggle and effort. Quietly appealing to their emotions can work if they see that your desires or aversions are strong enough.

Caring for the Aging Taurus Parent

Although Taurus parents would prefer to take care of themselves, they will be gratified by and, generally speaking, accepting of the insistent offers of their children to help look after them. In very pragmatic terms, they see their children's help as returning a favor for parental care they rendered in the past. However, Taurus parents have their pride, and so your involvement is best kept to the essentials rather than fussing over them continuously. Too often the child will want to give the Taurus parent what he or she considers best rather than what the parent would really like. Ultimately, Taurus parents like to spoil themselves in little ways without your help.

The Taurus Sibling

STRENGTHS

Forceful

Ethical

Respected

WEAKNESSES

Aggressive

Temperamental

Snappy

INTERACTIVE STYLE

Confrontational

Guarded

Concerned

Taurus siblings usually fight to keep their place in the family. Should the eldest child be a Taurus, their dominant side usually emerges. A middle or youngest Taurus child will resent being spoiled or coddled, wanting to be taken seriously and respected for their strength and moral fiber. Tauruses relate well to their siblings to a point, but ultimately they are more concerned with being left alone to develop their own interests. Also it is their friends, their possessions, and their activities that are unique and most important to them, so their siblings will have to remember not to transgression in these areas.

Rivalry/Closeness with the Taurus Sibling

Taurus siblings often develop rivalries with only one of their brothers or sisters, usually the one closest in age. This struggle will go on for years, eventually with neither child emerging as the winner. If the Taurus sibling is older, they will fight to hang on to the top-dog position; if the Taurus is younger, they may adopt a prickly or irritated attitude that shows a readiness to battle it out with the older child. Such confrontations can drive parents crazy, but like two knives being sharpened on each other, the Taurus and non-Taurus siblings will hone their confrontational and argumentative skills. In a fight, the Taurus sibling will rarely, if ever, give up willingly or choose to walk away.

Past Issues and the Taurus Sibling

Tauruses have long memories. It is not easy for them (perhaps impossible in most cases) to either forgive or forget disturbing past issues involving siblings. Slights and insults can be remembered for a lifetime and may be brought up in the heat of a dispute in adult life. Often such attachments hold Tauruses back in their development, so coming to peace with these issues can prove to be a major milestone. Good parents will realize this and encourage frank discussions on matters that are clearly bothering their Taurus offspring, perhaps even bringing the other sibling(s) in on the discussion, too.

Dealing with the Estranged Taurus Sibling

Estranged Taurus siblings will stubbornly refuse to resume contact or respond to overtures of friendship. It is not usually true that they just drift off, but rather that there is some specific issue that has been eating away at them for a long time. Sometimes provoking them, even deliberately, into losing their temper may be the dynamite charge needed to shake loose their emotional logjam. Once the air has cleared, it may be possible to have a frank discussion and even get back together, perhaps on a limited basis.

Money Issues (Borrowing Money, Wills, Etc.) and the Taurus Sibling

Taurus siblings want what is rightfully theirs and will fight to defend it. Particularly fond of objects with sentimental value, they will want to keep such items from the homes of their parents or other relatives as eternal reminders of the deceased and happy childhood memories. Tauruses are good about lending money to their siblings but are insistent about being paid back in a reasonable amount of time, usually because they need the funds themselves. Occasionally they will even forget to ask for it back, but will be quite pleased if the borrower remembers to reimburse them.

Holidays/Celebrations/Reunions and the Taurus Sibling

If Taurus siblings are on good terms with their families, they will want to play an important role in arranging get-togethers. Happy to be helpful in any way, Tauruses don't want to miss out on making important decisions (i.e., having things done the way they like them to be) or attending the festivities. Should they be excluded from such planning, they are likely to feel miffed and refuse to go to the event at all, or they will do so reluctantly. They should be allowed full rein in the areas of food and setting design, which are their strong suits. Taurus siblings can be counted on to be hard working and committed in such activities.

Vacationing with the Taurus Sibling

The Taurus sibling goes on vacation for only one reason— to have a good time. Thus, anything that interferes or even threatens to interfere with this goal will be met with stiff resistance. The Taurus idea of a great vacation is good food, a comfortable place to sleep (including camping), interesting side trips, challenging activities, natural surroundings, and good company. To guarantee the latter, Tauruses usually want to bring their own friend(s) along, which also provides a buffer against the usual family boredom. Usually when Taurus siblings are enjoying themselves, everyone else will have a good time, too. If not, watch out.

The Taurus Child

Taurus children can be pretty serious. As literalists, they expect you to keep your promises, and if you don't, they will usually raise quite a fuss. This seriousness pervades even their time at play, since there is nothing casual about their involvement in games and sports. A funny blend of activity and laziness, enthusiasm and detachment, chatter and silence, the behavior and moods of Taurus children are often difficult to predict. Of course they insist on having their own toys, games, and a secure and relaxed home turf to operate from, and they will become very unhappy if deprived of such things. Taurus children are willing to share with other kids only up to a certain point, and only on their own terms.

Personality Development and the Taurus Child

Some Taurus children never seem to change at all. Very sure of themselves already in their earliest years, they do learn from their experiences but somehow always maintain the essential core of their personality. Passing through the stages of childhood can be difficult for these stable individuals who are always more comfortable staying right where they are, rather than proceeding to the next level. No attempt should be made to push them or even encourage them to get ahead of themselves. Emotional difficulties inevitably arise in the life of any child, but Taurus children are especially prone to rebellion

Enthusiastic
Self-composed
Insistent

Unpredictable
Moody
Selfish

Serious
Committed
Demanding

and unhappiness if they are misunderstood by their parents. Ride through their storms with patience and understanding.

Hobbies/Interests/Career Paths for the Taurus Child

Taurus children are practical creatures who love to work with their hands. They have the special ability to watch what others do and then follow their lead through an interesting blend of imitation and originality. They demonstrate the old adage "What the eyes can see, the hands can do." Thus, it is helpful to introduce them to a wide range of hobbies and handicrafts (including music and dance, two Taurus specialties) since they bore easily and may become lazy and cranky if not challenged. Taurus children are proud of their accomplishments, but also need perks from their parents along the way to encourage them even further.

Discipline and the Taurus Child

As tough as Taurus kids seem to be, they are emotionally vulnerable when it comes to blame, criticism, and discipline, particularly when this last is unfairly imposed. For the most part, they tend to regulate their own behavior because, amazingly, they often develop a strong moral and ethical sense early in life and are able to stick to it. Their judgment of themselves is usually far more severe than that passed on them by parents, teachers, or siblings. As a parent, you would do well to withhold negative judgments when possible and become aware of how Taurus children evaluate their own actions.

Affection Level and the Taurus Child

Strangely enough, although many Taurus children are affectionate, they can have trouble showing and accepting it, particularly from overly effusive adults. Instead of making a big deal about it—which only makes Taurus children uncomfortable—try offering a normal daily diet of little hugs, smiles, and gentle tones of voice, which they can easily come to accept. If they are not overwhelmed by you, they can be encouraged to show affection through your acknowledgment of their touches or glances. Like flowers, Taurus children will blossom through such treatment. Taurus children who are either flooded by emotion or deprived of it can become psychologically blocked and extremely difficult to reach.

Dealing with the Taurus Child and Interactions with Siblings

In many respects, Taurus children are best left alone. They will decide on their own how they want to be dealt with, sending strong signals to parents and siblings in this regard. Taurus children are prepared to do only so much and go only so far; attempts to push them beyond these limits will arouse their stubbornness and, ultimately, their ire. Parents should never force them to play with siblings or friends. Taurus children will make it abundantly clear that such decisions are theirs to make, and theirs alone. Others will come to respect them for their emotional honesty and refusal to fake it.

Interacting with the Adult Taurus Child

Chances are that adult Tauruses will resemble child Tauruses in many respects, appearing unchanging and constant. Moreover, their good qualities usually improve and their bad qualities become only more deeply entrenched. As a result, both parents and siblings will have few doubts about what to expect from them, having experienced their reactions so many times in the past. A Taurus who has had an unhappy childhood often becomes an adult Taurus who cannot and will not cooperate, unable to release their resentment and hurt. A Taurus who has had a happy childhood will generally be cooperative, even eager to help out.

Gemini

BIRTHDATE MAY 22–JUNE 21

Geminis are mutable air signs, indicating their need for change and their tendency to flit from one activity or relationship to another. Ruled by Mercury, Geminis are communicators and oriented toward matters of the mind, including puzzles, games, computers, and deduction. Most Geminis are in constant and rapid motion, their minds moving with the speed of light and their bodies straining to catch up. Pinning down these elusive individuals to fixed commitments can prove a worthy challenge.

Work

GEMINI
May 22–June 21

The Gemini Boss

Few Geminis are comfortable giving orders or running an organization day to day. Instead, they enjoy being part of a team and sharing experiences on an equal level. Thus, although they are quite capable of taking on the work involved in being bosses, they are not born leaders and would much prefer to hang back and let things run on their own. Gemini bosses are very good at delegating authority, relying on a few capable employees to oversee the activities of their company. Such individuals are usually well rewarded and given a wide range of responsibilities. However, the Gemini boss likes to make the final decisions on all important matters.

Asking the Gemini Boss for a Raise

Although Gemini bosses are usually direct in letting you know how they feel about you, it is advised that you approach them fully prepared and cautiously. Catching them in the right mood is vital, and a casual approach is best; do not schedule an appointment but rather ambush them in the hall at a propitious moment and ask if they have a minute to talk. (Clever Gemini will probably already sense what you have in mind.) To put them at ease, first bring up another topic, or perhaps even two, before making your pitch. State your reasons why you deserve a raise succinctly and clearly. Be ready to negotiate.

Breaking Bad News to the Gemini Boss

It is best not to beat around the bush with regard to bad news. Once you have dropped the bomb, be sure to have a cogent damage-control scenario at your fingertips. Outline the implementation of such a plan. Prepare for the Gemini boss to make all kinds of objections, including a denial that things are as dark as you paint them. Watch the Gemini boss try to wriggle out of it by suggesting you may have misinterpreted the data. Gemini bosses are spin masters who can twist and turn facts to their advantage and even convince you in the process. Hold your ground, insist on being fully heard, and stress why immediate action needs to be taken to avoid disaster.

STRENGTHS
Lively
Communicative
Interesting

WEAKNESSES
Distracted
Superficial
Nervous

INTERACTIVE STYLE
Forward
Adaptable
Logical

Arranging Travel and/or Entertainment for the Gemini Boss

Short trips, domestic flights, and overall fun are staples of the Gemini diet. Thus, within reason, Gemini bosses will endorse travel plans that can benefit the company's image and lead to opening new markets. Pick unusual hotels with extras and surprises. Gemini bosses like to travel, but if that's not possible, they will send employees, enjoying the trip vicariously through their stories. They love office parties, at which they enjoy being the center of attention and telling funny stories. Never forget their birthdays; a surprise party is always appreciated. Keep the drinks light, and supply plenty of sweets and unusual pastries. Planning entertainment is always a good idea. Dance music should be phased in once the enjoyment level is high enough.

Decision-Making and the Gemini Boss

Gemini bosses like to share, and therefore they allow others to make decisions. They promote independence in others, as long as they are kept informed about what is going on. They do not particularly enjoy long formal meetings, preferring to outline their plans in a short and sweet fashion and expecting others to do the same. Never forget Gemini's impatience with long-winded or circuitous presentations. They will usually insist that important decisions be made on the basis of fact. Thus, past performance, rather than imagination, will make the best impression on them. Of course, all Gemini decisions are subject to change and usually are changed at least once.

Impressing and/or Motivating the Gemini Boss

The best way to impress Gemini bosses, or motivate them to follow your suggestions, is to make them curious. Show them only a tiny bit of what you have in mind and allow them to express interest. Play your cards close to the chest and show what you have only if they are willing to up the ante. Beware: A Gemini boss will often later take credit for your ideas. (A typical scenario: The employee presents his or her ideas. The Gemini boss says: "Gee, I'm glad I thought of that!") The cleverest way to get Gemini bosses to do your bidding is to subtly plant an idea in their minds by just casually mentioning it and later watch them "discover" it as their own.

Making Proposals and/or Giving Presentations to the Gemini Boss

To a Gemini boss, the way something is presented may be just as important as the content. Geminis love anything high-tech as well as hardware and software that can provide a glitzy or glamorous feel. Keep the tempo upbeat in your presentation, and feel free to jump from one topic to another. Avoid boredom or getting bogged down at all costs. Make only a few important points and devote the rest of your time to embellishing these with interesting facts and generally raising the level of enjoyment for all present. Be sure to allow the Gemini boss to interject remarks from time to time, and give those remarks a positive spin when you restate them.

The Gemini Employee

True multitaskers, Gemini employees love being busy. They specialize in doing several things at once for their boss and thinking up several new ideas or approaches to old projects. Their ability to juggle their work schedules and their versatility makes them excellent pinch-hitters, able to fill in for others at a moment's notice. This can even mean their physically moving around in the office, since, of all the signs, they are the least likely to be bound to their desks. The downside of all this is that Gemini employees get bored easily and may not have the stamina or follow-through to perform the same or similar functions day after day. They are particularly dexterous manually.

Interviewing and/or Hiring the Gemini Employee

Prospective Gemini employees are looking for a job in which their tasks are interesting enough but they have the freedom to meet others and investigate future possibilities. This gregarious sign does not like to get pinned down to a single position within the firm. If they are permanently anchored to a desk they will only be unhappy, eventually becoming a prime candidate for a nervous breakdown. That said, the Gemini interviewee will be happy to hear that, at least in the beginning of their tenure, their tasks are easy and well defined (as long as there is the guarantee of a broad palette of choices in the future). Salary is usually not as important as their work environment and benefits.

Breaking Bad News to or Firing the Gemini Employee

Getting fired may be something that Gemini employees actually welcome, since it could mean moving on to something new and different. However, they do not respond well to criticism or discussion of the poor quality of their work. Giving them concrete suggestions concerning where they might look for another job, an adequate reference, and perhaps a bit of severance pay will usually smooth their ruffled feathers. Breaking bad news to them should not be a big problem since they tend to give most results from their work a positive spin anyway.

Traveling with and Entertaining the Gemini Employee

Geminis love to travel and party, so these categories find the twins in their own element. Light and airy, their fun-loving personality enjoys nothing better than a change of scene or a rollicking office party. Here, their need to talk and entertain can come to the forefront. If a Gemini employee is sent to a convention or board meeting as a representative of the company, make sure they are well directed on the image of your company that you want conveyed. Supreme actors, Geminis are capable of assuming almost any role required under the tutelage of a good director. Their clothes should be kept on the conservative side to avoid gaudy or shocking displays.

Assigning Tasks to the Gemini Employee

Geminis are born problem solvers. However, Gemini workers do best with tasks that allow them to think outside the box. It is always the nutty, the unusual, or the unexpected that intrigues these people, so be sure not to make their new tasks overly repetitive or boring. Giving them freedom is okay as long as you make clear—as you would with a

STRENGTHS

Versatile

Adaptable

Active

WEAKNESSES

Flighty

Sarcastic

Argumentative

INTERACTIVE STYLE

Funny

Quick

Ironic

teenager—that along with this independence comes the responsibility for their behavior and performance. Make sure Gemini employees regularly touch base with a superior, not only at the beginning of a project but throughout it as well. They can spin out of control very quickly, so keep an eye on them, preferably without their knowledge to avoid cramping their style.

Motivating or Impressing the Gemini Employee

Gemini employees are most impressed and motivated by appeals to the faculty of thought. If you can explain to them in direct and logical terms what the situation is and how it can be managed or corrected they will head in the right direction with enthusiasm. Remember, however, that their need to reason often leads them to argument; if you are not careful, they will debate every point with you until the cows come home. Gemini workers are easily motivated by reward and impressed by your interest and confidence in their abilities. Thus, they are easy to convince that a new project will be not a burden but rather an exciting opportunity for them to enjoy and move ahead.

Managing, Directing, or Criticizing the Gemini Employee

More than any other sign, Geminis like to criticize others but are sensitive about receiving criticism. If you can direct them without criticizing their work, you will find them malleable and cooperative. Keep the tone of your remarks upbeat and positive. Be particularly aware that like unruly hair, a Gemini who has spun out of control is not a happy sight. This sign must be kept on the straight and narrow as much as possible, yet given enough freedom to do things his or her own way. As long as this precarious balance is kept, the Gemini employee will continue to make valuable contributions.

The Gemini Coworker

Gemini coworkers add a bit of spice to any group of which they are a part, as long as there are not too many of them. The proverbial barrel of monkeys is an apt phrase to describe the situation when too many Geminis congregate, making it difficult to get anything done. However, Gemini coworkers can be called upon to fill in for an absent colleague at a moment's notice, and this raises their value enormously from being just lively entertainers. Witty and loquacious, these folks will talk your ear off if you let them, which may prevent you from getting much done.

Approaching the Gemini Coworker for Advice

Geminis are only too happy to give advice, for they love solving problems. For the most part, they will volunteer counsel on their own. Constantly. Because of this trait, it is not often necessary to ask. Their analytic and upbeat approach will, at the very least, amuse you, even if their suggestions are less than sterling. Often they bring up issues and methods that you may not have thought of, so it can be helpful to hear them out even if you don't agree with either their premises or their conclusions. Nothing will hurt them more than your refusal to listen, since being abruptly cut off is the worst possible insult.

Approaching the Gemini Coworker for Help

Gemini coworkers are usually available to help and are particularly strong in two areas: dealing with language matters and performing manual tasks. The only problem is that most often they have to do things their own way. The result may be something that only they understand, and their way of achieving this result may make their methods incomprehensible. Thus repairing or reversing their efforts may be difficult or impossible. However, if they are well directed and take their time, they are capable of producing an excellent result that is right on the mark. Thinking on their feet is their specialty, with good or bad outcomes possible.

Traveling with and Entertaining the Gemini Coworker

In arranging entertainment for an office party or get-together after work, Geminis often prefer to do the entertaining themselves. Hard to control in this area, Geminis must be reminded that their job is to manage or arrange, rather than to be the center of attention. They are quite capable of a logical, analytic approach to organizational problems and challenges, both when booking entertainment and when making travel arrangements. They are good at details, excelling at investigating and exploring the best deals in flights, hotels, and food. Moreover, they can be adept in setting up workable schedules. They love to travel.

The Gemini Coworker Cooperating with Others

Gemini coworkers generally function well in group settings. They are social animals by nature. Making people feel and look better is their forte. In the forefront is their need to be appreciated for what they do. These are not people who can be expected to work anonymously behind the scenes. Their in-your-face style demands that they be recognized as important, even essential, cogs in the machinery. Not ones to dominate or take control, they are usually happy to be part of the team and to make it a fun ride for all involved. Their need to chatter will annoy some and amuse others, but Gemini repartee and banter will keep everyone on their toes.

Impressing and Motivating the Gemini Coworker

These loquacious souls are most impressed by the verbal skills and quick thinking of others. Of course they are bored by strong, silent types or slow movers. They tend to be impressed by sparkling personalities like themselves, and they are often motivated by verbal battles with such individuals. They strive to outdo others in speed, efficiency, logic, and cleverness, which can be a way for you to urge them to do their best. Highly competitive, they can accomplish Herculean feats to wind up on top with the highest grades for their work. Beware lest their energy be wasted in fruitless struggles and arguments, however.

Persuading and/or Criticizing the Gemini Coworker

Always appeal to the reason of Gemini coworkers. If you can persuade them of the logic of your arguments, they will listen. Paradoxically, they get very emotional over matters of the mind and may yell and scream if someone does not understand them. Let such attacks blow over, as they invariably will in short order. Criticism in small doses can be

(The Gemini Coworker)

STRENGTHS

Amusing

Handy

Inventive

WEAKNESSES

Upsetting

Blabbering

Unaware

INTERACTIVE STYLE

High-tempo

Upbeat

Interesting

tolerated, but constant nitpicking will rouse them to fury. Remember, their moods can change like the weather, so if you are unsuccessful in your efforts to get through to them, just come back later; you may be facing quite a different person or situation. Although they have excellent memories for slights, they tend not to hold serious grudges.

The Gemini Client

Gemini clients are likely to be as interested in details as in the overall game plan. Easily irritated and highly critical, they may be very demanding and not at all easy to deal with. They will expect to be kept up-to-date once a project is launched, always seeking demonstrable results and value for their money. Of particular importance to them are concrete results, since they will not be satisfied by promises of future gains or devious spins given to explain poor results. Should you be providing a service for them, they will pay particular attention to the written language and logic inherent in it; if you are making or selling one of their products, they will examine it very carefully for flaws. Geminis are difficult customers to fool.

Impressing the Gemini Client

Prospective Gemini clients will be truly impressed only by past performance. Preparing detailed lists and spreadsheets of weekly, monthly, and yearly sales is essential, even if only so that they give them a cursory glance in your presence. This is merely to acknowledge that what they need is there. Later, they will likely go over these results with a fine-tooth comb. All irrelevant facts will be sifted out, misleading number crunches ruthlessly exposed, and poor results shoved back at you. Thus, in your second meeting you must be prepared for a whole onslaught of negative facts.

Selling to the Gemini Client

Once you have attracted and interested Gemini clients, you must convince them of your ability to close the deal quickly and to meet most of their demands. It is best to move swiftly in preparing and signing contracts, rather than spending weeks working out complex legal and implementative issues (the same is true when preparing the product or service for public consumption). Remember that speed is of the essence for Gemini clients; to them, it is a direct indication of your ability to produce. Sell them on your plans in a logical, straightforward fashion. Turning on the charm does not usually help.

Your Appearance and the Gemini Client

Be careful to wear subdued clothing, avoiding loud colors that would be upsetting or distracting. Likewise, it is best to avoid strong perfume, cologne, or aftershave. However, Gemini clients will usually be very hip to the latest styles, and you definitely don't want to appear overly conservative or old-fashioned, which could give them the impression that your product or service is hopelessly out of date. It is the little touch or detail that their sharp eye will fall on—a fashionable pin, bracelet, watch, or other accessory, the stylish cut of your garments, and particularly your hairstyle. Gemini hair naturally tends to be wilder, so these clients will acknowledge any attempt on your part to keep yours under control.

Keeping the Gemini Client's Interest

Flirtatious or outright seductive behavior can keep a Gemini client interested over the months ahead. Geminis can be terrible flirts, and thus they appreciate this skill in others. Although actual contact with such a client is not advised, every meeting, phone call, or email can be spiced up with subtle innuendo, much like a dinner would be heightened with subdued spices. Game-playing is the forte of Geminis, and unlike other signs it is not necessarily the winning that urges them on but the pure fun of play itself. They instantly recognize and acknowledge a worthy opponent, and this respect can be directly reflected in their intention to keep a business relationship alive.

Breaking Bad News to the Gemini Client

Gemini clients are likely to accept bad news in a surprisingly unemotional manner. They can even be sympathetic to your claims to have done everything to ensure success (provided that they have acknowledged all along that you and your company have done your very best). As long as losses on both sides are manageable, Gemini clients are good at damage control and writing off losses. They could even suggest further work together, but with a change of game plan. Continued association with such a client is generally recommended. Warm mutual cooperation and the ability to learn from past mistakes can lead to future success.

Entertaining the Gemini Client

Gemini clients love to be spoiled. Business meetings with them, after the first or second office sit-down session, are best conducted in a bar or restaurant over a drink or meal. The ambience should be casual but upscale. Pick a location that you know well and that you feel is particularly suited to their personality. Thus, getting to know as much as possible about their personal likes and dislikes beforehand is crucial. Obviously, taking a vegetarian to a steakhouse or a fastidious drinker to a beer joint is not appropriate and will be highly counterproductive. Pick up the tab in an easy way and be sure they see you leave a generous tip, but only if the service merits it.

The Gemini Business Partner

Some think of them as loose cannons. Although Gemini's brilliant analytical skills are valued, their precipitous actions and talkativeness are often mistrusted. Gemini partners should be kept under control in this respect and often must be taught to play their cards closer to their chests. They are not always aware of who can hurt their partnership, and therefore their openness and overly trusting nature (or simply not caring who knows what) leaves both the other partner and the company or group they run vulnerable and at risk. As the sign of the twin, Geminis tend to treat their own partners as they would brothers, expecting to share with them but also expecting unquestioned loyalty and support.

STRENGTHS

Perceptive

Active

Analytical

WEAKNESSES

Loquacious

Careless

Unheeding

INTERACTIVE STYLE

Sharing

Open

Impressive

Setting Up the Business Partnership with Gemini

With a Gemini partner it is best to sign a contract before beginning any business dealings as a partnership. Geminis can be slippery customers and also changeable to the extreme. It may be hard to hold them to the original verbal agreement. A written contract should cover not only the structure and running of the organization (including percentages and duties) but also a highly detailed description of what happens if things go wrong. The structure of the contract will then carry over into the day-to-day running of the partnership, giving Gemini partners strict guidelines as to their behavior.

Tasking with the Gemini Business Partner

Generally speaking, Gemini partners do better when directed than directing. Their half of the partnership should be carefully laid out by the other partner, of course with the Gemini's agreement. In some ways, active Geminis are like a gun or fire hose: you just point them at the object and pull the trigger. Implementation is their forte, and though their planning skills can also be acute, it is equally possible that they will be skewed and lead to chaos. Partners who share a business with a Gemini are often most successful when they are conservative and careful, although not afraid to take the occasional gamble based on astute reckoning. Gemini–Gemini partnerships are not recommended because they can often lead to endless arguments and discussions.

Traveling with and Entertaining the Gemini Business Partner

The non-Gemini partner may be the one who makes travel plans for the partnership or who books restaurants and hotels, but usually the Gemini partner is best at making the trip and representing the company. A scenario usually emerges in which the non-Gemini partner stays home to mind the store while the Gemini partner roams the world, or at least the city, state, or country, drumming up new business and feeling out potential clients and opportunities. All of this information then gets passed back to the non-Gemini partner at the home base, who carefully and dispassionately determines the worth of each individual contact. This modus operandi can be highly successful.

Managing and Directing the Gemini Business Partner

The best way to manage or direct Gemini partners is to allow them to feel free while at the same time setting certain limits that do not cramp their style. Unhappy Geminis are not able to function at their highest level or, in extreme cases, to function at all. Complimenting them on their work and encouraging their active minds—basically, showing appreciation for what they do—and including small perks will keep them happy. In this respect, the Gemini can be treated as a child or adolescent and encouraged to please you and benefit the company. Task-oriented, a busy Gemini is usually a contented one.

Relating to the Gemini Business Partner in the Long Run

It is possible to hold on to these mutable partners as long as they feel valued. They will continue to work during lean times, even devoting months to projects that do not yield financial reward, as long as they find the work interesting and stimulating. On the other hand, when Geminis feel undervalued or unappreciated, they, like rabbits, tend to go hop, hop, hop. Bunnylike, they enjoy feeling secure and occasionally being petted (figuratively, of course). Few partners are more fun to work with or have around during good times. During difficult periods they must be reassured that everything is still okay, despite negative results, and that there is hope for the future.

Parting Ways with the Gemini Business Partner

Because of a Gemini partner's resiliency and tendency to land on their feet, dissolving the partnership need not necessarily be difficult or viewed negatively. In fact, it is often the Gemini partner who initiates the process, seeking change. This does not imply, however, that the breakup will be uncomplicated. Remember Geminis' love of detail; although these people may quickly agree to your offers and accede to contractual demands, they will usually review the fine print of such agreements with zeal and make talking (and often sticking) points of them. Legal and semi-legal discussions can be protracted for this reason. It's best to give in to the Gemini on such details and save your energy and attention for major issues.

The Gemini Competitor

Geminis are highly competitive. It is the challenge and the thrill of coming out ahead that drives them. Not sadistic in their joy of winning, they do no feel compelled to humiliate or tear down their opponent. However, with their barbed wit, sense of irony, sarcasm, quick minds, and sharp tongues they are quite capable of doing so, if required. With little preparation or aforethought, Gemini is instantly ready to leap into the fray. These highly competitive instincts are often best for any company to keep under strict control, since they can also backfire when their Gemini rep arouses opposition and deep antagonisms. After all, in the topsy-turvy world of business, today's enemy could become tomorrow's partner.

Countering the Gemini Competitor

Rather than taking the initiative in a one-on-one battle with a Gemini competitor, it is best to watch and wait. As would a good counter-puncher in boxing, let Gemini competitors attack and show what they've got before responding. It is when they are swinging wildly that Gemini opponents are most vulnerable. Sit back and calmly take pot shots, making your points in terse, succinct jabs. This can arouse your competitor's fury, giving you the opportunity to land the knockout blow. Keep in mind there is rarely anything personal involved for the Gemini partner, except the joy of combat.

Out-Planning the Gemini Competitor

Since Geminis are good planners, they usually do extensive research on your product or service in comparison to theirs, study public relations and advertising, examine sales

Ironic

Clever

Witty

Cutting

Resentment-
arousing

Hostile

Combative

Challenging

Sharp

in every category, and, in general, analyze every one of your strengths and weaknesses. Therefore you must be equally prepared in these areas in order to take them on and have a chance of winning. Anticipate the Gemini competitor's tactics. Particularly examine your company's weak points and make strides to eliminate them. One deficiency in Gemini competitors is that they often see only developments in the present or recent past with clarity. Thus you can frequently defeat your Gemini adversary by seeing the big picture, making plans for the long haul, and refusing to give up.

Impressing the Gemini Competitor in Person

When meeting with Gemini competitors, either one-on-one or in a group, it is best to counter their flamboyant style with a conservative one. Wear rich garments with subdued colors. In general, make an unruffled, unshakable appearance—neatly ordered hair, impeccably pressed clothing, and expensive accessories (watch, bracelet, pin). In contrast to Gemini clients, who could be put at ease by such an appearance, your Gemini competitors could be roused to fury by it. Let them boil in exasperation over your composed appearance and behavior, and then strike with a confident smile.

Undercutting and Outbidding the Gemini Competitor

Generally, Gemini opponents will seek to offer a client or the general public more value and freebies than you. They will always try to impress by the variety and quantity of these perks. You, on the other hand, would do best to take an opposite tack and not play their game. Concentrate on lowering your price and stressing volume sales, mass market, etc. In a bidding war for rights or product, let these adversaries show their hands, and hang in there until they exhaust themselves and drop out or are forced to overbid. Remember, the Gemini energy, although prodigious, is best combated by stubborn opposition.

Public Relations Wars with the Gemini Competitor

Gemini opponents will use every bit of glitz, glamour, and glitter to catch the public's eye. Trendy to the extreme, and tuned in to the public's insatiable desire for innovation, they will succeed in big initial sales and then often fold, having already racked up big profits. Your approach should be one that stresses past reliability, steady sales, small initial profit margins, and most of all a plan to build up over the years clientele that trusts your products for their dependability and reliability. Guarantees are important, as are endorsements by stars and ordinary folks alike. In your own ads, poke holes in your competitor's wild promises and demonstrate how they are not backed up by any reliable facts.

The Gemini Competitor and the Personal Approach

Gemini opponents may be deficient in this regard. Although glib and prone to promising the moon, they may not be able to thoroughly convince clients and consumers. There is always something a bit suspicious about them. To counter their many offers, substitute a warm, friendly, folksy approach, and your target audience will melt. Speak slowly and cover your talking points thoroughly to contrast with their high-energy, motor-mouth pitch. Seek to build a steady trust with the client that will inspire belief in your product or service. It may benefit you to offer longer guarantees as well.

Love

GEMINI
May 22–June 21

The Gemini First Date

Gemini first dates are up for trying almost anything once. Not easily shocked, these mutable partners are truly interested in what you like to do. It is good to take the lead with them up to a point (the point at which they are no longer having fun). They can enjoy experiences quite vicariously, particularly when they are, or think they are, dishing out the pleasure. Thus your enjoyment is a big ego boost for them. Excitement is their forte—it is the state in which they are happiest. Dullness is their worst enemy.

Wooing and Picking Up the Gemini First Date

Geminis are not at all averse to being picked up, despite the fact that their outgoing nature often leads them to initiate proceedings. Their sharp, roving eye will pick you out of a crowd, and before you know it they will have you engaged in quick, interesting conversation. "How can such a fascinating person be available?" you think. The answer is simple. Geminis are always available, even if they are married! If you are seeking a casual relationship or just a one-night stand, this could be the person for you.

Suggested Activities for the Gemini First Date

Geminis love to entertain and be entertained. Sometimes they like to do both at once, so if you settle down to watch a movie or two for the evening do not be surprised if their rapid-fire comments—or, at the very least, occasional witty remarks and laughter—accompany the film. Going out dancing, club hopping, or to a movie can be fun. They love social situations and the excitement of new activities. Later, there will be plenty of time for more intimate contact, if you wish.

Turn-Ons and Turn-Offs for the Gemini First Date

Gemini dates must feel appreciated. Nothing turns them on so much as that special sparkle in your eye when they tell you their favorite joke or see that you admire their appearance. If they wear a trendy hairstyle, cool clothes, or a pair of stylish shoes, they want you to notice and approve. Conversely, nothing turns them off more than being ignored. Note that it is not necessary for you to flatter them or shower them with compliments, since they find such behavior suspicious anyway.

STRENGTHS
Exciting
Interesting
Adventuresome

WEAKNESSES
Unaware
Selfish
Egotistical

INTERACTIVE STYLE
Upbeat
Verbal
Persuasive

Making "the Move" with the Gemini First Date

At that crucial point in the evening, just when you are debating whether or not to slide closer to Gemini or invite an advance, you may find your date right in your lap. Geminis have a sixth sense for such things and are masters of not only verbal but also nonverbal communication. Thus, keep in mind that when a thought enters your inbox, frequently a copy is forwarded immediately to theirs. First contact is usually pleasurable and can be surprisingly passionate. Cool reactions should not be taken as signs of disinterest or rejection, but simply as objective samplings or first tastes.

Impressing the Gemini First Date

Geminis are most impressed by knowledge and facts. Make sure you study up on their profession, hobby, or special interests, which you should know before the date. Asking intelligent questions that they can answer at length will turn them on. Even better is encouraging them to take you to one of their favorite haunts. Although appreciative, they may be uncertain in new surroundings, but on their own turf (which they hope you are unfamiliar with) they can assume one of their favorite roles—the motor-mouth tour guide. Prepare, and pretend to listen, but you only need to catch enough to frame your next question.

Brushing Off the Gemini First Date

Unless they are totally smitten with you, the easiest way to get rid of Gemini first dates is to hurt their ego by ignoring them, refusing to laugh at their witty remarks, grumbling, talking about yourself, saying you feel sick, or outright telling them you are having an awful time. More often than not, the date is not that important to them anyway. They may even catch someone's eye at the next table or in the next row that they like better, and when you turn around they could already be gone! If they are obsessed with you, however, they can be stickier than flypaper.

The Gemini Romantic Partner

Having Gemini romantic partners will certainly bring spice into your life, as well as a good dose of uncertainty, since it is difficult, if not impossible, to predict their behavior. Changing moods guarantee few dull moments but can put a crimp in your plans or undermine the structure of your relationship. Making appointments can be particularly difficult since, although they usually arrive on time (when they do show up), the greatest danger is that they will abruptly cancel an appointment they never really intended to keep anyway. Exasperating but fascinating, these ephemeral creatures will lead you on a merry chase.

Having a Discussion with the Gemini Romantic Partner

Geminis are not averse to talking, but they may not always take what you are saying very seriously. Although they may acknowledge it with a nod of the head or an "uh-huh," this is no real indication that they were listening. Should you pick a topic that either does not interest them or rubs them the wrong way, they will constantly change the subject to something they find more interesting. Should you persist in your efforts, they may either give you a sharp glance and move away, or tactfully recognize an object or person in the immediate area that requires their sudden attention.

Arguments with the Gemini Romantic Partner

With Geminis, the danger always exists that the discussion will turn contentious and become an argument. So skillful are these individuals with words, and so intent on winning in verbal repartee, that the issues being examined can get lost in the shuffle. Let them speak their piece and then gently guide them back to the main talking points. Keep your own comments short and sweet, aiming for maximum effect. When the Gemini first begrudgingly admits that you are right on any point (which could take anywhere from ten minutes to half an hour), this is a positive indication that they have heard you and that things are proceeding in the right direction.

Traveling with the Gemini Romantic Partner

Geminis like to travel light and move fast. Thus, any extra luggage you bring along is sure to arouse their criticism and ire. Be prepared to carry or roll your own bags, since they may simply refuse to help, arguing that you should have left most of it at home. Once under way—whether by car, plane, bus, or train—these loquacious souls will endeavor to keep you entertained for most of the trip with their demand that you appreciate their wit and brilliance and listen to their verbal pyrotechnics and idle chatter, as they jump from one subject to another. Falling asleep on them or even the occasional yawn is a big no-no, since it is the surest sign of boredom.

Sex with the Gemini Romantic Partner

Geminis like variety. Quality is generally more important than quantity, so they expect you always to be at your best for them. They will also expect you to know when they want sex and to present them with an interesting palette of experiences, or at least to be open to their need for experimentation. In general, they are easily aroused and therefore easily satisfied, at least in comparison with most other signs. Delayed gratification of pleasure is not one of their strong points, so their emotional intelligence tends to be low. Their tendency to talk before, after, and during sex may drive you up the wall, but you will have to put up with it if you are with a Gemini.

Affection and the Gemini Romantic Partner

Geminis are not overly affectionate or cuddly. They will often express affection in a particularly unemotional, even offhand way, so you will have to be very quick to catch it. It could take the form of a hurried smile, sharp glance, pat on the back, or even a sarcastic or ironic barb, although they mean well. In any case, their expression of affection does not usually take your expectations into account. Geminis have their own odd way of doing things, particularly in the emotional sphere, where they often feel awkward expressing themselves.

STRENGTHS

Fascinating

Spicy

Sparkling

WEAKNESSES

Unpredictable

Abrupt

Misleading

INTERACTIVE STYLE

Oblique

Persuasive

Flirtatious

LOVE

Humor and the Gemini Romantic Partner

Gemini romantic partners love to laugh. Unfortunately, the constant object of their humor may be you, which can become unbearable after a while. Any attempt on your part to object will inevitably be met with the charge that you have no sense of humor. Their humor is not only verbal, but it can extend to all sorts of practical jokes that occasionally even border on the sadistic. Viewing someone's unease and causing embarrassment can fill them with delight. Geminis are also terrible teases. They may be quick to admit that they were not being serious and thus poke fun at your having taken them seriously, particularly if you had reacted to them.

The Gemini Spouse

Gemini mates can threaten the stability and permanence of your marriage because of their individuality and intense need for freedom. Moreover, these twins frequently adopt a double standard, in which they are justified in going off on their own while you are not. Because of their amoral attitudes they rarely, if ever, see anything wrong with their behavior. Somehow you will usually wind up at home waiting for them to return. The best way to deal with such attitudes is to maintain your own right to be independent and refuse to clean up after them, literally and figuratively.

Wedding and Honeymoon with the Gemini Spouse

Being highly social, Geminis are usually lots of fun to marry. They will enjoy themselves and put out lots of energy to make the wedding a great success. By contrast, the honeymoon may prove somewhat of a letdown, since one-on-one personal interaction is not their strongest suit. Although sex can be exciting and highly varied, you may get the idea early on that they are not opening up to you at a deeper level. They can certainly do so over time, so it is better not to pressure them from the get-go. Also harping on the responsibilities of a married person during this early phase will not go over well.

Home and Day-to-Day Married Life with the Gemini Spouse

Maintenance is not Gemini's strongpoint, so they may look upon normal household tasks as meaningless drudgery. (Guess who usually winds up doing the work!) However, they are pragmatic enough to realize that cleaning up, putting things away, and, in general, organizing the domestic space must be done. It is best to make lists and outline their responsibilities, insisting that they keep to them and fulfill their obligations. They usually shine when thinking up new projects and ingenious solutions to problems. However, you will find yourself having to keep them on track and see that they follow through on their good intentions.

Finances and the Gemini Spouse

Geminis are not usually spendthrifts and, in fact, may prove to be quite stingy when it comes to cash outlays for domestic upkeep. Somehow, they cannot accept or grasp that the household budget must include unexciting and uninteresting items such as cleaning materials, repair items, insulation, roofing, plumbing, and the like. The trick is to get them personally interested and involved, since they are quite handy and react well to your appreciation of their work. Although Geminis can be kept to a strict budget, you will have to work hard at this, since their impulse to purchase unexpected and often impractical items is strong. Travel, entertainment, computer items, and fast or flashy cars have a fatal attraction for them.

Infidelity and the Gemini Spouse

Because it is one of the most likely astrological signs to stray, you are better off allowing Geminis to indulge their natural need to flirt, sometimes even outrageously. Should you come down too hard on them and forbid such behavior, you risk driving them to rebel by indulging in a full-blown affair. It is best to keep them on an invisible leash so that they feel free but know they may go only so far without incurring your ire. Geminis will usually get away with whatever they can without being caught, but their fear and guilt can also be easily aroused, and, therefore, they can place limits on their proclivities to wander.

Children and the Gemini Spouse

Being childlike themselves, Geminis are often surprisingly good parents—dedicated, involved, and fun to grow up with. They are particularly fond of sports, games, camping, and most recreational vacation activities. Although one or two children are usually all they can handle, some Geminis enjoy the company and adoration of more children, frequently treating them almost as friends or even brothers and sisters. The delights of watching their kids grow and experiencing new and unexpected happenings hold their interest over the long run. However, when the kids are old enough, the Gemini will tend not to hold on to them, nudging them out of the nest and urging them to fly on their own.

Divorce and the Gemini Spouse

Should you decide to dump Gemini mates, perhaps after forgiving their transgressions for the nth time, you may find their pragmatic, reasonable side surprisingly easy to deal with when sorting out property, cash, and legalities. On the other hand, Geminis can get out of control pretty quickly in the emotional sphere, an area where they do not feel at home. Carried away by jealousy, anger, or temporary hatred, an out-of-control Gemini may be about as easy to handle as a cyclone. However, Gemini mates' feelings calm down relatively quickly, and when the storm of emotions has blown itself out they will usually be up for a frank, constructive discussion.

The Gemini Lover

STRENGTHS

Free

Available

Intense

WEAKNESSES

Untrustworthy

Indiscreet

Overly talkative

INTERACTIVE STYLE

Direct

Reactive

Out-front

When having a secret love affair with a Gemini, expect a fleeting though intense involvement. This can work out for the better or worse depending on whether or not you wanted it to continue. The Gemini lover is less likely than most to be very dependable or to hang around for long. Furthermore, since Geminis need to talk about things that happen to them, they are unlikely to be willing or able to keep things secret. Do not be surprised if an embarrassing intimate detail lodges itself in someone's ear and then becomes salacious gossip spreading like wildfire through your social set.

Meeting the Gemini Lover

You can meet or pick up Gemini lovers in the most unexpected places. The initial contact is likely to be very short and may simply consist of a word or glance. Generally, they will get in touch with you directly following this or drop the word through a mutual acquaintance or friend that they are open to your advances. Their egos love flattery, so the fact that you find them attractive, interesting, or in any way intriguing is a big plus. More conventional settings like pickup bars, clubs, or dating websites or apps will include a high percentage of Geminis, so your chances of meeting one by accident are quite good. Geminis can usually be recognized by their lively characters, skillful communication, and need to impress.

Location and the Gemini Lover

Geminis are usually not particular about intimate settings and, in general, are more willing than most signs to get it on almost anywhere. This can even include public settings. Their extroverted character and more outrageous side allows handholding and kissing, and may even go further without causing them embarrassment. An afternoon or night together at their place can be truly entertaining, not only because of the actions involved, but also because you get to view their fascinating collections, including various objects, books, CDs and DVDs, and their latest computer software. At your place, these curious souls are likely to want to rummage through much of your private material, including clothes, hats, and shoes, to find out more about you.

Sex and the Gemini Lover

Geminis are generally easily turned on and easily satisfied. They may have all kinds of kinky interests, love to experiment, and have a fascination for a kaleidoscope of sexual activities, from the Kama Sutra to S&M. One can think of Gemini lovers as kids in a candy store or monkeys in a banana tree. What it all means to them is difficult to determine, but usually everything is done with humor and detachment, rather than really deep involvement. In some ways, you might feel like a spectator who has been invited to enjoy their show.

Holding On to the Gemini Lover

Like the proverbial rabbit, Geminis will stick around as long as they are appreciated, and if not, then simply hop, hop, hop away. Just when you have gotten used to them and all their strange habits, nervous mannerisms, and requirements . . . off they go. Geminis can slip through your fingers like water, and there is no surefire way to keep them with you. However, if you can find a good balance between caring too little and caring too much, they are likely to stick around, particularly if there is nowhere else at the moment where they are interested in going. Geminis' faithfulness, or lack thereof, is usually determined by their latest mood and agenda, which may or may not include you.

Entertaining the Gemini Lover

Geminis will love to appear in public with you, primarily to show you off. They expect you to look good, talk good, act good, and, in general, make them look good. Fond of films, clubs, dinners out, concerts, and almost any fun activity, they are truly action-oriented and not usually ones to yearn for a quiet evening at home. On the other hand, when they are home, they revel in the most up-to-date media, particularly computer software and a wide range of music and movies. Playful to the extreme, they are also fond of puzzles and board games. You might be wise to let them win occasionally, otherwise they are likely to get very cranky.

Breaking Up with the Gemini Lover

This is not usually a problem unless Gemini lovers are heavily addicted to you and your brand of sex and romance (in which case, they may refuse to leave). By the time you have wrestled and pondered with the momentous decision to dump them, you will probably turn around and find them already gone. They usually have radar out for rejection and will prefer to be the one who rejects rather than being rejected. However, they find such matters highly unpleasant, and in order to avoid confrontation they will probably quietly slip away before you even realize it. They will do their best to avoid difficulties, particularly emotional ones, preferring either to see you kept happy or, if you are not, simply to quit.

The Gemini Ex

For such independent and high-spirited souls, Gemini exes can turn surprisingly loyal, faithful, and even dependent once they are no longer involved with you romantically or maritally. It is strange to see them caring about you more as a friend than as a lover, but this, astonishingly, is often the case. Perhaps it is easier for them to give when not so much is required of them. Things will often work better if you do not put pressure on them after a breakup and instead wait to see if their goodwill is forthcoming without requesting or demanding it.

Establishing a Friendship with the Gemini Ex

The easiest way to establish a friendship with a Gemini ex is to attend events or activities—whether professional or social—where your ex will be present. Just the fact that you see each other will give the Gemini ex a chance to remain close without getting too close. Thus, the contact will be nonthreatening, just what the average Gemini likes best. Should you want to establish a full-blown friendship, it is recommended that you go easy, avoid sending too many mixed messages, and in general remain out-front and nonphysical, if possible.

Friendly
Caring
Giving

WEAKNESSES
Obstinate
Confrontational
Rebellious

INTERACTIVE STYLE
Engaging
Involved
Responsive

Issues of Getting Back Together with the Gemini Ex

Getting back together with your Gemini ex, at least on a trial basis and for a short time, is always a possibility, but it rarely works in the long run. You may even find your Gemini ex at your door a year after the breakup, insisting that he or she is returning to you and that it is ridiculous that you maintain an artificial separation when everyone knows you belong together. You must stand firm in your refusal here as well as in other situations in which they show themselves to be clearly out of touch with reality and disrespectful of your feelings.

Discussing Past Issues with the Gemini Ex

You can discuss the past objectively with Gemini exes in a cool, calm, and collected mood. However, should they become reactive or excitable, it is best to drop the subject before they lash out with blame and recrimination. If this does happen, however, it will usually pass as quickly as a summer storm, and the conversation can be postponed until a later date. Geminis are investigators, after all, and they are interested in getting to the heart of things, in the sense of solving a puzzle. Finding a pleasant public surrounding for your talk will help ease tensions.

Expressing Affection to the Gemini Ex

Be careful not to give your Gemini ex the wrong idea. Abstain from direct expressions of affection until your breakup has been official for some months. Geminis are quick movers and have reactive personalities—both high-strung and nervous—so keep the situation as cool as possible. Affection can be less physical and better expressed through a kind tone of voice or gentle smile rather than a hug or even a touch of the hand. Gifts should be avoided since they may imply an obligation for the Gemini to offer you something in return, therefore giving the impression that you are trying to buy your ex's feelings.

Defining the Present Relationship with the Gemini Ex

Establishing mutual guidelines with your Gemini ex is an excellent idea. Dos and don'ts should be openly discussed and decisions reached. Meet over two or even three relaxed sessions so that issues can be fully covered, without the pressure of making spot judgments or immediate decisions. Always give Geminis a chance to think things over, since they are prone to changing their minds. This can work out well if they initially object to your ideas but later have time to mull them over and see the wisdom of your arguments. It is best to keep friends and family up-to-date on your mutual decisions.

Sharing Custody with the Gemini Ex

Because of the hurt they have felt, Gemini exes will sometimes have a lukewarm attitude toward sharing custody of their children, putting their own bruised egos before their children's need for a second parent. Furthermore, they will probably move on quickly to a new, exciting relationship with a single person who does not particularly want to be saddled with kids. Be patient, since Gemini exes will start to act more responsibly as the children grow older and begin to touch their heartstrings. Geminis will eventually discover that relationships come and go, but children remain.

Friends and Family

GEMINI
May 22–June 21

The Gemini Friend

Although they are not just fair-weather friends, Geminis are much more fun to have around when things are going well. They tend to be skittish, nervous, and worried when faced with emergencies or long-standing problems, thus minimizing their usefulness to you. Gemini is one of the most playful signs in the zodiac, making your Gemini friend someone you want to take along when having a good time. Often adopting a light and nonserious attitude, Geminis can bring joy to almost any activity. Their rapid-fire chatter will let you know that they are enjoying themselves, too.

Asking for Help from the Gemini Friend

Gemini friends are frequently bewildered when asked for help. They are usually willing to lend assistance but may not know where to start or may suddenly head off in the wrong direction with you in tow. Being sympathetic or empathic is also not their specialty, and they prefer to come up with logical solutions to problems rather than lending emotional support. Although not cold per se, they may appear so because of this decidedly mental orientation. Also, their staying power is not high, since they can be easily sidetracked by another cry for help or the next new diversion that comes along.

Communication and Keeping in Touch with the Gemini Friend

Communication is Gemini's forte. If these friends are interested in you, communicating with them will not be a problem, presuming that you can keep up with their rapier-quick minds and chatter. They tend not to listen when rattling on, so you must periodically request that they slow down their monologue to listen and understand what you are trying to convey. Not always good at keeping touch, Gemini friends will assume you understand if they are busy with other activities for long periods. When they get back in touch, they will undoubtedly act as if nothing happened, carrying on as normal.

Borrowing Money from the Gemini Friend

Geminis are pretty good about lending money and also about giving you time to pay it back. However, the amount available may not be very impressive since they rarely have much cash on hand. By the time they remember to go to the bank or even to check their

STRENGTHS

Fun

Playful

Nonserious

WEAKNESSES

Nervous

Unreliable

Worried

INTERACTIVE STYLE

Loquacious

Demonstrative

Light

account you may have already found someone else more reliable. You certainly will not hurt their feelings or damage your relationship with them by asking for a loan, since they do not mind at all being asked.

Asking for Advice from the Gemini Friend

The advice given by Gemini friends is frequently not helpful, since it is rarely of the common sense, workable variety. They are likely to come up with all kinds of off-the-wall suggestions that sound fascinating but could never work. The more time they devote to thinking of such matters, the more far-out they get, until finally they may truly believe in their own delusions and be convinced that you should, too. Thus, be careful about asking Gemini friends for advice in the first place—it is frequently not worth the aggravation.

Visiting the Gemini Friend

Gemini friends are often happy to see you, but they may also (coincidentally) just be headed out the door. It is no easier to plan a visit since you may be left knocking or ringing the bell while they are off somewhere else having a good time, forgetful of your appointment with them. It is best to call them just before leaving to confirm that they will be there when you arrive. Do not keep them waiting too long, however, since your late arrival may be greeted by their absence or a stony silence.

Celebrations/Entertainment with the Gemini Friend

Geminis love celebrations and entertainment. However, they should not make all the arrangements since they can be forgetful and unreliable, although they will strive to overcome their natural nervousness and anxieties. Better that they be invited to the event rather than put in charge of it. They can usually be counted on to entertain guests with their verbal and physical humor, being fed by appreciation as a fire by fuel. Burning brightly, their energies can be counted on to light up a gathering of even the dullest souls.

The Gemini Roommate

Enjoy carnivals? Better get used to them because Gemini roommates are likely to transform your living space into one at any moment. Not only are they capable of staging the whole thing themselves for your benefit (and that of friends or other roommates) but they could very well have invited a whole cast of supporting characters to help them. If the whole thing starts to sound like a Fellini movie, then you are beginning to get the picture. Gemini roommates are quite fun as long as you don't have a lot of serious work to do, or anything else that demands concentration, for that matter.

Sharing Financial Responsibilities with the Gemini Roommate

Responsibility is not a word that will necessarily appear in a Gemini roommate's dictionary. Fulfilling responsibilities—particularly the domestic kind—is not their idea of a good time, and for them, a good time comes first. Money comes and goes quickly, so if they have it, you better move fast and get funds for the rent, groceries, and utility bills before they spend it on their latest passion. Indeed, having them pay in advance may be the only way to avoid your being footed with all the bills. Not that all Geminis are thieves or con artists as many astrologers insist, but they may honestly forget to pay if you let them.

Cleaning and the Gemini Roommate

Geminis are capable of thorough cleaning if they set their mind to it. However, their minds are usually elsewhere occupied. Sticklers for detail, Geminis will certainly not be blind to what needs cleaning up, but somehow registering this fact and immediately ignoring it go hand in hand. Their inability to see their own mess is legendary. Should you confront them, they may simply tell you that the way they keep their room is their business. Further, if you insist they clean the common rooms they will probably infer, or outright state, that they are hardly ever home (which could be partially true) and that you made the mess. Guess who winds up doing the work?

Houseguests and the Gemini Roommate

The problem is not usually *your* houseguests, but theirs. Likely to invite newcomers at a fearful rate, they also are good at building up a stable of regulars you can always count on. Life is a continual cabaret for Geminis, so have plenty of food, drinks, and music on hand at all times. They also won't object to your inviting new or old faces over, since this just becomes a potential audience for their performances. Yes, you'll never walk alone with Gemini roommates, who can't get enough of their fellow human beings.

Parties and the Gemini Roommate

Because life is a cabaret to Geminis, the implications of throwing a party may just get hidden in the background. Problems may arise when it comes to paying for all the food and drink, but Geminis do not mind throwing their money around when they have it; otherwise, they just tell people to "BYO" or that the get-together is a potluck affair. Normally, food is not that important to them anyway, since their mouth is more often used for speaking than for eating. Since Geminis don't need a lot of sleep, be prepared for parties to last into the wee hours.

Privacy and the Gemini Roommate

Gemini roommates generally regard your need for privacy with suspicion. They may also not understand your respect for their privacy; after all, what do they have to hide? Most people mask private thoughts and feelings through silence or secrecy. In other words, they hide by not showing things. Amusingly enough, Geminis use a different hiding tactic; they hide by showing everything, and through endless distractions and changes of subject, you never really find out their deepest and darkest secrets. After all, they just told them to you the other day, didn't they?

Discussing Problems with the Gemini Roommate

Discussion is something Geminis enjoy, but it may be hard to keep them on the same subject for very long. Their attention span is short and life is so interesting that they often jump from one subject to another at a blistering pace. Their analytic skills are high; they

STRENGTHS
Entertaining
Fun
Inventive

WEAKNESSES
Distracting
Needy of attention
Irritating

INTERACTIVE STYLE
Changeable
Eclectic
Energetic

FRIENDS AND FAMILY

love to solve riddles, puzzles, and mysteries; and they will do their very best to get to the bottom of your problems, if you can pin Gemini roommates down. It is best not to make them the problem if you have one with them but rather to discuss it in the abstract and then leave it to them to make the connection later.

The Gemini Parent

STRENGTHS

Interested

Varied

Enthusiastic

WEAKNESSES

Worried

Stressed

Absent

INTERACTIVE STYLE

Positive

Engaged

Energetic

Generally speaking, Geminis make good parents. At least at the times when they are truly interested in their children. They have a wide range of interests and a rich emotional palette, and they relish their role as group leader in the family. However, their minds often can be preoccupied with other matters that definitely do not include the kids. At these times their children must be capable of looking after themselves since their Gemini parent will not be available. The responsibilities of financial support, maintenance, and education can weigh heavily on the Gemini mind, which is highly susceptible to worry and stress.

Discipline Style of the Gemini Parent

Gemini parents do not enjoy disciplining their own children. Consequently, they either neglect to do so or reject the notion altogether. Children of Gemini parents are likely to run wild a good deal of the time, unless their mate takes control, which is usually the case. This can set up a situation in which the children go to the Gemini parent to find a sympathetic ear and an easy touch, putting the other parent in an uncomfortably unpopular position. Gemini parents are likely to allow, and even encourage, freedom if they themselves were strictly disciplined as children.

Affection Level and the Gemini Parent

Although Geminis are not overly emotional people and they are cool in their interactions with their progeny, they genuinely enjoy children, including those of their friends. Expressing affection on a daily basis is possible for them, but they are rarely effusive. Their sympathy always has a detached air about it, as if they are rationally assessing the situation rather than simply reacting to it, particularly if a child is hurt or in danger. Children who need the total sympathy of their parents in such situations may feel disappointed and frustrated at the Gemini parent's response.

Money Issues and the Gemini Parent

Because making money is rarely their primary interest, most Gemini parents face financial problems at one time or another or, in certain cases, all the time. They often insist that their children not waste money and appear tightfisted to those who know them. The refrigerator is unlikely to appear as an overflowing cornucopia nor is their outlay of cash for items they see as luxuries. Too often Gemini parents will impulsively and spend money the family has been carefully saving, splurging on an unrealistic item or project.

Crises and the Gemini Parent

When involved in true crises, Gemini parents are all too likely to overreact. Losing their cool in public situations can prove highly embarrassing to their mates and children. Their high-strung nervous systems and quick hands frequently allow them to save the day, but disasters can also quickly materialize as well when they are headed in the wrong direction, usually at warp speed. When they take the time to sit down and discuss or think about a proper response, they can be at their very best, considering the matter from every angle. However, their lack of deep emotional concern can be disturbing.

Holidays/Family Gatherings and the Gemini Parent

When they try to do all the prep work themselves, Gemini parents inevitably get over-stressed. Thus it is best to avoid such situations either by taking them out of the loop altogether or severely restricting their involvement, something they can usually accept with relief. Although enthusiastic about their immediate family, extensive larger family gatherings leave them cold, and they will often try to wriggle out of them. Few enjoy holidays and time off as much as Geminis, but they are extremely particular in their likes and dislikes of them. Do not plan surprises hoping Geminis will take them the right way.

Caring for the Aging Gemini Parent

Geminis tend to get less practical the older they get and, therefore, more unrealistic about their abilities. They usually want to just enjoy themselves, particularly in social interactions with people of all ages who are available to listen to their steady flow of ideas. Having a ready ear for them can become the principal requirement for being their friend or favorite child. Setting them up with a wide variety of books, games, puzzles, and internet activities will go a long way to keeping them happy. Thus, two-way human interaction is not really that important to aging Gemini parents.

The Gemini Sibling

Few things are sadder to contemplate than a Gemini only child. Gemini children love to have brothers and sisters around them, and if denied, they are likely to fill that void with friends and small animals, who become their surrogate siblings. (If further isolated, they will have no choice but to live in a fairy-tale world peopled by their stuffed animals and fantasy friends.) As part of a family unit, the Gemini sibling can be counted on to bring energy and an urge to explore the family group. They will often be set off by their creative use of language, which others can find quite contagious.

Rivalry/Closeness with the Gemini Sibling

Although Geminis can be quite competitive, it is usually the challenge of winning the game through personal achievement that is most important to them rather than beating their opponent. This is demonstrated by the zest with which they play solo computer games that test their skill and intelligence. Thus, they tend to be allies rather than rivals with their siblings, and they particularly enjoy group sports in which they can pair up

STRENGTHS

Curious

Energetic

Creative

WEAKNESSES

Isolated

Unrealistic

Withdrawn

INTERACTIVE STYLE

Social

Contributing

Verbal

with a brother or sister on their team. Here their true spirit of rivalry comes out, fully expressed against their traditional opponents. The height of achievement for Geminis would be scoring the winning run, basket, or touchdown in such a contest.

Past Issues and the Gemini Sibling

Gemini siblings can easily forgive and forget. Chances are that whatever is bothering you was never that important to them anyway. Gemini siblings are easily irritated, but their upset soon passes. This may actually be the crux of the problem, particularly if you are the one who cannot forget an unfortunate incident. It can be particularly galling to be reminded that your Gemini sibling does not really care about it and never has. Try to understand that it is only the event, not you, which meant less than nothing to them.

Dealing with the Estranged Gemini Sibling

Estranged Gemini siblings often drift away from the brothers and sisters they were never particularly close with while keeping their bonds intact with their favorites. Should they have been forced to break a close bond, it should be remembered that Gemini is the sign of the twins, and their desire to restore the close relationship they once had with a brother or sister can almost be as powerful as a biological urge. Because of this, sooner or later they will be open to reestablishing a relationship. In the case of distant siblings, the best that can be hoped for is cordiality and the occasional email, phone call, or family reunion.

Money Issues (Borrowing Money, Wills, Etc.) and the Gemini Sibling

For the most part, Gemini siblings do not care about being left money by a deceased parent. They will surely take offense if you infer that they tried to get their hands on it while the parent was still alive. Borrowing money from Gemini siblings is usually not a problem since they enjoy sharing what they have with family members. For most Geminis, money is not something to be hoarded but allowed to circulate freely. Situations arise when Gemini siblings seem to be taken advantage of financially by an overly needy brother or sister, but in fact the Gemini may not see it that way at all.

Holidays/Celebrations/Reunions and the Gemini Sibling

Gemini siblings enjoy celebrating festive occasions as long as all of their brothers and sisters are taking part. Often, a favorite cousin or two can take the place of a sibling as their sidekicks in such gatherings. The worst situation is when a Gemini is forced to face the celebration alone. Here, they tend to withdraw from the world of adults and seek to escape however they can. Too often they will retreat into their own unhappy shell, refusing to emerge. Do not even invite them unless a tried-and-true playmate is present.

Vacationing with the Gemini Sibling

Wrapped in the bosom of the family, Gemini siblings will usually have a great time on family vacations. Rarely the leaders in such endeavors, they are quite content to bask in the warmth of companionship and take part in adventures, explorations, contests, and general merrymaking. Continual play is what Geminis feed on. Their need to sleep on such excursions is slight, and they may keep the parents and siblings up half the night with their shenanigans. Make sure they get plenty of hard physical exercise during the day to guarantee a good night's rest for all.

The Gemini Child

The Gemini child needs lots of parental input. Interested in just about everything that goes on around them, Gemini children should be offered a wide range of activities. Gemini children can be delights or horrors, depending on their mood and yours. Nothing can be more maddening than their continual interruptions when you are trying to concentrate on something. You will experience great relief when you finally see your Gemini child absorbed in a solitary pursuit—or asleep.

Personality Development and the Gemini Child

Being high maintenance, Gemini children will suffer if they are not offered a broad palette of experiences and opportunities, plus the corresponding high-energy input needed for implementation. Skillful guidance will also be required, as well as good judgment if the Gemini child is to come to full flower. Such children must be given enough freedom but at the same time be required to fulfill obligations—fair ones, of course. Among these is the demand that they complete certain day-to-day tasks, including cleaning and straightening their room. Spoiling them can be as great a mistake as neglecting them.

Hobbies/Interests/Career Paths for the Gemini Child

The Gemini child often has a great interest in and talent for language. This can mean developing their written and verbal skills in their mother tongue but also in foreign languages. Such development could lead directly to a career in creative writing, journalism, editing, publishing, internet systems, or software development. Furthermore, Gemini children are also talented musically. Being particularly skillful with their hands and fingers, they can excel at a wide variety of musical instruments. A career in music performance, education, broadcasting, management, or composition and arranging are all possibilities. Often a Gemini child's principal hobby later blossoms into a career.

Discipline and the Gemini Child

Particularly for a Gemini child, discipline should denote guidance and structure rather than punishment. In this sense, Gemini children are particularly in need of discipline from an understanding parent, otherwise they are likely to fritter away their energies in a multitude of activities carried on at a superficial level. Learning self-discipline is most important for Geminis so that they can direct their energies in the most productive fashion, ultimately without having a parent or teacher standing over them. Many Geminis are self-taught, primarily using the skills of self-discipline they have acquired in their formative years to learn on their own.

STRENGTHS

Lively

Delightful

Fascinated

WEAKNESSES

Irritating

Needy

Horrid

INTERACTIVE STYLE

Demanding

Sparkling

Absorbed

Affection Level and the Gemini Child

Gemini children do not need constant perks or displays of affection. Just knowing that you admire or approve of what they are doing is usually enough. Constant disapproval is likely to damage them emotionally, so go easy on the negativity. A nod of the head, a smile, or a couple of kind words are usually enough for them. Equally important to the development of Gemini children is their own need to express affection, not only to parents and siblings but also to their pets. In many ways, their need to express affection is usually more pronounced than their need to receive it.

Dealing with the Gemini Child and Interactions with Siblings

Gemini children should be left alone to work out their sibling problems in their own way. It is best if parents do not get involved, and particularly that they do not force Gemini children to feel what they do not feel or act in a certain proscribed manner. A younger Gemini child is often highly criticized or even squashed by dominant older siblings, although in certain cases, a youngest Gemini child can be valued as a talented jewel in the family. An older Gemini child is not usually interested in dominating younger siblings and can be quite understanding and constructive in contributing to their development.

Interacting with the Adult Gemini Child

Adult Gemini children have strict ideas about the success or failure of their own upbringing and also concerning the behavior of their parents in general. Highly critical, they are quick to point out parental shortcomings as well as breakdowns that may have occurred in the sibling structure of the family. Usually up for discussions and debates, these individuals can be approached at any time for their opinions, and they will often offer to take part in group discussions. Most often their approach is analytical and detached rather than emotional, although they may need to blow off steam initially.

Cancer

BIRTHDATE **JUNE 22–JULY 22**

Ruled by the moon, these cardinal water signs are highly sensitive to the feelings of others and feel disappointment deeply. Because of the Moon's influence on the ocean's tides and the reclusive nature of the crab, Cancers are thought to be emotional people who often need to hide from the world. Yet, like the crab, they can become aggressive when disturbed and are also persuasive in getting their way, particularly when it comes to their living space, their food, and their loved ones.

Work

STRENGTHS

Low-key

Easy

Harmonious

WEAKNESSES

Overly demanding

Expectant

Particular

INTERACTIVE STYLE

Persuasive

Feeling

Empathic

The Cancer Boss

It can be a mistake to deny or underestimate the dominant qualities of the Cancer boss. Extremely particular about how things are done, Cancer bosses can be very demanding, albeit in a low-key manner. They expect their employees to understand their wishes and even to anticipate them. It is not so much rules and orders that count most for Cancer bosses, but rather the fact that everyone is on the same emotional wavelength. Not fond of trouble, Cancer bosses want things to run smoothly, and this fact, rather than power tripping per se, underlies their need for their dominance to be unquestioned.

Asking the Cancer Boss for a Raise

It is extremely difficult to talk a Cancer boss into giving you a raise. Cancer bosses usually have a good idea of whether or not you deserve it, although in the past they may have given away little indication of their feelings on this subject. Most often your raising this subject with them will have been anticipated, and you get the feeling they have been waiting for you to mention it. Should you choose the right moment to approach them—particularly at a time when your star is on the rise in the department—they may grant you a raise with surprising ease, even outlining your new salary, benefits, or position in some detail.

Breaking Bad News to the Cancer Boss

Cancer bosses tend to be moody, and here it is of utmost importance that you do not catch them in either a bad mood or an overly jovial one. Keep a sharp eye on their schedule and maintain close contact with their personal assistant. Choose a time when they are most relaxed and emotionally neutral. Preface your remarks with an outline of the historical aspects of the subject. Encourage Cancer bosses to ask questions, particularly concerning what can be done in the present moment to limit the damage done and perhaps turn the company's seeming disadvantage to its advantage.

Arranging Travel and/or Entertainment for the Cancer Boss

Cancer bosses are so particular that it is best if you have a separate conference with their personal assistant to determine exactly what their preferences are. Once these are known, they can be relied on in the future, for Cancers are very much creatures of habit.

Cancer bosses do not generally favor large outlays of cash to keep them happy and comfortable on the road. They think in economical rather than lavish terms, as long as the discomfort level is not high, particularly when it comes to their seating and their bed. Good food can do wonders for their disposition.

Decision-Making and the Cancer Boss

It is in this area that the dominant side of Cancer bosses emerges. These people are decision-makers who will not allow their authority to be questioned. However, they will usually take the time and trouble before making such final decisions to consult their employees, often devoting a whole meeting to meaningful discussion on the topic at hand. In this respect, they think of their decision as a final summation of the group feeling and general consensus of opinion. They are very wary of making unpopular decisions that will endanger their position of supremacy in the future.

Impressing and/or Motivating the Cancer Boss

Cancer bosses can at times be recalcitrant, slow moving, and unresponsive. It is best to attempt to motivate them without needing to impress them unduly. You should concentrate on trying to persuade them that there is some danger in waiting too long to implement a strategy everyone has already agreed on. If there is not yet full agreement, get them to schedule a group meeting within a week. Once the Cancer boss's emotions are aroused and engaged, they will finally begin to realize the importance of your plans and start to move forward with finality.

Making Proposals and/or Giving Presentations to the Cancer Boss

Keeping in mind the sensitivity and possible irritability of Cancer bosses, you should be extremely careful not to rub them the wrong way. The manner in which you present your proposal or make your presentation is thus every bit as important as, and in some cases even more important than, the content or point of view you wish to convey. If you start to sense that you have taken the wrong approach, have a fall-back plan handy and/or be prepared to improvise an adjustment to reduce their irritation. Once you see that they are responsive, proceed fearlessly with your delivery.

The Cancer Employee

Cancer employees are particularly good at desk jobs where they have the time to work on text. Best left uninterrupted, they can steadily churn out large blocks of paperwork over time in a consistent and high-quality fashion. Cancer employees seem to be devoted to their tasks and have unquestioned loyalty to the company. In fact, they have their own ideas on how things are going, but they usually watch and listen patiently, keeping their thoughts to themselves. If encouraged to speak out, they will do so, but only after repeated gentle prodding. Their observations are usually worth heeding.

Observant
Devoted
Concentrated

Confusing
Ambiguous
Silent

Uninvolved
Private
Reclusive

Interviewing and/or Hiring the Cancer Employee

Cancer interviewees rarely blow their own trumpet. They figure that their past record speaks for itself, and therefore they do not need to impress you. Not ones to come on in a verbal rush, they will usually wait for you to ask them specific questions rather than offering information on their own or attempting to guide the interview. They may give the impression of being nebulous, hard to pin down, and at times perhaps not even entirely there, but in fact they are taking in everything that is going on. They do not let you into their private world easily.

Breaking Bad News to or Firing the Cancer Employee

Cancer employees are extremely sensitive to bad news and will probably take it personally. Likely to feel guilty, they may immediately assume that if things are going in the wrong direction, it is at least partially their own fault. So sensitive are their emotional antennae that they will usually know immediately if you are about to break bad news or fire them, so don't waste your breath on lengthy introductions or other verbal preparations. They may even initially show sympathy toward the company's point of view, but most often will harbor long-standing and deep resentments.

Traveling with and Entertaining the Cancer Employee

Cancers are most comfortable working out of a home base. Although they can enjoy an occasional trip or party, they are best left at their workstation to complete their tasks. Cancers' imaginations are so active that they can experience the wide world of experience without going anywhere physically. They are extremely useful in planning or setting up projects rather than being the ones chosen to implement them. They have a special talent for picking the right person to do the appropriate job. Thus, you can trust and count on their judgment in most situations.

Assigning Tasks to the Cancer Employee

Always dutiful, Cancer employees will do their best with assigned tasks. However, they also know a lot about themselves, their capabilities, and their interests. Should they voice doubts concerning their ability to complete an assigned task, it is best to listen to them rather than brush off their objections or attempt to convince them otherwise. Even if you should succeed in getting them to agree to do something against their better judgment, it is their initial reservations that will usually prove correct in the long run.

Motivating or Impressing the Cancer Employee

True water signs, Cancers are difficult to push. It is hard to know how to approach them and where exactly to exert pressure without encountering resistance or, even worse, no resistance. Do not mistake their lack of objection for acquiescence. Time will be needed for your efforts to sink in, and even then they may prove unsuccessful. For the most part, Cancer employees must be self-motivated to get the job done. Once they have convinced themselves that a certain course of action is correct, they are capable of taking it all the way.

Managing, Directing, or Criticizing the Cancer Employee

Generally, Cancer employees must be handled much more carefully than most when you are attempting to give them direction or criticize their performance. Their feelings are easily hurt, so particular attention must be paid to the emotional reaction your statements may engender in them. Take care to speak in a calm, gentle fashion and to avoid personal subjects that could be taken the wrong way. If you are able to convey your meaning and intent without ruffling their feathers, you will have made a good start. If they are in a bad mood to begin with, back off and try again another time.

The Cancer Coworker

Approach Cancer coworkers on little cat feet. Prone to living in their own world, they are often deep in their imaginative thoughts when not outright absorbed in their work. Once a feeling of camaraderie or at least polite mutual attention is achieved, you may proceed with your question, observation, or request. Suddenly startling Cancer coworkers will most likely throw them off-balance and cause them to retreat into their shell. When committed to any projects at work, whether of a professional or nonprofessional nature, they can be counted on to radiate good feelings to all those around them.

Approaching the Cancer Coworker for Advice

Generally speaking, Cancer coworkers do not offer advice unless you ask them for it. Even then they can be reticent, even shy, about expressing opinions that could influence your behavior. Their modesty extends to almost every area of their work, so they appear not to be ruled by ego considerations. Lacking conceit or bravado, they frequently go in the other direction, appearing to lack confidence. In fact, they will give you solicited advice only if they truly believe they can help. This is most often in areas they feel they have special expertise in and a good feeling for.

Approaching the Cancer Coworker for Help

Although they may not immediately jump up when approached for help, Cancer coworkers can be counted on to lend their physical presence to small- or large-scale projects where they are needed. It is best to approach them a short time before they are actually needed, in order to let your request sink in, and to give them time to prepare for offering help in the best manner possible. Strong supporters of causes they believe in, they will go that extra mile for you in forwarding the implementation and execution of such projects. They are not types to quit when the going gets tough.

Traveling with and Entertaining the Cancer Coworker

Cancer coworkers are not easy to travel with because they are extremely particular about what they eat, where they sleep, and how they do things in general. In other words, they have demands and requirements that must be met not only when traveling but also when being entertained or setting up office celebrations. Cancer coworkers are not at all party animals, but because they have a tendency to be withdrawn, they especially enjoy them-

STRENGTHS
Sympathetic
Imaginative
Modest

WEAKNESSES
Distant
Off-balance
Withdrawn

INTERACTIVE STYLE
Low-key
Moody
Soft-spoken

selves when they can forget their introversion and let their hair down when participating in social functions. Unfortunately, their reactions cannot be predicted beforehand.

Cancer Coworker Cooperating with Others

Being such private people, Cancer coworkers don't always thrive in social involvements with groups. But in a professional situation, they will pull their weight, making unobtrusive contributions and being quietly helpful. Their ability to cooperate with others is dependent on the presence of good feeling and goodwill as well as a positive attitude toward the group. No matter how difficult the task, Cancers will not shirk their responsibilities once these emotional needs are met. In good situations, they may even assume a leadership role, inspiring great loyalty in their followers.

Impressing and Motivating the Cancer Coworker

As indicated, Cancer coworkers are not easily led when it comes to demanding something beyond their usual dedication to everyday tasks. Once their heartstrings are touched, however, they can be both motivated and impressed. No strangers to pain, Cancer coworkers have great sympathy for the feelings of others, particularly those who truly need them. Thus, they may be impressed and motivated when a colleague is down in the dumps or just going through a difficult time. They are often found on the side of the office misfit or outcast whose problems they can sympathize with.

Persuading and/or Criticizing the Cancer Coworker

Cancer coworkers react with hurt and withdrawal when they are the object of aggressive or sharp criticism. When stung by such verbal assaults or offhand slights, they are sure to become very recalcitrant to you in the future, often refusing to be persuaded even when your arguments are sound. Remember that in any conflict between head (logic, thought, reason) and heart (feelings, sympathies, emotions), the latter almost always assumes precedence for Cancer coworkers. Even when they themselves appeal to logic and reason, you can feel this strong emotional bias in their approach. On the other hand, they can be sharply critical to others and refuse to let up in their demands.

The Cancer Client

Cancer clients are difficult to please, not because they are overbearing or demanding but because they are so particular. On certain days it seems that nothing you present to them is right, even if profits and growth can be demonstrated. Do not expect to win them over by relying on facts and figures, but rather try to read their emotional state to see what they are in the mood for. In other words, be prepared to depart from your well-prepared presentation at the drop of a hat whenever necessary. If you are quick on your feet and receptive to their feelings, you will stand a better chance of success.

Impressing the Cancer Client

The best way to reach Cancer clients is by listening carefully to what they say and being sympathetic to their complaints. Only once you are tuned in to them and on the same wavelength will true communication be possible. They are impressed less by a cool, logical attitude that claims to make objective sense and more by one that is open to cooperation and compromise. You can also appeal to their imagination by presenting proposals that attract their powers of fantasy, often through daring, colorful, and expressive visual effects in the public relations department.

Selling to the Cancer Client

After presenting an unusual proposal—one that should be marked with flair and pizzazz—leave something to the Cancer client's active imagination. Another gambit is to plant the seed of an idea in their minds and in a subsequent meeting allow them to claim credit for it, often in the form of a new proposal based on your original suggestion. It is so important to read the Cancer client emotionally to know how he or she is feeling. To factor such understanding into your sell is essential, along with knowing how your Cancer client thinks in various situations. Cancer reasoning may not be entirely logical, but with study it can become predictable.

Your Appearance and the Cancer Client

Cancer clients have a wild, kooky side that may often lead them to dress in unusual styles. In order to build a bond of empathy, you should avoid bland or overly conservative dress and sport an unusual hairstyle, remarkable shoes, or a vividly colored outfit. When you see their smile you will know that you have succeeded. You will earn perks for taking a chance with your appearance rather than playing it safe. It is advisable for you to be clean and well groomed, but all cologne or other fragrances should be muted, although distinct. In your speech and movements, try to adjust to their tempo rather than overriding or ignoring them.

Keeping the Cancer Client's Interest

Cancer clients love to hear stories about various personal escapades, of both a business and a personal nature. Thus entertainment of all kinds will be appreciated, from telling jokes to outright flirting. If you can fascinate Cancer clients you may have won half the battle. Carried away by your convincing manner or seductive speech, they will be more open to any hard facts you want to get across. It is quite possible to accomplish this in their office or yours, rather than needing to wine and dine them. Leave them looking forward to the next enjoyable session.

Breaking Bad News to the Cancer Client

Remember that Cancers are no strangers to negativity, pain, and discomfort. Not that they are asking for it, but you do not have to beg their pardon or forgiveness for

STRENGTHS

Convivial

Appreciative

Imaginative

WEAKNESSES

Kooky

Strange

Illogical

INTERACTIVE STYLE

Fussy

Particular

Difficult

expressing negative results. The complexities of a problem will interest them, suiting the subtle twists and turns of their own personalities. By asking them to join you in helping to solve a problem, no matter how big, you will form a bond that can carry you through bad times together, as a unit. Never propose a solution that you will handle entirely alone, nor dump the whole thing in their lap. Cooperation is key.

Entertaining the Cancer Client

Oddly enough, Cancer clients may be happiest when doing something for you, rather than the other way around. Even if you are treating, leave certain areas open for their contributions and even allow them to occasionally take the lead. Seeing that they have pleased you, rather than vice versa, gives them the greater kick. The best you can hope for is that likes and dislikes can be discovered and shared in the course of an evening, leading to a convivial atmosphere with low-key good feeling on both sides.

The Cancer Business Partner

Cancers make excellent partners as long as you can be sure you are both on the same page most of the time. Prone to flights of fancy, Cancers are quite capable of dropping their more practical approach when something imaginative strongly appeals to them. Positively, this can mean that their ability to think outside the box brings your group forward in spectacular fashion; negatively, it can lead just as dramatically to disaster. The trick is for you to carefully evaluate each new project they come up with. Excellent at guarding the home base, Cancer partners are good tending to inside work such as planning, research, analysis, and development while you are busy working to sell and implement your product or service on the outside.

Setting Up the Business Partnership with Cancer

Contract-wise, Cancers will be agreeable to provisions that will guarantee the rights of both of you and ensure an equal stake in both risks and profits. It is best to set up the partnership carefully from a legal point of view, of course anticipating any difficulties that might arise. Keeping the contract conservative is advised, so it may be necessary to tone down any unusual or wild ideas your prospective Cancer partner comes up with. On the other hand, you should be sensitive to their preferences and responsive to their demands. Normally, Cancer partners can be counted on to keep to their word.

Tasking with the Cancer Business Partner

Listen to their ideas on tasking and then make your own evaluations of their strengths and weaknesses. Cancers are not always objective about their abilities, although they have a good idea of their likes and dislikes. Make sure they are not given a major role in an area that they enjoy but for which they are not suited. Accomplishing this task will involve not stepping on their toes or insulting them, and it will save you trouble in the long run. The important thing is that you take the time to explain. Be patient and sure that they absolutely understand what you are saying and that they agree fully.

Traveling with and Entertaining the Cancer Business Partner

As long as you are responsive to their needs and preferences, Cancer partners will be appeased. Try not to put them on a strict, demanding schedule, and be sure to leave time for breaks and rest since they tire easily when put under stress. Slowing down the pace of doing business will guarantee their fullest degree of participation. Cancers love to enjoy themselves in quiet, intimate settings. It is very important that you do not run off and leave them too much. Giving them your undivided attention from time to time will prove highly reassuring, furnishing them with the feeling of security they need.

Managing and Directing the Cancer Business Partner

Once Cancer partners know what they are supposed to do, they can be left alone, particularly in home-based work tasks performed in familiar surroundings. Leave Cancer partners free as much as possible in setting up the home base, making it in some ways a true domestic haven. They will guard their rights in this respect, so try not to interfere with their approaches, which could be a bit unorthodox to say the least. Only if you find that their in-house methods are financially unsound should you intervene and aim to restructure them. Modifying rather than aiming to scrap their ideas in this case is recommended.

Relating to the Cancer Business Partner in the Long Run

Cancer partners are usually in it for the long haul. Even if dull and unexciting, their steady input year after year can be counted on. Not overly fond of change, Cancers are particularly good at performing the same tasks in a highly reliable fashion. When irritations and difficulties arise, a soothing, sympathetic, and understanding approach is recommended. Cancer partners can get on your nerves at times, so your patience will be tested in this regard. Usually leaving them for a while to make a business trip or work on an outside project solves the problem.

Parting Ways with the Cancer Business Partner

As long as this can be done with good feelings, or at least without strong negative feelings, you are doing okay. The problem usually is that Cancer partners take everything so personally that they are likely to feel hurt, bewildered, rejected, and ultimately angry or depressed. To help avoid this, be sure not to break with them suddenly, but prepare them for your parting carefully over time, once you realize it is inevitable. Keep everything as objective as possible, but do treat their emotional state with respect by being responsive and sympathetic to their feelings whenever you can.

The Cancer Competitor

Masters at the art of subterfuge, Cancer competitors can be pretty difficult to read. By holding back a great deal and throwing out false leads, they manage to camouflage their true intentions. Sneaky may be a hard word to describe them, but there are few limits to how devious a Cancer competitor can be. They also have a seductive and persuasive

STRENGTHS
Convincing
Seductive
Fascinating

WEAKNESSES
Sneaky
Misleading
Negative

INTERACTIVE STYLE
Challenging
Controlling
Paralyzing

quality that can fascinate their opponents and at least temporarily paralyze their will to resist. Although they may seem relaxed, even passive, Cancer competitors can lash out aggressively when directly challenged.

Countering the Cancer Competitor

You should draw out Cancer competitors rather than try to confront them immediately. Allow them to show their hand as fully as possible, misleading and full of false clues as it may be. At least in this way you will have a good chance to study their deceptive methods. Of course do not take their content literally but rather look behind it to discover the truth that lurks in the shadows. Furthermore, their body language, facial expressions, and tone of voice will often yield more information about them than the facts they are trying to convey. Take time to plan your counterattacks effectively.

Out-Planning the Cancer Competitor

Convince your Cancer competitors that you believe what they have told you. Even give them the idea that your reactions will be based on that fact. In the meantime, you can best out-plan your Cancer competitors by being just as secretive and wily as they are. Behind a false front of inactivity and indecision, you should be at work actively planning your campaign. When you strike, hit hard at their most vulnerable points. Keep hammering away until they are finally forced to retreat or give in. Once you have punched a solid hole in their defense, they will begin to act more truthfully and reasonably.

Impressing the Cancer Competitor in Person

Keep your responses short and to the point. Because of their psychological acumen, Cancer competitors want you to talk as much as possible so that they can use your words against you in the future. By denying them this opportunity, you can capitalize on their confusion when you refuse to react. Should they turn on the charm, you can return the favor and play their seductive game, being careful not to fall for their devious ploys. By playing the strong and silent role you will impress them with your ability to resist and endure.

Undercutting and Outbidding the Cancer Competitor

Underneath the outer assurance and charm of Cancer competitors lies a thick layer of insecurity and doubt. The best way to undercut your Cancer foes is to arouse this insecurity by making them doubt their own methods, causing them to be particularly frustrated by the lack of effect their methods are having on you. Using irony, wit, andsubtle sarcasm, you will awaken their doubts about themselves and their products or services. Once you have managed to accomplish this task, you can continue to push their buttons at will and, like a good poker player, come out ahead when bluffing and bidding.

Public Relations Wars with the Cancer Competitor

The best way to counter Cancer competitors' imaginative public relation campaigns is to concentrate on poking holes in their grand schemes. Rather than mounting counterclaims in favor of the superiority of your product over theirs, continue to score hits that demonstrate their lack of practical thinking in the quality of their goods. By showing up their false claims and discrediting their products, you will leave them feeling helpless. Only then should you begin building the public relations claims of your own commodities, which will impact both the public and clients alike with telling effect.

The Cancer Competitor and the Personal Approach

Cancer competitors are masters of the personal approach. Therefore, it is better to leave this to them and concentrate on the empirical and objective. Strip your statements of any overtly emotional tone, relying as much as possible on data and figures. Let the facts speak for themselves, rather than trying to give them a practical spin. Encourage the emotional reactions of your Cancer competitors and let them wear themselves out in opposing the welter of feelings they stir up around them. Proceed with confidence and self-assurance, purging all doubt from your delivery.

Love

STRENGTHS

Demonstrative

Feeling

Loving

WEAKNESSES

Possessive

Clinging

Pretending

INTERACTIVE STYLE

Subtle

Watchful

Evaluating

The Cancer First Date

Being creatures of deep feeling, Cancers do not take relationships and emotional matters lightly. That said, Cancers are capable of pretending to have a good time and of fooling around without feeling anything deeply. But when they fall, they fall hard. If your Cancer first date expresses feeling toward you, accept it as a compliment to be treasured and never belittled. Cancer first dates will leave little doubt whether they want to see you again. If they really go for you, you may have trouble getting rid of them.

Wooing and Picking Up the Cancer First Date

Cancers love to be sought after, particularly if they like you. Rarely will they take the lead, leaving it up to you to pick them up or ask them out. The problem is that they are so particular in their likes and dislikes that it is difficult for you to read how you are doing at any given moment. Often they are unsure of their feelings in the early part of a relationship and need time to figure you out and let things sink in. Easily disappointed and puzzled, Cancer first dates are not terribly sure of themselves, although they are guided by their strong tastes and preferences.

Suggested Activities for the Cancer First Date

If you can find a concert, club, restaurant, or event that they like beforehand, then go to it, rather than taking them out to something you like. Should you decide anyway to take them to one of your favorite spots, be prepared that they may not like it at all and that the whole evening could be ruined. Wherever you go, don't spend the whole time telling them how wonderful something is, because it is impossible to convince them of it if they just don't like it. If in doubt, invite them over to your place and cook them a delicious dinner, followed by a quiet evening together.

Turn-Ons and Turn-Offs for the Cancer First Date

Cancer first dates vary with their likes and dislikes, but in all cases they feel strongly about both. Relating to Cancer first dates is simple: Find out what they like and give it to them. If you notice things they dislike, or if they tell you what they don't like, avoid these activities, locations, or interests like the plague. Do not discuss these matters with them or try to change their minds. Once they begin to trust you and know that you respect their judgment, you can think of moving to the next level with them.

Making "the Move" with the Cancer First Date

In most cases, it is best to avoid making the first move. These folks are really into the subtle nuances of feelings. They have antennae out for your intentions and often know what you are about to do before you do. They can also powerfully influence your feelings without your being aware of it. Watch them and listen to them carefully for clues to how you are doing. Usually by the second or third date you will know how far you are permitted to go with them.

Impressing the Cancer First Date

Cancers will be most impressed by your empathy for them and your sensitivity to their wishes. If you try to show off your knowledge, looks, personality, or connections, you may be digging your own grave. Cancers like to find out things about you on their own without being told. They are also likely to give unsolicited opinions on certain subjects should you mistake their meaning or overreach yourself. Since Cancer first dates will be highly critical of your actions, severe blunders may not be rewarded by a second chance.

Brushing Off the Cancer First Date

Unless they really flip over you, Cancer first dates can easily be brushed off by a bad look, hard remark, or brusque treatment, so sensitive are they to the feelings of others. If they like you, it will be difficult or impossible to rid yourself of them quickly. They will ignore all the warning signs and even interpret your negative actions positively. Once you ask them out and they have their sights set on you, the tender traps they set and the webs they spin to hold you are infinitely varied and can become quite pleasurable.

The Cancer Romantic Partner

Cancers enjoy being in a steady relationship. Very much creatures of habit, they get used to having their partners at their beck and call. As a result, they will count on them for everything from financial help to sex. Liking things to go well, these folks are affectionate and kind as long as they get their way. When denied their wishes, they get very crabby and irritable, often withdrawing into their shell and striking out in anger and resentment. Like their symbol, the crab, they are highly self-protective but are also no strangers to pain.

Having a Discussion with the Cancer Romantic Partner

Cancers do not mind talking about their feelings, but they are better at expressing them than analyzing them. Since emotional problems inevitably arise with Cancer romantic partner, it usually is best to get them out in the open, although often they will hide emotional problems and hold them inside. It will be up to you to find the right time and place for meaningful discussions since your Cancer partner will not usually take the lead in this matter. It will be difficult, but try to keep things objective or they may rage out of control.

STRENGTHS
Affectionate
Kind
Giving

WEAKNESSES
Irritable
Selfish
Withdrawn

INTERACTIVE STYLE
Self-protective
Accepting
Dependent

Arguments with the Cancer Romantic Partner

Arguments with Cancers tend to go on and on. Even if there is a temporary truce or agreement, do not expect that you have seen the end of a contentious issue between you two. Like a dog with a bone, your Cancer romantic partner is not able to easily let go. Arguments tend to take the form of endless bickering and low-key confrontation, only occasionally building to a grand climax. Such background noise can wear you down and put constant pressure on the relationship. Best to avoid tit-for-tat by simply letting them have the last word.

Traveling with the Cancer Romantic Partner

Some traveling with Cancers can be enjoyable, but not too much. Sooner or later they will long to return to the comfort and security of their home nest. They tire easily after a few days of traveling, tending to become exhausted and unhappy. They are, however, capable of putting up with a lot, and in emergencies they can be counted on to stick with you. This devotional side can carry you both through some difficult times while in transit. Try to plan your journey to include comfortable rest stops where they can regain their composure.

Sex with the Cancer Romantic Partner

Sex can be enjoyable with a Cancer romantic partner. As long as they are getting a fair amount of what they really like, they are generally up for pleasing you and being responsive to your needs. They also have a tendency in this area toward self-sacrifice, but beware that this does not eventually develop into self-pity and resentment, for it will eventually boomerang. In extreme cases, Cancers can make themselves very unhappy and not always be fully aware of the situation, particularly when they have idealized their partner or the relationship from the outset.

Affection and the Cancer Romantic Partner

Generally speaking, affection comes easier to Cancers than sex. They can have a very soothing effect on the relationship, constantly seeking to avert crises. This quality of wanting to ignore problems and avoid trouble can sometimes lead them to be almost fearfully affectionate and attentive, particularly if they are afraid of an outbreak of criticism or outright violence on the part of their partner. Thus the expression of affection can become a manipulative tool or a sure sign of wanting to deny or avoid the truth about a relationship.

Humor and the Cancer Romantic Partner

Cancers can enjoy laughter, particularly their own, but it does not always signal that they are having fun. Often it is nervous laughter, an attempt on their part to blot out something nearby that is bothering them. One type of humor they really enjoy is sharing private one-liners, gags, making faces, and other responses shared only by the two of you. This kind of inside or private joke is reassuring to them but frequently irritating to other friends and family members in their company.

The Cancer Spouse

Cancer spouses are intent on building a secure home base. Usually interested in almost everything about the place where they live, they will strive to get things exactly the way they want. Knowing that they will be spending as much time at home as possible, they wisely seek from the beginning to plan their domicile for efficiency and pleasure, down to the last detail. When they come up against fixed restrictions of space or location, they can get very frustrated over not being able to change them. Cancer spouses must be free to spend money for constant domestic improvements and keep up with maintenance as well.

Wedding and Honeymoon with the Cancer Spouse

Cancer spouses need to feel at home, and they are unlikely to take well to a long honeymoon in unfamiliar surroundings. Therefore, it is often a good idea to plan a honeymoon in a spot known to them, perhaps one they have visited from time to time over the years. In most cases, romance is not as important to them as the setting of the action. They have probably already made up their minds on the living space you will be returning to and have plans for fixing it up and making it just the way they want it to be.

Home and Day-to-Day Married Life with the Cancer Spouse

Once Cancer spouses have settled into their nest, they can be quite satisfied and happy. This happiness will be directly reflected in their attitude toward their marriage partner, but conversely so will any unhappiness they feel. Like the Moon, these lunar creatures reflect their feelings onto others, so it is best to keep them in a good mood. Make sure that a significant part of the budget—other than rent or mortgage and utilities—is available to them on a weekly basis to make new purchases. Cancers love food and are excellent cooks, so you will reap the benefits.

Finances and the Cancer Spouse

Not happy about having to account for every penny they spend or ask your permission to do so, Cancer spouses must be free (within reason) to handle finances on their own without the constant threat of criticism or interrogations. On the other hand, they can be very critical themselves about what their spouse does with the household money. It is best to leave as many domestic matters as possible up to Cancer spouses, but to get them to agree on a budget, particularly on the percentages spent for various activities. Cancers are capable of limiting their spending, even of hoarding, once they get the idea.

Infidelity and the Cancer Spouse

Cancers are likely to be there for you most of the time, but if they go off on their own, they do not want to be questioned about it. Should they truly step out on you, it will

STRENGTHS

Planning

Efficient

Domestic

WEAKNESSES

Frustrated

One-track

Controlling

INTERACTIVE STYLE

Protective

Maintaining

Confident

probably remain a secret, perhaps even shrouded in mystery over the years. "Did they or didn't they?" will be the big question you are unlikely to ever answer. Should you directly confront them with any indiscretion or outright infidelity, Cancer spouses are likely to refuse to answer and even threaten to leave if you show doubt and distrust.

Children and the Cancer Spouse

Cancers can make excellent parents in the areas of caring, devotion, and empathy. Yet Cancers can also smother their children, not allowing them the freedom they so desperately crave. Binding their children to them with hoops of steel, they frequently keep them from growing up into true adults in order to hold on to them tightly. With Cancers, it is not so much a matter of control as their refusal and, in some cases, inability to let go. Too often Cancer parents feel they should make all of the important decisions for their children, without question.

Divorce and the Cancer Spouse

Breaking up with Cancer spouses can be an extremely painful process. Because they feel so deeply and create strong emotional bonds with their partners, Cancers often need to maintain a working relationship with their spouses after the divorce. Generally speaking, they will fight for any object in the house—including the house itself, of course—to which they feel entitled. Since they have already invested so much of their time and energy in domestic matters anyway, they are likely to ask for most of it. If possible, it is best to leave them the home and the children and try to move on to greener pastures.

The Cancer Lover

Cancers are quite good at the art of concealment and are attracted to secretive relationships. Quite capable of keeping up their end of the bargain, Cancer lovers often make such a relationship possible and gratifying because of their discretion. Generally speaking, Cancer lovers see nothing wrong with giving their all in love, and then returning afterward to their partner or spouse with a clear conscience. Often the emotional expression they achieve with you will positively influence their primary relationship and enhance its quality in the long run. Cancer love affairs can stretch on for weeks or even years.

Meeting the Cancer Lover

It is best to have a special place where you can have regular meetings with your Cancer lover—one that is undisturbed and extremely private. Cancers must feel comfortable there and not feel anything cheap or sleazy about it. Sophistication comes naturally to most Cancers and, with it, a demand for quality. Moreover, they like to have quality time alone with you and not be rushed or fitted into a prescribed time slot. For them, it is not just sex but the honest expression of emotion that is most important. The slow expression and growth of affection can be more important than a sudden burst of hot passion.

Location and the Cancer Lover

Generally speaking, Cancers will not be comfortable either in their living space or in yours. Extremely particular about where and how they express their love, they often prefer to meet in a neutral setting that does not carry strong past associations. Such a place can become not exactly a new home for them but an escape where they can relax and withdraw from the busy world around them. Things will work out best if you provide such a location so that they do not have to be bothered by such matters.

Sex and the Cancer Lover

Cancers are highly physical creatures in a love affair, and they can wax very emotional and passionate. However, sensuality, rather than sexuality, is their forte. For them, the act of touching another's body is the ultimate in sensual pleasure, and allowing another to touch them is an expression of trust and deep intimacy. Cancers specialize in long, draw-out kisses and embraces, but also in developing quite complex and entangling routines over time. Mutual—as opposed to one-sided—expressions are preferred. Cancers enjoy getting to know their lovers as minutely as possible, pursuing intimacies in a thorough, subtle, and detailed fashion.

Holding On to the Cancer Lover

If Cancer lovers are truly in love with their partner, there will be no difficulty holding on to them, since it is they who will do everything in their power to hold on to you. Because of their strongly empathic powers, they will instantly sense when you are truly responsive and when you are faking it or pulling back from them emotionally. Should they feel they are losing you, they will tighten the ties that bind and often make it difficult or even impossible for you to escape. There are no lengths to which Cancer lovers will not go to hold on to the ones they love. Shameless, they are frank in their expressions of feeling.

Entertaining the Cancer Lover

In most cases, no entertainment is necessary. Cancer lovers are into weaving their magical spell around you, in enchanting and seducing you utterly. All other matters are secondary to this, as love is usually their highest ideal. All you are expected to do is to respond to them and give yourself completely to the love affair. Chatter and talk in general are to be kept subordinate to intimate looks, caresses, murmurs of affection, and sighs of pleasure. Being appreciative of them in the present moment is the principal requirement here. Steady eye contact especially turns them on.

Breaking Up with the Cancer Lover

Cancer lovers have to be absolutely convinced that their love relationship is completely over before they will give it up. If they are still in love with you, it will be extremely difficult for you to unilaterally break up the relationship. If, on the other hand, you are still in love with them and the thrill is gone for them, they can be quite ruthless in dropping you like a hot potato. Thus, the timing and manner of breaking up is usually in the hands of Cancer lovers rather than their partners.

(The Cancer Lover)

STRENGTHS

Discreet

Diplomatic

Clear

WEAKNESSES

Deceptive

Concealing

Prevaricating

INTERACTIVE STYLE

Self-assured

Unambiguous

Feeling

The Cancer Ex

STRENGTHS

Self-assured

Empowered

Giving

WEAKNESSES

Resentful

Rejected

Negative

INTERACTIVE STYLE

Guarded

Quiet

Careful

It is important to know who dumped whom or whether the breakup was by mutual agreement without animosity. If it's the latter scenario, there is no real problem. If Cancer exes are the ones who do the dumping, they may be surprisingly easy to deal with, since they are not feeling rejected and may even have been empowered by the experience. If, however, they are the ones who have been dumped, all kinds of aggressive, negative, and hurtful tendencies may surface. Resentment is likely to play a large part here, particularly when they feel they have been rejected through no fault of their own. Their feelings of having been unfairly treated can create blocks that last for years.

Establishing a Friendship with the Cancer Ex

At least a year or two is likely to elapse after the breakup before the Cancer ex is ready to be your friend. Once Cancer exes close the door on a relationship, it remains closed, and an entirely new doorway will have to be built. Extremely guarded the second time around, Cancers will be overly careful about giving almost anything away again to the same person. Of course friendships will be easier if Cancer exes have been adequately recompensed for the terrible pain they have felt. It's best to acknowledge your faults and responsibilities to them.

Issues of Getting Back Together with the Cancer Ex

This is extremely difficult unless you are the injured party and they have emerged virtually blameless and emotionally intact. In the latter case you could begin by gradually dropping your anger and resentment (or quietly expressing it just a few times), becoming friends, and proceeding from there. If your Cancer ex is still in love with you, there is a chance for reconciliation, as long as you do not take unfair advantage of their feelings. Keeping everything low-key, even casual, is recommended, and rather than commenting on or discussing what is taking place, allow the wonder of the new situation to overcome you both. Let it happen on its own—don't push.

Discussing Past Issues with the Cancer Ex

It is best if you don't raise past issues with Cancer exes. The past is a very tricky and sensitive area for Cancers; they do not easily forget or forgive. It is a very good sign if Cancer exes begin to reminisce or wax nostalgic about the old days, but don't jump the gun. Show that the feeling is mutual with a fond look or a smile. This will be sufficient encouragement for them. When they do raise past issues, allow them to express themselves fully rather than turning cold or changing the subject. When questioned on the subject, answer as calmly and truthfully as you can.

Expressing Affection to the Cancer Ex

Only be the first to express affection if you can do it in an extremely tactful and subtle manner. Otherwise, let them make the first move. So finely tuned to feelings are Cancers that they will pick up on the slightest softness or warmth on your part, so no need to overdo it—which would most likely arouse an immediate negative response. Just listening to them and being sympathetic to their feelings will, in itself, be viewed as an expression of affection. Remain attentive enough that you do not miss the first affectionate gesture that comes from their direction. Missing it could be a serious blunder.

Defining the Present Relationship with the Cancer Ex

Sharp definitions are not possible for most Cancer exes. Because of their watery nature, they are most often swimming around in a sea of feeling that resists being pinned down in a logical fashion. Making decisions that they can stick to may be very difficult for Cancer exes, even if they have all the best intentions. The best way to deal with this issue is to play things by ear, taking the present relationship one step at a time. By not planning ahead, and living day to day, you will prove to them that you can be trusted with their moods and feelings.

Sharing Custody with the Cancer Ex

If Cancer exes are convinced that you are a good person with the best interest of the children at heart, there will be few problems. However, if they have doubts about your character based on past performance, they will be very difficult to deal with on this subject. Build trust slowly by demonstrating consistency of a positive sort and allow past injuries to heal while a new bond is forming. Should the children be living with your ex, be responsive to the rules set up by the court or the demands the Cancer ex makes on you. If the children are with you, allow the Cancer ex to play a significant role in their lives, but be on the lookout for manipulative and controlling behavior.

Friends and Family

STRENGTHS
Interested
Patient
Dedicated

WEAKNESSES
Nosy
Needy
Hidden

INTERACTIVE STYLE
Receptive
Personal
Curious

The Cancer Friend

Although Cancers can make excellent friends, they are likely to want you all to themselves and not share you with mutual friends. Cancer friends have to know they are not only your good but your best friend. While you are out gallivanting they will wait patiently for you to get back to them. A lengthy telephone report from you will do, but they prefer the cozy atmosphere of their living space for you to spill the beans about all your recent shenanigans. Do not expect them to share their own experiences so easily, for they tend to keep personal matters to themselves. However, in acute need, they can become quite dependent on your support.

Asking for Help from the Cancer Friend

Cancer friends feel they are there to help others. Generous in giving time and attention to your needs, Cancers are among the most receptive and empathic of friends. However, when it comes to springing into action, they tend to hold back and be cautious. Thus their support tends to be more emotional than dynamic. They are particularly good at furnishing you with a private space where you can hide out and lick your wounds. Protective, they will do whatever they can in such a situation to keep you from harm. Their sympathy and understanding can usually be counted on.

Communication and Keeping in Touch with the Cancer Friend

Because of Cancer's frequently passive orientation, it will usually be up to you to take the necessary steps to ensure regular communication and contact with Cancer friends. They will be gratified to hear from you, even if a long time has passed since you last spoke. Communication is not essential from their point of view, since carrying you in their heart seems enough for them, and they often lack the acute need to express their feelings to you. Sending them an occasional text message or email will be appreciated. Likewise, if you go on a trip, sending a nice postcard with some kind thoughts expressed would also be looked upon favorably by a Cancer friend.

Borrowing Money from the Cancer Friend

Cancer friends can be very generous in lending money. They do, however, find it very awkward to ask for it back, so be sure you reimburse them for their loan according to your initial agreement to avoid hurting their feelings or their wallet. If you don't repay them, they are likely to sink into a silent depression, leaving no doubt in your mind what is wrong. Such occasions can lead to estrangement or even the end of the relationship, not so much because of the money but because you have insulted them. Remember, insensitivity ranks high as a sin in the minds of most Cancers, particularly with regard to their close friends.

Asking for Advice from the Cancer Friend

Cancer friends are happy to give advice and often do so unsolicited and in an unreserved fashion. When they see you acting improperly or in a hurtful way to yourself, they will be quick to advise you to change course. Nor do they consider such advice to be casual or take-it-or-leave-it. They will persist until you finally follow their advice or reject it—if the latter, they may not be so quick to help you again in this area. Generally speaking, their advice is helpful, but you must be careful that they are not just speaking about themselves rather than being objective.

Visiting the Cancer Friend

For Cancer friends, visiting is very important, particularly when the meeting place is at their house. Only in their own space can their warmest and most receptive side find expression. Security is very important for Cancer friends, and sharing this feeling with others can be gratifying to all concerned. They will no doubt delight in feeding you as well as sharing all the latest news and gossip. Generally speaking, you will leave Cancer friends feeling better than when you entered, unless you are intent on upsetting them, in which case you should spare yourself the trouble of a visit altogether.

Celebrations/Entertainment with the Cancer Friend

When Cancer friends do decide to go out, they want to have a really good time. Do not, however, try to drag them to celebrations that they fully expect not to enjoy. You will find them either confronting you with a last-minute refusal to go (no doubt on the grounds of feeling ill) or attending the event wearing a face that leaves no doubt about their having a lousy time. Cancers love to hold celebrations and throw parties, but they tend to want to do all the cooking and preparing themselves. They are quite capable of doing all of this, but they can also suffer a post-party breakdown and be unavailable for some days thereafter.

The Cancer Roommate

Because of Cancers' attachment to the home and all things domestic, they are likely to take a keen interest in your mutual living space and will seek to make it a refuge against the world. Their comfort-loving side and passion for food will make beds, bedding,

STRENGTHS

Domestic

Involved

Supportive

WEAKNESSES

Withdrawn

Fearful

Isolated

INTERACTIVE STYLE

Protective

Nurturing

Helpful

couches, dining, meals, heat, and hot water special priorities. The Cancer home is a nest, a hideout, a private sanctuary, so having you as a roommate is one of the biggest compliments Cancer roommates can offer. Invasion of their privacy (they simply must have their own room, but can share a common living space) is something they will not tolerate, but hopefully they will extend the same privacy to you.

Sharing Financial Responsibilities with the Cancer Roommate

Cancers can be quite good at handling money. Giving them the responsibility of paying the rent and utility bills after collecting your share is an acknowledgment of their capabilities and will usually sit well with them. On the other hand, you may have to establish a strict budget for food and other household expenses, since their elaborate tastes can easily run out of hand. Just tell them how much you are prepared to pay each month or even have a cash jar into which you put your share and let them spend as much as they want in addition to their split.

Cleaning and the Cancer Roommate

Once they get started, Cancer roommates can be excellent cleaners. The only problem is motivating them to begin, since they are notorious procrastinators in this regard. They are quite capable of living amid disorder, even approaching the chaotic, and turning a blind eye to it. Often scheduling a party or visit will wake them up to the necessity of cleaning up. Their work is usually efficient, and they have the stamina and concentration to hang in there and finish things once they put their minds to it. Another way to prepare them for cleaning day is to show some interest in the cleaning materials required and make sure they are added to the shopping list. Afterward, leave the materials in an obvious place where they can be seen.

Houseguests and the Cancer Roommate

Cancer roommates can get irritated if their peace and privacy are constantly disturbed. Their nervousness on the subject can make them so touchy that they become difficult to live with. You will have to pay special attention to the frequency of visits and the effect your visitors have on your Cancer roommate. Kept within reason, such visits can prove pleasurable for all concerned, since Cancer roommates are also proud to show their living space and to have it appreciated by others. Cancers love conviviality, so occasional guests for dinner, drinks, and a relaxed evening can be highly enjoyable.

Parties and the Cancer Roommate

Somehow, Cancer roommates always get deeply involved in parties and celebrations. Their culinary and organizational skills come to the fore here. Shopping, decorating, cleaning, sending invitations, and cooking take on a whole new aura for special events. Do not try to deny them any of the responsibilities they take on, since they will only feel disappointed or even ignored if you do too much. Socializing is not always easy for Cancers, and throwing a party can be a chance to fully indulge their social side. If things go well, they will be talking about the event for days thereafter and be up for a repeat in the future.

Privacy and the Cancer Roommate

Extremely private, Cancers cannot and should not be intruded upon. Once Cancer crabs enter their caves, they are very difficult to pry out. There will be periods of hours, days, and occasionally even a week when Cancer roommates should just be left alone and not disturbed by you or anyone else. Once you show that you are sympathetic to their needs, they will respond with warmth and show helpfulness when you are feeling needy. Do not object to their habit of locking their door and understand that, at times, just knocking on it may be seen as a major intrusion.

Discussing Problems with the Cancer Roommate

The watery side of Cancers often makes it difficult to pin them down for discussions of specific issues. After a few initial rebuffs to randomly raising problems for discussion, you may feel the need to schedule a full-blown meeting expressly for this purpose. Even though they may duck out of such sessions at the last moment, keep at it undeterred until they finally sit down with you. Making a list of the subjects to be discussed and even taking notes at such a session will be productive and counteract some of the Cancer vagaries and lack of focus. Once Cancers recognize the need to act to resolve certain problems, they can be counted on to do their share of the necessary work.

The Cancer Parent

Cancers can be among the most loving and caring of parents. Affectionate and protective, they easily satisfy the needs of their children to be nurtured and protected. However, they can also be overprotective and thus can frustrate or impede the needs of their offspring to emerge as individuals in their own right. Cancer parents must learn the hard lesson of letting go, allowing their children the freedom that is rightfully theirs. Because their loving support is such a tender trap, their children frequently succumb to it and become unduly dependent on their Cancer parents.

Discipline Style of the Cancer Parent

Ideally, because of their vast empathy for their children, not much discipline is possible or even necessary for Cancer parents to impose. Normally, they will have a heart-to-heart talk with their kids concerning an indiscretion or rule-breaking and things can be settled peacefully. However, when pushed, Cancer parents can be quite severe in imposing punishment on their children, usually in the form of grounding them. Cancer parents like to think their rules are well-known and therefore broken only intentionally, which should be a rare occurrence. They are open to listening to explanations and accepting excuses, at least the first time a rule is broken.

Affection Level and the Cancer Parent

Cancer parents are, as a rule, highly affectionate. For them it is quite natural and easy to express affection to their children. Their offspring soon learn that when affection is not being expressed, there is something wrong, and as children frequently do, they put

STRENGTHS

Nurturing

Loving

Caring

WEAKNESSES

Overprotective

Controlling

Smothering

INTERACTIVE STYLE

Supporting

Contributing

Interested

the blame on themselves. The Cancer parent may have to explain to the kids that their distance and lack of emotional expression has nothing to do with them, but with some other area of their lives. Cancer parents not only are able to express affection but also love receiving it in the form of hugs, kisses, and smiles.

Money Issues and the Cancer Parent

Cancer parents usually give their children a weekly allowance but will insist that they stick to it and not ask for additional cash on a regular basis. They will be responsive, however, to the needs of a child for a particular item of clothing, dues for a club, or a very special entertainment treat, as long as they are able to afford it financially. Cancer parents are so giving and sympathetic that they will often offer an extra outlay of cash before their children can bring themselves to ask for it.

Crises and the Cancer Parent

Cancer parents do everything they can to head off crises before they happen. Empathic with their children, they tend to know when something is wrong and will act to solve the problem or at the very least to exercise damage control. Although they can be relaxed, comforting, and reassuring, Cancers can move pretty quickly in an emergency situation and thus can be counted on in a pinch. However, because of overprotective attitudes, they can also get nervous and eventually overreact in their zeal to come to the aid of their offspring. Keeping cool in a crisis is something they have to work on.

Holidays/Family Gatherings and the Cancer Parent

Cancer parents do not view life as a perpetual family holiday. There are chores to be done, homework to finish, and one's personal appearance to be attended to. That said, their serious approach to raising children eases up when it comes to holidays and family get-togethers, where they can really let their hair down and allow their kids to have a great time. This does not include letting them run wild, however, since their protective instincts surface to keep their kids safe from danger. Swimming around in good feelings at a family celebration or holiday is a sure cure for Cancer crankiness or depression.

Caring for the Aging Cancer Parent

Because caring for their children is such an important part of their lives when they are younger parents, aging Cancers appreciate the necessity of being well looked after. But because they know the enormous outlay of time and energy required, they infrequently ask their children to take care of them. Normally they will try to get by on their own, certainly in their own home, or be persuaded to move into a smaller apartment, one closer to family members. Rarely will aging Cancer parents react well to the suggestion that they move into a home for the elderly. The older they get, the more difficult Cancers find it to share space with others.

The Cancer Sibling

Unless they are the oldest siblings, in which case their dominant and aggressive side is likely to emerge, Cancers often fit into a multisibling family with grace and ease. Prone to be spoiled by their more active brothers and sisters, Cancer siblings are usually content to play a secondary role, doing their own thing quietly and unobtrusively. They are likely to have a favorite sibling to whom they attach themselves, almost to the point of becoming their shadow. Cancer siblings often stand out from the other children because of their acute parental needs, particularly if they have a chronic physical, mental, or emotional condition.

Rivalry/Closeness with the Cancer Sibling

Cancers do not, as a rule, specialize in sibling rivalry, being content with what they have and who they are. If pushed, Cancers will compete and often win out, but overt aggression is not usually their style unless seriously provoked. Cancers tend to be close to siblings with whom they share common feelings, whether of joy or suffering. Should Cancer siblings be the eldest, they will exercise their dominance without fostering competition and exert strongly protective energies toward their younger brothers and sisters, particularly from the taunts and unfair challenges of older schoolmates.

Past Issues and the Cancer Sibling

Cancer siblings have long memories, particularly when it comes to holding on to resentments about past issues. Time usually does little to erase such unpleasant memories, so if their fellow siblings wish to clear up such matters, they will have to take the lead in raising them for discussion. More often than not, Cancer siblings will complicate matters by evading such attempts, outright refusing to answer or denying that such issues are really unimportant to them. Yet in the emotional life of almost every Cancer there are past issues that must be discussed or dealt with to avoid blocks in adult development.

Dealing with the Estranged Cancer Sibling

This is a difficult one. When Cancer siblings become estranged, like true crabs, they tend to withdraw and pull into their shell. Once they are in this defensive posture, it is extremely difficult to lure them out. Only by establishing trust with them over a long period can their siblings hope to reach them and bring them back into the family fold. To complicate matters, there is often not just one single cause for such behavior, but a whole complex network of chronic emotional disturbances that is responsible. Proceed with persistence, patience, and understanding to unravel the difficulties one by one.

Money Issues (Borrowing Money, Wills, Etc.) and the Cancer Sibling

Cancer siblings will usually demand what is rightfully theirs—but no more—when it comes to inheritances. Particularly if they were emotionally close to the deceased, the money may even be spent by them in accordance with the supposed or stated wishes of the departed. As far as approaching Cancer siblings for money, brothers and sisters may find them a bit tightfisted and unwilling to part easily with hard-earned cash. In case of an emergency or a shared expense involving the parents, Cancer siblings can be counted

STRENGTHS

Sensitive

Affectionate

Cuddly

WEAKNESSES

Dependent

Needy

Attached

INTERACTIVE STYLE

Affectionate

Removed

Self-absorbed

on to foot their share of the bill, but may have to be asked for it rather than offering it on their own.

Holidays/Celebrations/Reunions and the Cancer Sibling

If Cancer siblings have been on good terms with the others in the family, they will pitch in and help at the festivities, particularly if they are in a celebratory mood. If they are cranky or withdrawn, they will have to be prodded a bit. However, a recent or long-standing disagreement with one of the siblings can keep Cancers from attending or taking part at all. This issue is best addressed beforehand and not left to fester until the great day arrives. Once Cancers can put this conflict behind them, they can contribute their positive energies to the fullest.

Vacationing with the Cancer Sibling

As long as you are sensitive to Cancer siblings' needs, particularly their strong likes and dislikes, things can go very well. Cancers enjoy family vacations, but when they need to withdraw to their own space (which should be available) they must be allowed to do so. Particularly fond of swimming or bathing of all types, this water sign is known for its predilection for vacations near the sea, lakes, or rivers. Cancers can enjoy the sun as much as any, but they also enjoy languishing in cool green grass under a shady tree.

The Cancer Child

Cancer children can become overly dependent on their parents. Because of their intense need for security, Cancer children need a great deal of parental support, guidance, and protection. Frequently, Cancer children feel at the mercy of a hostile world that does not understand them or honor their feelings. The understanding parents of such children must seek to introduce their children to the world and teach them the social skills necessary to cope with it. Developing true independence is the Cancer child's greatest challenge. Thus, the parents' involvement in minimizing dependence and maximizing responsible freedom is essential.

Personality Development and the Cancer Child

Cancer children are unusual and have the capabilities to develop into their own people were it not for the acute dependency they usually manifest on parents, siblings, or other family members. Wrapped in the bosom of the family, Cancer children will experience few problems. In order for their personality to unfold, all social activities such as school, clubs, sports, culture, and internet contacts should be emphasized. This will counter their natural tendency to be alone and also place some checks on their unbridled fantasy life, which thrives in isolation from the world.

Hobbies/Interests/Career Paths for the Cancer Child

Hobbies that bring Cancers in contact with their peers should obviously be encouraged rather than ones that isolate them from the world. Their natural interests should be noted and followed. For example, if they have a love of music and the talent to match, rather than starting them on a solo instrument like piano, it might be better to try a string, brass, or woodwind instrument that they can play in an orchestra with other children, or drums or electric guitar with a rock band. Cancers can be excellent editors and often find satisfying careers in publishing. They also respond to physical challenges and need adventure to counterbalance their penchant for fantasy.

Discipline and the Cancer Child

Rather than being a system of dos and don'ts, punctuated by rewards and punishments, discipline for Cancer children should involve setting up structures and guidelines in which they can operate. Prone to drift and dream, Cancer kids respond positively to their energies being stimulated and channeled in a positive direction. By creating standards and requirements for them to meet, the parents of Cancer children can nudge (never force) them into productive activities where the results of their work are there for all to see. The pride of achievement can become a powerful motivating force in the future.

Affection Level and the Cancer Child

Cancer children's need for affection is high. Yet so particular are they about being approached emotionally and physically that only the most sensitive and perceptive of adults may be able to get through to them. Nothing turns off a Cancer child more than being spoken to or touched in the wrong way. Parents who are truly tuned in to their Cancer children know this and are able to consistently take the right approach. Thus, knowing how to express affection to Cancer children is just as important as the affection itself.

Dealing with the Cancer Child and Interactions with Siblings

A Cancer child should never be spoken to harshly or critically when in the company of siblings or friends. Adults should know enough to take them aside and speak to them directly, personally, and with kindness. Although parents should keep an eye on their Cancer children's interactions with other kids, particularly their siblings, parents should not constantly interfere to rectify a situation, but instead learn to back off and let their Cancer children handle their own business as much as possible. This attitude promotes trust between parents and their Cancer children.

Interacting with the Adult Cancer Child

Cancers tend to live very much in the past; therefore they often carry unhealed scars from childhood traumas in their psyches. If the interaction is between a family member and adult Cancer children, just the presence of this parent, sibling, or other family member can trigger the emergence of old scripts and feelings. For this reason, it can sometimes work better to contact adult Cancer children by email or telephone to minimize negative stimuli. As wounds heal with increased trust and love, more time may be spent interacting with them in person.

STRENGTHS

Challenged
Self-involved
Freedom-seeking

WEAKNESSES

Overprotected
Needy
Asocial

INTERACTIVE STYLE

Dependent
Original
Dreamy

FRIENDS AND FAMILY

Leo

BIRTHDATE JULY 23–AUGUST 23

Symbolized by the blazing and radiant sun, the fixed fire sign of Leo spreads its creative warmth over all within its sphere of influence. Leos pride themselves on keeping their fire under control and making judgment calls that can benefit others. Passionate emotionally, those born under this sign will not be denied what they desire and are prepared to fight for it if necessary. Leos demand the respect of others and will prove reliable by following through on their commitments.

Work

LEO
July 23–August 23

The Leo Boss

Born leaders, Leos exult in assuming the top positions of any company. Ownership is not the most important thing for them, however—so as long as they are CEOs or directors, they are happy to be employees. Leo bosses try to be fair and impartial, succeeding in doing so as long as their authority is not questioned nor their job threatened. As they see it, they are simply representing everyone under them, trying to get them the best possible salaries, working conditions, advancement opportunities, and benefits. Leos take great pride in their work, so when the company is being congratulated by stockholders, boards of directors, or owners, they are happy to accept for everyone else.

Asking the Leo Boss for a Raise
In the mind of the Leo boss, either you are ready for a raise or you are not. Leo bosses will counter your request for a raise with a detailed study of your past performance. If you deserve it, they will work as hard as they can to secure it for you within the limits of their budget and planning. Most often, if they cannot grant a raise immediately, they will at least give you an idea whether and when a raise would be possible and what you need to do to get it. Should you point out that one of your less-deserving associates has gotten a raise, they will be careful to point out objectively why that was so.

Breaking Bad News to the Leo Boss
If it is the kind of news that Leo bosses will not take personally as a reflection on their work or leadership, you can state it in very objective terms and let them deal with it. If, however, Leo bosses feel personally let down by an employee responsible for the bad situation or if they assume responsibility for the failure themselves, you had best soften the blow by taking them out for a drink or meal in a comfortable, well-lit atmosphere. Leo bosses can even surprise you in such an ambiance by laughing it off or confessing they are secretly glad that the disaster occurred or that the project is finally finished.

Arranging Travel and/or Entertainment for the Leo Boss
Leos feel ashamed and embarrassed staying in cheap or sleazy surroundings. Their royal nature demands something upscale, worthy of their noble air. First-class travel accom-

STRENGTHS
Fair
Proud
Commanding

WEAKNESSES
Egotistical
Power-hungry
Self-centered

INTERACTIVE STYLE
Friendly
Open
Generous

modations and four-star hotels are a must. Therefore, better to schedule fewer trips with greater outlays for posh living and dining accommodations than more trips on a budget. In other words, when Leos do something, they believe in doing it right. Usually they will supplement these special trips with a personal outlay for a couple of new outfits, including shoes, hats, and business suits.

Decision-Making and the Leo Boss

Leos make all-important decisions themselves but cleverly make you think you have also taken part. As long as the two of you agree, there is no problem—they are happy to share the decision with you. Be prepared, however, that if you have come up with the crucial suggestion or clinching argument, they might say, "Hey, I'm glad I thought of that." After all, why shouldn't they get the credit since ultimately they represent you and all the other workers anyway? The royal "we" (as when the king or queen says, "We are not pleased") must have been invented by a Leo.

Impressing and/or Motivating the Leo Boss

Best to motivate Leo bosses indirectly. Rather than coming right out with a suggestion or urging them repeatedly over time, it is best to plant an idea in their minds casually, in passing, and let it germinate there for a while. Doing this repeatedly will impress them and also give the added bonus that they can take credit for developing and, in some cases, having discovered it themselves. Leo bosses can come to depend on such little offerings on your part and feel the need to keep you around when they are preparing for a big meeting.

Making Proposals and/or Giving Presentations to the Leo Boss

When making a formal proposal or giving an important presentation to Leo bosses, try to pull out all the stops and create something grand. It is not enough to just state your case simply. Use style, verve, fanfare, and hopefully conviction in order to persuade them to your cause. Remember that they will judge the quality of everything you present. If you appear with flawed, sloppy, or slipshod materials, it will not matter how convincing or compelling your ideas are. Bad spelling or fuzzy screens all diminish your credibility in the eyes of Leo bosses.

The Leo Employee

Faithful to the extreme, Leo employees can be counted on to invest lots of time and energy in their work and to remain loyal to the group or company in which they participate. They are quite capable of sticking to a job or task, often being found in a given profession for an entire lifetime. Not only is this a matter of loyalty, but it is also indicative of their resistance to change and their getting used to being recognized for their expertise and trusted well as being counted on to produce tangible results. Ambition often urges them to seek reward, both financial and in the form of promotions. For most Leos, professionally, the only possible direction is up.

Interviewing and/or Hiring the Leo Employee

Leo interviewees will normally present themselves at their best and seek to emphasize their past experience and achievements. Although they may seem low-key, the power behind their quiet words will be evident. They are also capable of occasional dramatic outbursts that reveal a bit of their underlying volcanic energies. It is important to tell them any drawbacks or negative points they will have to reckon with in their new position. Eventhough they may ignore them, they can never say they were not cautioned beforehand.

Breaking Bad News to or Firing the Leo Employee

Leos tend to identify strongly with their profession and the group they work with, so being sacked from their job or receiving bad news can hit them pretty hard. Leo employees tend to take a positive attitude toward things, so much so that they block out anything they consider negative. Therefore, feeding them periodic hints of an upcoming blow to their professional aspirations may simply be ignored. This often necessitates a rather blunt statement on the part of their boss—it may be brutal, but at least it will be comprehended.

Traveling with and Entertaining the Leo Employee

Leo employees generally appreciate travel, but get worn down quickly by too much of it. They do not need a lot of entertainment since they are natural explorers who like to find their own way. Do not be surprised if they go off on their own and leave you to your own devices. There will still be opportunities for them to enjoy themselves with you or the group as long as they have the freedom to do their own thing. Do not constrain them through excessive requirements that limit their choice.

Assigning Tasks to the Leo Employee

Good at completing given tasks, Leos are usually helped rather than hindered by clear instructions about methods they need to employ and what is expected of them in general. Leaving things a bit fuzzy can result in their becoming either overly aggressive or individualistic in their approach or else uncertain and unsure of themselves. Neither of these alternatives leaves you with a happy Leo on your hands. Once you have given them explicit instructions, you will not need to check their work regularly, as they can be counted on to deliver the desired result.

Motivating or Impressing the Leo Employee

Most Leo employees do not need motivating. Their enthusiastic energies will carry them through the most demanding of endeavors. Also do not seek to impress them, since Leos are usually only fully impressed by their own efforts and successes. Both motivating and impressing a Leo contradict the basic Leo rule of being dominant and on top at all times. Should you find Leo employees admiring what you do, you may take this as an unusually

(The Leo Employee)

STRENGTHS
Ambitious
Faithful
Committed

WEAKNESSES
Insensitive
Pushy
Inflexible

INTERACTIVE STYLE
Frank
Dynamic
Positive

high compliment. However, from then on they will probably take your Herculean efforts for granted. On the other hand, Leo employees need you to be impressed with them.

Managing, Directing, or Criticizing the Leo Employee

Constantly managing or directing the efforts of Leo employees is not advised. Should you always be in their face with explanations and "helpful" suggestions, they may take this as a grave insult, implying that they were too stupid to understand the first time. Likewise, one word of criticism is usually enough. Lengthy diatribes may cause them to go deaf in both ears, sulk because they feel humiliated, or arouse their anger, which can be formidable. Sending them a short memo rather than confronting them verbally or face-to-face is recommended. Leo employees pride themselves on being able to understand the wishes of their superiors without being reminded.

The Leo Coworker

Although Leos are not overly social, they can serve as an important part of any working organization, particularly as a higher link in the command chain. Usually dissatisfied with remaining too long at low-level positions, they will seek to rise in the organization and may thereby arouse the resentment of their colleagues. Should they be denied advancement, they may further arouse jealousy by departing for another firm that shows more appreciation of their abilities. Thus their ambition will usually hinder them from fitting the stereotype of the faithful employee and close coworker.

Approaching the Leo Coworker for Advice

Leo coworkers can be surprisingly sympathetic and will often do their best to give helpful advice. However, they usually impose a strict limit on their time, since they are wary of being sidetracked from their work. The best way to approach them is to set a lunch date in a relatively private spot away from prying ears. Here you can pour out your heart and, if necessary, schedule a second meeting to more thoroughly discuss their helpful ideas, once they have had time to formulate them.

Approaching the Leo Coworker for Help

When it comes to approaching Leo coworkers for help, they may be wary of getting involved if such help in any way impinges upon their position in the work group; otherwise they will help. However, keep in mind that Leo coworkers will never get involved in actions that could diminish their status or lessen their chances for future advancement. Not usually undermining or misleading, they will rarely sabotage your efforts by offering false advice. They may also quite honestly state at the outset that they are not the ones to approach and might suggest another coworker who could be of greater help.

Traveling with and Entertaining the Leo Coworker

Remember that Leos are very dominant and find it difficult to take a backseat to anyone for very long, particularly a coworker. Recognizing their need to put themselves first will make things a bit easier in terms of traveling with or entertaining them. If you are unable to handle their big personalities from the start, you might avoid getting stuck in such a situation with Leo coworkers. That said, they will always do their share of the work required in making travel plans or setting up a party, but are sure to do things their own way, assuming that you will also enjoy the results.

The Leo Coworker Cooperating with Others

Leo coworkers are not the most cooperative individuals within a work group unless they are specifically ordered by the boss to pursue a well-defined path. Highly competitive, they usually seek to emerge from any group endeavor as the shining star responsible for its success. Should the project fail, they will rarely assume responsibility, but they will claim that their efforts were undermined by the incompetence of others. Reward-oriented, they can be enlisted as team players if recognition or a bonus of some kind is offered as a potential reward. Their prodigious energies, if well directed, often prove valuable to the group.

Impressing and Motivating the Leo Coworker

Attracted to challenge, Leo coworkers can be best motivated by putting their abilities to the test. Stating the difficulties or even the impossibilities of the project beforehand will arouse their fighting spirit. Making clear that no one could be expected to accomplish such a test could, in itself, motivate them to give their all in an effort to accomplish it. Likewise, Leos are most impressed by outstanding feats on the part of others and similarly challenged to equal or surpass such efforts in the future. Comparing them negatively with a coworker will usually spur them on even further.

Persuading and/or Criticizing the Leo Coworker

Leo coworkers can be most effectively criticized or persuaded if you are able to offer them something they like in return. They are particularly vulnerable to offers of a raise or a higher position in the firm—or even a hint that such an advancement might come their way. Therefore they can be easily convinced to accept criticism or follow a given course of action that would accomplish such an end. Making such changes could prove quite difficult for them, but using a carrot-on-the-stick approach, holding out the promise of advanced status or prestige, will usually motivate them to give it their best shot.

The Leo Client

Leo clients usually know exactly what they want, so you had better be in the mood to listen and, if possible, follow their lead. Direct, they will usually ask you outright whether you can guarantee the results they seek and, if so, how they can be sure you can deliver the goods. Leo clients are very results-oriented and often do not care so much how you achieve results as long as your methods do not backfire on them. Unlikely to take a chance unless desperate, they have probably already done some research on you or they would not be approaching you at all.

Confident
Insistent
Results-oriented

Amoral
Selfish
Self-impressed

Compelling
Opportunistic
Confident

Impressing the Leo Client

Leos are impressed by how well you listen to them and by your ability to think quickly on your feet. If you can improvise a practical method to implement their demands and meet their needs, they are likely to give you the green light to go ahead. Moreover, if they believe strongly enough in your abilities, they will make a large budget available to you to fully implement your plans. Leos often make their decisions on the spot, so if they say they need time to think about things, you may have failed to sell them on your service, product, or abilities.

Selling to the Leo Client

Leo clients admire good salesmanship, often thinking that if you can sell them, you also will be able to sell consumers, too. Likely to play devil's advocate, they will set up objections just to see how you handle them, which often produces new, valuable ideas and approaches. They will have no qualms about using your suggestions themselves and even taking credit for them in the future, whether or not they decide to do business with you. Leo clients often expect you to be equally opportunistic in directing the energies and ideas of others toward a positive conclusion when you are representing them.

Your Appearance and the Leo Client

It's best not to outshine Leo clients, so keep your appearance subdued. They will silently acknowledge your compliments about their clothes or accessories or quick glances of admiration and deferential attitude. Should they get aggressive, it is best to fall silent, change the subject, or back off rather than ratcheting up the confrontation level. However, should they keep at it, even to the point of becoming insulting or abusive, you should very sharply draw the line and caution them to proceed no further.

Keeping the Leo Client's Interest

Often Leo clients can be fascinated by your verbal abilities and timing. A few well-chosen words are preferred over lengthy statements. Injecting a bit of irony, humor, or sarcasm, accompanied by an occasional cryptic comment that just begs to be questioned, will also serve to keep their interest. Should they go so far as to ask for an explanation of one of these statements, you will know that you have hooked them. Repeating such tactics will not diminish their efficacy. Like a good performer with an audience, leave Leo clients begging for more.

Breaking Bad News to the Leo Client

Give Leo clients the good news first, no matter how diminutive it may be. Take the bad news apart and present it point by point, rather than coming out with one negative statement at the outset. Give each point a positive spin, but do not try to cover up facts or tell outright lies. Going deeply into details may serve to awaken these clients' new creative ideas concerning damage control. If they trust you and believe in your methods, they may give you yet another opportunity to rectify what did not work the first time.

Entertaining the Leo Client

Leo clients love to be spoiled, so present them with companionship, meals, or outright gifts with a grand flourish. They respond to being fussed over, but be prepared to back off at their first sign of irritation. At all performances or screenings, front row seats, or any other location where they can be seen and admired, are preferred. Giving them your complete attention is required. This includes laughing at their jokes (and perhaps adding a comment on one to show you understood it), making a lot of steady eye contact, and anticipating their moves with polite gestures. Sharing insulting comments about others often makes for enjoyable repartee.

The Leo Business Partner

Leos can be among the most trustworthy and reliable of partners. However, they are likely to go off in their own direction periodically, thinking they are acting for both of you but in fact being oblivious to your wishes. They may even return from such forays and proudly present you with their results, certain that you will be pleased. Such moments can put partnerships with Leos at grave risk. When not sidetracked by such "attacks," they are capable of performing their daily tasks competently and with vigor. Because Leo partners sometimes have difficulty listening, make sure that they understand what you mean to convey—either by putting it in writing or asking them to summarize.

Setting Up the Business Partnership with Leo

Leos often need to be convinced of the advantage of such an alliance. Confident of their abilities to act independently, they are not quick to see why a partnership is necessary. Once they make their commitment, however, you will find them cooperative, although demanding, in creating the structure of the organization. Tight legal restrictions and conditions are recommended because of Leo partners' penchant for independent action. The first year or two of the partnership will be the hardest, for, like a spirited horse, Leos must get accustomed to pulling the company carriage in the right direction.

Tasking with the Leo Business Partner

In partnerships, allow Leo partners as much leeway as possible in picking their own tasks. Allow them to operate independently as much as possible. Hopefully, they will return the favor and grant you the same freedom, but Leos can also be very commanding and controlling. Thus a double-standard situation may be set up—beneficial to them, detrimental to you. The most difficult part of tasking is having daily or weekly meetings, since Leos are not comfortable having to explain or justify their actions on a regular basis.

Traveling with and Entertaining the Leo Business Partner

Leo partners can be great fun to travel with. Their enthusiasm, humor, and good feelings in general give a positive thrust to many business endeavors. However, they do not handle negativity well, and if things are going badly they are likely to get upset and depressed. Rousing them from such a state is difficult or impossible. Therefore, during good times

STRENGTHS

Trustworthy
Reliable
Loyal

WEAKNESSES

Flighty
Distracted
Unheeding

INTERACTIVE STYLE

Individualistic
Cooperative
Vigorous

they are best left alone and appreciated and when the going gets rough simply left alone if possible. Leos do not need entertaining, in general. You will have to be understanding when they need to go off on their own and do their own thing.

Managing and Directing the Leo Business Partner

For the most part, managing and directing Leo partners is next to impossible. They may give the impression of having agreed with your proposals relative to their work but then go off on the opposite track. Later, if confronted with their actions, they will indicate they did not understand you well or found it necessary to change direction for the good of the company. Therefore, restrict your management of Leos to agreements on division of labor and pursuing broad areas such as sales, public relations, marketing, etc., while accepting that they will employ their own methods in discharging their duties.

Relating to the Leo Business Partner in the Long Run

If you can accept their need for independence, your partnership with Leos can last for years. But if constant friction is present from the start, you will be lucky to survive one or, at most, two years as their partner. If things go well and the company prospers, the only problem you may run into is their irritating habit of taking credit for successes and of ignoring your contributions, even your presence, when dealing with clients and employees alike. You may be unwillingly cast as the silent partner, or the "other one," and may, in fact, be forced to accept such a role to avoid conflict.

Parting Ways with the Leo Business Partner

Breaking up with Leo partners can be a great relief, particularly if their overbearing nature and refusal to be managed have created difficulties of high magnitude over the years. Be prepared for them to show little or no concern for your future welfare. However, splitting up profits and the established infrastructure of the company may be surprisingly easy because of their haste to get on with their next job, which is quite likely already set up. Thus, their seemingly giving attitudes cannot be ascribed to their generosity or need for fairness but to their impatience to move forward.

The Leo Competitor

Leo competitors are formidable opponents. Familiar with winning, these fighters are accustomed to getting the results they want. Their will to succeed is matched only by their grit and stamina to hang in there, wearing down their opponents no matter what it takes. Thus you can be proud if you are able to stave off their insistent attacks and hold your own against them. In order to triumph you will have to be highly inventive and equally persistent in your efforts. Leo competitors can desire financial gain, of course, but their primary motivation is coming out victorious in the struggle. They value their pride and fighting spirit more than anything else.

Countering the Leo Competitor

One way to approach this situation is to set yourself up as an immovable object to oppose Leos' irresistible force. Such direct confrontations can wear you down, however, and Leos' persistence can erode your defenses over time. Often, it is best to seek more subtle means to counter their persistent attacks. Study their approach, learn their methods (which tend to be repetitive), and try various countering techniques until you find the ones that work to slow them down. Once they are moving slowly enough for you to hit them at last, put everything you have into one final blow—hopefully the winning coup de grace.

Out-Planning the Leo Competitor

Leo competitors can be successfully manipulated into swinging wildly and dropping their guard when annoyed and irritated. Finding their weak spots can often be accomplished by repeatedly pushing their buttons. While they are engaged in swatting away your mosquito-like buzzings, you can be engaged in outflanking them, hopefully unnoticed. Best to keep such forays low-key, since their abilities to counter your attacks are no doubt prodigious. Infiltration of their organization is always a possibility if you can find one of their employees who is susceptible to your advances. Getting advance warnings of their plans through espionage can result in success.

Impressing the Leo Competitor in Person

It is often best not to impress Leo competitors at all, but instead lead them to think you are a less than sterling opponent—a pushover. By playing the role of the idiot or jerk, and convincing them of your ineptitude, you may fool them into thinking that you are not worthy of their best efforts, and they may grow overconfident. In the heat of battle, withdrawing astutely from engagements not worth your while could convey your cowardice, further encouraging them to underestimate your powers in the future. In-person confrontations are best kept low-key on your end.

Undercutting and Outbidding the Leo Competitor

Instead of trying to outbid Leos for valuable properties, it is often best to confuse Leo competitors by showing great interest in those that seem to have little or no value at all. While they are laughing at your stupidity in such choices, you could work your magic to bring a whole new product into being, confusing them even further. Since Leos hate to admit they made a mistake by underestimating you, they will not often make the same error twice. Therefore, the most successful gestures in undercutting them may be the first ones, so give those your best shot.

Public Relations Wars with the Leo Competitor

Leos tend to overindulge in grand public-relations gestures. Rather than opposing them directly with large-scale campaigns of your own, it is best to wear them down by encouraging even further overspending that will deplete their coffers. This can best be accomplished by clever public-relations jabs and insinuations of your own that undermine their product or service and their approach to promote it. Raising doubts about its true effi-

(The Leo Competitor)

STRENGTHS
Self-possessed
Persistent
Gritty

WEAKNESSES
Overconfident
Self-unaware
Repetitive

INTERACTIVE STYLE
Combative
Challenging
Confrontational

cacy may sting them and arouse a flood of denial, putting them clearly on the defensive, an area in which they are not so strong. Keep baiting them unceasingly for best results.

The Leo Competitor and the Personal Approach

Leos are very vulnerable to flattery. By buttering them up and watching them swell with pride, you can often succeed in breaching their defenses. They may find themselves liking you, even contemplating luring you away from your company or group to work for them or perhaps become their partner. Outright seductive approaches can work well with Leos since such overtures tend to rouse their large egos. Once you have them hooked on your brains, looks, or abilities, Leo competitors can be manipulated with surprising ease. Do not put yourself in their clutches intentionally, however, since their fury in discovering your duplicity will be unforgiving and annihilating.

Love

The Leo First Date

Should you ignite Leo's fire on the first date, the only problem you may face afterward is trying to put it out. Traditionally standoffish, on a first date Leos will usually adopt a pragmatic attitude: Let's see what you are made of. Therefore, a Leo first date is turned into a kind of tryout in which you are measured and judged. If acceptable, further developments are possible; if you fail the test, you are out. Remember, it is generally the Leo who does the rejecting, not you. Should you break this rule, beware of the consequences sure to be showered on you by the spurned Leo first date.

Wooing and Picking Up the Leo First Date

If you are interested in succeeding with Leo first dates, you had better look your very best, both when picking them up and when wooing them. Also be careful of what you say and how you say it. Idle chatter is not likely to get you anywhere, although Leo first dates may employ it as a tactic to feel you out in a neutral fashion. Although Leos are always open to compliments, they will also be suspicious of your attempts to impress them, and they will back off if they think you do not mean what you say. They know all the tricks of flattery and seduction well and are astute enough to recognize them.

Suggested Activities for the Leo First Date

Leo first dates like to go out and have a good time. A quiet evening at home is not their speed for an initial encounter. For a first date, Leos like to be free to move and make choices and usually will refuse to be trapped into being alone with you. Going to a party is ideal, since they will also have a chance to be the center of attention. Curb any expression of jealousy, since it will immediately throw a damper on their mood and make them feel uptight and restricted. When they are giving their performance, just be content to become another appreciative member of their audience.

Turn-Ons and Turn-Offs for the Leo First Date

Most Leos will want you to look good on your first date. They must be proud of the person they are with, never ashamed. Your clothes, hairstyle, shoes, and skin should not appear shabby or run-down. If they give you a compliment on any of the aforemen-

STRENGTHS

Discriminating

Noncommittal

Astute

WEAKNESSES

Judgmental

Rejecting

Standoffish

INTERACTIVE STYLE

Watchful

Patient

Observant

tioned, you can be sure you have passed the first hurdle to their heart. They are also turned on by your verbal abilities, particularly if you can impress a hostess, waiter, or mutual friend. If you get on the wrong footing with a third person, do not expect your Leo first date to bail you out.

Making "the Move" with the Leo First Date

Leo first dates will send you enough signals to inform you of their wishes. Their green light will flash through a tone of voice, a special glance, or a gesture signaling their readiness for you to advance. Generally speaking, it is best not to attempt to go too far with them without such an invitation, but to remain observant. Because rejection is not a word in the dictionary of most Leos, they will distance themselves quite quickly if they feel you are losing interest. Should they mention seeing you again, you will be expected to make the move either at that moment or on the next date.

Impressing the Leo First Date

Leo first dates will be impressed by a warm, sunny, open disposition in most cases. These individuals are not into pain and suffering, no matter how interesting and intriguing others may find it on a first date. Basically, they want to have a good time, and if you can have it with them, so much the better. Never dampen their abundant enthusiasm, as you would surely be met by a stony silence should you do so. Leo first dates do not care for excuses, apologies, or backing down from a confrontation. They expect you to be there one hundred percent and to give your all in mutual activities.

Brushing Off the Leo First Date

After a first date that you both enjoy, Leos will usually have the patience to wait a couple of weeks until you contact them again. However, if you fail to call them within this timeframe they have two choices: Accept your silence as a brush-off or take the initiative themselves. Once they have accepted that you have brushed them off, their pride will rarely allow them to continue further. Should they decide to contact you, a hint of disinterest or a lame excuse on your part will usually serve to get rid of them for good.

The Leo Romantic Partner

Leos are involved, committed, enthusiastic, and, in general, supportive of your relationship with them, to a point. They can be counted on not only on weekends but occasionally during the week as well, as long as you do not interfere with their ambitious career plans. Avoid situations in which they must choose between devoting time to you or to their job, since if they choose you it may be because they feel pressured to do so. Remember that although Leos may hate to lose you, they are always confident in their abilities to find a replacement.

Having a Discussion with the Leo Romantic Partner

Leo romantic partners do not mind having discussions on topics they approve of at the time and in the place of their choice. Not overly chatty, Leos prefer devoting the full force of their energies to having fun and expressing their romantic feelings. Because they are usually in constant and rapid motion, it is difficult to pin them down long enough to discuss that important matter that has been on your mind for a while. Tending to be evasive, they will strongly avoid subjects they do not wish to discuss through a variety of means, from changing the subject to outright refusal to speak.

Arguments with the Leo Romantic Partner

If provoked enough, Leos will argue, but they prefer not to. Should you insist on arguing, you will probably get more than you bargained for from these fiery individuals. Surprisingly good with few words, Leos know how to hurt their opponents and may lash out if severely threatened. For them, such a battle is one with no holds barred. Normally, they consider picking fights beneath them, an indication of their feelings of superiority in most situations. Should you force them to decide between having a discussion or having a battle with you, be prepared for them to pick the latter to avoid having the former.

Traveling with the Leo Romantic Partner

Leos will only truly enjoy traveling with you if they can be proud of you, not only your appearance, but also your kindness, attention to them, and generosity. Nothing is more embarrassing to them than having you repeatedly count your pennies and back down from making substantial outlays of cash. Any hint of cheapness turns them off, particularly when traveling on vacation. They feel that they are giving a lot and that you should do so also. Do not show up for a trip looking shabby or disheveled, since they will look on your appearance as a direct reflection of theirs.

Sex with the Leo Romantic Partner

This is one area that can be highly gratifying, if you are up to it. Leos tend to be sexually oriented, so they will generally expect frequent sex of a high quality, which takes into account their special needs and wants. There will be little doubt left in your mind that you are pleasing them since they will actively spur on the proceedings both physically and verbally. Not at all shy when it comes to such matters, Leos want what they want when they want it.

Affection and the Leo Romantic Partner

Leos are generally passionate rather than sensuous types, preferring outright sexual expressions to affectionate ones. They like to maintain a cool persona in public, so they will avoid hugs, snuggles, fond looks, and other overtly affectionate gestures. This may also carry over into times when you are alone with them. To Leos, being overly affectionate is not only unnecessary, but it can actually irritate them and turn them off entirely. You will have to educate them about your own special needs in this department if they are not forthcoming. Be prepared to encounter some resistance.

(The Leo Romantic Partner)

STRENGTHS
Confident
Enthusiastic
Supportive

WEAKNESSES
Career-oriented
Ambitious
Egotistical

INTERACTIVE STYLE
Proud
Demanding
Pushy

Humor and the Leo Romantic Partner

Although Leo romantic partners like to have fun, they are not usually endowed with a particularly good sense of humor. Frequently, they do not understand jokes, which must be explained to them. Too often they take certain subjects so seriously that any attempt to make light of them is met with stony silence or even fury. Making fun of them is, of course, completely off limits, since most proud Leos have difficulty in laughing at themselves. This really can get in the way of their appreciation of witty repartee because they are apt to take things personally.

The Leo Spouse

Leo spouses tend to be loyal and will remain so for years. Loyal, however, does not necessarily mean faithful, and at the first sign of disinterest on the part of their mates, the days of their faithfulness may be numbered. Leos need to be treated regally, royally, put up on a pedestal and worshipped like the king or queen that they are. Supreme actors, Leos can continue in such a marriage for the sake of their children, their social status, or their career, but their hearts and thoughts may be elsewhere. Treat Leo spouses well—very well—and your efforts will be rewarded and your gifts returned many times over.

Wedding and Honeymoon with the Leo Spouse

Leo spouses treat the honeymoon as a once-in-a-lifetime experience and expect you to pull out all the stops. Anything short of your total attention, participation, financial commitment, and complete devotion to them, and only them, is unacceptable. Do not play games in trying to arouse their jealousy through flirting, or you will find the lion in your face, which is not a pleasant sight. Leos like things to go smoothly without blunders or disappointments from your direction. The wedding should flow seamlessly into the honeymoon and then further into setting up house.

Home and Day-to-Day Married Life with the Leo Spouse

Leos like to have a free hand in choosing where the two of you will live, not only the city and neighborhood, but also the dwelling itself. Having a house usually appeals to Leos, but they will often settle for an apartment until the kids and some extra cash come along. However, both of the latter had better materialize within a couple of years to keep them happy. If you wonder where you fit into all of this, you should feel honored that you will share in the joys of all the Leo requirements by being chosen as the instrument of their satisfaction.

Finances and the Leo Spouse

Leos love to spend money, pure and simple. Whether it is yours or theirs is not important to them, although they do love you to spoil them. If you keep common bank accounts, be prepared for them to dive into these repositories at will and often on a whim. Impulsive individuals, Leos who are smitten with desire for an object or activity will grab whatever cash is at hand. This fact may prompt you to keep a separate account in your name only to pay the bills and give you a bit of money of your own.

Infidelity and the Leo Spouse

Although they can be sorely tempted by a new face, Leos will generally remain faithful as long as they are happy. They must be forgiven the occasional indiscretion, which they certainly will not announce, but if discovered will probably just laugh off. If you are able to overlook their occasional sexual hijinks with others, so much the better. Should you make a big deal of these pranks or threaten to leave them (or indulge in such freedom yourself), be prepared for Leos' full furies. Leos demand understanding—which is synonymous with turning a blind eye or, in extreme cases, forgiving them completely.

Children and the Leo Spouse

Most Leos do not consider a home complete without children. Those who do decide they do not want kids will often have a couple of nieces or nephews, or even pets, on which to lavish their affections. Should you decide to have kids in the house, Leos prefer their own, but if that is not possible or desirable they will make devoted parents to adopted children or stepchildren as well. They will not tolerate defiance to their discipline or rules, and they will expect your solidarity in dealing with such matters. Generally, they prefer to spoil or punish the kids themselves, without your interference.

Divorce and the Leo Spouse

Because Leos generally refuse to be rejected, they may react to your hints about unhappiness, lack of communication, or the relationship just not working by taking the lead in the act of divorce. Rather than waiting for the hammer to come down, they are more likely to wind up wielding it themselves. Thus, if you want to hold onto a Leo spouse, make sure that you appear happy and content. Of course this does not guarantee that your spouse feel the same way, but normally Leos can be satisfied by having their demands met (which they will make abundantly clear).

The Leo Lover

Masters at the art of deception, Leo lovers are likely to studiously keep your love relationship with them from the prying eyes of third parties, whoever they may be. Moreover, they will be very critical of your spreading the word about them, to the point of breaking things off with you over such indiscretions. Passionate in romantic matters, Leos give all they have in matters of love with a theatrical flourish, wanting to impress you with the depth of their commitment. An unforgettable affair with a Leo lover is likely to haunt you for a lifetime.

(The Leo Spouse)

STRENGTHS

Loyal

Attentive

Hard-working

WEAKNESSES

Demanding

Self-centered

Unfaithful

INTERACTIVE STYLE

Direct

Committed

Generous

STRENGTHS
Extroverted
Demonstrative
Giving

WEAKNESSES
Deceptive
Critical
Unforgiving

INTERACTIVE STYLE
Passionate
Private
Discreet

Meeting the Leo Lover

Leo lovers are risk takers—the excitement or danger of a hidden love affair draws them like a magnet. Yet they will take care in setting up meetings with you to avoid disruptions in their existing relationships and hurt to all concerned. Their attitude is generally that what they do is their business and nobody else's. They have their own private values, which often do not correspond with society's and therefore can be branded by others as immoral. They will usually opt for meeting places of a more private nature and avoid being seen with you in public whenever possible.

Location and the Leo Lover

Generally, Leos will prefer to meet at your place or at a neutral location that lacks powerful associations for them. Although taking their time is important to them, they will also occasionally settle for a quick meeting, finding this better than none at all. Although action-oriented, Leos find it extremely important to feel comfortable enough in this location to hold discussions with you, not only about personal matters but also other topics that interest them. They should not be pushed or pressured to get down to physical realities, for they follow their own natural rhythms.

Sex and the Leo Lover

Although sexually enthusiastic, romance is equally important to Leo lovers. On any given occasion, although sex is not a requirement, expressing romantic feelings definitely is. Leo's attitude is that sex is a very natural thing and will be indulged when both partners are in the mood. They may be bewildered by any resentment or anger you feel about being neglected sexually. They are quite capable of giving you what you want without really feeling a whole lot themselves. They do not look on this as faking it, but rather just dealing with realities as best they can and avoiding trouble.

Holding On to the Leo Lover

The Leo lover usually has few strict requirements when it comes to matters of love, being quite agreeable most of the time. Love affairs with Leos can go on for years, with them constantly adjusting to new situations and changes in other relationships that take place. Usually self-assured sexually, Leos have little need to impress, but at the same time they are acutely aware of whether or not you are enjoying yourself. Thus one of the best ways to hold on to Leo lovers is to leave no doubt in your mind that you want and need them and appreciate them fully.

Entertaining the Leo Lover

As long as Leo lovers find the surroundings comfortable and free from any sleazy associations, they will require little entertaining aside from your presence. They will expect you, however, to be at your best, showing a sparkling personality and pleasant demeanor. Although Leos often fall for depressive and highly complex types, they are generally made unhappy by such relationships and will eventually break them off through sheer force of will. Gifts and sharing fun activities are appreciated and enjoyed, but just laughter and smiles can be all the entertainment that is needed to keep Leo lovers happy.

Breaking Up with the Leo Lover

Leo lovers want to know when the relationship is over and prefer that such a decision be made by mutual agreement. Their pride does not allow them to be overtly dumped, so they will usually come up with a rationalization after the fact that will leave them at peace with themselves. They much prefer to avoid unpleasantness in breakups, but if pushed hard enough by their exes, they can certainly give as good as they get. The attitude of most Leos toward breakups is surprisingly peaceful and nonvindictive—considering their fiery temperaments—and they are quite agreeable to wishing you well if you feel the same way about them.

The Leo Ex

If Leo exes feel well-treated by you, they are likely to be generous and affable. If not, they can show a remarkable amount of coldness and unconcern with respect to your position. In such a situation, although compassion is lacking, Leos will rarely become aggressive or turn vindictive unless they have been severely roughed up. It is usually best to calm a nervous Leo with objective assurances of your positive intent first and then to behave politely on a personal level, avoiding sarcasm or insults. Often the Leo ex will want to move on quickly to the next partner; you should not let your ex's obvious displays of enthusiasm for this person push your buttons.

Establishing a Friendship with the Leo Ex

Unless you harbor ill will against your Leo ex, there should be few problems establishing a friendship here. Most Leo exes are open to moving on, rarely getting hung up on old issues or holding on to grudges. Most often they will adopt a wait-and-see approach, in which they observe your demeanor and either adjust to or react against it. Should your approach be neutral, Leo exes often take the first step in making an offer of friendship, which could be, after a knock-down drag-out period, quite welcome. Your immediate acceptance of the peace pipe could set a positive tone of goodwill for the future.

Issues of Getting Back Together with the Leo Ex

In order to even consider getting back together again, Leo exes need positive assurances, perhaps even in writing or recorded on video, that you will not make the same mistakes again. Financial promises will have an effect on them, but they would be offended by any attempt on your part to buy their love. Highly idealistic in such matters, Leos usually need to feel a return of the spark of romance rather than just taking the easy way out by accepting an attractive offer. If Leo exes play hard to get, persistence and understanding on your part can wear down their resistance and serve as proof of your serious intentions.

Discussing Past Issues with the Leo Ex

It is best to avoid such discussions with Leo exes, since they are usually eager to avoid getting hung up on old scripts. An occasional reference to the past will be tolerated, but should you decide to dig a bit deeper, you will usually encounter extreme resistance

STRENGTHS

Generous

Affable

Concerned

WEAKNESSES

Cold

Uncompassionate

Provoking

INTERACTIVE STYLE

Attentive

Fair

Polite

LOVE

or provoke a quick rebuff. The best way to approach a matter that you feel should be addressed is to make them smile or laugh about a past situation in which you both felt a bit awkward or lost. This could prove an entrée to a further examination of the matter, as long as it does not become overly serious.

Expressing Affection to the Leo Ex

Leos certainly have a warm and affectionate side that responds to positive treatment. It is best for you to establish some trust, however, before you make any moves in that direction. Generally, long periods of time are necessary to heal Leo's wounds, so for at least the first year it is best not to attempt to get too close to them emotionally. Any hint of a premature expression of affection could result in a setback and make this period of healing even longer. However, your patience will be rewarded eventually if you can hang in there and wait.

Defining the Present Relationship with the Leo Ex

It is best not to set up too many rules and regulations, since most Leos believe that promises were made to be broken. On the other hand, Leos will usually try hard to keep up their end of a deal and can be counted on to fulfill their obligations once they have seriously agreed to do so. Beware of any idle chatter or expressions of intent, since Leo generosity can be more an expression of momentary hopefulness than a reliable guarantee. The glow of Leo's good feelings can evaporate practically overnight and be replaced by something less palatable.

Sharing Custody with the Leo Ex

Leos are very possessive of and protective toward their children. Most often they will strive to win sole custody and agree to your seeing the kids only on weekends or even less frequently. Should you succeed in getting the children to live with you, Leo exes will battle to see them as much as possible and never give up their eventual goal of sharing custody equally, or even reversing the court's decision. In this one area, getting Leos to agree to strict rules and regulations may be necessary to keep their impulsive and insistent energies under control.

Friends and Family

LEO
July 23–August 23

The Leo Friend

Leos are legendary for making excellent friends. Their loyalty, devotion, and support can be outstanding, and they are known for standing by their closest friends in both good times and bad. Their need to be needed is not overly great, so they will also quite happily leave you alone for long periods, if you prefer it that way, without the friendship suffering. On the other hand, they enjoy a daily check-in or interaction with their best friends and love to share the latest news and gossip. They prefer actual meetings to virtual ones, but since your schedules may be busy, the odd text message or phone call will suffice until you can see each other again.

Asking for Help from the Leo Friend

"Hey, that's what friends are for" is a typical Leo friend's reply to your thanks, stated or implied. Since lines of communication are open with Leo friends, you usually have only to ask in order to receive their help. Dynamic Leos are often very busy, so it is good to give them as much advance notice as possible. Furthermore, you should be careful not to take advantage of their good nature, for several reasons. First of all, you can become too dependent on them. Second, you keep yourself from developing as a capable and independent-thinking person. In this respect, a Leo friend that is too good to you can prove to be undermining to your own capabilities.

Communication and Keeping in Touch with the Leo Friend

Leos prefer not having communication unless it is really desired by both parties. Thus, they don't feel obliged to keep in touch. They are understanding when it comes to your need to be alone at times and expect you to be the same way. They will expect, however, that you do inform them about important matters or ones in which they have already invested time or advice. Also, they can get upset about mixed messages, hearing the truth from a third party, or being left out of the loop altogether. True straight shooters, they want to hear it directly from you without distortion or elaboration.

STRENGTHS
Loyal
Devoted
Supportive

WEAKNESSES
Distracted
Forgetful
Poorly judging

INTERACTIVE STYLE
Available
Open
Breezy

Borrowing Money from the Leo Friend

Naturally generous, Leos will help out as often and as much as they can. However, they will expect to be paid back, and nonpayment on your part can signal the beginning of the end of a beautiful friendship. If the loan is a small amount, problems usually do not arise, though this should never degenerate into daily handouts. In the case of large sums, it would be best for you to sign an IOU or formal agreement, certainly in the case of investments. Leos friends provide not only their cash but also their abundant energies in times of need.

Asking for Advice from the Leo Friend

Being consulted for advice in important matters is highly gratifying to most Leos. However, the difficulty you may encounter here is that Leos' advice is not always the best, for their judgment can, at times, be clouded by what they wish to be true rather than what is true. Furthermore, although they are trying to be helpful, the results may not reflect their good intentions. Following such a scenario, Leo friends can feel slighted if you ignore their advice in the future or pull back from it on any given occasion. For this reason, you should be careful when asking for Leo's advice, unless you are fully prepared to follow it.

Visiting the Leo Friend

Often Leos will prefer to visit you at your place or meet at a café for a cup of coffee. This can reflect their need to get out of the house or to take a break after work, or their unwillingness to expose you to their domestic negligence. Don't be surprised if they are late; Leos are seldom exactly on time. Try to relax while you are waiting, since they may very well be a bit hassled by the time they get there and can use your calm as a comforting emotional cushion. Meeting a Leo friend several times a week is quite possible and can be mutually rewarding.

Celebrations/Entertainment with the Leo Friend

Leos generally enjoy parties of all types. However, they usually prefer celebrations with friends and meeting new people to traditional, boring family affairs. Asking for their help in organizing the party is not always the best idea, though, since even with all their best intentions, they may not come through with generous offers to assist in setting things up. Often preoccupied, Leos may even remember only at the last minute that they had promised to attend and as a result may make a grand entrance right in the middle of things. If you really are counting on their help, it is often best to pick them up on the way and bring them with you.

The Leo Roommate

Leo dominance can often raise problems. No matter where Leos live—dorm, shared apartment, or house—they see themselves as the king or queen of "their" space. As long as you understand this need for them to believe in their royal position, there will be few problems. In fact, they will roll up their sleeves and dig into whatever projects need getting done, from a stack of dirty dishes to a pile of laundry. Do not challenge their authority or engage in useless competition unless you just want to make trouble. Leos do not do well when beset by worries, so try to protect them from negativity whenever possible and let their sunny side shine through.

Sharing Financial Responsibilities with the Leo Roommate

The question is not if Leo roommates will pay, but when. Unfortunately, their rent and utility money may have already been spent by the time you need to collect it. (You should do the collecting, by the way, for Leo may have already ignored or forgotten about it.) It's best to hit them up for it as soon as their paycheck arrives, if possible. Bringing up the subject of unpaid bills is always difficult with Leos, who either promise to pay tomorrow or beat a hasty retreat when such distasteful subjects arise. Figure out a clever way to get them to pay on time and train them to make regular contributions to shopping and other household expenses.

Cleaning and the Leo Roommate

Cleaning is not usually high on Leo's priority list. Your Leo roommate is capable of creating monumental messes, not out of inconsideration, but usually just unawareness. Thus, Leos could be living in something that, objectively viewed, could resemble a war zone, and they wouldn't even know it. The problem is that they just get used to sleeping in an unmade bed or tripping over their towels. That said, they are usually careful enough to step around objects arranged on the floor rather than on them, creating navigable avenues of transit. However, getting them to pick things up may have to be left to the occasional empty Saturday afternoon during which you can finally get through to them on the subject.

Houseguests and the Leo Roommate

Leo roommates are often eager to show "their" home to their colleagues, family, or friends. It is probably best if you are absent during such guided tours since your presence would be entirely extraneous anyway. Should you need to be there, it would be best to shut yourself up in your room, removing yourself from the guided tour altogether. Just ignore hearing "my" this and "my" that as much as possible. Leos simply need to impress. Conversely, Leos will be extremely uncomfortable among a convention of your friends, probably exiting while mentioning an important engagement.

Parties and the Leo Roommate

It is necessary to create the guest list so that equal representation is achieved for each of the roommates. Thus, if there are only two of you, then half the invites should go to your guests and half to the Leo's. Even if this results in one group massing in one area and the other flocking to another, it is better than seeing the emergence of antagonisms,

STRENGTHS

Sunny
Helpful
Optimistic

WEAKNESSES

Worry-prone
Bossy
Argumentative

INTERACTIVE STYLE

Dominant
Regal
Overpowering

favoritism, and conflicts (however polite). Sometimes it is better to let Leo roommates take over the whole party with their friends and you do the same at another time with yours, avoiding the problem of mixing altogether.

Privacy and the Leo Roommate

Leo roommates do not mind your being around as long as you behave yourself. On the other hand, restricting yourself to your room may often work out even better. Unfortunately, Leo's idea of privacy really is synonymous with dominating the space and making it their "private" domain. At certain times you may begin to wonder why you are even paying an equal share since the Leo roommate seems to be getting the most benefits. But hey, you are lucky to be living with such a terrific person now, aren't you?

Discussing Problems with the Leo Roommate

Most Leos cannot handle what they consider negativity from others, and unfortunately raising problems is often regarded as making trouble. This can make it extremely difficult to talk about something that has gone dreadfully wrong. The Leo capacity to ignore such troublesome issues seems, at times, unlimited. Try to lead up to such matters gradually or discuss just one small point at a time, seeking to cover the entire issue over a course of weeks, if not months. Your greatest successes in this area will come over the long haul, so try to avoid losing patience and dumping your frustrations in one go, thereby provoking a monumental and often ongoing dispute.

The Leo Parent

Just like lions of a pride with their cubs, Leo parents are fiercely protective of their offspring. Because Leos always think they know better, their children can be suffocated by their overwhelming presence in daily life. Although Leo parents seldom leave anything to chance, they may not always be available, since their careers and extracurricular activities are so important to them. This means that modern Leo parents will leave their children in the care of preschools and schools, or babysitters, or even bring a grandparent or other family member into the house to help look after them. In such situations, Leo parents can effectively oversee the welfare of their children without spending a lot of time personally caring for them.

Discipline Style of the Leo Parent

Too often Leo parents let their children run wild, due to either their absence or their belief that kids should be free to express themselves. Of course they have ironclad rules that must not be transgressed, usually concerning matters of safety—from making sure doors and windows are locked to looking both ways before crossing the street. Such rules are often stated as instructions to those they hire to tend to their kids, but they are often drilled into children's minds by Leo parents. When it comes to punishment, warmhearted Leos may appear severe but in fact are totally forgiving. Rarely physical in their discipline, Leos convey their displeasure with a sharp look or brief warning.

Affection Level and the Leo Parent

Most Leo parents are highly affectionate with their children. Kisses, hugs, and a gentle tone of voice are usually the rule. Rarely will Leos use withdrawal of affection as a weapon, primarily because of their own strong needs to express it. Fond of engaging in leisure-time activities with their kids, Leos will enjoy visiting amusement parks, camping, swimming, and exploring the many challenges offered by natural surroundings. Leos love to bask in the affections of their little ones, and, as a result, their kids are frequently seen fiercely clutching their hand or even climbing all over them. To children of a Leo parent, their mom or dad truly belongs to them.

Money Issues and the Leo Parent

Few parents are as generous as Leos with their children. This may be observed not only in their giving attitudes toward higher education and weddings, but also in the outright pursuit of pleasure. In a way, this attitude is not as altruistic as it seems, for the enjoyment they receive from their generosity is extreme and well worth the expense for them. Furthermore, the perks they receive from neighbors, friends, and family are highly gratifying. It is important to Leos that their generosity be acknowledged and not overlooked.

Crises and the Leo Parent

Crises usually arise in the absence of Leo parents since they are away so much of the time. Notified of an emergency, Leo parents will drop everything and rush to the aid of their stricken child. However, if the problem is not severe, they usually have the presence of mind to wait until the appropriate time to speak to either the caregiver (teacher, babysitter, family member) or the child, and sometimes to both in the presence of the other, when necessary. Leo parents know intuitively that staying relaxed is important and that overreacting can exaggerate the problem.

Holidays/Family Gatherings and the Leo Parent

Leo parents can be counted on occasionally to help out with planning family gatherings, but not too often. This is not just because of their busy schedules, but also because of their dislike of playing a small part in group activities beyond their control. The Leo philosophy is usually to do something one hundred percent as the boss or not do it at all. They will, however, devote themselves to the planning and execution of holiday activities and fully enjoy them as well. Few parents enjoy holidays with their children and friends more than Leos. Cookouts, scenic trips, and warm destinations featuring sea and sand are among their favorites.

Caring for the Aging Leo Parent

Aging Leo parents will enjoy being taken care of, but will also—even at an advanced age—want to take care of grandchildren or other family members. Somehow they are kept young by such activities. More than others, Leos do not like feeling old and useless; they need to be wanted and needed. In a funny way, then, caring for aging Leo parents can involve letting them do the caring. The principal problem that frequently arises is that aging Leo parents overestimate their capabilities, putting themselves under stress

(The Leo Parent)

STRENGTHS
Protective
Concerned
Responsible

WEAKNESSES
Smothering
Omniscient
Absent

INTERACTIVE STYLE
Challenging
Dominant
Authoritative

and causing health problems, and in some cases even endangering those they are caring for. They will almost always deny these facts and fight any attempts to disengage them from their tasks.

The Leo Sibling

STRENGTHS

Commanding

Rewarded

Respected

WEAKNESSES

Overly demanding

Strident

Selfish

INTERACTIVE STYLE

Combative

Confrontational

Indomitable

Leo siblings will fight to maintain, or to better, their position in the family, often by battling with older brothers and sisters. Not usually content with just preserving what is theirs, Leo siblings tend to assume a leadership role and make their presence felt. They also have strong desires to be recognized by their parents and to have their important contributions to the family both acknowledged and rewarded. Leo siblings also enjoy being unofficial family representatives, thus demanding the respect of other families for their own.

Rivalry/Closeness with the Leo Sibling

Rivalries with Leo siblings can go on for many years. Not ones to back down from a struggle, Leos will stubbornly and insistently oppose their sibling competitors. As they see it, there is only one pie available, and they will make sure they get a big slice of it. In larger families, there are often a couple of siblings who are quieter and not at all interested in drawing attention to themselves or seeking reward. It is precisely with these unassuming siblings that Leos tend to form the closest bonds, often acting as their protectors and defenders.

Past Issues and the Leo Sibling

It is difficult for most Leo siblings to forgive and forget. They are likely to be controlled by old scripts in which they were badly treated in the family dramas. One of their greatest challenges as adults is to free themselves from these thought patterns, not necessarily to forget but certainly to forgive. Often their memories fix on a single incident—usually involving one specific sibling—that sticks in their craw and will not be dislodged. Such an event may become an excuse that Leos invoke whenever a serious failure needs explanation. In this respect, Leo siblings can get stuck in the past, and unless they deal with such issues they may find it difficult to move ahead on their life path.

Dealing with the Estranged Leo Sibling

Estranged Leo siblings can be wooed back into the fold. In most cases, the best method is to acknowledge that they, and only they, can help the family out of a tough situation. Once they believe they are needed and can provide unique help, Leos will often decide to lend a helping hand. In the course of doing so, old conflicts, as well as sympathies, will inevitably emerge, creating internal conflicts in them. This can result in the end of their estrangement, but can also bring new strife and struggle into the family.

Money Issues (Borrowing Money, Wills, Etc.) and the Leo Sibling

Being highly competitive and combative, Leos will demand to get what is theirs when it comes to inheritances. They may even try to take over the proceedings and demand more for their work in representing their siblings. Should you need to borrow money from your Leo siblings, be sure that you can cogently present your reasons for approaching them and your need for doing so. Often generous to a fault, Leo siblings can lend money without many thoughts about it being paid back, particularly if you are a brother or sister with whom they were close growing up. It is recommended that borrowed money be returned as soon as possible, however, to avoid future recriminations.

Holidays/Celebrations/Reunions and the Leo Sibling

Leo siblings are often the moving force behind family get-togethers. Although they are not overly fond of throwing or even attending repetitive and boring birthday parties, they can get excited about special events, particularly surprise parties thrown for an unsuspecting parent or sibling. Furthermore, they love to be surprised themselves and will brighten up considerably when others prepare a secret celebration and manage to catch them unaware. Although Leos love to get presents, the party will be accepted as a big present in and of itself. Good feelings thus engendered can continue to brighten Leo spirits in the weeks and months ahead.

Vacationing with the Leo Sibling

Vacation is a Leo specialty. Great lovers of travel, Leo siblings will look forward to and actively plan such activities joyfully well in advance. They may have trouble controlling their excitement, but they may be wary of appearing to lose their cool and therefore will pretend to treat things matter-of-factly. Drawn like a magnet to white sandy beaches, clear ocean waters, blue skies, and, above all, warm weather, you will usually know from the beginning what their preferences are. Should they be forced to visit a spot or engage in activities they do not fully enjoy, be prepared to have a sulky lion on your hands, as vacationing Leo siblings are not overly self-sacrificing.

The Leo Child

The average Leo child will expect what all the other kids have—and more. Aware of their own special energies, Leo children take the attitude that parents, teachers, and others in authority are lucky to have them. Strong, self-assured, and confident, Leo children aim to be standouts in whatever activities they take part. Although they are not necessarily oriented in an academic direction, their contributions in school can be considerable, not only in sports but also in school politics, where they often display leadership abilities. They are also likely to occupy a prominent position in their social group, where their more flamboyant side can find full expression.

Personality Development and the Leo Child

Even subdued Leo children will reach a point in their development where they burst out with the unmistakable energy and panache of their sign. Such kids will always have a quiet side to retreat to, but once recharged they will again leap into the fray. Frequently, Leo children can be picked out in a crowd of young children as the ones with the most

STRENGTHS

Outgoing

Confident

Popular

WEAKNESSES

Egotistical

Loud

Disliked

INTERACTIVE STYLE

Self-assured

Recognizable

Unmistakable

energy and will to win. Leo children do not do well by themselves and particularly needy social interaction in order to achieve a well-balanced personality. Their need to lead, impress, and interact with others is like a whetstone on which they can sharpen their talents. Keeping them away from other children in overprotected surroundings or relative isolation is exceedingly cruel treatment for Leo children.

Hobbies/Interests/Career Paths for the Leo Child

As super-achievers, Leo children thrive on challenge, particularly of a physical nature but also involving other areas of life as well. Because of their penchant for leadership, they do well in careers and activities where they can function not only as leaders, but also as representatives of the group. Frequently, their upward mobility results in a corresponding upward movement in the groups they lead. However, since they are frequently victims of hubris (overweening pride) they can also be held responsible for group failures. One of their greatest challenges is understanding and recognizing their limitations.

Discipline and the Leo Child

Although Leo children hate discipline more than most, and frequently rebel against its application to themselves and those they love, they will acknowledge the need for structure in their childhood days once they grow up. The wildness of Leo energy just cries out for direction so that it is not dissipated in rebellion and useless or counterproductive activities. Having a parent or teacher who keeps them in check can be essential to the Leo youngster, guiding them in adopting more constructive behavior. Mental training is key here, for Leo children frequently do not think before they act.

Affection Level and the Leo Child

Although Leo children may push away overly affectionate parents and strongly deny their need for such feelings, they secretly crave affection, but only in a form in which they are able to accept it. Moreover, their need to give affection is often expressed in their attitudes toward pets, small friends, or siblings and generally to those who are defenseless. Classic protectors of those in need, Leo children can express affection toward (but also receive it from) creatures weaker than they. Particularly fond of nonphysical forms of affection, they brighten up considerably when given a smile, gentle touch, or eye contact that expresses approval.

Dealing with the Leo Child and Interactions with Siblings

Leo children can often become little parents to one or more of their siblings. It is best if their actual parents do not interfere in such behavior as long as it remains a positive influence, but parents should keep an eye on things. Such childhood experiences often can be a chance for Leo children to hone their parenting skills, eventually resulting in them becoming good parents to their own children once they grow up. In the case of combative relationships with their siblings, Leos' dynamic force may have to be blunted for the sake of mutual preservation. Sooner or later, overly aggressive Leo children will have to learn other means of dealing with their siblings than simply bowling them over.

Interacting with the Adult Leo Child

If Leo children grow up into true Leo adults, interactions will be, at best, predictable and productive. But if the Leo adult is a child who never grew up, the same problems that beset them as children will be projected on their adult contacts. Difficulties in making friends and keeping them are foremost among these, along with a rebellious streak that cannot bear the rules and regulations laid down by bosses and other authority figures. Hopefully, by the time they become adults, Leo children will adopt a less selfish, self-centered, and egotistical persona that recognizes the value of acceptance, empathy, and sharing.

Virgo

BIRTHDATE AUGUST 24–SEPTEMBER 22

Like Gemini, Virgo is a mutable sign ruled by the speedy planet Mercury, but its element is earth. Well grounded when at their best, Virgos are practical thinkers capable of bringing structure to the lives of those around them. However, when beset by their sensitive nervous and digestive systems, Virgos can become their own worst enemy. Virgos are wonderful organizers who are appreciated by any group of which they are a part, but their private lives are their own and they can be very secretive about them.

Work

VIRGO
August 24–September 22

The Virgo Boss

Virgo bosses are highly pragmatic and generally realists. Thus the intent or ideals behind your actions are not nearly as important to them as the results. Facts and figures play a large role in their thinking, so be sure you have these at your fingertips when you are summoned to their offices. Excuses will be accepted only if they can be backed up with logic and acceptable evidence. Do not seek to arouse the Virgo boss's sympathy or under-standing, and keep your interactions as unemotional as possible. Virgo bosses highly value their time, as well as yours, so try not to waste it in idle banter.

Asking the Virgo Boss for a Raise

Bring as much supporting evidence as you can that shows your dedication to your job and the positive results you have booked. Do not be surprised if your Virgo boss already has these at his or her fingertips, since investigation and vetting are Virgo specialties. Furthermore, be able to show that you can act more effectively in a higher-paid posi-tion and be of greater value to the company. No doubt your Virgo boss will ask you a few questions to test your mettle. Be sure to answer succinctly and to the point. Avoid digressing, joking, or abruptly changing the subject.

Breaking Bad News to the Virgo Boss

Although Virgos rarely get emotional, suddenly presenting them with bad news can throw them off balance and immediately arouse their ire. The first question they will ask is usually, "How did that happen?" and the second is, "Who was responsible?" Fixing blame is extremely important to a Virgo boss, and once they are convinced that one person was responsible, they will zero in with laser-like intensity. Criticism from a normally calm Virgo boss can appear to others as a maniacal whiplashing in which charges are levied with dazzling speed. Only if victims can parry each of these blows with equal dexterity do they stand a chance of professional survival.

Arranging Travel and/or Entertainment for the Virgo Boss

In matters of travel, Virgos absolutely insist on having things set up in an orderly fashion. Trying to make excuses for an oversight is rarely acceptable. Since such bloopers only

STRENGTHS

Pragmatic

Realistic

Matter-of-fact

WEAKNESSES

Unresponsive

Unsympathetic

Cold

INTERACTIVE STYLE

Literal

Concise

Economical

arouse a storm of invective anyway, it is best just to say you are sorry and fall back on plan B as seamlessly as possible. Virgo's entertainment needs are generally sparse and easy to meet, that is, once you know a lot about their likes and dislikes. Virgos are extremely picky, so be sure you have made a checklist of their preferences beforehand, and follow it to the letter.

Decision-Making and the Virgo Boss

Virgo bosses are happy for you to make decisions as long as they have a firmly empirical basis. They do not want you to waffle or be vague in expressing or implementing them, preferring you to be either right or wrong rather than trying to cover all your bases. Written—rather than spoken—decisions carry the most weight with Virgos, including the date on which they were made, which employees and materials are to be involved, budgetary facts and figures, and all other relevant details. Although they may take only a quick look at your plan in your presence, you can be sure they will go over it with a magnifying glass in private.

Impressing and/or Motivating the Virgo Boss

Many Virgo bosses are impressed by facts, and facts alone. They love lists, spreadsheets, agendas, and all structural aids that make your facts more cogent and easy to understand. When presenting facts verbally, keep your presentation brief and never sugarcoat. Remember that Virgos like to make up their own minds about things and do not need you to tell them how great your plans are. Impressing them will motivate the Virgo boss to go that extra mile for you.

Making Proposals and/or Giving Presentations to the Virgo Boss

Begin with an introduction that states the intent and scope of your proposal in the form of a short overview. From there, proceed to the most important points, being sure to number them in consecutive order. Following each of these, be prepared to answer pointed questions that will undoubtedly deal with small details. Finally, present a summary of your budgetary, personnel, and time demands for implementation. Virgo bosses tend to be quite stingy in such matters, always preferring frugality and economy to largesse, so expect that they will pare both your needs and available resources to a bare minimum.

The Virgo Employee

Virgo employees take their work seriously and generally turn in good quality at a high professional level. They are dependable and trustworthy, even if a trifle dull. Because Virgos are the most private of people, their work usually serves as an important social outlet. As a result, for Virgos work represents a job for which they get paid as well as an opportunity to interact with their fellow human beings on a daily basis. Frequently, their best friends are numbered among their colleagues. Discussions over lunch, interchanges at the water cooler or coffee machine, and an after-work drink are important social opportunities.

Interviewing and/or Hiring the Virgo Employee

It will usually be easy to determine what prospective Virgo employees can and cannot do, both from their resumes and first interviews. Rarely will Virgos attempt to present themselves as something they are not just to get the job. Realists first and foremost, they know that both employer and employee must have a clear idea of what is in store for them in a potential work situation together. Usually their questions are quite penetrating but also extremely revealing of their priorities. Above all, Virgos want to be assured of an adequate level of security being offered to them in the company.

Breaking Bad News to or Firing the Virgo Employee

Virgos frequently have a hidden inferiority complex that can overwhelm them when confronted with failure in the form of bad news or the threat of being fired. It is not at all uncommon for them to go into a tailspin, even to the point of emotional collapse. Thus the prudent boss or director will be careful when breaking bad news to Virgos in order to avoid any direct blame. Your best course of action is simply to deal with facts and figures that show the impossibility of continuing on the same course. If approached in this way, Virgos are quite capable of correcting their approach and going on to serve the organization well in the future.

Traveling with and Entertaining the Virgo Employee

Although they are picky, Virgo employees have a good sense of what is and is not possible within the company budget. Thrifty by nature, they will rarely spend more than they have to, even when the money is available. Entertainment is not usually high on the priority list of Virgo employees, who will easily settle for some interesting conversation and a relaxed drink. They are strong on organization and planning, and therefore they are quite capable of arranging the whole trip either for just themselves or for groups. Travel is something they look forward to as a reward for their hard in-house work.

Assigning Tasks to the Virgo Employee

If tasks are carefully set out and explained, Virgo employees are fully capable of implementing them. Literalists, they will follow instructions to the letter. As a result, it is best not to leave too much to their imaginations but to spell things out fully, often best expressed in following a series of steps. They will have occasional questions and should feel free to consult their superiors when problems arise. Better at working alone than with groups, they should be given a job that will benefit from a thorough approach and require individual care and attention.

Motivating or Impressing the Virgo Employee

Virgos in general are thought-oriented. All matters concerning intelligence, mental agility, puzzles, and problems that can be unraveled and solved particularly appeal to them. Thus they will be best motivated by projects that have a high degree of logic inherent in them and by bosses who know how to use their brains to the advantage of the company. Virgos cannot bear working with slow and stupid people and will always want to work side by side with intelligent ones. The more difficult the problem that needs to be solved, the more motivated the Virgo employee will be to deal with it.

STRENGTHS
Serious
Professional
Trustworthy

WEAKNESSES
Dull
Needy
Uninteresting

INTERACTIVE STYLE
Responsible
Helpful
Dutiful

Managing, Directing, or Criticizing the Virgo Employee

Virgo employees can accept and benefit from constructive criticism if it is offered in the right spirit. Very critical themselves, Virgos know the value of digging out mistakes in anyone's work and demonstrating how they may be corrected. As long as bosses stay objective in managing and directing Virgo employees, and avoid expressing anger or making outright accusations, they will find Virgos willing instruments in implementing orders from above. Reward-oriented, Virgos will usually be satisfied with a small word of thanks or praise for a job well done, but a promotion or bonus is even better.

The Virgo Coworker

STRENGTHS
Helpful
Honest
Polite

WEAKNESSES
Insensitive
Unfeeling
Unsympathetic

INTERACTIVE STYLE
Modest
Unassuming
Hard working

Virgos can grow very close to their coworkers in any organization, not only as professionals but also as friends or acquaintances. Although they may prefer working alone, Virgo coworkers are proud of their achievements as part of a team. In such groups they rarely, if ever, seek to assume a leadership role but normally are content to play a modest part. Hard workers, they will seldom let their colleagues down or dump work on them that they would rather not handle themselves. Although Virgos are polite, tactful, and considerate in most matters, they can also be insensitive to emotional nuance in their attempt to stick to the factual and literal.

Approaching the Virgo Coworker for Advice

Virgo coworkers are best approached for professional rather than personal advice. Not specialists in human psychology, Virgos can completely misread a situation and offer counsel that may prove disastrous if followed literally. Especially sharp in professional matters involving schedules, complex instructions, and technical detail, Virgo coworkers will usually take the time to help you unravel orders that are difficult to understand or implement. Their razor-sharp minds have a way of cutting through obscure references and finding workable methods that will yield tangible results. If they talk or think too quickly for you, just ask them to slow down and take time to explain things in a simple fashion.

Approaching the Virgo Coworker for Help

Not usually ones to immediately spring into action, Virgos will need to reflect on your request, particularly the effects such an action might have on their professional standing. If they think that helping you will do them no harm, they will probably give their consent. Lending aid may come slowly, but they will follow through on their promises, for the most part. However, be prepared for them to limit the scope or duration of their involvement at any time, because they sometimes need to scale back their help for any number of reasons.

Traveling with and Entertaining the Virgo Coworker

When traveling with Virgo coworkers, you will find that they enjoy the pleasure of your company just as much as any special entertainment planned for their benefit. If the two of you are getting along well, they will enjoy sharing normal daily activities with you.

Used to taking a secondary role, your Virgo coworker will be happy to defer to you in most matters and allow you to take the lead in making decisions. Show kindness and consideration to Virgo coworkers, and they will always go that extra mile in helping you out. Should they suddenly become withdrawn and moody, do not question them, but let them work themselves out of it.

The Virgo Coworker Cooperating with Others
Virgo coworkers are extremely cooperative in working with others as long as they are not ignored or taken for granted. Although their needs for perks and rewards are not overly high, they will gain satisfaction from praise offered to the group of which they are a part. Rarely rebellious, Virgo coworkers will speak out only if treated in a blatantly unfair or dishonest way. They are particularly sensitive about broken promises, since they take the spoken word to be legal and binding. Complaining is necessary for their psychic health, so try to ignore their little frustrations and irritations.

Impressing and Motivating the Virgo Coworker
Virgos will be best motivated to give their all by being part of a hard-working group where everyone pulls his or her own weight. Annoyed by shirkers and freeloaders, the Virgo coworker will be particularly angered by charming or superficial individuals seeking a free ride and using manipulative means to get out of doing their fair share. Should such wastrels surface in a group, Virgo coworkers can be the obvious choice to speak to these individuals in no uncertain terms and get them back on track. Virgos are nothing if not persistent, and they will not rest until the group is working at maximum efficiency.

Persuading and/or Criticizing the Virgo Coworker
Virgo coworkers can be convinced only by common sense and logical argument. Appeals to their emotions generally fall flat. Should you wish to level criticism at Virgo coworkers, it is best to take them aside and patiently criticize their methods point by point, in a constructive manner. These sessions' occurrence should be kept to an absolute minimum, however, since frequent carping makes them nervous and wears them down. Persuading Virgo coworkers of the correctness of your approach is best confined to short explanations over time. Virgos are not always easy to convince in one go and need to see that your methods work before they will be ready to adopt them.

The Virgo Client
Virgo clients are likely to be very particular and picky. Working with them will require a great deal of concentration, since they will want their instructions followed to the last detail. You will be expected to dot every "i" and cross every "t," for they will go over your reports with a magnifying glass. You should gently urge them to look at the big picture and sense the underlying approach or philosophy you are following, but do not expect too much from them in this regard. They will rarely commend you on your work, but just the fact that they continue as your client should be accepted as thanks in and of itself.

Detail-oriented
Focused
Thorough

WEAKNESSES
Picky
Particular
Ungrateful

INTERACTIVE STYLE
Factual
Observant
Analytical

Impressing the Virgo Client

Virgo clients will require that you adopt the same kind of analytical and thorough approach that they use. Thus it may be useful for you to get an outline of a previous project they have developed so that you can view their methodology. Once you have covered that and are ready to begin with your project, Virgos will be impressed only with your dedication in covering every point that they mentioned in their instructions. They will usually expect regular updates to get an idea of your progress. At any point they may blow the whistle and stop you to correct and redirect your efforts, so be prepared.

Selling to the Virgo Client

Once you have proven yourself to the Virgo client, selling a new project or product will rarely be a problem. Building your credibility with them must come first, however, so make sure that your initial project is a success. Your pitch to them should, above all, be logical and reveal no contradictions or inconsistencies. Be upbeat and positive, but at the same time do not gloss over or ignore potential difficulties, such as keeping costs down or meeting deadlines. Your past record with other clients will be an important selling point, particularly if you have improved the standing of one of their competitors in the past.

Your Appearance and the Virgo Client

It is best not to wear loud or overly stylish clothes that could distract Virgo clients from concentrating on the material you present to them. Strong cologne or perfume, sexy styles, or trendy hairstyles can also be counterproductive. Present yourself as a reliable person who is ready to listen. This latter trait can be bolstered by taking thorough notes and asking intelligent questions. Virgos are often annoyed by their listeners' impatience, wandering attention, and, above all, inability to understand the main points. They hate to repeat themselves, so try to get straight what they say the first time around.

Keeping the Virgo Client's Interest

Virgo clients are quite attached to their own way of doing things, so showing curiosity in this area and asking their advice about how they would handle matters will serve to keep their interest. Avoid trying to spice up your meetings with anecdotes or jokes, and most important, do not go off on tangents or continually change the subject. Attracted by complexity and puzzles, a Virgo's interest can be captured by challenging them mentally. Complexity is something that fascinates them, and your mental agility in dealing with problem areas will serve to rivet their attention.

Breaking Bad News to the Virgo Client

Virgo clients can take bad news as long as you have a list of reasons that explain, in logical fashion, why the failure took place. By presenting these reasons one by one and showing how they can be prevented (or, at the very least, minimized) in the future, you can convince your Virgo client to give you a second chance. Virgo clients can wax quite enthusiastic about new approaches to an old problem, particularly inexpensive ones that only serve to tweak their own approaches (instead of writing them off completely). Thus, adopting slight changes of direction while still keeping to their original intentions go down best with them.

Entertaining the Virgo Client

It is quite possible for Virgo clients to loosen up, let their hair down, and enjoy themselves thoroughly once you get them away from the professional setting and off the subject of business. They want to maintain a strict separation between their personal and professional life, but they just don't know how. By allowing them to forget their careers for a while and fully indulge in hedonistic pursuits, you will be doing them a great favor—one they will not easily forget. Once they get hooked on your entertainment style, they may continue to do business with you, always looking forward to the leisure-time bonuses that you have in store for them.

The Virgo Business Partner

Generally speaking, Virgos make good business partners. Notwithstanding, the more changeable side of Virgo manifests in partners born under this sign. Hard to predict, they can confound their partners periodically by doing an unexpected about-face. This isn't necessarily due to their calculated attitudes but more with acting on impulse, frequently surprising even themselves. Thus it is often hard to be absolutely sure of what to expect from Virgo partners. Since by nature Virgos are private and keep a lot to themselves, it may be difficult to know what they are thinking.

Setting Up the Business Partnership with Virgo

Virgos like to know beforehand what is expected of them. Therefore, in any partnership with them, the division of labor should be thoroughly discussed, planned, and put into writing. Rarely will Virgos agree to take on assignments that they are not sure they can handle. Delivering the goods is what they are after; thus they are decidedly results-oriented. They are also likely to expect the same or more from their partner(s) as well. Paradoxically, however, the best partners for them are opposites whose strongest suits are in the areas of theory, imagination, and intuition.

Tasking with the Virgo Business Partner

Allow Virgo partners to work on their own as much as possible. Furthermore, should it be necessary to assemble a staff of specialists to help them and implement their ideas, it is best to leave the choice of assistants to them. Virgos generally have good instincts for those they can work with and those they cannot. Should you need assistance from your Virgo partner on one of your own projects, he or she will be ready to lend a helping hand. However, you must avoid interrupting their work as much as possible; once their concentration is broken, it may be difficult for them to quickly regain focus.

Traveling with and Entertaining the Virgo Business Partner

Feelings of camaraderie between you and your Virgo partner can grow on trips together. This in and of itself is a good reason to suggest one or two business trips a year with each other. Although they have strong preferences, most Virgo partners will defer to you on your choice of hotel, restaurants, or mode of travel. In case you show disinterest or inde-

STRENGTHS
Faithful
Composed
Discreet

WEAKNESSES
Impulsive
Unpredictable
Confounding

INTERACTIVE STYLE
Private
Low-key
Surprising

cision in this regard, they will be capable of giving direction. For most Virgo partners, it is not necessary to have entertainment scheduled every night; most often one single outstanding show or other performance on the trip will be sufficient.

Managing and Directing the Virgo Business Partner

In some respects, Virgos can be unmanageable, but in others they are surprisingly agreeable. A lot, of course, depends on their individual makeup, but when you see them showing resistance to being directed, you should immediately back off and seek a less direct and confrontational approach. Likewise, you should not take advantage of their seeming willingness to follow orders, since they may feel resentment that will only surface much later. Rather than asking a Virgo directly, "Do you mind doing that?" you should instead try to sense the answer without posing the question. Your sensitivity to Virgos' wants and needs will be highly appreciated and tend to grease their squeaky wheels.

Relating to the Virgo Business Partner in the Long Run

Problems with Virgo partners often surface only after a long time. Because of this, you may feel good about how things are going in the partnership and then one day be startled by a Virgo outburst of anger, specifically directed at you. In order to avoid such episodes, gently encourage Virgo business partners to express their negative feelings occasionally and then take their statements seriously. The only problem with this approach is that Virgos love to complain, and you may be opening a can of worms by encouraging them in this regard.

Parting Ways with the Virgo Business Partner

Virgos can get attached to both their partnerships and their partners. Yet they can be realistic enough to accept when things are just not working out. If you are the one who is unhappy, while they are quite content, you might try making concrete suggestions for change that would work better for you. Should they disagree or be unable to meet such demands, this can become a reason for a parting that they can understand and accept. If they are the unhappy party, they may suffer for months or years without saying anything at all, then one day announce unexpectedly that they have had enough.

The Virgo Competitor

Virgo competitors can be extremely clever and are likely to prove formidable opponents on the mental level. Fond of matching wits with their opponents, they will seek to confuse, bewilder, and exasperate using whatever tactics they need to sow the seeds of disorder. This is usually done subtly, while they themselves remain cool, calm, and collected on their side of the fence. Once their weapons have taken effect, they will proceed with their original plans for their own product or service in an innocent manner, as if nothing at all had happened.

Countering the Virgo Competitor

The best way to counter Virgo competitors' sneaky tricks is to give them back their own tactics in spades. At the first sign of their intervention into your public relations and marketing campaigns, you should silently declare all-out war and go on the attack, seeking to undermine their own plans the way they sought to destabilize yours. At the same time, you should institute damage control at home, vigorously countering their aggressive behavior and also quickly mending whatever holes they have made in your nets. Your quick response will unnerve them and make them vulnerable.

Out-Planning the Virgo Competitor

Virgos' greatest talents emerge in their planning, so it is best not to attempt to counter them directly in this area. Better to wait until the structure of their plans becomes clear and then seek ways to oppose them directly on each point. Usually if you can punch a hole in their armor in one or two areas you can cause them to doubt the efficacy of their entire plan. Once this is accomplished, they are sure to institute changes and you will have gained the tempo in your interactions. From then on their actions may be limited to reactions to your tactics. Confusion often results when these competitors are put on the defensive.

Impressing the Virgo Competitor in Person

Because Virgo's style is so secretive, you should aim for the opposite approach. Remaining breezy and open will usually irritate your Virgo competitors and throw them off-balance. While they are surprised (and probably chuckling over your stupidity at being such an all-revealing blabbermouth), you can take advantage of their being off-balance. Throw out as many false clues and contradictory statements as you like to blow their cool; when they begin to react, they may reveal many of their hidden intentions.

Undercutting and Outbidding the Virgo Competitor

Often Virgo competitors are engaged in doing their real dealings behind the scenes, sometimes even having their company's interests represented unofficially by others. Best to counter them directly here by engaging in a bit of research (and espionage) to undermine their tactics. In all-out bidding wars, Virgo competitors are best countered with bluffing, since they are likely to take your actions literally. Once you have committed yourself to making high bids, you can usually succeed in driving up their counter-bids until you finally withdraw, leaving them the dubious winner of an overinflated bidding war you were never interested in winning anyway.

Public Relations Wars with the Virgo Competitor

Virgo competitors are usually clever enough to analyze your approach and then to counter it point by point. One way to frustrate them is to adopt the same approach and hold back on your public relations and marketing until the very last minute. Often you will win such a war of nerves and force them to take a stand or show their hand. They will seek to get you to react by pushing your buttons with false or misleading statements about your company. Take the high ground and refuse to react to such jibes and taunts.

(The Virgo Competitor)

STRENGTHS

Clever

Formidable

Subtle

WEAKNESSES

Overconfident

Misleading

Untrustworthy

INTERACTIVE STYLE

Devious

Secretive

Sneaky

Also refuse to adopt underhanded approaches; don't criticize their products, but instead seek to promote yours.

The Virgo Competitor and the Personal Approach

Most Virgo competitors seek to be objective. They are usually very protective and secretive when it comes to personal matters. Even an oblique reference to something in their private lives can upset them greatly. Thus, avoid such topics studiously during times of truce and peace. However, in an all-out war with such opponents, you may very well employ the personal approach as a weapon. Virgos are at their worst when angry, and they open themselves to further attack as well as exposing their sensitivities and subjecting their delicate nervous systems to extreme stress.

Love

The Virgo First Date

Virgos can be particularly noncommittal and standoffish on the first date. Highly critical and guarded, they usually keep their feelings to themselves, giving little away about whether they like you or not. It is best not to intrude on their space. Do not crowd them or push them to say if they are having a good time or not. Virgo first dates will want to impress you with their appearance, so be sure to remark on how nice they look. You will be expected to make things interesting for them by indulging in wit, irony, wordplay, and conversation featuring interesting topics and insightful commentary. When they fall silent, it doesn't necessarily imply anything negative about you, so just go on with your spiel.

Wooing and Picking Up the Virgo First Date

Although most Virgos will be open to being asked out for a first date, they will probably make it clear that the first moment you meet is not the best time to talk. Schedule a telephone conversation a few days later in which your first extensive meeting can be planned. Often it is best just to take a walk or have a relaxed cup of coffee or drink with them rather than schedule an elaborate date featuring dinner and entertainment. This will give the discriminating Virgo a good chance to look you over and decide if further involvement is desired.

Suggested Activities for the Virgo First Date

After having initially met, spoken on the phone, and gone for a walk or drink, you are now ready to move on to the first full-blown date. Here you should pull out all the stops, not sparing trouble or expense to impress your Virgo date and make sure you both have a great time. Find out what kinds of music, food, or other activities Virgo first dates like, since there is nothing worse than sitting out their disapproval or lack of enjoyment because of a poor choice on your part. Virgos are good complainers, so you will know immediately where you stand and perhaps be able to change course in time.

STRENGTHS
Tasteful
Discriminating
Attractive

WEAKNESSES
Closed
Unemotional
Silent

INTERACTIVE STYLE
Cool
Unimpressed
Unflappable

Turn-Ons and Turn-Offs for the Virgo First Date

Turn-offs are easier to discuss. Virgo first dates are so selective and picky that practically anything can turn them off. For example, they may like something you offer, but it may come at the wrong time or in the wrong place. Since their rejection is such an unpredictable thing, even for them, it will be necessary to just take your chances. What will really turn them on is your ability to read their present state and mood and be able to improvise something that pleases them on the spot, right then and there.

Making "the Move" with the Virgo First Date

Being tuned in to *kairos* (knowing the right time to do something) is essential before making the move with a Virgo. Virgo first dates will fully respond only if things are exactly right; any feelings that the moment is not correct will inevitably result in your being pushed away, both physically and emotionally. Encouraging them to make the move is not usually a viable alternative, since they will rarely commit themselves so early on. Nor will holding back when they seem to be open to your move. Thus you will have to be the one to take a chance and act sooner or later, risking rejection.

Impressing the Virgo First Date

Virgos are often impressed by thorough preparation. If you have your act together, you will have passed over the first hurdle. Such preparations include not only making reservations, buying tickets, arranging comfortable transportation, and guaranteeing a certain amount of privacy, but also looking good enough to accompany them on a night out. Virgos simply expect things to go well, and when they don't, they can show a lack of sympathy and understanding. Doing your best is not enough—things must be perfect. Such demanding attitudes can stimulate some to higher achievement but turn others off completely.

Brushing Off the Virgo First Date

In many cases, Virgo first dates could not care less about being brushed off. Both of you will know by the end of your first evening together, and often sooner, whether or not things have clicked. True realists, Virgo first dates will rarely want to continue with someone who is obviously not the right person for them, or vice versa. It is not necessary to think up elaborate excuses for not getting back in touch with these clear-thinking and logical individuals. Stating the truth in such situations does not usually faze them in the least.

The Virgo Romantic Partner

The fringe benefits of Virgo romantic partners become apparent when scheduling travel, making arrangements and reservations, and planning for the future. Virgos will leave little room for error in their shrewd calculations and need to put such matters in order. Sometimes you will wish they did not need to pin down everything so precisely and left a bit of wiggle room for last-minute changes, but for the most part, they will spare you a lot of time and trouble. Generally, Virgos serve the relationship rather than their partners and strive to preserve its integrity as well as its limits.

Having a Discussion with the Virgo Romantic Partner

Virgos will hold you to promises you have made and pressure you to keep to your original plans. Thus any discussions involving a change of mind on your part will be dealt with severely. Virgos will prefer to discuss specific points rather than just rambling on, although they do have a weakness for juicy tidbits of gossip. The most enjoyable discussions you will have with them are the ones that cause them to smile and laugh, since at such times they will drop their sterner attitudes and truly let their hair down.

Arguments with the Virgo Romantic Partner

Forget about winning an argument with Virgos. Not only will they use logic to punch holes in your arguments with devastating effect, but they will also simply stonewall efforts on your part either to oppose their will or to wriggle out of responsibilities. A paradox exists here: Although their arguments are logical, their behavior may be not at all rational. When driven to it, they will just say "no" and refuse to listen to any common-sense arguments at all. This strange combination of rationality and irrationality makes them formidable opponents. They also tend to neither forgive nor forget easily.

Traveling with the Virgo Romantic Partner

What a pleasure to sit in a car, airplane, or train and know that everything from tickets to refreshments has been already taken care of by your Virgo romantic partner. Virgos hate being caught up short, and as a result, preparation is their long suit. Although serious miscalculations are unusual, Virgos will just shrug them off as unfortunate accidents, not wanting to take the blame themselves. Although interesting conversation is appreciated, idle chatter can wear Virgos down and make them very nervous and grumpy. Keep them in a good mood with witty wordplay, solving puzzles, and playing games.

Sex with the Virgo Romantic Partner

Even the strictest of Virgos (and often precisely the most uptight ones) tend to let it all hang out in private. Even venturing into kinky and strange sexual realms, they can be surprisingly aggressive and responsive when they get you alone, most often on their own turf. The experience of being attacked in the bedroom (or any other room) by a seemingly staid, even prudish, Virgo can be quite a memorable one. Revealing themselves in private when and where they choose to is a true Virgo specialty. Do not refer to it later or try to tease them about their behavior since the Virgo sense of humor has strict limits.

Affection and the Virgo Romantic Partner

Most Virgos dislike open displays of affection in public. More passionate than sensuous, Virgos are generally not fond of touching or being embraced on a regular basis and may also shrink from your attempts to kiss them, even on the cheek. Although they have a reputation for being cold, most Virgos will brighten at a smile or kind word addressed to them, when they are in the mood for it. Things will go best with your Virgo when you can read that flashing red warning light that says: Keep away or *noli me tangere* (don't touch me).

(The Virgo Romantic Partner)

STRENGTHS

Structured

Orderly

Prepared

WEAKNESSES

Compulsive

Tight

Unyielding

INTERACTIVE STYLE

Calculated

Precise

Orderly

LOVE

Humor and the Virgo Romantic Partner

Some people insist that Virgos have no sense of humor, labeling them highly critical, picky, sensitive, and condemning. Some even refuse to say anything good about Virgos at all, insisting that their negativity will eventually destroy the romance in any love relationship. Although this is overstating the case, it cannot be denied that strict and serious attitudes do often keep Virgos from fully relaxing and enjoying themselves. But those who know how to make their Virgo romantic partners laugh will usually have few complaints about them.

The Virgo Spouse

Even the most independent Virgos are able to quite naturally move into the sphere of marriage and become excellent homemakers and providers. Although they can drive their mates crazy with their insistence on order, they are often curiously lax in cleaning up their own private work and living space. Such areas may seem sloppy but, in fact, are arranged according to some strange Virgo logic, recognized only by them. Although Virgo spouses will work hard, they won't necessarily like it, often preferring to do the minimum of what is required and then relax and enjoy themselves. They shine in emergency situations and are there when needed.

Wedding and Honeymoon with the Virgo Spouse

Although Virgo spouses like to have everything well arranged for their weddings and honeymoons, they prefer to have someone else handle things. They are not at all averse to making plans or stating their requirements and wishes, but when it comes to implementation they like to have someone else do it, for once in their lives being able to stand back, or rather sit or lie back and relax. Also, when alone with their new spouse they prefer not to be pressured in any area—they're on what may be the first real vacation they have had in a long while.

Home and Day-to-Day Married Life with the Virgo Spouse

Virgos can be very insistent in their demands. Thus it is better to oppose them as little as possible and to make sure they are at least temporarily satisfied with your behavior. The alternative is not a pleasant one. When Virgo demands are not met, you better prepare for a deluge of criticism, complaint, invective, or a coldness rivaled only by the chilly winds of the Arctic. Virgos are notoriously hard to please, so it is best to try to follow the rules they lay down whenever possible, without questioning them.

Finances and the Virgo Spouse

Virgo spouses can be very good at cutting corners, finding bargains, squirreling away surprisingly large savings, and doing without. They are also prone to being stingy in outlays of cash and demanding that their partners also hold on to the family money rather than spending it. Virgos get angry when their mates spend unnecessarily, even to the point of not speaking to them or withdrawing physically. Both making budgets and following them (and of course insisting that you do so as well) come naturally to most Virgos.

Infidelity and the Virgo Spouse

For such strictly opinionated and rule-oriented people, Virgos can be surprisingly amoral in their attitudes toward infidelity. When they are sure of their mate's devotion and love, they are quite capable of overlooking an occasional indiscretion. However, they will rarely forget any of the details of such infidelities and may later use them as weapons against their spouse. They also see nothing wrong with having their own occasional flirtation or fling, as long as all private matters are kept secret. As a matter of fact, Virgos do not see sex as the most important thing in a marriage, and therefore it is not worth getting terribly upset about.

Children and the Virgo Spouse

Virgos are excellent at looking after the daily needs of their children. Particularly detail-oriented, they will want to check every area of their children's psyche and anatomy to make sure everything is all right with them. They will also pay attention to their clothing, homework, and food habits. They are quite adept at getting them ready for school and making sure they are not left alone when young. As their children grow older, Virgo parents are amenable to granting them independence and are relieved not to have to attend to them so assiduously. However, Virgo parents usually keep a keen eye out for trouble.

Divorce and the Virgo Spouse

Virgo spouses are particularly unforgiving in the matter of divorce. They will usually try to keep the kids, the house, the bank account, and anything else they can get their hands on. Their attitude is usually that they worked the hardest and therefore should be given most of what accumulated (with the exception of debts and bills). A blindness to the needs of their spouse usually accompanies such an attitude, but beyond that, they normally do not seek to injure or inflict emotional hurt. The fact that they do injure emotionally is in most cases due not to their intention to wound, but rather to their insensitivity and indifference.

The Virgo Lover

Virgo lovers are easily upset and cannot be counted on to maintain stability in a romantic relationship. Frequently nervous about holding on to their partners, Virgos convey their insecurities through actions that reveal their doubting and critical nature at work, undermining their feelings. Most often such negative thoughts are directed toward themselves but can also be separately aimed at either their partner's attitudes or the very nature of

STRENGTHS

Attractive

Thoughtful

Capable

WEAKNESSES

Insecure

Doubting

Unstable

INTERACTIVE STYLE

Unassuming

Private

Critical

the relationship. When feeling positive about things, the natural beauty of Virgo lovers shines through, highlighting and complementing their intellect and capable and responsible nature.

Meeting the Virgo Lover

Frequently you will hear about a potential Virgo lover from a mutual friend or family member who finds him or her interesting and thinks you two should meet. In the same way, the Virgo's interest in you may have been aroused. An air of expectation has probably built up on both sides before the first meeting, serving to heighten the intensity of actual contact. In addition, the feelings that both of you have toward the person who introduced you can serve not only as an excuse or reason to meet, but also to furnish the cement that holds the relationship together, particularly in the early stages.

Location and the Virgo Lover

Virgos will have to spend a lot of time at your place before they begin to feel truly comfortable there. At first it is probably best if they invite you to their place, which in and of itself is a high compliment and an indication of their degree of interest. Even an invitation from a Virgo to come in after knocking on the door is an expression of trust, but it also shows an interest on their part for you to get to know them better. Be extremely respectful of their space and rarely, if ever, handle objects or rummage through their books, papers, or refrigerator when they are absent or out of the room.

Sex and the Virgo Lover

Virgos enjoy sex as long as everything that occurs is kept between the two of you and never repeated to anyone. Should information about their lovemaking style, however complimentary, get back to them, they may be extremely upset. Likewise, keep tight-lipped about things they say, particularly shared confidences. Virgo lovers will usually respond in kind, honoring your privacy as well. In general, secret love affairs are often highly attractive to Virgos, who are turned on sexually by these clandestine adventures. Enjoy them to the fullest, but be aware that if you betray Virgo lovers in any way, you should expect extreme jealousy and aggressive, swift reprisals.

Holding On to the Virgo Lover

If you proceed on a constant course with Virgo lovers, once you are deeply involved and intimately familiar with their likes and dislikes you can usually hold on to them. The reasons for breakups with Virgo lovers are often related to the simple diminishing of the intensity of feelings over time. However, Virgos lovers are frequently already married or in a steady relationship when you meet them, and once their need for a fling has passed, be prepared for them to return to their original partner, dumping you in the process. In retrospect, it may seem that they sought out and needed not you specifically, but only the affair itself.

Entertaining the Virgo Lover

Virgo lovers like to have your full attention when you are together, but they also enjoy playing games, doing puzzles, solving problems, and discussing a variety of topics.

Interesting varieties of lovemaking and mental activities are particularly attractive to them. Never seek to penetrate their veil of mystery directly, but instead show them that you are fascinated by it through expressing interest in a subtle, indirect manner. Such interest is often all the entertainment they require when you are alone. When you go out in public together, keep in mind their predilection for quality in dining, seating at shows, and means of transportation.

Breaking Up with the Virgo Lover

Most often, breakups with Virgo lovers will be initiated by them after the relationship has outlived its usefulness. This may sound cold-blooded, but frequently an affair with a Virgo lover will be based on pragmatic considerations, because Virgos are honest as well as realistic. Should you decide to break up with a Virgo, they are likely to accept such a decision without a struggle, knowing that another lover is probably waiting just around the next corner. The actual breaking up is best done face to face in a straightforward manner that avoids deception or game-playing.

The Virgo Ex

Virgo exes are not usually very enthusiastic about continuing relationships with their former mates. Too often they are filled with negative feelings and prefer to simply break cleanly with the past. Good with lawyers and legal issues, they will pursue every avenue to assure themselves of being adequately compensated and also cared for in the case of gaining custody of children. They prefer to keep things very cool and matter-of-fact with their exes without emotional displays, although they can be prone to irritation and anger, particularly when they feel wronged or unfairly treated.

Establishing a Friendship with the Virgo Ex

Do not expect to get too close with your Virgo ex. Trying to establish a new emotional bond is usually doomed from the start. The Virgo attitude in such matters follows the old adage: "Once bitten, twice shy." Usually, the best you can hope for is an objective understanding of the other's position, mutual respect, and an absence or cessation of resentment and hostility. All physical contact should be studiously avoided. Virgo exes can get particularly nasty if you try to come on to them or reach out emotionally. Stirring up old feelings will usually only lead to incriminations and rancor.

Issues of Getting Back Together with the Virgo Ex

Only after a long period of reestablishing respect and trust should such a possibility even be considered. Do not be surprised if they demand verbal and written assurances from you that they will be treated fairly before they let you near them or begin to discuss getting back together. You must be prepared to set aside your feelings of pride and also to freely admit past failures and your intention to change. However, they will not believe all the promises in the world unless you can back them up with deeds.

STRENGTHS
Clear-thinking
Decisive
Unambiguous

WEAKNESSES
Condemning
Unenthusiastic
Resentful

INTERACTIVE STYLE
Cool
Matter-of-fact
Detached

LOVE

Discussing Past Issues with the Virgo Ex

Past issues can be discussed only if you are prepared to analyze, listen, accept, and, above all, see the point of view of your Virgo ex. If you display any sign of anger or other strong emotion, you should be prepared for Virgo exes to turn their backs on you and walk out. Sometimes it is better not to go down the road of past issues at all, since once they begin the journey with you, Virgos are unlikely to want to stop until the subject is fully, and usually painfully, exhausted. Like a dog with a bone, your Virgo ex will not easily let go of such a topic, continuing on it for days, weeks, and even months.

Expressing Affection to the Virgo Ex

Rarely, if ever, should you take the lead in this activity. Although you may end up waiting a couple of years, it is best to let the Virgo make the first move. Appreciate even the slightest smile, lingering eye contact, or touch of the hand, and above all do not overreact to such overtures. As a matter of fact, you would do better to ignore them altogether. Your best approach may be to begin to express affection through writing, where your physical presence is not so strongly felt.

Defining the Present Relationship with the Virgo Ex

Virgo exes are masters at defining such relationships; therefore the setting up of ground rules for behavior and speech should be left to them. Being able to keep strictly to these caveats will be the best way for you to prove your good intentions. At crucial moments you can even point to your achievements in this area as examples of your goodwill and desire to make things work. Never make a promise that you are not prepared to keep. To Virgos, your word is your bond.

Sharing Custody with the Virgo Ex

Structure comes naturally to all Virgos. They will feel most comfortable when a fixed pattern of visitation or sharing has been firmly established. Flexibility is not usually possible, even when the children make demands on the advent of a particularly special occasion. Furthermore, Virgo's insistence on your keeping to legally binding agreements concerning the children is usually ironclad. Displays of emotion on your part are likely to turn them off, so work on avoiding expression of your feelings, from empathic concern to outright outbursts of joy or anger. Both positive and negative emotions are likely to be condemned equally.

Friends and Family

VIRGO
August 24–September 22

The Virgo Friend

Virgo friends can be extremely supportive and helpful. They seem to know when you really need them, and even if they have been out of touch with you for some time, they often pop up at just the right moment. Although Virgos in general can be very needy individuals, Virgo friends find it difficult to ask for direct assistance. Such appeals are a long time coming, so when they finally do come, they should be taken seriously. Contact with Virgo friends need not be frequent, but once every few weeks or every couple of months it is good to give them a call or send an email bringing them up-to-date on your activities.

Asking for Help from the Virgo Friend

Help is available from Virgo friends only at certain times, namely when everything in their life is together and they are willing enough to give it. Because they are so often involved with their own personal problems, however, they are not always in a stable enough emotional state even to help themselves. With such sensitive nervous and digestive systems, Virgos are often in a state of suffering or, at the very least, mild upset. Therefore, it is necessary to check out their physical, mental, and emotional states before requesting help. Should they be well enough, do not hesitate to ask.

Communication and Keeping in Touch with the Virgo Friend

Virgo communication is characteristically direct and to the point, but beneath the surface there may be other issues lurking. Conversations with Virgos therefore often take place on several different levels at the same time. After such an interchange you will want to go over the conversation in your mind and read a bit between the lines. Frequency of communication is not important to most Virgos, but constancy is. Should a schedule involving contact every week or every month emerge, Virgos will expect you to keep to it. Usually a leisurely evening together or extensive telephone conversation will prove sufficient for a substantial period of time.

STRENGTHS
Supportive
Helpful
Constant

WEAKNESSES
Needy
Difficult
Judgmental

INTERACTIVE STYLE
Caring
Critical
Involved

Borrowing Money from the Virgo Friend

There is an unwritten law with many Virgo friends that says: "If I don't borrow money from you, don't borrow it from me." In the case of Virgo friends who have never borrowed from you in the past, your approaching them for a loan could be met with a chilly reception. The fact that they are flush with funds or destitute at any particular time is not the overriding factor in their disbursing funds. They want to know what it is for, whether it would be a good idea for you to spend it, and how and when you intend to pay it back. With these and other conditions imposed on loans, you might wish to look elsewhere for money.

Asking for Advice from the Virgo Friend

Virgo friends can be very helpful with advice, since they think logically and are able to anticipate the problems that might arise from following a given course of action. However, they are sure to ask you later whether or not you followed their valuable advice, and if you have not, they might choose not to offer their help again. Virgos tend to be both judgmental and critical, and after receiving advice from them you might not wish to have your behavior scrutinized. Think carefully before asking for or accepting their counsel, since it could become the beginning of the end of a beautiful friendship.

Visiting the Virgo Friend

Visits with Virgo friends should be held at a time and place of their choosing, as long as such matters do not assume a great position of importance for you. Particular about almost everything, Virgos can quickly get uncomfortable and nervous if they are not sure whether or not they really want to do something a certain way. Therefore, it is best not to talk them into making any arrangements they are obviously feeling resistant to. Pressuring them will only make things worse and may even precipitate a catastrophe that requires a long recovery period on both sides.

Celebrations/Entertainment with the Virgo Friend

Although excellent planners and organizers, Virgo friends cannot always be counted on to be in a good mood when the event arrives. Frequently they play an important part in its preparation only to fall victim to an excruciating headache or nervous stomach that keeps them from attending at all. Actually, they would often prefer it that way, to tell the truth. Social gatherings are not really their strong suit, and they prefer to meet with people one-on-one or, at the most, a few at a time. However, should you need them to accompany you or provide protection, they will perform this role admirably.

The Virgo Roommate

Virgo roommates generally do not seek to play the dominant role in a day-to-day living situation. However, their bottom-line requirements are usually strict enough that their presence is strongly felt. Certainly not self-effacing, Virgos believe they are there to help and uphold domestic stability. Rarely will they work to bring uncertainty, chaos, or overt rebellion, but if they are repeatedly crossed or ignored, they will certainly dig in their heels and refuse to budge. They can be extremely unforgiving of their roommates' mistakes and rarely, if ever, overlook a slight, no matter how seemingly trivial.

Sharing Financial Responsibilities with the Virgo Roommate

Virgos are not well-known for their generosity. Therefore, they are prepared to meet their obligations but may very well refuse to pay one cent more than agreed upon. They are likely to be very hard on roommates who cannot meet their end of the bargain, even lashing out in blame and invective. Because of their strict and unyielding attitudes toward financial responsibilities, they ensure that the rent, utility, and phone bills, at the very least, will be paid on time. When it comes to food and extras, however, they may insist that their roommate(s) follow a prudent course and not overspend.

Cleaning and the Virgo Roommate

Actually, despite their clean-crazy reputations, Virgos can be as messy as anyone else. But they will clean up, and often in short order. This does not mean, however, that they will clean up your mess, too. Often a strict geographical dividing line clearly shows where they left off. They do not like nagging others to clean up; rather they will usually issue the cleaning command in short and not-so-sweet terms. The real strength of Virgo roommates cleaning-wise is that they have a place for everything and believe that everything should be in its place as much as possible when not in use.

Houseguests and the Virgo Roommate

Often Virgos cast a wary eye on your houseguests, viewing them as potential trouble-makers that they will have to clean up after. On the other hand, Virgos can be extremely giving and considerate to their own family members and friends who are staying for a few days. Overstaying is a real no-no for most Virgos, as they get nervous when guests start enjoying themselves too much. Financially, they are not at all shy about asking or implying that others help out with contributions for food and even for utilities when a visit drags on.

Parties and the Virgo Roommate

Virgo roommates enjoy letting their hair down occasionally. They can certainly be as wild, boisterous, and sexually demonstrative as anyone else at the party, and frequently more so. Yet when the commotion dies down, their sense for structure and order kicks in almost immediately as they start straightening, putting away, and gently ushering guests out the door. Often Virgo roommates will take on and successfully execute all the responsibilities for the party themselves, without expecting any thanks. However, this is only when others fail to help, for they are very grateful when they are lent a helping hand.

Privacy and the Virgo Roommate

Virgos are extremely private and secretive people. They will demand that their own space be inviolable, but they will be quite open to sharing common rooms like the living room, bathroom, and kitchen. Their room must never be entered under any circumstances, short of fire, and they expect you always to call them or knock on their door (but please,

STRENGTHS

Stable

Conscientious

Orderly

WEAKNESSES

Unforgiving

Rigid

Vindictive

INTERACTIVE STYLE

Purposeful

Logical

Responsible

FRIENDS AND FAMILY

not too often). When they use the internet or talk on a common computer or phone, they do not want you looking over their shoulders or listening in. Maximum privacy should be granted to them early in the morning, late at night, and of course between these times.

Discussing Problems with the Virgo Roommate

As long as conversations remain calm and rational and stick to the main points, Virgo roommates have a lot of faith in problems being solved. They will prefer having discussions with you on any particular issue as long as you have thought about it beforehand and have given their point of view serious consideration. Rather than trying to pin them down in passing and improvising a talk on the spot, they prefer that you make an appointment so that they can give their full attention to the issue and, above all, collect their thoughts and prepare for mild debate. Their faith in logic and common-sense solutions to almost any problem is unshakable.

The Virgo Parent

Fond of making rules and regulations, Virgo parents seek to protect and defend their children. They are likely to structure every aspect of their lives in an effort to spare them pain and keep them from harm. Such controlling attitudes are not always appreciated by their children as they grow up and seek to be more independent. Virgo parents too often foster rebellion by refusing to acknowledge such demands for freedom, insisting on their children's absolute obedience while they are still underage. Wise children will not oppose Virgo parents directly, but will seek to keep their own wishes and activities to themselves whenever possible.

Discipline Style of the Virgo Parent

Because of their strict attitudes in forbidding certain activities, Virgo parents are forced to have certain disciplinary methods and forms of punishment in reserve if their rules are broken. Normally, grounding is punishment enough. However, Virgo parents are clever enough to also reward their children for obeying them, particularly when heeding their advice or following their instructions yields a positive result. They will usually seek to create a feeling of solidarity with their children, sharing their proud family attitudes with them. Virgo parents are happiest when their children also view them as friends.

Affection Level and the Virgo Parent

Virgo parents may not be overly ostentatious with displays of affection but often show it in little ways. Children who are keyed into their Virgo parents easily recognize such signs and treasure them. Even the strictest of Virgo parents has a softer side that reveals itself now and then. When it comes to their children expressing affection toward them, Virgo parents may be standoffish or even rebuff such displays of feeling, but later will appreciate them when they are alone. Ironically, for such pragmatic individuals, Virgo parents can more easily express affection sporadically for no reason at all, rather than giving it as a reward.

Money Issues and the Virgo Parent

Virgo parents are very strict in outlays of cash to their children, not only because they are thrifty, but because they want to instill good habits in them. Normally they will grant a small allowance; however, they will also keep an eye on how it is spent. If a child wishes to purchase a special item, the Virgo parent will insist that he or she save up for it and buy it with his or her own money, often made babysitting, delivering newspapers, or mowing lawns. In the case of a very expensive item, Virgo parents will often help by paying their child to perform a needed task.

Crises and the Virgo Parent

Since Virgo parents have very sensitive nervous systems, they may overreact to a situation, creating a crisis where none exists. Sensible children will not expose their Virgo parents to such upsets, but rather handle the situation themselves. In the event of a real emergency, however, Virgo parents usually remain calm and move efficiently to rectify matters. Being worriers, they may find it difficult to let go of their fears for their children's safety, thus sometimes unknowingly bringing on small catastrophes rather than preventing them. Virgo parents must learn that repressed fear can act psychologically to attract the very dangers they are trying to protect against.

Holidays/Family Gatherings and the Virgo Parent

Virgo parents know how to prepare thoroughly for any holiday or family get-together. Although their children appreciate not having much to do themselves, at the same time they often long to experience the spontaneous joy of impulsive action and may come to feel that excessive planning makes things dull and predictable. Unfortunately, Virgo parents tend to do things the same way every time, in a highly predictable fashion that gets boring after a while. Lovers of tradition and ritual, Virgo parents tend to see the family as upholding their more conservative side.

Caring for the Aging Virgo Parent

Virgo parents tend to get fussy as they get older. Consequently, it may be hard to care for them and keep up with their likes and dislikes. Complainers, aging Virgo parents need to express their preferences, worries, and concerns rather than bottling them up and getting depressed—also not pleasant for a caretaker to face. It is best to put agreements in writing, so Virgo parents can be reminded of what they originally consented to, particularly in the case of an aging Virgo parent whose memory is impaired. The best way to keep an aging Virgo parent in line is to employ good old common sense.

The Virgo Sibling

STRENGTHS

Adaptable

Supportive

Contributing

WEAKNESSES

Silent

Passive

Touchy

INTERACTIVE STYLE

Helpful

Friendly

Reserved

Do not mistake the quietude of a Virgo sibling for weakness. Usually quite sure of their own power, Virgo siblings do not seek to direct attention to themselves needlessly. Content to work on their own, they will rarely ask for help of any kind unless they truly need it. Virgo siblings can adjust well to their place in the pecking order: as the oldest they will be more assertive, as the middle they will be more adaptable, and as the youngest they will be agreeable and often delightful. Their family loyalties are high, and they will stick by their siblings through thick and thin.

Rivalry/Closeness with the Virgo Sibling

Virgo siblings are usually content with their position in the family. They do not need to engage in endless sibling rivalry to establish their position or feel sure of it. They put their energies to work within the family structure without complaint or need for recognition. Their reward usually comes in service itself, and in this area, they can be quite unselfish. However, reward is important to them also, and they will demand their fair share in return for their efforts. Although Virgos feel close to their siblings, they are often among the first to leave the nest and establish themselves on their own.

Past Issues and the Virgo Sibling

Virgo siblings can be quite unforgiving when they feel wronged. Moreover, their judgmental and critical attitudes are likely to descend on their fellow siblings with terrifying force and can throw a real wet blanket over the family's mood. Until such issues are addressed and worked out, the family will continue along a troubled path. Above all else, Virgos stand for justice, which, as they see it, is something due to all, and when injustice rears its ugly head they will be there to cut it off. The punishment they mete out for wrongdoing usually involves coldness, silence, and ignoring the culprit, but they can get physical, too.

Dealing with the Estranged Virgo Sibling

Most estranged Virgo siblings are unapproachable. Once they have judged others, they assume an aloof and impenetrable stance that is difficult, if not impossible, to breach. Thus, reaching out to them over a period of time demands a lot of patience. It is possible to get through, little by little, over months or even years of applying pressure sensitively, however. Apologizing to them often helps, but also holding out the olive branch and urging all concerned to finally put an end to family discord can be effective as well. Once they reenter the fold, they can do so completely, without reservations.

Money Issues (Borrowing Money, Wills, Etc.) and the Virgo Sibling

Virgo siblings are quite strict in money matters, particularly when it comes to inheritances. Not only will they insist on everyone being treated fairly, but they will certainly stand up to receive their own fair share. Should they be involved as a trustee or custodian of a family estate, they will also want to be recompensed adequately. Virgos are not fond of either borrowing or lending money, but when they need it for vital matters, often involving their nuclear family, they will not hesitate to ask for it or even seek legal means to break a will.

Holidays/Celebrations/Reunions and the Virgo Sibling

Virgo siblings are known to be dutiful, and they can be counted on to do their share of the work in the preparation of family get-togethers. They are particularly fond of reunions when family members have not seen one another for a long time. Here their organizational skills really shine, and often they will make their own dwelling the principal meeting point, even to the point of miraculously finding domestic niches where everyone can sleep and park their luggage. In the case of older family, such as parents or aunts and uncles, they will even give up their own beds and sleep on a mat on the floor for a night or two.

Vacationing with the Virgo Sibling

Virgo siblings do not enjoy leaving much to chance when it comes to vacations. They are fully aware of bothersome preferences of certain family members that are particularly repugnant to them, and from the start, they will make it clear that they do not wish to participate if such undesirable paths are to be taken. Thus, they wind up insisting that things be done their way by rejecting anyone else's way. Although their irritation factor is high, their personal demands are normally reasonable and quite conservative in nature. Basically, they just don't want to be exposed to uncertainty or any crazy or disturbing behavior that could ruin their vacation.

The Virgo Child

Dutiful children, Virgos can be the mainstay of the family, making their contributions year after year without complaint. Yet, if they feel unappreciated, taken for granted, or downright ignored, sooner or later their resentment will build to an intolerable level and finally explode. Thus it is best to take notice of them and give them perks for their helpfulness. Although Virgo children can be models of good behavior, they also have a highly critical and judgmental side when it comes to their parents. Literalists, Virgo children will insist that parents keep their word. Parents of these children quickly learn that they must not make promises lightly.

Personality Development and the Virgo Child

Virgo children do not seem to change very much or very quickly as they grow up. The core of their personality remains the same, although, of course, their interests and activities change quite a bit. Their appearance can also go through extreme transformations, as they are not afraid of making radical changes. Virgo children have set beliefs that emerge at a very early age, beliefs that they will not forsake no matter what. Fierce in their moral attitudes, few children can be as disapproving as Virgos when others indulge in what they see as unethical behavior. Unfair parental treatment of fellow siblings, pets, and friends will simply not be tolerated without strong protest from a Virgo child.

STRENGTHS

Dutiful

Cooperative

Obedient

WEAKNESSES

Stubborn

Disapproving

Rejecting

INTERACTIVE STYLE

Reserved

Watchful

Careful

Hobbies/Interests/Career Paths for the Virgo Child

Virgo children often seek careers involving service such as health care, social work, teaching, and publishing. They are also good at amassing large sums of money and knowing how to invest it, so they make excellent bankers, stockbrokers, and business-people. Growing up, their hobbies are extremely important to them. Whether collectors or fanatical devotees of video games, sports, fashion, or film, they frequently give more energy to such pursuits than to their schoolwork. That said, Virgos are usually good students whose organizational skills ensure passing and often superior grades.

Discipline and the Virgo Child

Usually discipline is not necessary with Virgo children, who are very much aware of what is and is not allowed. Rarely will they plead ignorance of or make excuses for outright transgressions. Virgo children usually break rules with full knowledge of what they are getting into, including the consequences. When and if discipline must be meted out, they will usually accept it without complaint. However, should disciplinary action be taken unfairly or unnecessarily, they will protect the mistreated sibling or friend with every ounce of their strength.

Affection Level and the Virgo Child

Although affection is not the most important thing to Virgo children, they are very responsive to it. Family members who express endearment with a hug or kind word genuinely touch the hearts of Virgo children. They are extremely fond of pets and other small creatures, and even normally unaffectionate Virgo children will lavish affection on them and unreservedly show their feelings on a daily basis. Often Virgo children have a favorite sibling or parent with whom they can share their affections, but such preferences often can lead to familial jealousies, in some cases, even extreme ones.

Dealing with the Virgo Child and Interactions with Siblings

If Virgo children are treated fairly by parents and siblings, they will not cause problems. In the case of unfair treatment, Virgo children will simply not accept it, and problems will continue to arise until wrongs are righted. Virgo children do not have to be pushed or reminded of duties or obligations; usually they are the ones who do the reminding, in quite an adult manner. Particularly good at remembering holidays, birthdays, and special occasions of all kinds, Virgo children will take the lead in rounding everyone up for celebrations. Lighting a fire under lazy or resistant family members to get them to take part in activities is a Virgo specialty.

Interacting with the Adult Virgo Child

Sometimes Virgo children are so mature in their attitudes that they seem already grown up at an early age. In these cases, there is little difference between the Virgo child and the adult version of this person. We might say on inspection that the adult Virgo child is just a wee bit more adult. One reason that Virgo children are often more mature has to do with their seriousness, a quality that persists and often intensifies into their adult lives. This is one reason why it is very important for adult Virgo children to have fun and really let their hair down once in a while. Adult Virgo children highly value friends and family members with whom they are able to enjoy themselves in a lighthearted manner.

Libra

BIRTHDATE **SEPTEMBER 23–OCTOBER 22**

Like Tauruses, Libras are beauty lovers ruled by the planet Venus. Extremely talented socially, Libras know a great deal about how to make friends and deal with the complexities of human nature. This does not make them social butterflies, since many prefer to be alone, but their karma in this lifetime seems to lead them to professions where they can utilize their talents in dealing with people. Libra's great challenge in life is to maintain balance, represented by their symbol, the Scales.

Work

The Libra Boss

The only things Libra bosses value more than being liked by their employees is being well liked by them. This intense need for popularity often betrays them and can even undermine their efforts. Instead of keeping their eye on the ball and striving for positive results, too often they are interested in their personal gratification. At times their need for admiration seems boundless; those who know this are able to manipulate them through alternately giving and withholding praise. The struggle of Libra bosses to create successful companies is often against that most difficult of enemies—themselves.

Asking the Libra Boss for a Raise

It is important for those on the way up in a company headed by a Libra boss to never seek to outshine their master. As long as Libra bosses do not feel threatened by their more ambitious employees, they will often grant them raises and promotions. The clever employee of a Libra boss will soon realize that their true allegiance should not be to the company but to its presiding officer. Libra bosses expect unquestioned personal loyalty from those who work for them—a kind of unflinching support that only increases over the years.

Breaking Bad News to the Libra Boss

Frequently, good feelings are even more important to a Libra boss than good results. Conversely, Libra bosses can accept bad news as long as the feelings involved are truly shared by all concerned. Thus Libra bosses can gain as much emotional satisfaction from weeping together over bad news as from celebrating together over good news. After being presented with bad news, Libra bosses definitely do not want to be left alone. Sharing is key to the makeup of the Libra psyche, without which almost everything becomes meaningless. Rarely does a Libra boss say "I"—more often it is "We."

Arranging Travel and/or Entertainment for the Libra Boss

Libras function well in groups, and this affects their predisposition toward traveling and celebrating with others. At sit-downs, particular attention should be given to those seated at the Libra boss's table as well as to those who are placed in closest proximity. Likewise, although Libra bosses will occupy their own room in a hotel when on the road (at least in

STRENGTHS

Popular

Charismatic

Likeable

WEAKNESSES

Conceited

Needy

Self-defeating

INTERACTIVE STYLE

Agreeable

Charming

Magnetic

the afternoon of their arrival), others accompanying them on the trip should not choose a room on another floor but instead select a room near their leader. All social considerations that enhance sharing and personal interaction should be given top priority.

Decision-Making and the Libra Boss

Many Libra bosses will be sure to include not only top-level advisors in policy meetings but also some lower-level workers as well. Appearing to be democratic is much more important to Libra bosses than displaying an autocratic side. Libra bosses do not see themselves as kings or queens ruling the roost, but rather as central figures in a group that works hard, plays hard, and functions always as a mutually dependent and beneficial organization. Of course Libra bosses will not shrink from making final decisions, but the full participation of employees in formulating such decisions is essential.

Impressing and/or Motivating the Libra Boss

Libra bosses are most impressed by selfless behavior that contributes to the common good of the working group. They are turned off by selfish or self-aggrandizing behavior or the traditional climbing of the success ladder by stepping on others' fingers and shoulders. Likewise, you can best motivate Libra bosses by assuring them they have the support of the group on issues that will benefit management and workers alike. The whole idea of pulling together appeals most strongly to them, often resulting in everyone going that extra mile for one another rather than just working extra hours to fatten their own paychecks.

Making Proposals and/or Giving Presentations to the Libra Boss

Libras are very impressed by external appearances, and this means that presentations need to be attractive, inventive, and beautifully presented. In making such a presentation, every element should be carefully scrutinized beforehand, since the shoddy appearance or execution of any given item could be an indication of the low quality of the proposal as a whole. Text handouts should be clear and free of mistakes; audio-visual materials should be colorful, clear, and, if possible, digitalized and programmed intelligently. Finally, your appearance should be meticulously crafted. Remember that Libra bosses will voice company concerns but also want to know how group tasks will be divided and implemented.

The Libra Employee

Libra employees are not necessarily overly social. Although they have a decided talent for dealing with people, they often prefer to work alone, finding that their ability to concentrate depends to a great extent on screening out distractions. Often perfectionists, they will rarely allow their high standards to be compromised by the personal demands and endless babble of others. But undeniably their work karma seems bound up with other people, no matter how much they may try to deny it. Their understanding of human nature is often highly prized by colleagues and bosses alike.

Interviewing and/or Hiring the Libra Employee

Prospective Libra employees like to have their talents and experience acknowledged. Once this is settled, they will expect corresponding remuneration and a position that suits their abilities. This latter point is sometimes even more important to them than money, since they want to be given the opportunity to shine in their careers as well as to achieve status within the company. During a first interview, they will usually be careful to ask about the conditions under which they will be working and the people they will come in contact with daily. Being able to feel part of a team is important to them.

Breaking Bad News to or Firing the Libra Employee

Most Libra employees have a high opinion of their professional abilities. Consequently, being confronted with their shortcomings or outright failures is not easy for them to bear. However, if they are transferred to another department or faced with a wage cut, it is possible that this announcement will not be taken as bad news at all, particularly if it means less pressure and more congenial working conditions. Most Libra employees are not overly hard workers. They enjoy fulfilling easier tasks that put them under less strain and allow for relaxation and friendly relations with colleagues.

Traveling with and Entertaining the Libra Employee

Although not all Libra employees are party animals, they will enjoy social occasions and entertainment as much as anyone else and, frequently, more than most. All Libras love to have fun and consider travel and entertainment as rewards for the work they do. Indeed, such activities are necessities for Libras and looked upon professionally as important benefits of their jobs. Libra employees like to keep it light, which includes traveling light and illuminating social occasions with wit and humor. Count on a Libra employee to make things more enjoyable for everyone concerned.

Assigning Tasks to the Libra Employee

Avoid assigning crushing or overly challenging tasks to the average Libra employee. At work, Libras have an undeniable tendency to take things easy, and they will become most unhappy if forced to produce large quantities of work day after day with no relief. The situations they like best are twofold—either to be given manageable or easy tasks that do not put them under much strain, or to have interesting assignments where they are challenged to work hard followed by rest periods or slowdowns in the tempo of their work.

Motivating or Impressing the Libra Employee

Libra employees treasure their vacation time and love having holidays and days off. Therefore, guaranteeing them more breaks or lengthening their vacation period can be a strong motivating factor. They are most impressed by bosses and coworkers who accomplish their tasks easily and with brilliance, rather than those who simply plod along and gain results through sheer determination and hard work. Libra employees are also impressed by those colleagues who are pleasant and full of good humor and are turned off by overly serious sourpusses who rarely have a smile or kind word for anyone.

(The Libra Employee)

STRENGTHS
Understanding
Clever
Perfectionistic

WEAKNESSES
Rejecting
Cutting
Unrealistic

INTERACTIVE STYLE
Energetic
Feisty
Relaxed

Managing, Directing, or Criticizing the Libra Employee

Managing and directing Libra employees can be easily accomplished as long as you keep the instructions short and sweet, leaving them to their own devices and not nagging them (unless you do so in an upbeat and lighthearted way). Criticism is difficult for most Libra employees to accept, since their perfectionistic attitudes make additional demands unnecessary—at least in their minds. When Libra employees show poor judgment (which can be frequently), they may have to be told to change their approach 180 degrees, since they tend to go off in entirely the wrong direction from time to time.

The Libra Coworker

Libra coworkers can usually be counted on to brighten everyone's day. Their good humor is often apparent in a smile or witty remark. Although Libra coworkers enjoy the company of others, they are still able to produce high-quality work when left on their own. Their social side emerges when in a group, particularly when taking part in activities with three or four colleagues. Libras not only enjoy social contacts but also know how to function as part of a team. When they do make errors of judgment, however, they are likely to pull everyone else out of line with them, due to their charm and the magnetic influence of their personalities.

Approaching the Libra Coworker for Advice

Libra advice must not always be taken literally, since it is often given with a twinkle in the eye. Libra wisdom is sometimes not well grounded in either experience or reality. Certainly in the case of a colleague they are not particularly fond of, Libras are capable of giving misleading counsel that can send their poor coworker scurrying off in the wrong direction. Fond of practical jokes, slapstick humor, and sarcastic references, Libras give counsel that must not be taken at face value. Thus, their ability to inject humor in almost any situation will be appreciated only when given with positive intent.

Approaching the Libra Coworker for Help

Libra coworkers are not usually the ones you want to approach first for help. They are often far too wrapped up in their own world to take the time to spring to someone's aid or pledge themselves to make personal commitments. If, however, they are uniquely suited to help—being the only ones available with the expertise or know-how—they can be approached on a limited basis. Rarely will Libra coworkers return the favor and ask others to help them in return, usually finding it beneath them and detrimental to their professional image or social standing.

Traveling with and Entertaining the Libra Coworker

Libra coworkers are more fun than a barrel of monkeys when it comes to sharing good times. They are not only capable of enjoying themselves but also adept in seeing that others do as well. By contrast, they are not so much fun to be around when things become demanding or serious, or when they are simply not having a great time. Like flowers touched by frost, they seem to wilt and shrivel up, their good moods evaporating almost instantly. Once this behavior is experienced, colleagues are often under pressure to guarantee that their Libra coworkers are continuously amused.

The Libra Coworker Cooperating with Others

Although socially adept, many Libra coworkers are so feisty that they find cooperation not only difficult, but also undesirable. Libras have an unmistakably nutty side that causes them to approach problems in a manner different from everyone else. They also have a tendency to create problems when they do not exist and to work at fixing things that others find are running just fine. Truth be told, it is often a desire to make things run even better that urges them on. When everything is operating smoothly, they can be a valuable part of any group effort, as long as their kooky views are not taken too seriously.

Impressing and Motivating the Libra Coworker

The carrot-on-the-stick philosophy works well to motivate Libra coworkers. Normally, the rewards they seek are ones that let them proceed at a leisurely pace and give them time off rather than promises of monetary reward. Libra coworkers are happiest when things are running smoothly and others leave them alone. However, they do like to be free to interject their views and crack jokes. They are most impressed with colleagues who understand and appreciate their sense of humor. Nothing is more important to Libra coworkers than sharing good times.

Persuading and/or Criticizing the Libra Coworker

Sometimes Libra coworkers will allow themselves to be cajoled or even pushed into following orders for a while to avoid further conflict. However, you can be sure that as soon as possible they will resume their highly individual approach. Libras are quite capable of laughing at themselves, so if criticism is brought in a light and even funny manner, they may seem to accept it. But it is also often the case that remarks made at their expense tend to rankle them, building up long-lasting resentments over time. Later on, they are likely to suddenly lash out at the offender with a volley of barbs, at last having found an opportunity to take their revenge.

The Libra Client

Working for Libra clients can be an enjoyable experience. Normally polite, delightful, and cheerful, they will put on a good face and see no need to reveal or discuss any of their personal problems. Likewise, they will not usually go deep into business difficulties but will present you with a clear picture of what they want done and how to do it. You should adopt a similarly upbeat attitude toward work, since Libras react well to enthusiasm, particularly concerning their own unusual plans. Your adopting of unconventional attitudes will not upset them and frequently will serve to make their assessment of your capabilities even more positive.

STRENGTHS
Enthusiastic
Polite
Delightful

WEAKNESSES
Fantasy-prone
Impersonal
Superficial

INTERACTIVE STYLE
Seductive
Attractive
Positive

Impressing the Libra Client

Libra clients will first and foremost be impressed by those who take them seriously and in whom they arouse admiration. Libra clients are suckers for flattery, and for them, perhaps the greatest compliment you can give is that you find them fascinating and their ideas interesting. However, not all their ideas are workable, so modifying or criticizing these in a first session may turn them off so much so that they drop you. Therefore, keep upbeat and save modifications for a later stage in your work together, particularly when things are going well.

Selling to the Libra Client

Libra clients are not easy to convince, unless your basic business premises are the same. Normally, a Libra client will not have to be sold at all, since if you are in agreement on basics, they will be open to and accepting of your proposals. They will also be prepared to free up cash for an extra level of investment should they really go for your approach. Avoid trying to put the big sell on them, not only because it will be unnecessary but also because such an approach will just turn them off and prove counterproductive.

Your Appearance and the Libra Client

Libra clients pride themselves on their appearance, so it is best not to outshine them in this respect. You should look good, but not *too* good. Normally, they will never comment on your appearance, but you can be sure that they are registering every detail. Frequently, upon their return to their company they will answer queries about you from their colleagues and superiors with a simple statement describing how you looked and sounded. Keep well-balanced, responsive, tidy, and together, avoiding overly flamboyant or provocative clothing. Be sure there are no wrinkles, spots, or water marks on your garments, and keep your hair neatly presentable.

Keeping the Libra Client's Interest

Holding Libra's interest is best accomplished by keeping your interest fixed on them. All you need to do is listen to them carefully and remain responsive. Let them raise a subject and then be prepared to fly with it in the right direction. By always allowing them to take the lead, you will show your ability to understand them and follow their instructions. If you want to go into detail on a given subject, just throw out a one-liner or even ask them directly if an explication of this area might interest them. Only proceed if they truly want to know more; otherwise you may be digging a deep hole for yourself to climb out of.

Breaking Bad News to the Libra Client

Present bad news without excuses, but not in an alarming manner. Remain cool and well-balanced, adopting a "We're both experienced businesspeople and can handle a setback like this" attitude. In case they get alarmed, have an alternate set of figures available that could give a more positive spin to what has happened. Moreover, showing that a failure could in fact be a blessing in disguise will intrigue these clients enough to get out of an otherwise rough situation. Normally they are not interested in lengthy postmortems or explanations of what went wrong.

Entertaining the Libra Client

Libra clients love to be wined, dined, and generally spoiled in many ways, depending on their personal preferences. The only problem is that they may begin to look at you as the principal entertainment before the evening is over. Although the value of mutual seduction cannot be eliminated when dealing with charming Libra clients, it is a lot cleaner and professionally beneficial to make a strict separation between personal and business involvement. Drawing the line in the sand sooner rather than later—perhaps by dropping a rather broad hint—will help keep things properly in balance.

The Libra Business Partner

Libra business partners can be wonderful to work with, but they are also highly critical of themselves and those close to them professionally. Extremely demanding perfectionists, Libras, as charming and agreeable as they may be, can also drive you wild with their demands. Although they uphold their end of any partnership, Libras will evoke many ambivalent feelings, sometimes causing them to become a love–hate object for you. One of the most difficult traits of Libra business partners is their endless indecision, usually a result of their always wanting to consider the other side of the matter.

Setting Up the Business Partnership with Libra

Most Libra business partners are extremely versatile and able to pinch-hit at a moment's notice, even in areas outside their normal realm of expertise. Therefore, you would do well to direct your own efforts to specialized areas and give Libras as much space as possible to express their many talents. With projects requiring mutual input, Libra business partners do well when the other person is a rock of solidarity and dependability. Libra's energies can be worn down quickly, and they tend to express themselves in spurts rather than regularly over the long haul.

Tasking with the Libra Business Partner

Because of Libra's strong social skills and knowledge of the human personality, it is best to leave projects involving contact with others to them, particularly when representing the partnership in outside projects. Your tasks should have more to do with working out of the home base on objective activities that involve maintenance, planning, and marketing while leaving public relations, advertising, presentations, and sales to them. Rather than sharing common jobs with Libra business partners, it would work better to maintain a strict separation of tasks assigned to each of you through common agreement. When needed, however, Libras know how to share and help out, too.

Traveling with and Entertaining the Libra Business Partner

Both travel and entertainment can be definite pluses with Libra business partners. Few signs of the zodiac can be more fun than Libras when they are in the right mood. Notorious spendthrifts, their cash and credit card outlays are kept under control, unless they are spending the company's rather than their own money. Because of their seduc-

STRENGTHS
Wonderful
Charming
Agreeable

WEAKNESSES
Demanding
Indecisive
Procrastinating

INTERACTIVE STYLE
Fair
Balanced
Friendly

tive talents and social needs, the two of you are not likely to be alone for long. You will have to be understanding of their needs to hog the spotlight, but also of their penchant to disappear suddenly with their latest friend in tow.

Managing and Directing the Libra Business Partner

Although Libra business partners will listen to what you have to say, they are very difficult to manage and direct. Since their activity level is so high, they may have already acted before you can pin them down to make mutual plans. However, their contemplative side and difficulty in making long-term decisions will give you a chance to discuss specific issues and advise them on future actions. The best way to slow them down is to get them to consider the opposite point of view. Thus, beginning with "On the other hand . . ." in response to their assertions is often the most effective way to bring them down to earth and stimulate their thoughts.

Relating to the Libra Business Partner in the Long Run

Libra business partners are capable of commitment and long-term involvements as long as they feel appreciated and are fairly treated by you. The real problem can be their unremitting criticism and their penchant to fix things that are best left alone. Born tinkerers, Libras have the maddening tendency to create unfinished projects that they constantly return to, just when you thought things had finally been resolved and completed. Be patient with them in this respect, for they are unlikely to change. It is best that you resolutely move on to the next item on the agenda and allow them to catch up when they can.

Parting Ways with the Libra Business Partner

Breakups with Libra business partners often arouse ambiguous feelings. You are likely to feel both regret and relief at the same time. The breakup usually seems to favor Libra partners, since they invariably protect their own feelings well and have a curious way of rationalizing after the fact—not unlike the fox in Aesop's tale who, unable to reach the grapes, dismissed them as probably being sour anyway. Your feelings are another matter, and your Libra partner's concerns about you are likely to be almost non-existent. Realistic in breakup matters, Libras usually see the mutual advantages of such splits and will be fair in the division of property and profits—less so about debts, which may be left for you to pay.

The Libra Competitor

Libra competitors aim to win. Yet they can curiously undermine their own position and even betray ideals that were once important to them. They may become their own worst enemy. Libra competitors sometimes appear to be confident and self-assured while they secretly harbor grave doubts and insecurities. Most often these doubts are not about their products or services—which are most often of high quality—but about themselves, and at a deep level. Most Libras are often not aware of their insecurities, nor of themselves, and they proceed on their merry way without giving such matters much thought.

Countering the Libra Competitor

Libra competitors run hot and cold. Prone to go off on tangents, follow false clues, and misdirect their efforts, Libra competitors can frequently be countered by simply watching them make mistakes without commenting or even raising opposition to them. When on a roll, Libras must be countered directly or they will overwhelm you with their lucky efforts. One of the best ways to do this is to send out false clues about your plans while keeping your real plans hidden. This will encourage your Libra competitor to go off entirely on the wrong track in an effort to stop your advance.

Out-Planning the Libra Competitor

Libra competitors are very much creatures of habit who tend to do things the same way, particularly using methods that have been tried and true in the past. Thus the best way to out-plan them is to study their past campaigns and to pay particular attention to the specific approaches that guaranteed their greatest successes. By arousing their inner insecurities—chiefly through casting doubt on the efficacy of their favorite plans—you can leave them feeling helpless and alone. Indecision is Libra's greatest enemy, and if you can catch them off-guard while trying to make up their mind, you can usually breach their defenses decisively.

Impressing the Libra Competitor in Person

It is best not to try to impress Libra competitors, but rather to refuse to be impressed by them at all. Treating them in a brusque or cavalier fashion is the best way to disrupt their seemingly balanced aplomb. Once Libra competitors get you to react, they have you by the throat; to keep them from pushing your buttons, you must grow a whole new set of buttons that they cannot push so easily. Never lose your cool with Libra competitors, particularly in person, but remain self-composed and calm no matter what wild statements or shenanigans they indulge in. Their frustration will be apparent, and you can safely watch them getting tied up in knots.

Undercutting and Outbidding the Libra Competitor

The best way to undercut Libra competitors in bidding wars is by stimulating their self-doubt. Like a good poker player, you should bluff whenever you can, making them feel that the cards they are holding are not good enough to counter what is in your hand. Never show them what you are holding in reserve, but certainly alert them that something pretty powerful is there. Likewise, they can frequently be outbid by forcing their offers to rise until they finally drop out, usually at an early stage. Should they overreact and continue to bid high, you should drop out at the very last minute, leaving them holding the bag.

Public Relations Wars with the Libra Competitor

Since Libra competitors can be experts at public relations and advertising, you are likely to lose all-out wars with them. Sometimes it is better to let them dominate the field and overinvest in largely overkill campaigns, wearing them out financially. During this time you can put your money into marketing and sales, convincing wholesalers to buy and

STRENGTHS

Convincing

Fascinating

Distracting

WEAKNESSES

Misdirected

Insecure

Unaware

INTERACTIVE STYLE

Tough

Unyielding

Determined

push your products, rather than trying to win over the general public through expensive advertising campaigns. Do not emphasize the bad points about your Libra competitor's products but rather the good things about your own.

The Libra Competitor and the Personal Approach

Knowing facts about your Libra competitor's personal life can place powerful weapons into your hands. The best way to upset Libra competitors in direct confrontations is, after having remained objective and unruffled for a period of time, to suddenly come in with an indirect reference to an area of their personal lives, one they find particularly upsetting. If they fall for the bait and get terribly worked up, or just clam up and turn red in the face, you can immediately apologize and explain that such a reference wasn't intentional. This will only infuriate them further and undermine whatever objectivity they were striving for in their business arguments. They may even have to request an adjournment to pull themselves together.

Love

The Libra First Date

Libras are among the most seductive lovers in the zodiac. If they like you, they don't waste time going about their appointed task—to charm the pants off you right off the bat. Be prepared to be dazzled, and challenged, as it will be difficult to keep your hands off these highly attractive individuals. When on a first date with a Libra, you may feel like the luckiest person in the world. Part of their tremendous attractive power is that Libras make you feel good, even honored, to be with them. However, your feelings of "lucky me!" can quickly change to "poor me" in subsequent dates. It is best to try to maintain some objectivity during the first date with a Libra in order to avoid being swept off your feet.

Wooing and Picking Up the Libra First Date

You may think you are picking up the Libra first date when, in fact, the very opposite could be true. When Libras flash that green light, it may be terribly difficult to resist at least trying to pick them up. Wooing them can be a complex process during which you are wrapped ever more tightly in their encircling web. A quality of intrigue surrounds all first contact with Libras; a kind of complicity is implied in their attitude, suggesting that only you are important and that you are already intimate, without any physical contact whatsoever. Reality frequently flies to the four winds when under their spell.

Suggested Activities for the Libra First Date

You may be enjoying your Libra first date so much that you forget all about mundane matters such as making reservations. Although you may prefer to keep the date simple, indulging in conversations and congratulating yourself on your good luck, your Libra first date might be growing progressively bored with you. Therefore, it is important that you keep your eye on practical matters as well, particularly on providing suitable entertainment in return for the enjoyment you are being granted. A concert, a pleasant meal, a trip to a favorite spot—all will be appreciated by your Libra first date.

Turn-Ons and Turn-Offs for the Libra First Date

Libra first dates will require you to be enchanted. Just appreciating them is not enough. They need to see that sparkle in your eye and that entranced, open-mouthed admiration

STRENGTHS
Highly attractive
Seductive
Charming

WEAKNESSES
Misleading
Undermining
False

INTERACTIVE STYLE
Dazzling
Judgmental
Magnetic

that betoken your complete interest and involvement. Anything short of this will turn them off to the point that they feel they are just wasting their time on you. Whether or not they are turned on by you depends on a number of factors: how you look, how you talk, how you act, even how you smell. If you concentrate on these personal factors, rather than trying to impress them with money, you should be able to draw them in.

Making "the Move" with the Libra First Date

Making the first move on a Libra first date, and then being rejected in that effort, may be part of the usual scenario. It clearly shows the Libra that you are interested, but also puts them in the driver's seat. Be persistent in your efforts, since this is also expected. Eventually, they are likely to allow some contact, but they will always leave you hanging, hoping for more. Be extremely careful not to muss their makeup or rumple their hair, since one look in the mirror will brand you as the erring culprit. Knocking over a glass of water or wine on any part of them may put a quick end to your efforts and the evening.

Impressing the Libra First Date

Libras are impressed by status. Therefore, whom you know may be more important than what you know. Arranging a "chance" meeting with a well-known acquaintance could become the highlight of your Libra first date. Another plus could be when a manager or maître d' at a chic restaurant greets you by name upon your entrance. Staging a scene where a "fan" comes to your table for your autograph or just to say hello would be great if it happened spontaneously, but if obviously contrived this would only arouse suspicion and will likely backfire.

Brushing Off the Libra First Date

Showing disinterest in your Libra first date is usually sufficient to brush them off. When you lose interest in them, Libra first dates will automatically lose interest in you. By contrast, telling them in one way or another that you do not find them sexually attractive (even if phrased to show admiration of other qualities they have) can wound their egos and stimulate them to seduce you just out of spite. This kind of one-upmanship is a distinct trait of most Libras, for they like to be the ones who do the choosing and the rejecting.

The Libra Romantic Partner

If you are to be a Libra's romantic partner, you had better talk, act, and look good. Libras are very choosy when it comes to those they want to be seen with in public; they also expect to be treated well and shown a good time. You can expect rewards from Libras, but it will be clear that your constant appreciation is expected without any thought of receiving anything in return. That said, Libras are very giving in relationships, and those who have their love and full attention are indeed blessed. Problems arise when Libras become unhappy, and these difficulties should not be ignored but addressed as soon as possible, before things get out of hand.

Having a Discussion with the Libra Romantic Partner

Libras try to be fair, although they do not always succeed. In making the effort to be just they will often engage in lengthy conversations to explain or justify their behavior. They fully expect you to act in kind and want to know all about your motives, intentions, and goals after you have committed a transgression or sinned outright. After you argue your case, they will be the judge, and you should expect not only a verdict for wrongdoing but also that it will be carried out. Libras are not ones to make idle threats that they do not intend to follow through on.

Arguments with the Libra Romantic Partner

Libras are good with words. Also, because their judgmental minds generally see both sides of the story, they are not likely to be swayed by irrational, selfish, or one-sided points of view. Generally speaking, Libras will seek an equitable solution, one that is accepted favorably by both sides. If engaged in an argument with your Libra romantic partner, after a while you may get the idea that your presence is a bit superfluous, so well do they cover all the bases and consider all angles. Libras like to resolve arguments and leave no ends dangling.

Traveling with the Libra Romantic Partner

When traveling with a Libra, you will be expected to remain alert and attentive. Should you drift off into never-never land or let your attention stray to a new interest, you could suddenly be brought back to reality by an elbow in the ribs or a sharp squeeze of the hand. Although Libras are permitted to show interest in others and invite a third party to join your twosome, you are not. This is simply because their judgment is considered impeccable when it comes to other people, while their partner's is rated less than perfect. Making new friends is a Libra specialty, particularly while traveling, so you might as well get used to it.

Sex with the Libra Romantic Partner

Libras are very sexual creatures, so they like not only having sex but also talking about it. Not averse to rating their partners, they will discuss their own past exploits, make comparisons, and let you know how you are doing, even during the act. Libra romantic partners will examine and analyze every aspect of foreplay and intercourse. They are open to experimentation, being inventive in all sexual matters, but often consider it their duty to teach you how to do things. Their stamina is legendary, so between lovemaking and talking, don't expect to get much sleep when spending the night with your Libra romantic partner.

Affection and the Libra Romantic Partner

Libras are not exactly cuddly, but that doesn't necessarily mean they are cold, either. They exhibit a funny kind of affection that is not always immediately recognizable as such. Irony, wit, and sarcasm may be their way of showing you that they care, and of course you may not always appreciate their unique manner of expressing closeness or good feeling. When in the company of others, they can display affection that may be

(The Libra Romantic Partner)

STRENGTHS

Giving

Affectionate

Loving

WEAKNESSES

Unhappy

Needy

Selfish

INTERACTIVE STYLE

Selective

Expectant

Affectionate

interpreted as insulting, when in fact all they are doing is playing or kidding around. Accepting their gambit and returning the favor is generally taken in good fun.

Humor and the Libra Romantic Partner

Libras first and foremost want to have a good time. Since most of them are fun-loving creatures, you would expect Libra romantic partner to have a well-developed sense of humor. However, the jokes they tell and play are often at the expense of the other person. Libras particularly enjoy seeing others uncomfortable or knocked off-balance. (Although not really sadistic, they do have an appreciation of practical jokes.) Truth be told, Libras are happiest when everyone present joins in the fun.

The Libra Spouse

STRENGTHS
Socially adept
Supervising
Pleasing

WEAKNESSES
Overly controlling
Frustrated
Bizarre

INTERACTIVE STYLE
Directorial
Involved
Unflappable

Libra spouses are particularly good at arranging the social life of the family. Planning dinners, organizing get-togethers with friends and family, setting up holiday and vacation celebrations, and overseeing the relationships of their children are all Libra specialties. Generally speaking, however, Libra spouses are more interested in their own nuclear families than with those of their parents and siblings. In their homes they tend to be the boss and, therefore, the court of last resort when it comes to complaints and problems. Pleasing their spouses is very important, and if they are unable to do so, they can experience extreme frustration, often leading to depression.

Wedding and Honeymoon with the Libra Spouse

Every aspect of the wedding and honeymoon interests Libra spouses, who can become instantly dissatisfied if things are not done the right way. However, they can usually make quick adjustments in both their own and their spouse's behavior and move on to the next issue. Libras are easily irritated and bothered, so others should make an effort not to upset their hyperactive nervous systems, handling things themselves as much as possible rather than bombarding Libra with problems. Libra spouses love to let their hair down and finally let it all hang out, in both intimate and social situations.

Home and Day-to-Day Married Life with the Libra Spouse

Although not particularly good at, or interested in, cleaning, Libra spouses still expect their homes to look beautiful. So, as you can imagine, it is their partner's duty to keep it that way. Libra spouses feel they are making enough contributions, both aesthetic and financial, that they needn't take care of all the little maintenance tasks that pop up. They are very good at directing their spouses and constantly finding new tasks for them to perform, while occupying themselves with more important matters.

Finances and the Libra Spouse

Libra spouses are convinced they are very good with money. Because of this belief, they will usually appoint themselves to the positions of banker, financial advisor, and business brain, much to the consternation of their mates. In no area more than finances are Libra spouses likely to get out of control and head in entirely the wrong direction. Yet they refuse to recognize this fact and can bring the family to the brink of ruin through their unique combination of being both a spendthrift and a flawed economist while blithely ignoring or denying the consequences of their actions.

Infidelity and the Libra Spouse

Having a little fun on the side is not regarded as infidelity by most Libra spouses. Should you become terribly upset with their antics or threaten to leave, they are likely to simply laugh it off as having been of no consequence and to mildly berate you for having taken their actions so seriously. Libra spouses are not particularly good at hiding their deeds, and they can be painfully frank and open in relating them. Normally, Libra spouses do not require that their mates be strictly faithful, either, so long as they don't find out about dalliances.

Children and the Libra Spouse

Libras enjoy having a whole bunch of kids around the house, preferably their own, although their children's friends are usually both present and welcome. Wonderful at managing all sorts of social situations, Libra parents actually enjoy carting their offspring around and guaranteeing that they have a good time when engaging in a host of after-school activities. They are not always present at these, however, since their busy and often frenetic schedule necessitates having a host of babysitters, nannies, and above all a cooperative, obedient, caring, and sharing marriage partner.

Divorce and the Libra Spouse

As long as custody matters are thoroughly discussed, finances worked out, and mutual property fairly and justly divided, Libra spouses can enjoy the process of divorce (once emotional matters are under control). They often treat divorce the same way they handled the marriage, that is, by overseeing the whole thing down to the last detail. Keep an eye on them, however, when they take the lead, since their enthusiasm and occasionally bizarre ideas may confuse and complicate things, particularly if their legal representatives share their skewed point of view.

The Libra Lover

Libra lovers are particularly prone to suffer the fatal consequences of falling in love with love. Highly unrealistic in such matters, they experience the world of love as a church in which one pays tribute to that which is most holy. Consequently, they view their loved one as a divinity to be worshiped and adored. Libras could be considered the high priests and priestesses of this religion, and all the popular songs ever written about romance could be considered their Bible. Being chosen by such a lover brings a frightening amount of responsibility, but it is also accompanied by a great deal of pleasure and can be a quite enjoyable ego massage.

Romantic

Sensual

Ecstatic

Unrealistic

Fantasy-prone

Suffering

Convinced

Claiming

Overwhelming

Meeting the Libra Lover

The actual place or circumstance of meeting is not really important. It will usually assume the importance of a magical moment in the lives of two people, a lyric epiphany not to be forgotten. Falling in love at first sight is often the way it happens, with both parties equally smitten. However, the Libra lover almost immediately seizes the opportunity and takes the lead, being more of the expert in such matters. Libra lovers have few doubts about how to proceed and are happy to serve as the tour guide on this exploration of romance and love.

Location and the Libra Lover

Since Libras are usually the more romantic partner of a couple, they love to be carried away to your chambers, where they can be further enthralled. Even if your place is a wreck, they will view it as a kind of palace; nevertheless, it would be best to set aside at least a few minutes or hours to make it a bit more presentable. It is therefore recommended that you postpone your first meeting until you have a little more time to clean up and make your space more inviting. Libra lovers are also capable of bringing you home, but the well-known atmosphere will likely carry associations of past conquests.

Sex and the Libra Lover

Although Libra lovers are quite capable of waiting, their naturally ardent inclination is to get right down to it. Usually some innocent form of foreplay, or at the very least, affection, will begin on the way home, and by the time you two arrive, passions are often at the kindling point. Taking off the other person's clothes is the usual scenario, although torrid feelings may cause you both to undress yourselves on the way to the bedroom, leaving a trail of clothes behind. Libra lovers do not necessarily require the use of a bed, but sooner or later you will reach it and be able to relax in greater comfort for the duration of the experience.

Holding On to the Libra Lover

The question of how to hold on to these love-struck creatures is easily answered. As long as Libra lovers remain in love with you, they are unlikely to leave the relationship. Once they are cold to you, however, it will be impossible to hold on to such folks for very long. Should they meet the new love of their life when their feelings for you are waning (often inevitable under such circumstances), you may be rather rudely dumped. You could ask, in a bewildered fashion, "What did I do wrong?!" But the answer is usually the same: "Nothing."

Entertaining the Libra Lover

Love is usually entertainment enough for a Libra lover. However, such social creatures eventually want to be seen with you, and thus the whole relationship may be sacrificed to this need since it necessitates breaking with clandestine patterns and exercising discretion. Once the two of you appear in public, it is best to give it the spin of friendship to avoid hurting partners and family alike. Open displays of affection should be avoided, although secret smiles and an easy sensuality may tell the whole story anyway. Prepare for loose tongues to start wagging.

Breaking Up with the Libra Lover

This can happen pretty quickly, since you are unlikely to be either the first or the last in a seemingly endless parade of lovers. Should you be the one who decides you have had enough, you should expect sobbing, tears, protests, pleas, and finally displays of tempestuous anger, perhaps depleting your stores of glass and china, thus giving "breaking" up a whole new dimension. Libra lovers simply cannot believe or accept that anyone would be interested in spurning their affections, so they will probably find an excuse for your doing so. Your one source of consolation may be the ability to say ironically: "I was lucky enough to be one of many satisfied souls, however fleeting."

The Libra Ex

Libra exes are likely to leave their partners a bit bewildered and confused. Moreover, so subtly powerful is the net in which Libras catch their mates and lovers that it is difficult for these partners to let go of their fascination with the charms of the Libra ex and to escape intact. The Libra ex thus continues to exert powers over those they leave or outright reject far beyond the time of the breakup. Should Libra exes be the ones rejected, they usually have far more advanced recuperative powers, sometimes just treating their past relationship as nothing more than a hiccup in their busy love lives.

Establishing a Friendship with the Libra Ex

Libra exes are not averse to establishing friendships with their former spouses and lovers. They much prefer having the latter as friends rather than enemies, and they know how to smooth ruffled feathers and grease squeaky wheels in order to make things less awkward for all concerned. Libras can be highly diplomatic, weighing and balancing all the complex social and personal forces at work. Although their attitudes can be highly selfish, they are also able to empathize with others and understand their plight. However unsympathetic or cool they seem, Libras can never be accused of not understanding what is going on.

Issues of Getting Back Together with the Libra Ex

Caught in Libra's web—perhaps hurt and confused—a rebuffed individual might long to get back together. Most often this longing is neither realistic nor desirable, and Libra exes, being experts in the field, certainly know it. Unless they are in the mood for playing with the feelings of their exes, Libras will put a halt to any attempt reconcile and will do so with finality. This tendency to play, however, is quite marked in some Libras, who delight in miring their exes in the treacherous quicksands of love and longing.

Discussing Past Issues with the Libra Ex

Libras are always up for talking about the past, but their talk has a decidedly judgmental air, tending to evaluate and often condemn the actions of their ex-spouses and lovers. After one or two such sessions, their opponents have usually had enough, perhaps regretting ever raising past issues in the first place. Moreover, they may be left with the brunt

STRENGTHS
Self-assured
Self-sufficient
Knowing

WEAKNESSES
Hurtful
Confusing
Bewildering

INTERACTIVE STYLE
Entrancing
Magical
Desirable

of the anger and frustration stirred up by these discussions—negative feelings that do not disappear so quickly. Therefore, with Libras it is better to concentrate on positive memories only and to reminisce solely about the good times.

Expressing Affection to the Libra Ex

Libra exes frequently have no objection to sharing affection and even sex after a relationship is over. In doing so, they frequently ignore the feelings of the other person, who naturally looks upon Libra's emotional expressions as indicative of their openness to reuniting or a statement that the relationship is still ongoing. Libras are curious in that they can close the door and truly end a relationship, yet keep it alive for the other person. This sort of double standard frequently gets them in hot water and can make Libra exes the object of dislike, anger, or even hatred.

Defining the Present Relationship with the Libra Ex

This proposition is often difficult. Sometimes Libras are clear about their feelings and sometimes they are not, most often finding it difficult to make up their minds. Such ambiguity is not much fun to deal with, since you never really know where you stand. The fact that they do not either is certainly of little comfort. Confusion, misunderstanding, and deception are likely to reign, leading to uncertainty and chaos. The best attitude to take is a well-grounded one that does not shift or readjust with each new stance of the Libra ex.

Sharing Custody with the Libra Ex

Most Libra exes seek to be fair in matters of custody. They see the real value of children having two parents and also the benefits of cultivating the friendship rather than the enmity of their former spouses. Diplomatic to the extreme, Libra exes will be willing to compromise, but beneath this seemingly cooperative and charming air lies a stubborn determination to get their own way. Moreover, Libra exes are clever tacticians who know when to push and when to yield. They are also not above using their seductive charms to further their demands.

Friends and Family

The Libra Friend

"Friends to the end . . . and this is the end." Does this assessment of how Libra friends act ring true? Well, it is undeniable that Libra friendships are often limited in duration and can end quickly and unpredictably. Whether or not Libras are always responsible is not the point, but they do have a tendency to plunge into intense relationships and, at some point, begin to back out of them without informing the other party of their intentions. Most Libras feel they are acting fairly and making judgments that are realistic for all concerned. However, this does not make things easier for their friends, who may feel they have been harshly evaluated and unceremoniously dumped.

Asking for Help from the Libra Friend

Libra friends can be incredibly giving. Moreover, their generosity seems to be unconditional, until they want back whatever they have given or lent to you. Calling in a loan or loaned object can fall out of the blue. No use asking what you have done, since this behavior rarely has anything to do with your actions but more with the moods of your Libra friends. Libras often give generously of their skills, time, and energy, but, alas, their perfectionistic tendencies often attract them to work on things that are already running just fine.

Communication and Keeping in Touch with the Libra Friend

Libras tend to live in their own world, populated by their many friends and acquaintances. Therefore, one way to keep in touch is through this network they have created. Like a spider web, a tug on one of its strands will elicit reactions from all involved, particularly from the Libra at its center. Word gets around so fast that the Libra friend will contact you without fail or much delay. Forget about private communication, since Libra friends have a way of broadcasting the news to all within hearing range.

Borrowing Money from the Libra Friend

Libras will lend money when asked, if they have it. Sometimes they will even offer it unsolicited when they see the extent of your need. Frequently they do not look on it as a loan at all; they simply give without further definitions, conditions, or strings attached.

STRENGTHS
Intense
Involved
Evaluative

WEAKNESSES
Rejecting
Harsh
Withdrawing

INTERACTIVE STYLE
Quick
Unpredictable
Surprising

They also do not give to others with the idea of setting up a mutual credit line that they also can tap into one day. Normally, what they get in return is the simple satisfaction of having helped but also the points they have gained within their circle of friends for having saved someone's skin. Libra friends hate seeing those close to them looking destitute because it reflects badly on their own social status.

Asking for Advice from the Libra Friend

Helpful to the extreme in giving advice, Libra friends frequently provide very valuable counsel, and in hindsight they may be credited with saving the day. Libras are born judges and evaluators, able to look at both sides of the story and then render objective evaluations of even the most trying matters. Libras are often chosen as mediators, and many people trust them enough to submit to their arbitration, knowing that their binding decisions will be rendered dispassionately and without bias. Rarely will Libra friends seek advice from you, since they are wary of accepting opinions they do not think are as carefully weighed as their own.

Visiting the Libra Friend

Libra friends are very proud to show off what they have, including, of course, the color and design schemes of their living and work spaces. But they will rarely formally invite people over. This is due less to a need to be alone and more to wanting to have a lot of time to fully prepare for a major exhibition. Libras hate to be seen in anything but the best light, being particularly sensitive to criticism. Libra friends are more likely to hold a big party and show off their accomplishments, achievements, and style in one go, rather than sending out periodic invitations. Their greatest reward is hearing that everyone was talking about what a marvelous time they had.

Celebrations/Entertainment with the Libra Friend

Despite that friends constantly drop in, many Libras prefer to go out, either in public or to visit their many acquaintances. This also gives them a chance to show off their new clothes, jewelry, cologne or perfume, and the latest car or electronic gadget. Being left off the party list or ignored at social gatherings is the worst fate that can befall Libra friends, at least in the realm of get-togethers. Libras need to dazzle, seduce, and charm those they meet—in essence, to be the life of the party. Rarely are they happier than when standing at the center of a circle of admirers.

The Libra Roommate

Other than finding it difficult to get work done or have a moment's peace, the experience of having a Libra roommate can be enjoyable with rarely a dull moment. Libras are not away from their friends for very long, which means they do not come and go anywhere alone. Listening to the marching tread of this group on the stairs can become annoying pretty quickly, but there is little you can do but accept it and pray that the neighbors complain. During the rare times when friends are not accompanying them,

Libra roommates spend their time talking about themselves and their latest experiences. Either Libra roommates will make a more social person out of you, or you will wind up hiding in your room with the stereo turned up.

Sharing Financial Responsibilities with the Libra Roommate

Libras will share financial responsibilities when they are flush with cash, but they become desperate when they reach the limits of their checking accounts and max out their credit cards. Usually they will ask you to cover their share of the rent and utilities, promising to make it up to you next month. Truth be told, they usually manage to accomplish this. However, whenever that time of the month rolls around you may cringe a bit and feel nervous about asking when they do not offer to pay. Once you get used to the regular rhythm of their needs, matters do not appear so dire, but they do put you under constant pressure to have extra cash on hand.

Cleaning and the Libra Roommate

As a rule, Libras are quite tidy, if only because their aesthetic sense and desire to keep up appearances demand it. Libra roommates will pitch in and help with cleaning projects that involve two or three people, but if they had their druthers, they would prefer to simply do their share of the cleaning alone. Their own rooms are most often kept tidy, but not spectacularly neat. Libra roommates are the ones most likely to sweep dirt under the rug (telling themselves, "It's just for the time being"). Great procrastinators, Libra roommates have a habit of putting off cleaning projects for days and even weeks.

Houseguests and the Libra Roommate

Because of Libra's penchant for having friends over, you will often get the distinct idea that houseguests are perpetually present. Thus, a fine line exists between a visit and a protracted stay. Should you subtly suggest that perhaps your Libra roommate pay a bit more for food, shelter, and utilities, you may find yourself confronted with an accusation of being an antisocial party pooper. Libras are convinced that they are actually saving you money by providing constant free entertainment. The strain of having so much fun can become tiring after a while, leaving you longing for some peace and quiet.

Parties and the Libra Roommate

Libra roommates rarely need to throw parties, since there is usually one going on anyway. Predictably, soon after the entrance of Libra's group there will be calls for someone (perhaps you?) to go out for beer or wine or pizza. Although this relieves you of having to cook, it can have drastic consequences in terms of weight gain and sleep loss. You might just slip out to a rendezvous of your own, but being forced to do this night after night makes you doubt whether you are really living there at all. Your only hope may be sitting your Libra roommate down and creating a weekly planner that includes your activities, too.

Privacy and the Libra Roommate

Your privacy may not exist, whereas theirs is unnecessary. Closing and locking the door to your room becomes isolation rather than privacy, and ultra-social Libra roommates

(The Libra Roommate)

STRENGTHS

Entertaining

Enjoyable

Social

WEAKNESSES

Bothersome

Annoying

Distracting

INTERACTIVE STYLE

Involved

Participating

Managerial

and friends may even interpret this as an act of hostility. You may have to seek privacy elsewhere and simply accept the fact that you live in a train station or bus terminal. Of course, you may find that you are enjoying yourself, too, as long as you get a couple of nights a week alone (hopefully when your Libra roommate and company leave). You often ask yourself of Libra roommates: "Don't they ever want to be alone?" The answer is always the same: No.

Discussing Problems with the Libra Roommate

Libra roommates love to talk, but pinning them down to a discussion—particularly when the topic is your grievances—may be difficult. They will probably turn things around so that the discussion becomes centered on what they see as your lifelong problems, rather than ones of their making. To themselves, Libra roommates are just acting normally, expressing the human social impulse. You are the weirdo—grouchy, uptight, irritable, and hopelessly cut off from other human beings. After a while, you will realize that such discussions are just a waste of time. For the sake of self-preservation and survival, you must simply put your foot down, stick up for yourself, and, ignoring all insults and barbs, get things in order the way you need them to be.

The Libra Parent

STRENGTHS
Goal-oriented
Ambitious
Supportive

WEAKNESSES
Pushy
Stressful
Demanding

INTERACTIVE STYLE
Insistent
Involved
Evaluating

Libra parents are extremely sensitive about their social standing. They want their children to look good and associate with the "right" kind of children. Libra parents are very much involved in planning their children's careers; therefore, they take a keen interest in their educations, carefully monitoring grades and other academic parameters. Proud of their offspring when successful, Libras do not hesitate to take credit for their kids' achievements. They will make all sorts of sacrifices of their time and money to ensure that their children get ahead, including extracurricular activities that stress achievement.

Discipline Style of the Libra Parent

Libra parents are stern judges of their children's behavior, but only in matters that really count to them. Homework must be done and good grades achieved. However, they give their kids great latitude when it comes to play and having a good time. Rarely will they punish their children severely for coming in late or spending too much time online, watching TV, or playing video games. Notably sensitive about social standing, they will not hesitate to ground their kids for serious transgressions of normal social behavior or otherwise giving the family a bad name.

Affection Level and the Libra Parent

Libra parents love to cuddle their kids when they are young. Although this affection level decreases with age, they still usually have a kind word and a smile for their offspring, at least when things are going well. Libra parents will not consciously withhold affection as a punishment, but the level of their affection is usually directly proportional to the degree of cooperation of their children. Children who please their Libra parents on a regular basis can usually count on a corresponding expression of good feeling from them. Libra parents often enjoy expressing mutual affection along with their children toward pets and other small creatures.

Money Issues and the Libra Parent
The average Libra parent will see the need for a weekly allowance paid to each child. This will be in addition to lunch money, transportation, and, often, a clothing budget. Although their children are free to spend their allowance as they wish, Libra parents are likely to keep an eye on new purchases and expenditures in order to evaluate their positive or negative effects. Quite capable of diminishing or cutting down regular cash outlays, Libra parents make it abundantly clear that money should not be thrown away on useless or downright harmful pursuits.

Crises and the Libra Parent
Because they are excitable and demonstrative personalities, Libra parents frequently overreact and precipitate crises where none exist. Highly dramatic, they can easily display their emotions in public places, such as a crowded shopping center or in the street, causing great embarrassment for their children. Their kids soon learn to keep most upsetting matters to themselves, rather than share them with Libra parents, who are sure to overreact. For this reason, the children of Libra parents often develop as independent, self-sufficient, and capable people who infrequently ask for outside aid.

Holidays/Family Gatherings and the Libra Parent
Libra parents are in their element when it comes to such social events. Particularly good at planning, Libra parents can be counted on to arrange things down to the last detail and to guarantee that all present—particularly their own children—will have a great time. Libra parents are able to put themselves into other people's shoes and discover what gives them the greatest pleasure and also what turns them off. Consequently, family members look forward to special events such as birthdays, trips, and picnics or cookouts in which Libras play a significant role.

Caring for the Aging Libra Parent
As long as you are sure that aging Libra parents have a good friend or two close by, your worries can diminish considerably. Although Libra parents can be left on their own for a time, they will noticeably brighten and even improve health-wise through daily contact with friends of their own age. Libra parents do well in retirement communities in which they have their own home but also the opportunity to mix socially whenever they wish. Elderly Libra parents enjoy sharing experiences with their peers and are particularly fond of taking part in and contributing to special social events.

The Libra Sibling

STRENGTHS

Flamboyant

Sparkling

Contributing

WEAKNESSES

Attention-seeking

Sad

Sulking

INTERACTIVE STYLE

Bright

Active

Cheerful

Libra siblings demand attention not only from their parents, but also from their other siblings. Their way of doing so is usually through their intense activity and sparkling manner. Should they be deprived of attention, they will usually become even more flamboyant. If this does not work, they are likely to sulk and get mildly depressed. But with one eye on the other members of the family, they will usually succeed in being noticed, and ultimately appreciated. Libras love to make contributions to the group and revel in special family activities with their brothers and sisters.

Rivalry/Closeness with the Libra Sibling

Libras often engage in sibling rivalry. Although they enjoy locking horns with brothers and sisters, they normally do so in a playful manner. Once they have the attention of their parents, they are happy and content. Not ones to lord it over their fellow siblings, Libras like just to be noticed and to take part equally in most activities. They are not leaders or bossy individuals, for the most part (although they always make their voices heard), particularly when it comes to planning events and making decisions. Libras love being part of a big family and often openly show affection for their siblings.

Past Issues and the Libra Sibling

Libras are pretty good about forgiving and forgetting. Once they have dealt with the matter in their own way—countering or punishing an offender, passing judgment, finding a compromise solution—they are free to move on without harboring resentments. Libra siblings live very much in the present and do not have the time or inclination to dwell on past issues or be held back by them. They can have problems with brothers or sisters who harbor past resentments, however, and their own free-and-easy attitude can be misunderstood or condemned by more serious family members.

Dealing with the Estranged Libra Sibling

Libra siblings are not usually estranged from other family members unless they have been ostracized from the group. Therefore, if an estranged Libra sibling is to be brought back into the fold, it is the job of the brothers and sisters to make them feel welcome again. Rarely will Libra siblings seek to reject the rest of the family, and they will respond with relief when difficult issues can be settled and conflicts ended. Normally, contact should be made with an estranged Libra sibling through the brother or sister who took the lead in the rejecting process, and once this is done, things can move ahead smoothly toward normalization.

Money Issues (Borrowing Money, Wills, Etc.) and the Libra Sibling

Libras are born judges and mediators, always seeking a fair balance between the rights of all concerned. Usually taking the lead in the matters of inheritance and other issues connected with the death of the parents, they want to see thorny issues settled and a peaceful outcome prevail. Often other brothers and sisters recognize these abilities in their Libra siblings and turn to them to play a prominent role in such matters, or, at the very least, to give advice and counsel. When approached for loans, Libra siblings are generally open to lending money but will feel more comfortable when a mutually agreeable schedule is made for paying it back.

Holidays/Celebrations/Reunions and the Libra Sibling

Libra siblings love taking part in these activities and frequently take the lead in setting things up. They are particularly fond of reunions when they are older, since they sincerely miss their brothers and sisters living far away and love to see them every once in a while to catch up and reminisce about the old days. Spending holidays together is particularly enjoyable, and such moments often involve their own children and cousins having a great time. Celebrations find Libra siblings in their true social element, reveling in games, meals, and spirited conversation.

Vacationing with the Libra Sibling

Libra siblings are very fond of occasional vacations with their brothers and sisters. They look forward to such activities for months on end—dreaming, planning, and helping as the day draws near. They are easily disappointed, however, should the parents drop their original plans or scale them back because of financial problems. Nevertheless, they are inventive enough to rise to the occasion and help figure out viable alternatives. When older, Libra siblings are excellent organizers in summoning the clan to one spot from distant locations—coordinating available vacation days, travel plans, vacation rentals, and such.

The Libra Child

The Libra child is obedient but demanding. The single demand that Libra children invariably make is that they be the center of attention. Performers on life's stage, Libra kids want to be appreciated, acknowledged, recognized, and rewarded with the love and affection of their parents. In return, they have much to offer—continuous nonstop entertainment being only one of the many benefits of Libra children. Whether singing, dancing, drawing, writing, or devising new games and inventing novel activities, there is rarely a dull moment with a Libra child around. Their creative talents are particularly marked, but they must be kept under control lest they run out of hand.

Personality Development and the Libra Child

Libra children need the guidance and wisdom of their parents in order to develop properly. They have a marked tendency toward wildness and out-of-control behavior, and their parents will be doing them a disserve by giving them free rein to act as they please. With patient and understanding supervision, Libra children can be guided through the stages of growth that are particularly challenging to them and will win out in the end,

STRENGTHS

Entertaining

Creative

Inventive

WEAKNESSES

Needy

Uncontrollable

Self-centered

INTERACTIVE STYLE

Playful

Light

Sharing

evidenced by a well-balanced adult persona. The alternative can be disastrous: a child constantly teetering on the edge of chaotic behavior and anarchic to the extreme in challenging social authorities.

Hobbies/Interests/Career Paths for the Libra Child

No matter how introverted or isolated a Libra child may seem, you can be sure their destiny is ultimately connected with other human beings. Although this may ultimately be true of all of us, Libra kids have a special talent in social situations. Therefore, they are especially good as group leaders, teachers, and social workers of all types, including psychologists and counselors. Even when young, other children quite naturally come to them for help and advice. Being able to help their playmates, school chums, and acquaintances in this manner gives great satisfaction to Libra children.

Discipline and the Libra Child

For discipline, read *guidance*. Libra children do not react in a healthy way toward being punished and may suffer deep psychological trauma. Parents must never take the easy way of shouting at or hitting them; rather, use a quiet, patient, firm, but understanding manner seek to curb the wayward energies of their Libra children. The greatest gift a parent can give Libra children is to teach them the value of self-discipline. Once they grasp the concept that imposing order on themselves can carry them much further in the world, they will be firmly on the path of personal growth and career success.

Affection Level and the Libra Child

Like flowers turning toward the sun for light, Libra children turn to their parents for affection. Depriving them of it on a regular basis can cause them to become withdrawn and emotionally damaged. Likewise, Libra kids also need to be able to express affection toward their parents. Love—both giving and receiving—plays a major role in the daily lives of Libra children (more so than most children). Parents should beware of withholding affection from their Libra children as a punishment and also of using their power and favored status improperly in both physical and mental contacts.

Dealing with the Libra Child and Interactions with Siblings

This is a difficult one, since Libra children often indulge in intense sibling rivalry for the affection of their parents. Practically speaking, the easiest way to handle this problem is for a parent to pay attention to Libra children first; once it is apparent that they are satisfied, turn to their siblings. Since Libra children do, in fact, seek outright favoritism from their parents—and since they usually will not rest until they get it—their parents must find a way of giving attention without arousing the animosity of their other offspring. Of course, all the children should be treated equally whenever possible.

Interacting with the Adult Libra Child

In the best-case scenario, Libra children grow up to be well-balanced, responsible, and caring adults. However, the ones who are not fortunate enough to have had conscientious parental guidance are likely to run wild and be out of control a good deal of the time. Such Libra children can find their way in an adulthood marred by erratic behavior and a lack of stability in their lives. Interaction with these adult Libra children will involve great patience and understanding. It is best to allow them to come to you for guidance and help, rather than seeking to run their lives for them, which inevitably arouses insecurity and, ultimately, resentment.

Scorpio

BIRTHDATE **OCTOBER 23–NOVEMBER 21**

Scorpio is the fixed water sign, ruled by the dark planet Pluto and co-ruled by aggressive Mars. Like their namesake, Scorpios are best left alone since their capacity to inflict pain is pronounced. Scorpios can be very charming as well as aggressive, and their interest and abilities in the sexual sphere are well-known. Like Virgos, Scorpios lead hidden lives and often cultivate an air of mystery around them. Fatally attracted to money and power, Scorpios must learn the lessons of gentleness and kindness to others.

Work

SCORPIO
October 23–November 21

The Scorpio Boss

Scorpio bosses are serious individuals—hard-driving and dedicated to the company's success. Consequently, they set extremely high standards for their employees and expect them to give their very best every day. Scorpios do not accept excuses for shoddy or slipshod work, preferring a frank admission of failure over attempts to explain it away. Powerful and dominant, Scorpio bosses sit in the driver's seat at all times and do not allow their colleagues to question or undermine their authority. When reporting to their superiors or owners of the business, they seek to protect their own employees from unreasonable demands and insist on adequate and often abundant reward for their workers' dedicated efforts.

Asking the Scorpio Boss for a Raise

It is best to wait for Scorpio bosses to raise the subject, since they have an eye out for deserving efforts of their employees. Sometimes this can be done indirectly in a normal conversation, when the subjects of hard work and reward surface in dialogue. Never directly ask Scorpio bosses for a raise—allow them to mull things over once the matter has been mentioned. Normally, Scorpio bosses will get back to you within a couple weeks to a month, after which a short reminder can be considered, since they usually do have a lot on their minds.

Breaking Bad News to the Scorpio Boss

Best to tell it as it is, straight up, without trying to sugarcoat the pill. Although Scorpio bosses have notoriously bad tempers, even violent ones, they will only be angrier if you attempt to give things an unwarranted positive spin. Ultimately, no matter who is at fault, most Scorpio bosses will ultimately take responsibility for what happened, and when reporting to their superiors, they will generally shift the blame away from the employee(s) responsible and onto their own shoulders. Truly, they do feel as if all major failures ultimately rest with them.

STRENGTHS
Well-directed
Protective
Powerful

WEAKNESSES
Inflexible
Unforgiving
Harsh

INTERACTIVE STYLE
Serious
Hard-driving
Dominant

Arranging Travel and/or Entertainment for the Scorpio Boss

Scorpio bosses like good food and comfortable, even luxurious accommodations. These are likely to put and keep them in a good mood throughout the business trip, given that other matters go reasonably well. Notoriously late for appointments, Scorpio bosses may leave you to entertain a client or prospective business partner for quite some time before they finally show up for the meeting. This is a not-so-subtle manner that Scorpios frequently adopt to show their power in controlling the situation, at times delivered like a manifesto. Needless to say, as their assistant or companion on such a trip, you should never seek to outshine the master.

Decision-Making and the Scorpio Boss

There is nothing ambiguous about Scorpio decisions, but they often take time to appear. Not quick to make up their minds, Scorpio bosses like having a long time to chew matters over and make well-thought-out decisions. Never rush them in this process because it will not work and can also arouse their irritation and aggression. Once their mind is made up and their decision stated, it is most unlikely that they will ever change or go back on their word. Yet, curiously, they may leave themselves a secret loophole or way out. Holding a plan B (or even C) in reserve is a typical Scorpio trait, even though it is rarely implemented.

Impressing and/or Motivating the Scorpio Boss

Scorpio bosses are particularly impressed by efforts that are made not out of a desire for bonuses or other rewards, but simply because they are demanded by the work. Those who regularly go that extra mile are likely to impress Scorpio bosses the most. Conversely, Scorpio bosses are usually turned off by flamboyant individuals who seek to hog the spotlight and show off their talents. It is often quiet, unassuming employees who succeed in impressing Scorpios most through their untiring, unselfish, and faithful attitude.

Making Proposals and/or Giving Presentations to the Scorpio Boss

Usually Scorpio bosses already have their minds made up on most subjects. Therefore, your presentation will either reinforce what they already know and believe or contradict it. If the latter is the case, be prepared for an unremitting battle with no ground given; if it's the former, your Scorpio boss may give a nod to your efforts without seriously acknowledging them. It is usually through disagreement with Scorpio bosses rather than agreement with them—in the heat of fierce intellectual combat and interactive repartee—that truly useful ideas and approaches to problems emerge. All of the foregoing urges you to be well prepared, but also ready to fiercely defend your point of view.

The Scorpio Employee

Scorpio employees will get the job done when left to work on their own. They have their own ways of doing things, which are not necessarily shared or understood by their peers. Scorpio employees are likely to appear secretive, not being overly social or anxious to reveal much about their methods or their personal lives. Loyal to the company, Scorpio employees will always do their best to go beyond the normal call of duty. They get aggressive only when unduly or unfairly attacked or criticized, at which point they become formidable adversaries.

Interviewing and/or Hiring the Scorpio Employee

Scorpio interviewees are not ones to blow their own horn. In fact, interviewers may have to drag personal information out of them, beyond what is stated in their CV or resume. Prospective Scorpio employees are not overly curious about working conditions, but usually they will have a few criteria that must be met. Once they are satisfied about the reliability and security of the job they are being considered for, they will show more willingness to be open about themselves but will still hold back a great deal. Rarely will Scorpio interviewees misrepresent themselves or overestimate their abilities.

Breaking Bad News to or Firing the Scorpio Employee

Scorpio employees can become quite aggressive when accused of wrongdoing or threatened with firing, particularly when they have given their all in the daily discharging of their duties. They are able to take bad news, so employers and colleagues should not beat around the bush but instead present it straight out. Scorpios will usually be honest enough to accept or deny their degree of responsibility, but frequently they will remain quiet rather than engage in spirited arguments. Able to say what they have to convey in few words, Scorpios feel no great need to justify their behavior. Threats of being fired usually do not frighten or intimidate them.

Traveling with and Entertaining the Scorpio Employee

Because of their love of privacy, Scorpio employees most often prefer traveling alone. If it is absolutely necessary for them to travel with a companion, then the other person should not chatter or otherwise disturb Scorpios' introspective, quiet demeanor. Scorpio employees are easily irritated when traveling with others and can characteristically become silent and moody. When entertaining the Scorpio employee, it is best to inquire about their preferences beforehand and perhaps even do some research on the subject. Their closest colleagues should be able to yield information on the Scorpio employee's likes and dislikes.

Assigning Tasks to the Scorpio Employee

Scorpio employees tend to be specialists who perform certain tasks very well. They are not really fond of diversifying or filling the role of multitaskers, so it is best to examine their work history and consult them directly to find out if they are indeed the right person for the task at hand. Such research will be time well spent, because once Scorpio employees are put in the right niche, they will perform at a high standard in most cases. Conversely, if they are given the wrong job, you can expect a less than sterling performance, marked by bouts of discouragement and even depression. It is generally best not to make them part of a big group and whenever possible to leave them alone to complete their tasks.

(The Scorpio Employee)

STRENGTHS

Loyal

Committed

Discreet

WEAKNESSES

Hidden

Isolated

Aggressive

INTERACTIVE STYLE

Self-sufficient

Secretive

Reserved

Motivating or Impressing the Scorpio Employee

Scorpio employees are best motivated by having doable jobs well within their realm of competence. They like the security inherent in doing a job they can handle and not being overly challenged or stressed. Do not make the mistake of offering them a salary hike to complete work they are not particularly interested in doing. Scorpio employees will be impressed with your understanding of their needs and your refusal to subject them to doing work for which they are not suited, despite pressure from the bosses upstairs. If you protect their interests, they will go that extra mile for you.

Managing, Directing, or Criticizing the Scorpio Employee

Once instructed, Scorpio employees can be left to do their work on their own. They react very poorly to your constantly peering over their shoulders and are capable of delivering high-quality work on time without being continually checked—which only makes them nervous and negatively influences their performance. Scorpio employees can accept criticism if it is offered in the right way and in the right spirit. Highly sensitive emotionally, Scorpios should never be threatened, cajoled, or blamed in a direct manner; it is best to be as objective as possible in dealing with them. Even so, you will have to be careful not to offend, so pick your words carefully to avoid disturbing their feelings and eliciting an angry or aggressive response.

The Scorpio Coworker

Scorpio coworkers gravitate toward helping out with the most difficult and challenging tasks. No strangers to pain, Scorpios know how serious it can be to fall victim to circumstances and, worst of all, to one's own fears and anxieties. Rather than trying to comfort coworkers in need, Scorpios jump right in, roll up their sleeves, and get to work. Scorpio coworkers do not scare easily, nor are they daunted by seemingly insurmountable objects and complex tasks. Their interest is roused more by the challenge of the impossible than by the ease of routinely doable projects.

Approaching the Scorpio Coworker for Advice

Scorpio coworkers are able to give advice in just a few sentences. Normally, they will take time to chew over your words and then get back to you with their considered opinion. They should not be rushed or pressured in this process. Often their advice is based on their own experiences and those of coworkers in the company. Scorpios have long memories, remembering important details that others may have forgotten over the years. Thus they are able to access highly pertinent information. However, their verbalskills are not always their strongest suit, so listen carefully to understand what they are trying to tell you.

Approaching the Scorpio Coworker for Help

If Scorpio coworkers are convinced of both your suffering and their abilities to alleviate it, they will help you to the full extent of their abilities to do so. This help will not take the form of empty promises, either. Whether the required involvement is physical or financial, they are ready to put it on the line if they believe in your cause. A funny blend of idealist and pragmatist, crusader and empiricist, Scorpios can offer penetrating analysis and, at the same time, draw up battle plans for attacking and solving problems. Once committed to helping you, Scorpio coworkers will not rest until you are once more on top of the situation.

Traveling with and Entertaining the Scorpio Coworker

It is recommended that you travel primarily with those Scorpios you are already close with. Traveling with Scorpio coworkers who are also friends can be great fun, but adjusting to the demanding personal preferences and tastes of one you do not know at all can prove to be a less than enjoyable experience. Should you choose to dominate unknown Scorpios, you will meet resistance and often refusal to obey your commands, or even complete silence and a black mood. Should Scorpio coworkers take the lead, you may find yourself unable to enjoy their preferences in food, lodging, and transportation, trapped in a difficult, inescapable situation.

The Scorpio Coworker Cooperating with Others

Scorpio coworkers are not known for their cooperative behavior. Strong-minded, they usually have their own ideas about how things should be done. No amount of cajoling or threatening is likely to budge them one iota. That said, they can work smoothly with others, but only if they truly believe in the efficacy and justification of the chosen approach. Scorpio coworkers are not at all reticent about voicing their opinions if asked, but they do not easily reveal their true inner thoughts. Valuable members of any group, they should be consulted and their opinions given serious consideration before they are asked to serve in a team effort.

Impressing and Motivating the Scorpio Coworker

It is very difficult to motivate Scorpio coworkers—most often, attempting to do so is counterproductive. These powerful individuals must be self-motivated, a process best aided by accepting them as they are and assessing objectively whether their contributions could be suitably applied to the task at hand. Moreover, Scorpio coworkers are not easily impressed; they often take the attitude that they or their methods could accomplish things more effectively. Nor are Scorpio coworkers frequently conceited or overreaching; they have usually made a realistic assessment of their own abilities and know whether they can get results.

Persuading and/or Criticizing the Scorpio Coworker

Because Scorpio coworkers are tough customers, your criticism usually just bounces off. When hit in a sensitive spot, however, they are capable of lashing out in fury, giving their judges far more than they bargained for. Should they initially be opposed to your point of view, Scorpio coworkers can be persuaded to your cause over time, with patience and persistence. Change does not come easily to most Scorpios, but because of their tendency to mull things over in private, they will give your opinions and attitudes much thought. Whether or not they respond to your constructive criticism or attempts to persuade, you can be sure they will not ignore or forget your assertions.

(The Scorpio Coworker)

STRENGTHS
Helpful
Confrontational
Energetic

WEAKNESSES
Overbearing
Pain-ridden
Suffering

INTERACTIVE STYLE
Supportive
Sympathetic
Challenging

The Scorpio Client

STRENGTHS

Well-directed

Purposeful

Helpful

WEAKNESSES

Stressed

Demanding

Picky

INTERACTIVE STYLE

Straight-forward

Unambiguous

Commanding

Scorpio clients know exactly what they want and are insistent about getting it from you. If you want their continued business, you had better be able to satisfy them down to the last detail. A comprehensive plan and checklist are indispensable. Scorpio clients will not breathe down your neck as long as you supply them with regular progress reports. Nor are they in much of a rush; generally speaking, they prefer you to be thorough and take your time in implementing their requests. There will be no doubt, however, about who is the boss, and you will be expected to follow their requests and orders to a T.

Impressing the Scorpio Client

Scorpio clients are most impressed by your past performance as an individual and of your company as a whole. Before they invest their hard-earned cash in one of your products or services, they will want to examine your track record in detail. They will not necessarily accept the figures you submit without doing their own private research to corroborate them. Furthermore, they will have personal conversations with those who have worked with you before to verify your reliability. Without a strong history of success, you are unlikely to impress Scorpio clients or win their business.

Selling to the Scorpio Client

Once your business background has passed the test, you will be faced with the job of convincing the Scorpio client that your product or service is the very best. Heavily into quality, Scorpio clients are impressed not so much with your assets or share price on the big board but with what you can offer them. Not particularly seeking cheaper prices per se, Scorpio clients are willing to invest extra money if you can guarantee both quality and performance. Scorpio clients are security oriented, unlikely to gamble or take chances when it comes to production and meeting deadlines.

Your Appearance and the Scorpio Client

Scorpio clients want reliability and dependability from you. Therefore, your appearance should be conservative and reassuring, without any weird or unusual touches that could irritate them. Quite likely, their appearance will also be quite traditional and reserved, although quality-oriented. Should you be able to match them in these respects, you will already be building bridges of commonality and trust between you. The sooner the concept of "us" replaces the polarity of "me and you," the better. Things are likely to run more smoothly once this solidarity is established and a common approach is adopted.

Keeping the Scorpio Client's Interest

As long as you continue to produce measurable results and preserve the believability of your predictions for the future, Scorpio clients will continue giving you their business. This is about as far as they go, since they rarely show interest in you or what you are doing. Trust is number one. Once you earn that, they will not bother you by showing continual curiosity that involves asking questions or doing research to check up on your progress. Therefore, you should feel relieved when Scorpio clients show disinterest—accept it as a compliment, and do not seek to attract their attention.

Breaking Bad News to the Scorpio Client

Realists first, Scorpio clients can handle bad news. If you have established solidarity and trust with them, you can both deal with adverse developments in a spirit of mutual cooperation, immediately seeking to rectify matters through common efforts. This feeling that "we" need to find a solution and that "we" can handle it is much preferred over a sharp order or threat from a Scorpio client to set things right by yourself. Should it come to that point, however, Scorpios can be ruthless, even vindictive, threatening legal action and other reprisals. Working on building mutual trust and respect early on in your business relationship is essential to avoid conflict.

Entertaining the Scorpio Client

Scorpio clients will be most impressed by the best food, the best entertainment, and, in general, the highest quality you can afford. However, this does not mean throwing your money around, since you are likely to be judged a fool if you present something as superior that is in fact subpar. Spending money judiciously at a restaurant or club can be an indication of how economically astute you are in business dealings with your Scorpio client. If they have a good time, Scorpio clients can be very generous in return, wanting to reciprocate by picking up the tab the next time you meet socially.

The Scorpio Business Partner

Scorpio partners are good at assuming responsibilities, but you must be careful that they do not take over completely. Their competence is usually high, but so is their interest in running the show. Depending on the strength of your own personality, Scorpio partners can often overwhelm you and assume command. This in itself is not a bad thing, particularly if you are a more passive type. But more active personalities may find themselves in conflict with Scorpio partners and thereby waste a lot of time and energy that could be used for the partnership's benefit.

Setting Up the Business Partnership with Scorpio

More prudent than mistrustful, Scorpios generally feel it is in the mutual interest of you both to draw up a detailed contract that foresees problems and addresses what happens if and when things go wrong. This agreement should be both comprehensive and clear. If you have doubts about your Scorpio partner's dominating attitudes, your interests and active participation in the partnership should be guaranteed in such an agreement. Once such a contract is drawn up by a legal representative, signed by both parties, and registered, it may never be necessary to refer to it again.

Tasking with the Scorpio Business Partner

Before beginning each project, the roles played by both of you should be carefully worked out. Your strengths and weaknesses should be examined and the division of labor judiciously made to guarantee success. Once tasks are assigned, both partners should guard their provinces assiduously and not allow the other's activities to overlap their own.

STRENGTHS
Responsible
Experienced
Well-directed

WEAKNESSES
Overwhelming
Insensitive
Dictatorial

INTERACTIVE STYLE
Dominant
Commanding
Self-assured

Touching base daily is not usually required, but every two weeks or so a meeting should be held to assess the progress of the project and evaluate whether or not changes need to be made. Scorpio partners can procrastinate in some important areas while investing needless energies in others, so it is best to keep an eye on them.

Traveling with and Entertaining the Scorpio Business Partner

It is generally best for each of you to take turns representing the company in various meetings, with emphasis on your own areas of expertise. Traveling with your Scorpio business partner is not recommended in most cases and not necessary; greater progress can usually be made with one of you staying at the home base or pursuing other projects independently. Scorpios are best entertaining themselves and traveling alone, since their tastes and preferences are so strongly marked and their cooperative spirit on such ventures so limited. Adopting a secondary and deferential role to your Scorpio partner day after day on the road can prove quite trying.

Managing and Directing the Scorpio Business Partner

Scorpios cannot easily be directed. Managing their prodigious energies and strong points of view is also difficult. Rather than wasting time in such fruitless endeavors, it is best simply to come to some binding agreements initially and to hold your Scorpio business partners to them. By contrast, you may have to fight their dictatorial tendencies in attempting to manage you, though their advice and guidance can often be helpful and reassuring. However, if they make egregious errors and refuse to recognize them as such, confrontation may be unavoidable in order to avoid disaster.

Relating to the Scorpio Business Partner in the Long Run

Scorpio business partners are usually in for the long haul. They are capable of upholding their end of a bargain or corporation for many years. However, they may have issues with the way you handle things and are rarely shy about voicing them. Should you refuse to listen to such criticism, they will usually intensify their efforts until you do. Confrontational by nature, Scorpios are not easily avoided, and your normal avoidance mechanisms will be severely challenged. If you have complaints about their methods, behavior, or performance in general, you should raise them at the right moment and in a respectful manner. Otherwise they will be perceived as attacks to be defended against, usually through forceful counterattacks.

Parting Ways with the Scorpio Business Partner

The initial contract that you should have signed with your Scorpio partner will have to be followed to the letter. Normally, such issues as debts, real estate property, copyrights, division of assets and profits, and the like will be covered. At any expense, try to avoid arguments and all-out pitched battles involving acrimony and blame, since Scorpio total aggression is not a pleasant prospect to face. As long as things remain objective, polite, and agreeable, the dissolving of a partnership can be accomplished to both parties' satisfaction. Remember that Scorpios have long memories and are extremely tenacious, so it is best to settle all issues in the present and not leave important issues unsettled.

The Scorpio Competitor

Scorpio competitors do not like to lose. Their desire to come out on top is so strong that they are capable of unethical behavior, but only in the most extreme cases. This is because the primal joy they experience in defeating their opponents is fully experienced only when they win in a fair fight. Scorpio competitors feel at home and are actually relaxed in the heat of battle, which frequently unlocks their most abundant energies. Strategy is their forte, for a true Scorpio will never enter a conflict without meticulous, thorough, and crafty planning.

Countering the Scorpio Competitor

Scorpio competitors make tough opponents. Because of their aggressive nature, it is important to know how to oppose them, otherwise they can overwhelm you. Particularly good at waiting, they can come at you with lightning speed, after which they again adopt a defensive stance. It is this superb combination of offense and defense that makes them so difficult to counter. First and foremost, remain calm and do not expose your weak spots through hasty action. Second, be wary of falling for tricks and traps. Third, prepare for a long, tough fight rather than a quick, easy win. Match their thorough preparation with your own.

Out-Planning the Scorpio Competitor

In seeking to out-plan a Scorpio competitor, you will be engaging in a difficult struggle since planning is one of their fortes. Initially, give equal attention to your historical strengths and their traditional weaknesses. Find loopholes in their approach and carefully analyze the setbacks they have suffered in the hopes of revealing their Achilles heel. Build your own strengths to the point that you are sure of your abilities to wage a protracted battle. Only then should you turn to an examination of their greatest strengths (allowing you to anticipate their modes of attack and defense) and attend to your own historical vulnerabilities, which Scorpio competitors are sure to seek out.

Impressing the Scorpio Competitor in Person

Only approach your Scorpio competitors from a position of strength. Playing nice or using the ploy of appearing clueless will not fool most of them. They have a good nose for sniffing out dissimulation and tricks, rarely falling for traditional traps. True students of the art of war, they will be most impressed by a relaxed, quiet, and confident manner. Once they acknowledge you as an equal, you will have gained their respect, which will push them in the direction of a fair fight and diminish their need to use underhanded tactics. Your physical presence should not be overly intimidating, but seductive methods can be carefully employed as long as you remain aware of their expertise.

Undercutting and Outbidding the Scorpio Competitor

Scorpio competitors are good bluffers, but they rarely come to the bargaining table without ammunition in reserve. In outbidding them, you will find it difficult to read their intentions. Since they are so secretive, they frequently hide their real motives as well as the depth of their pockets. The best way to undercut them is to arouse their anger and

STRENGTHS
Fighting
Meticulous
Crafty

WEAKNESSES
Unethical
Cruel
Hurtful

INTERACTIVE STYLE
Thorough
Aggressive
Battling

knock them off balance. Although flailing Scorpio aggressors can be frightening in any confrontation, they leave openings through which they can be undercut and their powers sapped. However, they can be even scarier when their approach is cold-blooded—that intimidating look in their eye is the signal that you had better back off or face their full, well-directed fury.

Public Relations Wars with the Scorpio Competitor

Public relations campaigns are not usually Scorpio competitors' forte. Should it come to all-out war, their normal strengths of advanced planning and ruthless execution should be expected, but most Scorpios show uncertainty when asked to measure the public pulse. Although personally seductive, most Scorpio competitors do not know how to seduce the general public or to beat an opponent who understands what people like. Too often Scorpio competitors follow fixed rules and do not show the flexibility needed to counter your newest, scintillating, and varied approaches.

The Scorpio Competitor and the Personal Approach

Scorpios are dangerous opponents in the personal area. Because they understand their own motives and feelings so well, they are able to alternately attack and seduce their opponents, frequently leaving them helpless and bewildered. When securing results, their personal charm and magnetism can be employed in a very cool and calculated fashion. Moreover, they have a reputation for treachery that should not be forgotten. Watch out especially when they seem to be disinterested and let up in their efforts. It must have been a Scorpio who said: "Revenge is a dish best served cold."

Love

The Scorpio First Date

Although highly sexed, passionate people, Scorpios are quite capable of keeping themselves under control. Undeniably seductive, they will work their particular brand of magic in a subtle manner, which will not arouse alarm or concern. Yet they are always prepared to go further if this is truly your desire. Scorpios want to have a good look at you but are particularly prudent about revealing their true personalities and showing their intentions. You should make it clear that give and take is important in this area and that interaction is reciprocal, rather than a one-way street.

Wooing and Picking Up the Scorpio First Date

Scorpios are likely to be the ones to do the picking up and wooing. Even the least aggressive Scorpios will generally give the signal for you to proceed; thus they remain in control while seeming overtly passive. Scorpios are not shy about suggesting that a time be set for your initial rendezvous, but often propose a less public and more private place where they can get to know you better. Subsequent wooing by Scorpio first dates follows an inevitable pattern of subtle insistence that you meet again—on a regular basis if they really like you.

Suggested Activities for the Scorpio First Date

Scorpios are fond of quiet dinners in subdued settings. Lovers of good food and particularly attracted to exotic dishes, they will enjoy ethnic restaurants that feature such fare. Do not interpret their quiet or reserved demeanor as disinterest, since many Scorpio first dates enjoy letting things develop slowly. Not being in a rush can be misinterpreted as shyness, when in fact most Scorpio first dates are quite self-assured. Masters of the art of seduction, Scorpios know how to wait and not push, spinning their seductive webs in a most captivating and charming manner.

Turn-Ons and Turn-Offs for the Scorpio First Date

Most Scorpio first dates do not enjoy being questioned about themselves. If they deflect or ignore your personal questions, you should avoid the subject entirely. Extremely sensual, Scorpio first dates are turned on by fragrances, occasional touches or "acci-

STRENGTHS

Passionate

Controlled

Sexual

WEAKNESSES

Unrevealing

Prying

Secretive

INTERACTIVE STYLE

Prudent

Subtle

Observant

dental" close brushes, muted sexual innuendo, and low-key inviting glances. Although they are undeniably physical, they are often most excited by sophisticated behavior and turned off by not-so-subtle suggestions and actions. Showing respect for their silence and privacy, and not intruding on their reserved demeanor, is definitely a turn-on.

Making "the Move" with the Scorpio First Date

Generally Scorpio first dates will maneuver things so that you make the first move, no matter how slight it may be. Invariably, they will signal you to go further if they are turned on, but they do not expect aggressive behavior in return. Once Scorpio first dates are fully aroused, however, their full-blown passionate nature will emerge and leave no doubts about their extremely sexual orientation. Still waters run deep, and you had better be prepared for the all-out sexual expressions that Scorpios are capable of once you flash a fully illuminated and unambiguous green light.

Impressing the Scorpio First Date

Scorpio first dates will be especially impressed by your appearance. They are highly drawn to good-looking and sensuous individuals, even when they are not so attractive themselves. The appealing qualities of Scorpios grow on you, but they expect to be bowled over or, at the very least, highly intrigued by you from the outset. Scorpio first dates are quick to pick up on any suggestion that you are interested in furthering intimacy with them, but remember that their lack of immediate response could be a tactic, for they pride themselves on keeping their feelings under control at will.

Brushing Off the Scorpio First Date

Scorpio first dates are not easy to brush off if they find you highly attractive. They are persistent in pursuing their interests and may even have a fetish about never giving up. Making up a story about having a steady relationship usually just serves to stimulate them even more. They are challenge-oriented, so all roadblocks you throw up will invite a redoubling of their efforts. Often the best way is to refrain from outright refusal, but gradually scale things down over time before dropping them for good.

The Scorpio Romantic Partner

Scorpio romantic partners can be both jealous and possessive. They fully expect your unilateral involvement with them, and at the first sign of your interest in someone else, they are likely to either lash out in anger or become silent, withdrawn, and depressed. Scorpios figure that because they give a lot they should also get a lot, and that you are lucky to have them. Beyond that, for Scorpios love is a territorial thing—they just don't like someone messing with their chosen one. Also protective, they have a notable interest in the well-being of their loved ones and can show quiet concern for them in times of illness and need.

Having a Discussion with the Scorpio Romantic Partner

Many Scorpios are careful about what they say. They are quite aware that words have power and can be used against them in later discussions. No matter what they choose to discuss, you can be sure that, like an iceberg, there is a great deal of unspoken material lurking beneath the surface. Scorpios are also fond of using innuendo rather than direct statements, particularly when applying pressure. Thus their threats are most often veiled, but they should be taken seriously. Scorpios carry through with their intentions.

Arguments with the Scorpio Romantic Partner

Most Scorpios will not choose to start arguments, but once involved they can be counted on to finish them. For them an argument is just another form of battle (or in extreme cases, war) that must be won at all costs. Consequently, picking arguments with Scorpios is not advised, since the emotional fallout can be so severe. Keeping discussions from becoming arguments involves being sensitive and extremely aware, thereby keeping the level of invective under control. One way to prevent arguments from getting too heavy is to kid around and inject humor in the form of competitive wordplay and witty remarks that are not to be taken seriously.

Traveling with the Scorpio Romantic Partner

Scorpios are good at making plans and arrangements beforehand but do not always choose to do so. A curious kind of passivity in this area may emerge, forcing you to take initiative and put your preferences on the line. This can result in Scorpio's merciless criticism of your choices, using their well-honed sarcasm and irony, even to the extreme of belittling you. For these reasons, it is best if you insist that they take a more active role in planning a trip in the first place, thereby giving you some ammunition should disputes arise on your travels.

Sex with the Scorpio Romantic Partner

Scorpios have a notorious reputation for sexual interest, involvement, and performance. Frequently, they pride themselves on it, but not openly. Usually it manifests as a quiet self-confidence in sexual matters; they have the knowledge that they can come up with whatever their partner requires. Nor are they reticent to express their own wishes, which are well defined and frequently demanding. Their unavoidably unconventional and even kinky attitudes toward sex should not be surprising. Scorpios love to explore the highways and byways of the sexual terrain, leaving little to the imagination of their partners.

Affection and the Scorpio Romantic Partner

More passionate than sensuous, most Scorpios choose to fully express their feelings in stormy sessions rather than indulging in touchy-feely, casual contacts. Consequently, they are not overly cuddly or affectionate types. They often express affection through making jokes or even hurling insults, with a twinkle in their eyes. You are supposed to know that this is, in fact, affection, and Scorpios expect you never to be offended by it. They can go pretty far in this direction, and unless you kid them back or just keep cool, you are likely to feel terribly insulted and lose it, which could just arouse more derision.

(The Scorpio Romantic Partner)

STRENGTHS
Caring
Protective
Interested

WEAKNESSES
Jealous
Possessive
Angry

INTERACTIVE STYLE
Involved
Serious
Self-contained

LOVE

Humor and the Scorpio Romantic Partner

Scorpio humor is rather strange in that it often involves making fun of the other person. The wisecracks or other witty remarks they make are pointed and leave little doubt about whom and what they are directed at. Once Scorpios make such a statement they are likely to inflict further hurt (unintentionally, of course) by giving a provocative smile or even a full-throated chuckle or outright laugh. The trick is not to react negatively, but instead to laugh along with them. Lots of fun can be had when the two of you can trade jokes about the same person in private.

The Scorpio Spouse

Scorpios are usually loyal but not always faithful. That is to say, they regard their personal life as their own and resist being dictated to by their partner in particular, or society as a whole, when it comes to sexual freedom. Yet at the same time, they can loyally uphold their end of the marital responsibilities, leading somewhat of a double life. Secretive by nature, Scorpios will rarely, if ever, share information about their personal lives with family or friends. Scorpios love their homes and spend as much time there as possible, and they are not reluctant to invest in making them beautiful and comfortable.

Wedding and Honeymoon with the Scorpio Spouse

The sexual aspects of the honeymoon are very important to the Scorpio spouse. The pleasure afforded to their partners is important, but not essential to their own. Scorpios see their honeymoon as a passionate consummation of their desires. Consequently, if things are just mediocre or do not go well, they are likely to react with great disappointment, frustration, and depression, all of which they may attempt to hide. The wedding is usually seen as just a necessary preamble to the honeymoon, which is the really important part.

Home and Day-to-Day Married Life with the Scorpio Spouse

Scorpio spouses are not always aware of or responsive to the wishes of their marriage partners. They seem to live in their own private world even when in daily contact with their spouses. Often hard to reach, Scorpios will retreat to a private space, even if that is limited to a chair with a book or newspaper. Scorpio spouses are able to tune out at will, so you may find that they have not been listening to you for minutes, hours, or even days. However, during that time they have surely been listening to their inner voice and have been stimulated by their inner promptings. Therefore, do not blame yourself for their reactions; you may not even be involved.

Finances and the Scorpio Spouse

Scorpios love to spend money on food, drink, and expensive personal and household items. Fortunately, they are also good at making money, thus guaranteeing a regular cash flow. You must keep an eye on them, however, since not only can their spending run out of hand, but they are also attracted by all kinds of investment schemes that promise reward. Sometimes it is best to maintain a separation of certain accounts, incomes, and expenses with your Scorpio spouse, leaving a common daily household fund for both of you to use.

Infidelity and the Scorpio Spouse

Scorpios have high sexual needs that you may or may not be able to satisfy. Furthermore, they are drawn by intrigue, secret affairs, hidden romantic involvements, and the like. Even if you satisfy your Scorpio spouse sexually, they might still feel the need to indulge occasionally in extramarital activities. As Scorpios see it, they can be both loyal to you and stray once in a while without feeling that what they have done is immoral or unethical. Through all this, they are also capable of maintaining a hurtful double standard, insisting on your undivided attention while they show interest in others.

Children and the Scorpio Spouse

Scorpio spouses are very protective of their children, and when their kids are younger, they will rarely allow them out of their sight. Consequently, although their children grow up feeling secure, they also tend to be dominated and controlled by their Scorpio parents. The great challenge for the Scorpio spouse is to encourage independence in their children, even if it means fostering rebellion against their own edicts in certain cases. The psychological weaning process is often as painful for Scorpio spouses as it is for their progeny. In such a process, the older and wiser Scorpio parent should act to instill a feeling of responsibility and maturity in the children.

Divorce and the Scorpio Spouse

Unfortunately, the more negative aspects of the Scorpio personality can manifest here, particularly if the Scorpio spouse feels unfairly or poorly treated. Scorpios have an undeniably vindictive streak, which can cause them to hurt and carry out revengeful actions against their spouses. Formidable antagonists, you may find it difficult to oppose Scorpio spouses hell-bent on doing battle with you over a failed marriage. For these reasons, it is best to act respectfully and quietly avoid rousing the very worst actions of which they are capable. During divorce proceedings, contact your Scorpio spouse as little as possible, leaving most communication to the lawyers.

The Scorpio Lover

Many Scorpio lovers fit their amorous roles like a hand in a glove. Their dually passionate and secretive nature makes them ideal candidates for clandestine love affairs. This does not indicate a high frequency of involvements—quite the contrary. Most Scorpio lovers choose to get involved quite rarely and selectively, but usually very deeply. This fact often guarantees a certain amount of pain and suffering in addition to the joy or ecstasy they may experience. Their lovers will usually attest to the fact that Scorpios are very emotional, in fact often volcanic, although these feelings are usually kept under control and allowed to emerge in only the most intimate of situations.

STRENGTHS

Amorous

Intimate

Volcanic

WEAKNESSES

Painful

Suffering

Unhappy

INTERACTIVE STYLE

Private

Concealed

Attached

SCORPIO

Meeting the Scorpio Lover

Scorpio lovers have subtle ways to announce their interest in you. A chance remark to a mutual friend, a casual glance, or an obliquely flattering comment can all serve as signals. Later you may ask yourself, "Are they really interested or not?" Throwing you off balance can be a Scorpio tactic, often prompting you to show your hand while they keep their own cards hidden. Causing you embarrassment or even a trifle of discomfort can fit the plans of Scorpio lovers, since frequently they approach matters of love similarly to how they would go into battle. This makes you the adversary as well as the prize.

Location and the Scorpio Lover

Scorpio lovers are stimulated by having you over to their place. Their domicile is their den, their lair, and their web, in which they can entangle you and place you firmly in their clutches. Intrigue figures prominently here, with Scorpio lovers piquing your curiosity and urging you to know them better. Seduction is a specialty of many Scorpios, so you might as well enjoy it. Later, there will be enough time for regret or sorrow if things do not work out. You may find yourself being the aggressive one in such a situation, with your Scorpio lover responding in kind to produce a once-in-a-lifetime first experience.

Sex and the Scorpio Lover

Falling in love with a Scorpio can, at times, resemble an addictive experience. Whatever Scorpios have (if they could bottle it) would probably become a very popular elixir. Like a habituating drug, Scorpio love invites higher and higher dosages and can create true withdrawal symptoms when it is withheld. Although Scorpios can give the initial impression of being repressed, shy, or withdrawn, once they are involved in sexual contact their truly passionate nature will emerge. Before releasing such torridly eruptive energies, be sure you can handle the affair without blame or regrets.

Holding On to the Scorpio Lover

Normally this is not difficult if the two of you are into each other emotionally. As a matter of fact, getting your Scorpio lover to back off may become the problem. Be prepared for Scorpio lovers to want things to continue just as they are for a long time. This is especially true of the secret aspects of your meeting and a refusal to allow the world any view or entry into such private realms. Scorpio lovers can indulge in undercover communications, even employing codes and signals, when they want to get in touch with you.

Entertaining the Scorpio Lover

Scorpio lovers will make their personal preferences abundantly clear. Entertaining them can be as simple as running down their checklist. Unfortunately, this can leave your needs and wants out of the picture, so when entertaining these lovers, try to employ methods that guarantee mutual pleasure. Most entertainment will be of a private nature, since Scorpios will not usually go out of their way to be seen with you in public. Intimate dinners cooked by them replace visits to restaurants, while DVDs and CDs are preferred over going to the movies or attending concerts.

Breaking Up with the Scorpio Lover

Unfortunately, passionate relationships with Scorpio lovers often guarantee passionate breakups. Not necessarily theatrical, but certainly emotional, the breakup may bring about a great deal of pain for both parties. The problem is that the relationship and the breakup can leave scars that do not heal very quickly, thus throwing a pall over your future involvements or even your ability or interest to get involved again soon. Bitterness and frustration are both likely to surface. In combating them, dwell on the positive aspects of the relationship and refuse to give in to your negatively reactive feelings.

The Scorpio Ex

Scorpio exes are not easy to deal with. Their well-known need to take punishing revenge for your past actions, particularly insults to their prodigious egos, could urge them to hurtful actions. At some points, you will be sorely tested and must decide whether to wait things out defensively or to counterattack. Either way you will need to form a strategy, and this should be done in conjunction with your family, clergyman, accountant, lawyer, or friends. These individuals can also exert pressure on Scorpio exes to behave and show them that it is to their advantage to cooperate and negotiate.

Establishing a Friendship with the Scorpio Ex

Normally, deep friendships are impossible to institute after breakups with Scorpio exes. The best you can hope for is a cessation of overt hostilities and an uneasy truce. Unfortunately, Scorpios rarely, if ever, forgive or forget. Moreover, any sign of weakness on your part or an appeal for forgiveness may be met with scorn or additional punishments. Their attitude is: "You made your bed, now you must lie in it," so you should expect no help from them. The only area in which they may be forced to cooperate is lingering business and personal matters that require transfers of money.

Issues of Getting Back Together with the Scorpio Ex

Getting back together with a Scorpio ex is not recommended. Scorpios often have a deep need to inflict hurt, and this could be facilitated by once again coming into close contact with your Scorpio ex. Staying away from Scorpio exes and avoiding getting back together may be necessary for your emotional and psychological survival. There is nothing wrong with talking about your relationship from time to time, but be suspicious of any hints of perhaps being agreeable to a reconciliation. Since Scorpios know how to turn on the charm, you may have to exercise considerable self-restraint.

STRENGTHS

Negotiating
Cooperative
Proud

WEAKNESSES

Revengeful
Recalcitrant
Punishing

INTERACTIVE STYLE

Aggressive
Difficult
Accusing

Discussing Past Issues with the Scorpio Ex

Scorpios know exactly what happened, as they see it, so there is no need to remind them of it as far as they are concerned. Discussing past issues for most Scorpio exes is just like rubbing salt in an open wound. First of all, they will be suspicious of your motives in doing so and equally wary of your future plans involving them. Should you just want to reminisce and have an easy interchange or joke about pleasurable mutual activities, approach the subject with care; catching Scorpio exes in the right mood can help in this respect.

Expressing Affection to the Scorpio Ex

Scorpio exes may respond to your expressions of affection, but if this goes any further in a decidedly sexual direction, you may come to regret ever having started things in the first place. Remember that Scorpios regard the sexual arena as their own personal province, accompanied by a full knowledge of how to use these powers against you. It is therefore best to remain aloof, respectful, and objective when it comes to expressing any physical affection to Scorpio exes. A softened tone of voice or endearing glance may be the most that can be prudently allowed on both sides.

Defining the Present Relationship with the Scorpio Ex

It is best not to discuss the relationship with Scorpio exes, but rather give it your own personal definition, attempting to remain cool and fair, and urging them to do the same. Keep most interaction restricted to business, logistics, and financial matters, along with practical day-to-day family activities. Avoid alienating Scorpio exes by continuing to include them in family plans rather than excluding them. This is an effective way to provide some stability and social control so that emotions do not spin out of control. Sometimes one mutual friend can act as a go-between, helping to define the present relationship and defuse volatile situations.

Sharing Custody with the Scorpio Ex

You and your Scorpio ex must guard against using your children as weapons against each other in a breakup. Furthermore, it is usually best to have all custody matters strictly handled by legal representatives and courts rather than through personal contacts. The children should never be urged to take sides; indeed, the kids may be the very ones who can keep things running peacefully and even be helpful in handling problems that arise between their separated parents. In many cases, wise children can handle Scorpio exes much more efficiently and sensibly than the other parent can.

Friends and Family

The Scorpio Friend

Scorpios are very selective in their choice of friends, so if you are picked to be one, you should feel honored. Often Scorpios keep their best friends in reserve and save them for the best moments. Not particularly needy most of the time, Scorpio friends will usually contact you when they want to enjoy themselves, celebrate, or just go out on the town. They can be wonderful companions, but they build their friendships mostly on their own terms and often on their own turf. Those of a more versatile and mutable nature often get along best with them, for they are able to adapt quickly to their serious moods and to changes in their complex emotional states.

Asking for Help from the Scorpio Friend

Since most Scorpio friends do not approach you for help often or easily, they assume that you will not approach them for assistance very often, either. They can be relied on, however, in serious or crisis situations. Cool in emergencies, Scorpios can be lifesavers to their friends, both literally and figuratively. Once they hear an earnest tone in your voice, they will spring to your assistance and, if necessary, even go on the attack against those who are opposing you. Before unleashing these energies, however, you should think carefully about what the consequences of their actions might be.

Communication and Keeping in Touch with the Scorpio Friend

Scorpio friends are not high-maintenance. You can go for long periods of time without contacting them, and after such pauses they are generally very happy to hear from you. Because they are not needy of your attention, do not bother them with constant inquiries to see how they are. Most often such fussy behavior will just irritate them, preferring to be left alone. When they have something to share with you, they will get in touch. Although private and often introverted, Scorpios can be excellent communicators, able to get their often thought-provoking ideas across to others in few words.

Borrowing Money from the Scorpio Friend

Although possessive in many areas of life, Scorpio friends can be surprisingly easy about sharing money with those close to them. They hate meanness and pettiness above all;

STRENGTHS
Selective
Fun
Celebratory

WEAKNESSES
Testy
Emotionally labile
Moody

INTERACTIVE STYLE
Forceful
Thought-provoking
Defending

quibbling about sharing a bill after dinner is something they will avoid by just paying themselves. But beware: they will assume that your money is there for them, too, so if they need it, they may ask for it in an offhand way that sounds like a surgeon asking for a scalpel. Scorpios tend to be good with money—making it, handling it, and spending it. They are unhappy with being poor, since deprivation is not their idea of living a good life.

Asking for Advice from the Scorpio Friend

Scorpio friends will want time to think over your problem before giving advice. Their thoughtful and contemplative nature is not suited to offering sudden or superficial counsel. They do not need to be reminded of your having asked for advice; they will come up with a solution when they are good and ready. Scorpios often consider themselves worldly people who have a good knowledge of human psychology and the way things work in the world. Although this is true, you may not want to follow their advice blindly, since doing so could prove counterproductive.

Visiting the Scorpio Friend

Scorpios love when their friends come to visit. They usually have a great deal to share with them, both in the realm of conversation and in mutual enjoyment of music, sports, political satire, art, and of course food and drink. Going out for dinner with Scorpio friends on a regular basis can be highly enjoyable, although expensive, since their taste is excellent and their desire for quality is high. Although they will visit you occasionally, they are usually happier and more comfortable in their own quarters, which frequently resemble a secret hideout, den, or lair. Your enjoyment in such situations is of paramount importance to them.

Celebrations/Entertainment with the Scorpio Friend

For Scorpios, celebrations and entertainment are very special matters, not to be indulged in on a daily basis. They will look forward to such events with great anticipation. If attending a sporting event, concert, or show, they will invariably want to purchase the best seats and, therefore, assume that you will want to also. Frequently knowledgeable about these events, they will freely share their expertise with you, acting almost like a tour guide or font of information. If they take you along to an event in which they are emotionally involved, you will be required to let them take the lead and show your appreciation for their actions and observations.

The Scorpio Roommate

Privacy is usually the top priority for most Scorpio roommates. Not only is their room an inviolable territory, but they may come to look on the entire apartment or house as their own hidden den, one that just incidentally involves you to help pay rent and share expenses. Social activities may be difficult to implement with such an attitude. In addition, Scorpios like to control their environments, so at their most sensitive times, Scorpio roommates will seek to scale down your input—whether insisting that music and TV be played at a lower volume or even demanding that you cut the chatter and leave them in peace. Scorpios are notoriously grumpy upon awakening and often need infusions of black coffee to get them going.

Sharing Financial Responsibilities with the Scorpio Roommate

Approaching Scorpio roommates for their share of the rent, food, utilities, and other expenses can be difficult, even when they are capable of paying. The most difficult part may be raising the subject without them refusing to talk about it or deflecting your questions. The fact is that Scorpios can do things only when they are ready, and they resist being pushed. In a good month, they will place their contribution in cash in a conspicuous or customary spot and leave it to you to spend it or deliver it to the right address. Other than making a short reference to what they have left, you are unlikely to hear any more about it.

Cleaning and the Scorpio Roommate

Scorpios are not known for their interest in cleaning, although once they make up their minds to do it, they are quite capable workers in this area. Often they will agree to help clean common spaces, but balk at any suggestion that they make their own rooms more presentable. For them, their rooms are their private lairs where you might never be invited, and they resent even having their space under your scrutiny. The sight of closed doors is probably one that you will have to get used to, whether these roommates are present or not.

Houseguests and the Scorpio Roommate

Scorpio roommates are unlikely to invite guests to stop by often. However, at times they will have their closest friends or family members over to spend the night. You will be expected to easily accept these visitors and to make them feel welcome. Do not intrude on the time Scorpios spend with their guests, since they are very possessive of those who "belong" to them. Scorpio roommates will feel free to invite the occasional overnight visitor or engage in a sexual tryst whether or not they have afforded you an equal opportunity to do so.

Parties and the Scorpio Roommate

Though not overly social people, Scorpio roommates can still enjoy throwing an occasional party. They may even share responsibilities with you and put you on equal footing when it comes to creating a guest list. They will grow irritated, though, if your social life at home becomes too active, and they will make it abundantly clear that they need

STRENGTHS
Protective
Supportive
Involved

WEAKNESSES
Withdrawn
Uncommunicative
Closed

INTERACTIVE STYLE
Private
Reclusive
Controlling

FRIENDS AND FAMILY

privacy. Putting on a bad face and shutting doors with a bang, unhappy Scorpio room-mates will not do much to promote an upbeat mood when your guests start piling in. Therefore, you must be sensitive to their need for isolation and not stress them out with too much traffic.

Privacy and the Scorpio Roommate

Strangely enough, if things are going well between you and your Scorpio roommate, he or she may not insist on privacy when alone with you. This is the surest indication that Scorpio roommates feel close to you—so close, in fact, that they do not recognize you as a separate entity. The fact that they can view the two of you as a single unit is undoubtedly a compliment—coming from such private people—but it can also prove cloying and can be indicative of their need to possess and control you. This can put you in the funny position of insisting on your own privacy, something that Scorpios may, in fact, resist giving you.

Discussing Problems with the Scorpio Roommate

Not only are intimate discussions possible with Scorpio roommates, they also frequently prove helpful, not only in the advice given but also in cementing a deep personal bond between you. Rarely will Scorpio roommates approach you to discuss their own personal problems (unless they involve you), but they are good listeners when you run into diffi-culties (unless the difficulties involve them). As far as houseguests, financial matters, or distribution of tasks are concerned, most Scorpio roommates can be difficult to engage in conversation or discussion. Even if you make an appointment for a heart-to-heart talk on such matters, they may either arrive too late to allow serious discussion or not show up at all.

The Scorpio Parent

Most Scorpio parents raise their children according to very strict rules. They have many ideas about parenting—often formed before they even have children—and these fixed principles are implemented without variation or compromise. Extremely direct toward their children, they will insist that homework, household chores, and family obligations be discharged without question on a regular basis. Scorpio parents are proud of their kids and want to see them looking their very best, particularly when going off to school but also at family affairs and social events. They take the behavior of their children as a direct reflection on their abilities as parents, highly prizing a good reputation. A partnership that includes only one Scorpio parent usually works better than two Scorpio parents, because of their demanding natures and uncompromising attitudes.

Discipline Style of the Scorpio Parent

Scorpio parents can be severe in disciplinary matters. However, they make it abundantly clear to their children that they would rather not punish them at all. They announce that the choice is up to their children, either to avoid punishment by following the rules or to invite inevitable punishment by breaking them. Unambiguous rules are laid down by Scorpio parents from the outset, so that their children can never plead ignorance. A wide range of punishments, from grounding to a scowling glance, spanking, or shove, are administered on the spot without premeditation. However, more complex and longer-lasting punishments aimed at correcting the underlying problem can be meted out in the case of more severe transgressions.

Affection Level and the Scorpio Parent

Scorpio parents can be very affectionate toward their children, but usually only when they are behaving themselves. Scorpios are as consistent about giving affection as a reward as they are about administering discipline as a punishment, approaching these matters in a black-and-white manner. However, Scorpio parents can also joke by pretending to be angry, using their feigned threats and insults as an expression of true affection. When the Scorpio scowl first appears, their offspring learn how to read it and determines whether a storm or a laugh will follow.

Money Issues and the Scorpio Parent

Money is important to Scorpios, and consequently most Scorpio parents will take the time to teach their children how to use (and not misuse) it. Often tightfisted, Scorpio parents will not be overly generous with allowances, usually insisting that their children earn cash by performing household tasks. Furthermore, Scorpio parents will encourage their children to make money by babysitting, delivering newspapers, doing yardwork, and the like, but they also may severely supervise how these funds are spent. Some will encourage or even that demand their children put such earnings in a bank account for when future needs or desires arise, thus teaching them "good habits."

Crises and the Scorpio Parent

In crisis situations, Scorpio parents can be counted on to stand squarely behind their children. However, for cases in which the child is clearly at fault and someone else is hurt due to these actions, they may also be expected to deliver severe admonitions and punishments. Life can be a whole lot more pleasant for everyone concerned when such crises are kept to a minimum, because of the severity of the Scorpio parent's responses. Should the crisis involve Scorpio parents directly, the rest of the family will be expected to give their full support and understanding, otherwise they may suffer the consequences later, involving blame, anger, and resentment.

Holidays/Family Gatherings and the Scorpio Parent

Depending on work schedules, Scorpio parents may choose either to get fully involved in such activities or to leave the planning or execution entirely up to others. Although they can enjoy holidays and family gatherings, most Scorpio parents usually put their professions, domestic work projects, and prior commitments to friends first. Some family members can be upset, even insulted, by winding up second in line to these preferences. Scorpios usually figure that this is the other person's problem, not their own. Should Scorpio parents choose to fully engage in the planning of celebrations and vacations,

(The Scorpio Parent)

STRENGTHS

Protective

Advising

Encouraging

WEAKNESSES

Overprotective

Bossy

Repetitive

INTERACTIVE STYLE

Insistent

Demanding

Proud

FRIENDS AND FAMILY

their involvement is usually total—sometimes overly controlling and overbearing, albeit highly competent.

Caring for the Aging Scorpio Parent

Most aging Scorpio parents will ask their families to help them only with the barest necessities and leave the rest to them. Assuming that they have enough retirement income to live on, their needs may be restricted to weekly help with shopping and/or cleaning. In more severe cases, they would prefer the help of a professional nurse or healthcare worker for matters of personal hygiene and exercise over requesting such help from their loved ones. Scorpio parents love to see their grandchildren on a regular basis and will appreciate your bringing them to visit. Occasionally, they may be willing to visit your home, although not often, and only if you furnish the transportation coming and going.

The Scorpio Sibling

Scorpio siblings will make their presence felt in any family group. Their strong likes and dislikes alone are enough to guarantee this, but when you add an aggressive and controlling temperament, you realize they truly are a force to be reckoned with. Scorpio siblings do not usually hold in their objections or demands, instead letting their brothers and sisters know what is on their minds. Their position in the family is a highly significant factor. The eldest Scorpio siblings can be quite tyrannical over the younger ones, whereas a youngest Scorpio sibling can be of a sunnier disposition, cuddly even. It is often the second or middle Scorpio siblings who suffer the most should they be ignored or neglected.

Rivalry/Closeness with the Scorpio Sibling

Scorpio siblings can develop intense rivalries with their brothers and sisters, particularly when they are the youngest, clamoring to be heard and recognized. Nothing is more difficult for a Scorpio child than repeatedly losing games and athletic contests to older siblings. Such defeats can engender a desire in adult life to be first in everything and to win out at all costs, frequently against overwhelming odds. On the other hand, Scorpio siblings also can develop strong bonds with their brothers and sisters, bonds that last well into advanced adult life. Most often an interesting blend of rivalry and closeness exists between such individuals.

Past Issues and the Scorpio Sibling

Scorpios have long memories. This fact can work against them psychologically and create acute problems due to their inability to either forgive or forget past wrongs. Issues may be discussed, but actual incidents forged in their memories are the truly difficult matters to be dealt with, either by themselves or with the help of a counselor. Their desire to put such issues to rest is in itself a very positive step for Scorpio siblings to take. Once this decision is made, they can proceed slowly and carefully over many years to finally put these matters to rest. Such resolutions may be viewed as major triumphs in the lives of Scorpios.

Dealing with the Estranged Scorpio Sibling

Estranged Scorpio siblings are often difficult to reach psychologically. Repeated attempts must be made over a long period to get through to them. Great sensitivity must be displayed because bothering them too often may only irritate them or harden their resolve not to respond. A kind of persistence that takes their feelings into account, gently and persuasively, will begin to move them in the right direction. Underneath it all, many Scorpios have an unannounced desire to truly love and be loved by their siblings and to be accepted back into the bosom of the family (although they would probably never admit it).

Money Issues (Borrowing Money, Wills, Etc.) and the Scorpio Sibling

Scorpio siblings do not usually make demands beyond what they think is rightfully theirs. When treated unfairly or dishonestly, they go on the attack and give no ground to their enemies, who are often members of their own families. Beyond a need to be treated fairly, they also extend their moral and ethical values to cover other family members whose rights have been infringed on. Because they do not give up easily in these matters, issues of wills and inheritances can carry on for years. Generally speaking, Scorpios will financially help their siblings whenever possible.

Holidays/Celebrations/Reunions and the Scorpio Sibling

Scorpio siblings love to participate in reunions and other family celebrations. Depending on their busy schedules, they will also occasionally take part in spending holidays with siblings, particularly when the children (the cousins) get along well. Scorpios love the easy feeling of being part of a group and will be generous in their outlays of money and time to make sure such events are a success. To expect such enthusiasm from them on a regular basis is certainly in order, as long as the frequency does not exceed two or, at the most, three times a year.

Vacationing with the Scorpio Sibling

Scorpio siblings often prefer to vacation with their friends rather than with their brothers and sisters. When vacations range from two weeks to more than a month, old antagonisms and conflicts can surface, causing major disruptions. Brothers and sisters of Scorpios should be aware of this and avoid getting locked into fixed commitments about vacations. Should vacations last only a few days, and not be excessively frequent, everyone can certainly have fun, as long as a strict moratorium is imposed on all arguments, lest they run out of hand and ruin everyone's good time.

The Scorpio Child

Scorpio children can be the delight of any family, as long as they are treated fairly and not taken advantage of. Scorpio kids love their friends above all other people in the world and are even able to share them with brothers and sisters without becoming unduly possessive. Parents will find Scorpio children dutiful, aware, energetic, and sympathetic to their own personal problems. Frequently, a Scorpio child can become the leader of

STRENGTHS

Delightful

Dutiful

Energetic

WEAKNESSES

Easily upset

Argumentative

Unhappy

INTERACTIVE STYLE

Supportive

Helpful

Motivated

the family in the parents' absence or the driving force promoting group solidarity and support for the parents when they are present. Nothing is more pleasurable for them than joking around and having fun with adults and other children alike.

Personality Development and the Scorpio Child

Scorpio children display well- and sometimes fully formed personality traits at a very early age. Their characters emerge strongly after a year or two of life and can, amazingly, stay constant throughout an entire lifetime. Watching the personality development of a Scorpio child can be a fascinating process, since their feelings go so deep and the intricacies of their psychological states are so complex. Teachers, parents, other family members, and friends will be truly challenged in maintaining relationships with Scorpio children. Frequently unstoppable in their actions, Scorpios are forceful personalities that others must learn to deal with without using up energy in order to battle them to a standstill.

Hobbies/Interests/Career Paths for the Scorpio Child

The interests of Scorpio children are frequently a blend of the mental and physical. Attracted and responsive to challenge, most Scorpio kids are adept at overcoming difficulties, although they are also quite capable of enjoying more conventionally pleasurable activities. Quite often the latter serves as rewards for the former. Being deprived of simple sensuous enjoyments over a period of time can wear down their positive energies and make them unhappy, even bitter. Thus, reward in the form of candy, favorite foods, affection, or gifts are demands that must be met to keep Scorpio children in a good mood. Good career paths are those that offer challenge, adequate remuneration, and pleasant work surroundings.

Discipline and the Scorpio Child

Scorpio children react very badly to the need of teachers, parents, or other family members to take disciplinary action against them. Most Scorpio kids have a good idea of what is right and wrong and feel that punishment or discipline is simply unnecessary because they are entirely aware of what they have done. It is true that they can punish themselves much more than any adult can, and that they suffer deeply from mistakes they have made, particularly in their unfair or hurtful actions toward others. Scorpio children are able to bear pain, blame, and isolation better than most, even when such punishments are blatantly unfair.

Affection Level and the Scorpio Child

Scorpio children love to give and receive affection, selectively, although the form it takes can be quite unusual, even bizarre. Adult Scorpios can even be affectionate to their adversaries, a trait they may display in childhood during competitions or outright battles. Some of it has to do with the fact that they truly respect those who can stand up to their forceful personalities, and that the affection they share with their opponents is often a sign of mutual respect. Although touchy-feely creatures to some, they can appear quite prickly and standoffish to others, usually indicating that Scorpio children must develop a meaningful personal relationship before allowing people to get too close.

Dealing with the Scorpio Child and Interactions with Siblings

When Scorpio children take the lead, it is very important that they gain the respect of parents and siblings alike for doing so. Sometimes they can assume leadership of their family unit to the point of vying with the parents for control. Parents can sometimes be forced to direct their disciplinary actions, punishments, and admonishments against the Scorpio child, who has become the representative of the other siblings. Consequently, in such cases, Scorpio children are forced to grow up and assume mature and responsible attitudes early in their development, which can result in their being deprived of the joys of a carefree childhood.

Interacting with the Adult Scorpio Child

As indicated, Scorpio children can mature into adults at a very early age, depending on individual circumstances. Already quite mature in their teenage years, adult Scorpio children may be fully formed by this time and continue to display the same traits throughout the rest of their lives. In their confrontations with Scorpio children, parents are frequently amazed how they seem to be facing a little man or woman—who can be quite a formidable opponent. Maturity is something that Scorpios have a natural feeling for, since it complements their seriousness and depth of feeling as well as their intensely realistic view of the world.

Sagittarius

BIRTHDATE **NOVEMBER 22–DECEMBER 21**

Sagittarius is the mutable fire sign, ruled by the optimistic and highly expansive planet Jupiter. Most Sagittarians adopt an extremely positive view toward life and believe that almost anything is possible for those who have the courage to dare and dream. Idealists, they insist on ethical behavior and honesty from those they come into contact with, preferring to judge people by their motives rather than by the results they achieve. Sagittarians are natural protectors of small creatures and champions of the underdog.

Work

SAGITTARIUS
November 22–December 21

The Sagittarius Boss

Because of their high degree of independence and individualism, Sagittarians not always suited to the role of boss. They are prone to go off suddenly and often precipitously in their own direction under a full head of steam, so it may be difficult for their employees to keep up with them. Furthermore, they may not take the time to communicate their thoughts clearly to the company, preferring to let their actions speak for themselves. Not really team players, Sagittarius bosses assume command and then follow their hunches rather than carefully mapping out a campaign and delegating duties carefully.

Asking the Sagittarius Boss for a Raise

Being results-oriented, Sagittarius bosses may not have shown great interest in your manner of working or taken the time to listen to your recommendations and complaints. Therefore, it will be up to you to approach them and state your opinions, hoping they will get to know you better. Keep close contact with their assistants to find the most auspicious break in their whirlwind schedule. Do not waste a Sagittarius boss's time with idle chatter; state your viewpoints in a clear, concise, and unambiguous manner. At a later date approach them for a raise only if you truly merit one.

Breaking Bad News to the Sagittarius Boss

Sagittarius bosses have quick tempers that are likely to flare up when bad news is first presented. Do not try to calm them down, but allow them to vent their immediate anger. They may either lay the blame on you or seek to discuss the matter with you and reach mutual decisions designed for damage control. In such crisis situations you may form bonds with the Sagittarius boss, thus being the bearer of bad tidings may produce positive results. Should these plans work out, you may find your Sagittarius boss consulting you more and even seeking your advice.

Arranging Travel and/or Entertainment for the Sagittarius Boss

Because of their dynamic and hard-driving natures, Sagittarius bosses may spend a lot of time traveling but will not expect to be coddled or entertained. They rarely spend much time in any one place when on the road, so their schedules must be worked out skillfully

STRENGTHS

Intuitive

Forceful

Quick

WEAKNESSES

Uncommunicative

Unclear

Unsympathetic

INTERACTIVE STYLE

Independent

Individualistic

Impulsive

and efficiently to maximize their effectiveness. Sagittarius bosses just need to be put in the right place at the right time in order to fire their lightning bolts and then move on to the next confrontation. Accommodations need only be reasonably comfortable, certainly not luxurious. Keep in mind that they will want to work while traveling and during their hotel stays, so be sure there are electrical outlets, wireless connections, and high-speed internet hookups available.

Decision-Making and the Sagittarius Boss

Sagittarius bosses are known for making quick decisions. Sometimes they stick to them, sometimes not. For them, a decision is not necessarily binding and may assume the status of a trial attempt, to be changed or rejected if things do not work out. Therefore, you should not get overly upset if the Sagittarius boss makes decisions you feel are wrong, since in a few days, weeks, or months they are likely to see the light and amend their plans, making them more in keeping with your own. Do not immediately oppose a Sagittarius boss, but show patience and constraint—watch and wait.

Impressing and/or Motivating the Sagittarius Boss

Sagittarius bosses are best impressed by employees who do not try too hard to get their attention but produce undeniable results over time. Should they show interest in your work, particularly curiosity about the methods you have used to achieve success, feel free to openly share your ideas and approaches. If they come to the conclusion that you are on the same wavelength, the Sagittarius boss will feel confident about your abilities and very well might decide to entrust you with a plum of a project that your colleagues have been vying for.

Making Proposals and/or Giving Presentations to the Sagittarius Boss

Sagittarius bosses are not usually patient people, so you should keep your proposals succinct and your presentations short and sweet. They may not even choose to attend the entire meeting—arriving late, doing a whirlwind tour of the conference table (hopefully being seated briefly), and hearing a few of your words on their way out the door. Thus you may choose to abandon your text for the short time they are present and address your remarks specifically to them, in an improvisatory and hopefully inspirational manner. Your enthusiasm and optimism about your proposals will not be lost on them.

The Sagittarius Employee

Sagittarius employees can be hardworking and dedicated, but you must keep an eye on them since they are also capable of following their impulses at any moment. Frequently, they stay with a work group or company until they have acquired enough experience before going off on their own. The events that precipitate their inevitable move toward professional independence are frequently not planned or even of their own doing; fate simply takes a hand and furnishes the push they need to follow their path. Sagittarius employees can fill in and function well as temporary bosses of the work group of which they are a part.

Interviewing and/or Hiring the Sagittarius Employee

Sagittarius interviewees must be accepted as they are, since no amount of explaining or indoctrination will hold their individualistic temperaments in check for very long. Yet because they are so versatile (often indicated by their resumes or CVs), they are valuable multitaskers and pinch hitters, always able to assume temporary duties at a moment's notice. Although Sagittarius employees bore easily, they are quite capable of performing repetitive tasks for long periods. That said, they will respond more positively if you offer them a position in the firm that is interesting and exciting and that encourages individual initiative.

Breaking Bad News to or Firing the Sagittarius Employee

Because of their optimistic and positive attitudes, Sagittarius employees react poorly to criticism and blame. If the bad news is directly related to their actions, they may become unhappy and depressed; if it is due to the failure of others, they generally will jump in and help rectify matters. Should they be fired unfairly, they will demand talking things out with their employer. Highly moral and ethical in their approach, they want to make it clear that their motives were pure and their efforts sufficient. Sagittarians will actively seek a good recommendation for their next job.

Traveling with and Entertaining the Sagittarius Employee

It may be difficult to keep up with these dynamos when on the road. Sagittarius employees travel best on their own, although they enjoy having a companion or two along, as long as these coworkers do not hold them back or drag them down. Sagittarius employees enjoy being entertained by others, but because their tastes are selective in this area, it is often best to allow them to take the lead in providing the entertainment themselves. They require little help in making plans and organizing events, although their idiosyncratic methods and reasons for doing things a certain way are not always easy to fathom.

Assigning Tasks to the Sagittarius Employee

Make sure that Sagittarius employees listen to you carefully and fully understand what you expect them to do. The alternative is, of course, that they will walk out after your explanation and simply do it their own way. Insist that they write down—and in extreme cases, even sign—your instructions; also have them restate such instructions to show they have truly been listening. Also allow them to modify one or two points, per your approval, since this will go a long way toward making them feeling appreciated and valued for their unusual but frequently helpful suggestions.

Motivating or Impressing the Sagittarius Employee

Sagittarius employees will be even more impressed with your intentions than with your performance in many cases, particularly if things do not work out. Their ethical approach emphasizes the importance of clear thinking, pure motive, and, above all, honesty. Sagittarius employees value honesty not only in relation to others, but also in being honest with oneself. Nothing will disappoint them more than seeing bosses

(The Sagittarius Employee)

STRENGTHS

Versatile

Hardworking

Dedicated

WEAKNESSES

Hasty

Rebellious

Peculiar

INTERACTIVE STYLE

Energetic

Quick

Alert

deluding themselves or living in a fantasy world. They are perhaps most impressed by prompt and effective actions that, in retrospect, were performed for all the right reasons.

Managing, Directing, or Criticizing the Sagittarius Employee

Sagittarius employees must be skillfully managed, directed, or criticized to avoid arousing their opposition and antagonism. Remember that they usually have a very clear idea of what needs to be done and how this should be accomplished. Therefore, constantly correcting and criticizing them can take the edge off their enthusiasm and dull their performance. A discouraged, unappreciated Sagittarius can be a sorry sight, and you may later regret not having handled them with greater sensitivity and understanding. Moreover, you may have lost a most valuable ally or assistant who could have been called on to provide support in times of need.

The Sagittarius Coworker

Although Sagittarius coworkers do not generally feel comfortable working in corporate structures, they are usually friendly and cooperative when it comes to relating to their peers. Usually, they can be counted on for a good word and a smile. Their optimism is apparent, although when they are down in the dumps their feathers may appear more bedraggled than most. Hard workers, Sagittarians can be counted on by colleagues to lend a helping hand in almost any difficult situation. Their first instincts, however, are to solve problems on their own rather than joining in salvage efforts as group players.

Approaching the Sagittarius Coworker for Advice

Sagittarians are very idea-oriented and spend a lot of time thinking about things in a philosophical fashion. Consequently, they are frequently able to mull over your words and give good advice once they have had enough time to consider them thoroughly. Sagittarius coworkers can often give problems a different spin, seeing them from a very different point of view than most people. A positive spin can help revive your flagging spirits and give you hope; a negative spin is their attempt to warn you against self-delusion and false optimism. Do not approach Sagittarius coworkers for advice unless you are prepared to confront the truth, which is perhaps their highest priority.

Approaching the Sagittarius Coworker for Help

Sagittarius coworkers are prepared to back up their words with deeds. Action-oriented, they will jump into the fray on your side if they feel you are being unfairly treated or if they consider you their friend. They are champions of the underdog and do not mind battling at your side against seemingly overwhelming odds. Their prodigious energies can serve to buoy your spirits and give you more energy to fight, with such a good and faithful colleague at your side. Moreover, once problems are solved they will back off and not seek to control or unduly influence you.

Traveling with and Entertaining the Sagittarius Coworker

When good feelings exist between you and a Sagittarius coworker, traveling together can be a most enjoyable experience. Extremely convivial and friendly to their favorite coworkers, Sagittarians will have a friendly and positive demeanor that can make almost any trip or entertainment experience memorable. Good travelers, they will not hold you up or be overly demanding. If you are not familiar with them before your trip, by the end of your travels you may have become fast friends. Getting used to their interesting and often peculiar ways of thinking and behaving will, however, take a bit of time.

The Sagittarius Coworker Cooperating with Others

Although Sagittarius coworkers can be quite cooperative, their highly individualistic and frequently impulsive approach to things leads them to break with company rules, traditional modes of behavior, and more conservative perspectives. Consequently, by the time a task force has been formed to tackle a particular problem, they may have already figured it out and fixed it for good. It is particularly difficult for most Sagittarius coworkers to mute their efforts and accept a minor role in group endeavors, particularly if they know how to solve things quickly on their own. They have much to understand about being team players but are quick learners and can adapt well.

Impressing and Motivating the Sagittarius Coworker

If Sagittarius coworkers believe in a project, they will be highly motivated to give it their all. But if they have serious doubts, they are quite capable of withholding their energies and even slowing things down through their critical attitudes. Motivation is very important in dealing with such recalcitrant Sagittarius employees. You can curb their obstinate and headstrong tendencies by truly impressing them with the strength of your logic and the efficacy of your methods. However, they will still be suspicious of your motives, which can rankle them if they feel you are being dishonest, despite the fact that you are being successful.

Persuading and/or Criticizing the Sagittarius Coworker

Sagittarius coworkers are quite capable of accepting constructive criticism if it can help solve problems. Particularly receptive to useful tips, they will often try them out to see if they work. They are best persuaded if you know how and when to approach them; they can stubbornly refuse to listen when they are pushed or ordered to obey. Often the best time to get through to them is not when hard at work but during coffee breaks or, even better, when out together to eat or for an after-work drink. When in a relaxed mood, they are more prepared to be persuaded to at least listen and consider different points of view.

The Sagittarius Client

Sagittarius clients are certainly results-oriented and, as such, are not much interested in the wrappings of your presents but rather in the contents of the box. Any frills, promised benefits of dealing with them, or outright gifts will be viewed with suspicion. The same

STRENGTHS
Positive
Idealistic
Natural

WEAKNESSES
Suspicious
Unaccepting
Unrealistic

INTERACTIVE STYLE
Forthright
Honest
Informal

goes for their refusal to accept blatant promises and guarantees. Yet Sagittarian optimism and idealism can still shine through as long as both you and your Sagittarius clients stay on the same page. In the minds of most Sagittarians, positive thinking is always preferred to negative, reactionary, or timid attitudes, all other things being equal.

Impressing the Sagittarius Client

Sagittarius clients are impressed by your abilities to comprehend the depth and scope of their projects. They hate pettiness, small thinking, and fussiness, always preferring the big picture to minute analyses of details. You will find them very impatient if you choose to constantly get stuck on small issues and slow the forward progress of the project. Not that they encourage you to throw caution to the wind. Despite their positive approach, they will not urge you to be hasty when making major decisions or to suspend your critical attitudes. Sagittarius clients know that dangers lurk around every corner, and they believe in being prepared for them.

Selling to the Sagittarius Client

It is best not to try to sell Sagittarius clients on the benefits of using your products or services. They simply want their demands met with as little fuss as possible. Above all, they have to believe you and therefore will always demand that you be honest with them. They also want to be assured, in most cases, that you are not acting unethically, breaking any laws, or indulging in immoral behavior. Their names and reputations are important to them, and if you are to be involved with their business, they expect you to studiously avoid bringing them into disrepute.

Your Appearance and the Sagittarius Client

Your appearance is not nearly so important to them as their own. Highly aware of how they look and the impression they are making, Sagittarius clients want to be acknowledged directly or indirectly for their taste in clothes and modern, up-to-date attitudes. You will do best if you avoid pretentious behavior and do not seek to impress them with expensive clothes. In most cases, they will appear natural and informal in their dress and will be impressed by an absence of stiffness and elitism. A mutual recognition of natural attitudes on both sides will help get things off to a good start.

Keeping the Sagittarius Client's Interest

Sagittarius clients often have a weakness for technical matters, puzzles, and humorous or even silly wordplay, including puns and jokes. Because of their high degree of individuality—and their respect for it in others—they will often appreciate your offbeat or oddball approach to things and give their stamp of approval to efforts that flourish in environments far from the norm. When intrigued by your methods, they are more likely to back up their interest with financial commitments that can move your projects forward and produce results more quickly. Avoid depressing or upsetting topics when dealing with Sagittarius clients.

Breaking Bad News to the Sagittarius Client

Sagittarius clients do not want to hear bad news. Because of their natural optimism and idealism, they are likely to take such results very hard, seeing their dreams going up in smoke. Yet they are also quite resilient and able to come up with a plan B or an entirely new approach that can prove efficacious. You may be able to convince them that cutting back on expenditures or trimming a project to a more manageable size is always a possibility and that realizing their grand design is just being postponed for the time being. Generally speaking, Sagittarius clients have a way of landing on their feet and surviving apparent disasters.

Entertaining the Sagittarius Client

Sagittarius clients like to work hard and play hard. Unlikely to devote themselves to the pursuit of pleasure during their work hours, they are still up for a good lunch, drinks, intense conversations, a long walk or jog, or a tennis or golf game. Forget about trying to buy or even influence their interest in you or your company by entertaining them lavishly. They might regard such treatment not only as embarrassing to them but also somewhat unethical. Your personality, ideas, and company will be entertainment enough for them, obviating the need for cash outlays to guarantee their good time.

The Sagittarius Business Partner

Maintaining good feelings on a personal level is very important in forming a good working relationship with your Sagittarius business partner. Sagittarians like things to go easily, without stress, and at the same time to enjoy their daily contact with you. Often like a marriage, a partnership with a Sagittarius can yield joy but also serve as a never-ending source of challenge and interest. Sagittarius business partners expect honesty from you and also will insist that your intentions be pure and ethical, no matter how things work out. You can always open your heart to Sagittarius partners, although this is not necessary since your company can run smoothly on a highly objective and straightforward basis.

Setting Up the Business Partnership with Sagittarius

In setting up a partnership with a Sagittarius, everything should be out in the open, carefully stated, and all ambiguity or secret agendas studiously avoided. This will get things off to a good start and also furnish a clear reference point that can be revisited in the future. Another reason this is necessary is that Sagittarius business partners are known to change their minds without always being aware that they have done so. Moreover, at the same time they may feel the need to hold you to your original promises, creating a kind of double standard. For these reasons, a good lawyer who functions as legal representa-

STRENGTHS

Honest

Ethical

Straightforward

WEAKNESSES

Judgmental

Stressed

Upset

INTERACTIVE STYLE

Open

Energetic

Capable

tive for both of you should draw up a concise yet all-inclusive legally binding agreement that is signed by both parties.

Tasking with the Sagittarius Business Partner

Sagittarius business partners are versatile but tend to spread themselves thin, taking on too many things at once. Disciplining and structuring their wayward energies may be necessary. If you can keep them in line, Sagittarius partners can apply their enormous stores of energy to any task. Since they bore easily, be sure that their workload is interesting and that they do not get stuck in one boring or repetitive job. Thinking outside the box is their specialty, but you will have to keep their more unrealistic side from running out of hand.

Traveling with and Entertaining the Sagittarius Business Partner

Although good travelers, Sagittarius business partners have a surprising love of their home base, where they have set up their workplace and feel comfortable getting the job done in the best way possible. It is often best to leave them to travel alone and to arrange their own entertainment, since their tastes are highly individualistic and likely to raise conflicts if they are forced to do things in a way that is foreign to them. Sagittarius business partners need to be free to make their own choices, in particular, to walk out the door or hop into the car whenever they feel like it.

Managing and Directing the Sagittarius Business Partner

Although Sagittarius business partners can be difficult to manage or direct, doing so can be accomplished in a subtle manner, by leaving major decisions about their behavior to them but being there at the right moment to give them a nudge in the right direction. Frequently a passing comment can be a strong motivator for them, and they will later chew over what you have said. Highly philosophical and thoughtful, these partners need significant downtime to reflect on your observations and formulate their unique responses, which frequently means coming up with an entirely new and efficacious approach.

Relating to the Sagittarius Business Partner in the Long Run

Over the long haul, Sagittarius business partners will insist on you keeping your promises and remaining fully dedicated to your mutual work. At any sign of you letting up or backing off, they may become nervous and upset, quite capable of making accusations that manifest in the form of angry outbursts. All they really demand of their partners over the long run is that you remain honorable in their intentions, dedicated to the company, constant in their energy output and direction, and produce results. They will be most upset by distractions, idle dreams, lack of focus, constant excuses, and unnecessary demands.

Parting Ways with the Sagittarius Business Partner

Breakups with Sagittarius business partners can be very difficult if they feel you are guilty of unethical behavior. Rarely will they be selfish in the division of assets and real property, since they pride themselves on their fairness and honesty. Should you seek to gain an unfair percentage of the spoils, they will resist your efforts with formidable force.

In the case of considerable debts accrued by the partnership, they will insist that these be paid back to the last penny and that both of you discharge your responsibilities fully in consort. Parting on good terms is not always possible, but is certainly desirable from the point of view of your partner.

The Sagittarius Competitor

Sagittarius competitors can wear you down with their abundant energies. In order to keep up with them, you will have to stay vigilant and alert. Often attacking on more than one front, they will seek to advance their product or service through a number of means and, likewise, to undermine the merits of your company using a variety of methods. However, Sagittarius competitors do not always have the persistence to hang in there for the long term. Changeable in their moods and approaches, they are likely to shift the emphasis of their campaigns, unsettling your efforts to remain concentrated on one area at a time.

Countering the Sagittarius Competitor

Businesswise, the average Sagittarius competitor often seems more involved with concepts and principles than with the pursuit of financial gain per se. Sagittarius competitors are constantly coming up with new ideas and approaches, many of which do not make much sense or work out. However, the percentage of ideas that are successful, although not high, is daunting and effective. The hardest part about opposing Sagittarius competitors is countering their blitz techniques. Try to remain settled and do not react to each of their offensive efforts, since many will be abandoned quickly anyway.

Out-Planning the Sagittarius Competitor

Often the best way to out-plan Sagittarius competitors is to let them waste their time, money, and energy implementing their many ideas, then sit back and pick them off one by one and only deal with the most important and effective ones. Along with this selective counterattacking technique, you would do best to put your eggs in one basket by concentrating offensive efforts in one or two areas, using massed forces sporadically rather than continuously. Thanks to the element of surprise, you will force Sagittarius competitors to adopt a defensive posture, one in which they are not always comfortable or successful.

Impressing the Sagittarius Competitor in Person

Sagittarius competitors will have only contempt for deceit, dishonesty, and manipulation. They are often easier to deal with in a fair fight rather than when their fury is aroused by unethical behavior, so you would do well to keep your presentations open and aboveboard. This applies to your appearance as well, which should be kept fairly neutral and unprovocative. Often Sagittarius competitors seem more interested in winning for its own sake and upholding their ideals, so you should assume control of the high ground in the financial sector and impress them with your practical, astute, and measured approaches to any situation.

STRENGTHS
Energetic
Changeable
Unsettling

WEAKNESSES
Asocial
Overly aggressive
Scattered

INTERACTIVE STYLE
Undermining
Shifting
Confrontational

Undercutting and Outbidding the Sagittarius Competitor

Because of the Sagittarius competitor's enthusiastic and expansive approaches, you should let them wear themselves out with bidding on a number of issues across the board. Refuse to let them drive down your bids in order to attract clients, instead watching them gain ground in many areas that will only be quickly abandoned in the future. By taking this approach, you will allow them to make commitments they will be unable to fulfill. When you are seriously interested in defeating them in a bidding war, put everything you have into a few efforts. By undercutting their bids or outbidding them with suddenness and intensity of involvement, you may cause them to quickly back off and oppose you in a number of areas you do not really care about losing.

Public Relations Wars with the Sagittarius Competitor

Seek to punch holes in their campaigns by showing how unrealistic their approaches are in promoting unreliable products and services. Emphasizing their lack of commitment and consistency to their customers over the years can be an extremely effective method that undercuts their promises, particularly in the areas of maintenance and repair. Likewise, stress your own company's reliability and dependability in standing behind your products, and give examples of how you can be counted on. Give specific examples of your company's unwavering commitment to customers over the past few years.

The Sagittarius Competitor and the Personal Approach

Adopting a more personal approach can often unsettle and undermine the Sagittarius competitor. Not really specialists in business areas requiring social and personal inter-actions, they can be left behind when you succeed in establishing successful contacts with clients and the public alike. Coming to respect your social expertise, they may retreat behind a wall of objectivity and concentrate on hatching ever-new hooks with which to grab the public's attention. A warm, even folksy approach is often best for you to adopt, because an easy and personable attitude that is welcoming rather than challenging or off-putting is essential. Sagittarius competitors will have difficulty fathoming or opposing your low-key methods.

Love

The Sagittarius First Date

Sagittarius first dates can be charming, perhaps a bit aloof, but nevertheless engaging. They like to take their time in sizing you up from several points of view and specialize in injecting humor into their observations, asking questions with a twinkle in their eyes. At times, their light banter can turn serious, making you feel slightly uncomfortable, but most often, their changing the subject is inevitable after a protracted silence on your part. They are in constant rapid movement, so you will have to move quickly to keep up with Sagittarius first dates, who can often change their minds in an instant and send an unspoken message for you to follow their gyrations.

Wooing and Picking Up the Sagittarius First Date

Sagittarians are usually up for anything, so attracting their interest is not difficult. Holding on to them may be, however, since their changeable natures and problems with commitment guarantee an uncertain future in the earliest stages of a relationship. Getting Sagittarius first dates more interested in you can be accomplished by adopting an air of mystery, since these natural detectives enjoy ferreting out secrets and bringing hidden facts to light. Sagittarius first dates are also challenge-oriented, so your attempts to put them off will usually only spur them on—if they like you, that is. Sagittarians tend to persist until they get what they want.

Suggested Activities for the Sagittarius First Date

Usually the Sagittarius first date will come up with the idea of "doing something." Extremely physical, Sagittarius first dates will characteristically suggest strenuous activities that also serve the purpose of testing your ability to keep up with them. Should you pass the test, you can be sure that their interest will be piqued and that they will want to encourage regularly scheduled encounters in the future. After a long walk or run, swim, bike ride, or other strenuous activity, sitting down at a table to get to know each other better inevitably follows and can prove most enjoyable.

STRENGTHS

Charming

Humorous

Observant

WEAKNESSES

Teasing

Testing

Fickle

INTERACTIVE STYLE

Physical

Stimulating

Dynamic

Turn-Ons and Turn-Offs for the Sagittarius First Date

Sagittarius first dates are turned on if you can keep up with them and turned off if you cannot. Highly buoyant and optimistic, they are also quickly repelled by any negativity on your part, although occasional ironic barbs can gain their admiration. They can invoke a bit of a double standard when it comes to one area: they feel free to criticize you but resent any criticism directed at them. Because of their extremely physical nature, your appearance can be a real turn-on if they find you at all attractive.

Making "the Move" with the Sagittarius First Date

Generally speaking, making the move on Sagittarius first dates is not necessary or advisable. If they like you, they will not be at all shy about making the first move, and if they do not find you sexually attractive, any movement on your part will only turn them off. Thus it is best to adopt a wait-and-see attitude and to leave making the move completely up to them. If there is mutual sexual interest, remember that Sagittarius first dates are prepared to go all the way and to give their all without holding back.

Impressing the Sagittarius First Date

Sagittarius first dates will be most impressed by your natural demeanor and honesty, particularly by the purity of your motives. They do not like any kind of phoniness or artificiality. Thus they will react positively to traits or ideas that they do not necessarily share, showing respect for your candor and openness. There is no need to compliment Sagittarius first dates; indeed, they are suspicious of attempts to butter them up. The greatest compliment you can give is simply to look great, engage in spirited conversation, and make them feel proud of being seen in public with you.

Brushing Off the Sagittarius First Date

Since their feelings are easily hurt, it is not difficult to brush off a Sagittarius first date. They have even been known to precipitously head off in another direction if you make a remark they don't like. Sagittarians are prone to explode like a firecracker, so you may feel like you need to walk on eggshells after witnessing such a reaction. If they like you, they will let you know; then brushing them off will be more difficult since their pride may be wounded. But they can understand your need to be alone without feeling rejected.

The Sagittarius Romantic Partner

Sagittarians make ardent and intense romantic partners. Yet they can also be quite relaxed, enjoying conviviality and good humor and delighting in the many pleasures of life. Their positive orientations and excessive energies make them a valuable partner, one who will always seek the best in any situation and bring out the best in you. They are not good at handling disappointment, however, and may sink into depressions when things are not working out. Easily disappointed, their positivity can plummet when rejected, leaving them feeling hopeless and abandoned. But their buoyant spirits revive quickly, and their philosophy urges them to do better next time.

Having a Discussion with the Sagittarius Romantic Partner

Sagittarians are very fond of philosophical discussions. They not only have a lot to contribute to any conversation but also know they can learn a great deal from them. By contrast, they are not interested in idle chatter; being action-oriented, they know that deeds speak louder than words. Sagittarians are open to hearing other points of view but usually have strong ideas of their own. They will expect you to listen carefully to what they have to say and will get upset if you show a lack of attention.

Arguments with the Sagittarius Romantic Partner

Sagittarians do not give up easily in arguments. They will go on, sometimes for days, weeks, and even months, hammering home their points of view. This demonstrates their need not only to win but also to fully express their frequently moral pronouncements, which they are absolutely convinced are both true and helpful. They believe they can set things right, if only you give them a chance. Their romantic partners would often prefer to be left alone, but this is something that Sagittarians find difficult to do.

Traveling with the Sagittarius Romantic Partner

Surprisingly, Sagittarians can be homebodies, often preferring to relax in their home base, but when they decide to leave they can move like greased lightning. Keeping up can at times be difficult, even impossible, once they get an idea in their minds. Nor will they make your task of accompanying them any easier, being so intent on reaching their goals. It is best if you learn to read the warning signs that they are about to head off at full steam and be ready to move with them.

Sex with the Sagittarius Romantic Partner

More often passionate rather than sensuous types, Sagittarians do not usually dwell on the preliminaries or aftermaths of lovemaking. Direct, ardent, and sometimes overwhelming, they can be counted on to provide a high level of excitement. Fulfillment is not necessarily a constant accompaniment to such frenetic activities, for either of you, but such experiences will be memorable in most cases. Spontaneous expression is a Sagittarius specialty, and surprise is an essential characteristic of such behavior. Tame and predictable behavior on your part may turn them off or spur them to break through your defenses with extreme forms of arousal.

Affection and the Sagittarius Romantic Partner

Quite affectionate, Sagittarians have a peculiar way of expressing it. Their natural physical ease allows them to feel comfortable in close proximity to friends, but they may avoid touching, holding hands, or caressing those they love, preferring to postpone physical contact until they are sexually aroused. Thus, Sagittarians often prefer to show affection through a glance, smile, or soft laugh or chuckle that reveals their feelings of tenderness. Lovers of animals, they may find it easier to express affection toward a favorite pet than toward their romantic partners.

(The Sagittarius Romantic Partner)

STRENGTHS

Ardent

Good-humored

Positive

WEAKNESSES

Disappointed

Hopeless

Abandoned

INTERACTIVE STYLE

Optimistic

Philosophical

Improving

Humor and the Sagittarius Romantic Partner

Fond of kidding around, Sagittarians like nothing better than poking fun and telling funny stories, even if jokes are not their forte. They are truly in their element when the two of you are part of a social gathering, where they will become quite animated and extroverted. Not always the ones to take the lead, they are fond of responding in the form of one-liners that cast a witty and often ironic light on the statement they are reacting to. The actual act of laughing brings them an unusual amount of enjoyment, and its full-throated expression is a sure-fire sign that they are having a good time.

The Sagittarius Spouse

Sagittarius spouses are highly capable, but because of their career orientations and need to make their mark in the world (or at the very least within their social and professional sphere), they may not be at home or available to their mates and families most of the time. This can put a great deal of responsibility on their partners, who are often good at keeping things smoothly running around the house. If both you and your Sagittarius spouse are busy professionally and socially, having a housekeeper may prove necessary. Usually, having children (and ambitiously fostering their education and careers) can be the magnet that is needed to keep Sagittarius spouses more active domestically.

Wedding and Honeymoon with the Sagittarius Spouse

Weddings and honeymoons are generally not so important to Sagittarius spouses. Because of their busy schedules, they may not have time for a honeymoon after the wedding, but may carefully plan such an event later in the year or even the following year. Although they will go through with formalities involved in traditional weddings, if they had their druthers they would settle for a civil ceremony without a lot of fuss or hoopla; particularly if their spouses-to-be have their hearts set on a big family blowout, Sagittarians will dutifully play their part and even muster up a certain amount of enthusiasm.

Home and Day-to-Day Married Life with the Sagittarius Spouse

Don't count on seeing your Sagittarius spouse too often at home. They have busy schedules and often will be on a visiting basis as they quickly enter and, just as quickly, leave their residences. They are extremely independent, so you will have to pin them down to a fixed schedule and responsibilities. Great procrastinators, they will usually put off cleaning, straightening, and ordering their work and living spaces for as long as possible. This often indicates not their penchant for procrastination but the lack of importance they attach to such activities in general.

Finances and the Sagittarius Spouse

Sagittarians are not known for thrift, economy, or budgets. They tend to spend money when they have it, almost as if it is burning a hole in their pocket or purse. When they don't have it they are capable of living on quite little, something they would not necessarily do when things are at a sufficient financial level. Thus, they are thrifty only out of acute necessity. Sagittarians are most happy when a good cash flow is operative—they enjoy making and spending it in an easy, uncomplicated manner. They are more likely to spend on clothes and special items such as sporting equipment than on vacations or computer goods.

Infidelity and the Sagittarius Spouse

Sagittarius spouses are remarkably faithful. Should they stray, they usually undergo a good deal of self-torture and guilt before they are able to discuss a secret liaison openly with their mate. When at last they do, if ever, their emotions can come rushing out in a torrent. Honesty is so important to Sagittarians that often the reason they keep things secret is out of consideration (as they see it) for their mate, children, and other family members. Sagittarian spouses are not good at keeping secrets or being able to handle illicit affairs and should studiously avoid them.

Children and the Sagittarius Spouse

One of the great faults of Sagittarius parents is that they can be overly ambitious and pushy regarding their children's careers. Even if they deny it and claim that their children are free (which they frequently do), a closer look will reveal high expectations that must be met. Sagittarius parents feel very close to their children and often have a tendency to control their career decisions, even when they have raised their children to think for themselves and have allowed them a certain amount of freedom. Wise Sagittarius parents will avoid fostering rebellion in their children by refusing to judge and control them, which they are quite capable of doing if they try hard enough.

Divorce and the Sagittarius Spouse

Often Sagittarius spouses divorce simply because they need to be free. Thus, bad feelings toward their partners need not even be present to motivate their departure. Their intuition just dictates that it is time to move on in their self-development, and they can be quite cool and ruthless in not letting anything, including obligations to their children, stand in their way. Nor are they overly concerned about their spouses, who they seem to know will survive the ordeal. For many Sagittarians, divorce is just another fact of life, as was marriage earlier on.

The Sagittarius Lover

Sagittarius lovers often become easy prey for sexual predators, partially because they are extremely sympathetic to the plight of their lovers. If they feel the latter are lonely and unhappy, they will immediately respond in the same direct way they would to a small animal in distress. Extremely sympathetic and empathic, they can feel the pain of those whom they love and usually respond with affection and support. Sex follows quite naturally on the heels of such feelings and is often given rather than taken. Sagittarius lovers are sensitive and responsive to their lovers but can be extremely hurtful in the neglect and abandonment of their families when engaging in such extramarital activities.

STRENGTHS

Sympathetic

Empathic

Loving

WEAKNESSES

Neglectful

Abandoning

Hurtful

INTERACTIVE STYLE

Sexual

Responsive

Evocative

Meeting the Sagittarius Lover

Sagittarians most often meet their lovers by chance or through mutual friends. Having a sixth sense for lonely and unhappy individuals, they cannot resist taking an interest in them and perhaps even getting involved. Such involvements rarely become regular habits with them, but they do occur a few times in the lifetimes of most Sagittarians. (Less often will Sagittarius lovers seek to have affairs with those who are happy and contented in their lives.) They also send out signals about their own needs, but generally Sagittarius lovers suffer in silence in their marriages or lonely existences without running after others to alleviate their situation.

Location and the Sagittarius Lover

Generally, Sagittarius lovers will feel more comfortable at your place—at least in the initial phases of the affair. Since they most often see themselves as giving and helping in their displays of feeling, they may even regard their first visit as if making a house call to come to your aid. So great is the Sagittarian need to help others that they will rarely be able to hold back from trying to brighten up the lives and the living space of their lovers, whether sexual expression is part of the package or not. Frequently they will make several visits before the flames of true passion are kindled.

Sex and the Sagittarius Lover

Once Sagittarians are emotionally involved, they are ready to give their all to their lovers. However, if treated poorly, they will eventually abandon their efforts to help and seek to preserve their dignity, no matter how much their feathers were ruffled. Their wounded pride may urge them to seek another lover in turn, in order to make them again feel appreciated and valued. Thus in most cases it is not really sex itself that dictates their level of sexual involvement but more complex emotional and even ethical considerations.

Holding On to the Sagittarius Lover

Sagittarius lovers will remain faithful to those whom they have helped, provided that these individuals are not overly hurtful to them. Being appreciated is immensely important to Sagittarian lovers, and the best way to hold on to them is to let them know you value them in small ways, rather than in bombastic proclamations of love. Extremely observant, Sagittarians know when their lovers are faking and when they really mean what they say and do. Honesty is the best policy to follow with Sagittarius lovers. Their self-sacrifice can be a strong motivating factor in their continued commitment, as long as they feel you truly need them.

Entertaining the Sagittarius Lover

Sagittarius lovers enjoy being spoiled and entertained. A candlelight dinner or other romantic event is high on their list of priorities. Sagittarius lovers are magnetically drawn to private settings filled with mystery and adventure. They may find your place extremely interesting and want to go through your books, CDs, and personal effects in an effort to know and understand you better. This makes it easy to entertain them, since you only have to invite them over and let them wander around. They may even seek to help out on their first visit, even to the point of helping to straighten and clean up your place.

Breaking Up with the Sagittarius Lover

Once you show Sagittarius lovers that you do not need them anymore, they will leave. In a sense their job has been accomplished, and they can look for another poor, hurt creature to help—also giving their energy to others with whom an affair and sex are not part of the equation. Should you decide to change partners mid-affair, Sagittarius's wounded pride will usually guarantee an end to the relationship. At such a juncture, they may return to their original partners and once more bestow renewed attention on their children and friends.

The Sagittarius Ex

Pretty cool customers emotionally, Sagittarius exes are unlikely to indulge in open displays of feeling, as long as antagonisms and animosities do not surface. They prefer to remain objective about the current situation, neither waxing sentimental about the past nor being overly hopeful about the future. Although they are not averse to discussions, they will discourage emotional dependencies by keeping such interactions few, short, and if not sweet, then at least polite. Sagittarius exes believe that if both parties can show goodwill and cordiality, they stand a chance of working things out to the satisfaction of everyone concerned.

Establishing a Friendship with the Sagittarius Ex

Although not warm, such a friendship can prove effective in dealing with parental, domestic, and financial matters. A good working relationship can go a long way to defuse tensions and smooth over thorny past issues. Matters can be more complicated when Sagittarius exes have already found a new partner; greater acceptance and understanding will be required in this case to keep a friendship with them intact. Sagittarius exes can be remarkably passive in letting you take the lead and responding to your proposals rather than initiating action themselves. Do not apply pressure or rush Sagittarius exes, who need to feel free to decide on their own.

Issues of Getting Back Together with the Sagittarius Ex

Reconciliations with Sagittarius exes are possible but require much understanding and patience. When their pride or honor has been severely tested or outright damaged,

Polite

Cordial

Well-meaning

WEAKNESSES

Cold

Unemotional

Brusque

INTERACTIVE STYLE

Agreeable

Objective

Realistic

Sagittarius exes will not easily accept your offers of reconciliation. No amount of apologizing or making promises will convince them of your good intentions. Instead, they will wait and see how sincere you are and whether you are proceeding out of pure and honest motives. Taking a year or two, or even longer, to make up their minds is not unusual for Sagittarius exes, so you will have to be able to wait and show real sensitivity if they are unable or unwilling to come to a decision.

Discussing Past Issues with the Sagittarius Ex

Go easy here. Sagittarius exes are liable to get upset and emotionally worked up in the course of discussing past issues. Such upsets can abruptly reverse whatever positive trends have emerged since the breakup. Setbacks like these should be avoided at all costs—just quickly back off and change the subject when you see storm clouds gathering. If you must bring up certain issues, do so in writing, perhaps via email, encouraging them to respond in kind. Make your points succinctly and unambiguously while studiously avoiding manipulative tricks or laying on guilt trips. Listen carefully to what your Sagittarius ex is trying to tell you.

Expressing Affection to the Sagittarius Ex

You will probably face rejection should you decide to express affection openly to your Sagittarius ex. However, if they are able to break their silence, and should you see signs of their icy exterior beginning to thaw, you may take this as a precursor to an expression of affection. Do not overreact. Even if they gaze into your eyes or hold your hand, be aware that Sagittarius exes may just be testing you. They are also not above manipulating you with a display of emotion that they do not really feel but instinctively use as a controlling tactic, sometimes without even realizing it.

Defining the Present Relationship with the Sagittarius Ex

Although Sagittarius exes may agree to rules and guidelines, do not expect them to keep to them. When it comes to emotional matters, including romance, sex, and love, Sagittarians are extremely unpredictable and impulsive. They can keep cool, with their feelings under control, to a point; when their seething emotions become too much for them to handle, they are likely to break out in a fiery torrent, like a volcano erupting. Take a calming approach and refuse to respond with equal intensity, since anything done prematurely in such a highly charged situation may be severely regretted by both of you later on.

Sharing Custody with the Sagittarius Ex

Sagittarius exes usually have more to do with their lives than taking care of children, so they can be quite agreeable to sharing custody of the kids. Even if they insist on being the primary caretaker, they will accede to your offers to take the kids on weekends and special occasions and to pick them up after school from time to time. They can also be mollified and their resentment toward you lessened by repeated demonstrations of goodwill and by financial and logistical support rendered on a regular basis, freely given in a generous spirit, without them having to ask or threaten.

Friends and Family

The Sagittarius Friend

Sagittarius friends are fun to be with. They will in fact usually contact you when they are ready to have a good time and wish to share the experience. Not ones to complain or seek help from you on a regular basis, Sagittarius friends maintain an upbeat composure while keeping their troubles to themselves. As their friend, you might encourage them from time to time to discuss their problems, since suppressing their feelings and indulging in private worries can only lead to depression. They can at times be overly optimistic, necessitating that you bring them down to earth, no matter how painful such a process may be.

Asking for Help from the Sagittarius Friend

Sagittarius friends are there to help—that is, if you can catch them when you need them. Once you manage to get their attention—usually through leaving a voicemail or sending them a couple of text messages—they will be alerted to your difficulties and quickly appear at your door should you be in urgent need of help. There are few limits on the degree of aid they can offer once convinced that your needs are in fact as urgent as you say they are. Once you have passed through your crisis, Sagittarius friends will not usually stick around for very long.

Communication and Keeping in Touch with the Sagittarius Friend

Sagittarius friends customarily have little need for constant communication. They are solidly convinced of their friendships and do not see the use of continually reassuring others of their feelings or needing to be reassured themselves. Inevitably, however, Sagittarius friends will schedule an evening or afternoon together so that the two of you can catch up and share the latest news about yourselves and some interesting gossip about mutual acquaintances. Also, being that Sagittarians are creatures of habit (as far as their relationships are concerned, at least), you may set a regular monthly activity or meeting with them that fits into their work schedule.

STRENGTHS
Fun
Upbeat
Self-sufficient

WEAKNESSES
Unrealistic
Overly optimistic
Repressed

INTERACTIVE STYLE
Confident
Interested
Involved

Borrowing Money from the Sagittarius Friend

The financial situations of your Sagittarius friends are likely to be up and down. Although they are generous people and would share their last crust of bread with you, they may be broke on any given occasion when you are in financial need. If you do not know that they are out of cash, the experience of being turned down by them (and their disappointment and embarrassment of having to turn you down) can be painful for both of you. When they do have funds, they may give to you with no questions asked about repayment. Although they can even forget about small sums over time, you would do best to repay your Sagittarius friend promptly and not take advantage of their good nature.

Asking for Advice from the Sagittarius Friend

Sagittarius friends enjoy giving advice. They are more likely to keep such counsel brief and to the point, rather than going into long explanations or continually reminding you of it on subsequent meetings. Their attitude usually is that it is up to you whether you follow their advice or not. Their feelings will not be hurt if you ignore it, but should you get into the same problems over and over again, they may lose interest in continually warning you. As they see it, many of your troubles have a simple solution; they may therefore feel that you create your own troubles by continually making things more complicated than they are.

Visiting the Sagittarius Friend

Because Sagittarius friends are often in motion, it is not easy to find them at home, although once they have settled in, they will welcome visits from friends. Consequently it makes more sense to visit with them on the run by catching them between appointments at a local bar or restaurant on their path. Such visits are best kept short. Should you want to spend a quiet evening together, you are better off inviting them over to visit you, keeping in mind they may have to postpone your meeting if an appointment is made too far in advance.

Celebrations/Entertainment with the Sagittarius Friend

Sagittarius friends are fond of birthday and holiday celebrations. They will be up for hosting such events at their place, but they can also be available to pitch in with group endeavors away from home. Their role is often that of picking up items at the store, frequently being asked to dash out to buy last-minute or forgotten items. Fonder of small parties than large-scale sit-down dinners or reunions, Sagittarians love the intimacy of being with a few close friends for a quiet or boisterous evening, depending on their moods. Footing the bill is something they like to do when flush with cash, and their generosity in supplying good food and drink is legendary.

The Sagittarius Roommate

Sagittarius roommates can wear you down with their abundant enthusiasm. Also, when they are in a motormouth mood, you will desperately look for a way to shut them up, at least for the time being. Thankfully, they will be out and about most of the time, leaving you alone to be able to concentrate once more and recover from their energetic onslaughts. Sagittarius roommates may have difficulty handling negativity, either from you or the landlord, since they frequently sink into depressions when their expectations are not met or when unexpected disappointments surface. Sometimes they simply forget about rent, utilities, and food contributions, so just remind them to pay. They will not take offense to such inquiries.

Sharing Financial Responsibilities with the Sagittarius Roommate

With all the best intentions, Sagittarius roommates will agree to fully share financial responsibilities. Carrying through on this, however, is not always possible for them, particularly when they are switching jobs or seeking employment, both of which may be happening with great regularity. Sagittarius roommates can grow anxious when the end of the month rolls around and they are completely broke, and they will communicate their anxiety to you as well. Invariably they will ask you to cover for them and promise to pay you back as soon as possible. When they have work, Sagittarians are capable of fulfilling their obligations on time.

Cleaning and the Sagittarius Roommate

Sagittarians are renowned neither for their cleaning skills nor for their thirst to put things in order. Rather, they have their own peculiar ideas on straightening up and can even proudly display their results, leaving you astounded at how little they have accomplished in bringing order to the living situation. The Sagittarius roommate's ideas are thus quite peculiar, but once they set their minds to cleaning up, they can do a good job. Catching them at the right moment can be a formidable challenge. Be forewarned—cleaning is not usually high on their list of priorities.

Houseguests and the Sagittarius Roommate

Sagittarius roommates can be very welcoming to your guests, seeking to make them feel comfortable and relaxed. However, their whirlwind energies are not always conducive to making others feel at home; consequently, even the most placid souls can be jolted by the lightning bolts they cast. No doubt about it, Sagittarians can be provocative toward your guests, not out of negativity but from a need to check them out, to see if they can be trusted in the future. Often good judges of character, Sagittarians can spot dishonesty and phoniness a mile away, and they cannot refrain from launching barbs to deflate overblown egos.

Parties and the Sagittarius Roommate

Most Sagittarius roommates will enjoy throwing parties, both with you and on their own (in your absence). The only problem is that they may begin to hog the spotlight, particularly after they have had a few drinks or built up their enthusiastic enjoyment to a fever pitch. Going overboard is the invariable result, whether the consequences are glasses and plates dropping or the decibel level rising to unbearable heights. Sagittarius laughter is unforgettable and highly contagious. Normally, Sagittarius roommates are

(The Sagittarius Roommate)

STRENGTHS

Enthusiastic

Optimistic

Giving

WEAKNESSES

Talkative

Unheeding

Forgetful

INTERACTIVE STYLE

Frenetic

Hopeful

Forgiving

not satisfied until everyone present is having a great time. The next morning they may not remember anything of their actions.

Privacy and the Sagittarius Roommate

Sagittarius roommates rarely demand privacy. First of all, they enjoy social contact at home, and second they are able to concentrate or work with lots of activity around them. Sagittarius roommates are likely to get nervous when things are too quiet for days on end. They do not look on privacy as something they have to guarantee themselves, but as something they can share with you and even your friends. Beware of what you tell them, since they like to share your ideas and even secrets with others, as a means of encouraging you to be more open and less private.

Discussing Problems with the Sagittarius Roommate

Generally speaking, Sagittarius roommates are ready to offer a sympathetic ear. Good listeners, they may not immediately come up with a solution, but suddenly they will be lit up by a lightning flash of inspiration after some time. Beware of following these epiphanies literally, since too often Sagittarius roommates are giving their peculiar points of view rather than thinking about how you can deal with a particular problem. Do not feel constrained to follow their advice, since they will not take offense if you fail to do so. Ultimately, they feel that your problems are your business to take care of.

The Sagittarius Parent

Sagittarius parents are very giving toward their children. Not driven by feelings of responsibility but simply by their devotion and love, Sagittarius parents often enrich their domestic lives through the addition of household pets and a need to establish their families in beautiful natural surroundings. That said, many Sagittarius parents ultimately fail in their marriages despite the cement of their parent–child relationships. This is often due to their demanding natures, their inability to continue to compromise for too many years in a row, and their inherent restlessness, which can take them far afield. Once they have made up their minds to jump ship, either for a change of life or a new partner, they do so without looking back or having regrets.

Discipline Style of the Sagittarius Parent

Sagittarius parents can be severe with their children when they exhibit unethical or dishonest behavior. Just going against their wishes is not enough to really upset them, since they admire their progeny's shows of pluck and individuality. Rarely will Sagittarius parents discipline their children on a regular basis, nor will they exhibit punitive physical behavior unless driven to the end of their rope. One bad habit Sagittarius parents can engage in when angry is to become silent, which often affects their offspring more deeply and cruelly than physical punishment. Another is to lay on guilt trips or stir the pity pot.

Affection Level and the Sagittarius Parent

Sagittarius parents love to cuddle cats, dogs, and—yes—their kids, too. Physically oriented, Sagittarians enjoy close contact with those they love and believe that hugs are an important part of every daily encounter. They do not have tremendous needs, however, to receive affection from others, preferring to give it instead. They can remain remarkably cool and undemonstrative outside cuddly periods and not give a clear idea of how affectionate they can be. Sagittarius parents can also express affection through the familiarities of jokes, teasing behavior, and gentle derision.

Money Issues and the Sagittarius Parent

Sagittarius parents would rather starve and deprive themselves of necessities than deny their children what they need. Not necessarily prone to heaping gifts on their progeny or buying them only what they demand or crave, Sagittarius parents will be generous in areas that tend to build character and serve the purpose of developing educational and professional opportunities. In wanting the best for their children they frequently reveal their true intentions—to see their children get ahead and become successful. Such ambitions should not be allowed to get out of control, for they can rob the children of initiative and self-worth.

Crises and the Sagittarius Parent

Sagittarius parents are just as capable of engendering crises as they are of dealing with them. Sometimes it is precisely this fact that keeps them from seeing why the crises arose in the first place and from being able to resolve them. Many parents born under the sign of the archer miss the mark by a wide margin when aiming to come to their children's aid. Part of this is due to a clouding of their judgment, but also to their sensitive nervous systems, which can be so easily upset. Learning to remain cool under fire is a great challenge for Sagittarius parents.

Holidays/Family Gatherings and the Sagittarius Parent

Sagittarius parents who relate well to their brothers and sisters can pass along such good feelings to their children and nieces and nephews at any family get-together. The problem is that although their children and nieces and nephews may look forward to seeing one another over the years, the parents might not, frequently being upset by the uncompromising and alienating behavior of the Sagittarius member of the clan. Too often the Sagittarius parent comes to feel like an outsider at family gatherings, and when resentments or angry feelings arise, this creates problems for their children, who could be feeling quite at home until parental storm clouds gather.

Caring for the Aging Sagittarius Parent

Many Sagittarians become fussy and peculiar the older they get. Difficult to satisfy, they may resent any intrusion on their personal space, particularly by a well-meaning relative who is trying to put things in order. Aging Sagittarius parents will send out a strong signal to back off, and if this is not heeded, they may break off contact completely. Looking after aging Sagittarius parents requires great tact and care to avoid rousing them to fury.

(The Sagittarius Parent)

STRENGTHS
Giving
Loving
Natural

WEAKNESSES
Dissatisfied
Inconstant
Distracted

INTERACTIVE STYLE
Driven
Temperamental
Restless

Often the best approach is to leave them to their own devices while keeping a good eye on them and making sure their physical wants are satisfied and their safety guaranteed.

The Sagittarius Sibling

Too often Sagittarius siblings find themselves the odd ones out in their family groups. It can be difficult for their brothers and sisters to deal with Sagittarius siblings, since the latter's natural tendencies to protect them (if younger) are frequently unappreciated or outright rejected, and their urges to win out (if older) are likely to dominate. So different are they from their siblings that Sagittarians often stand out, even to the point of looking different from the others. Great respect must be paid to their individuality and a wide berth given to their unusual approaches to things if conflicts are to be avoided.

Rivalry/Closeness with the Sagittarius Sibling

Sagittarius siblings rarely, if ever, give up in a struggle with their brothers and sisters. This includes vying for their parents' attention, although Sagittarians are less concerned with being the favorite than they are with winning in games and contests. Self-confident and aggressive in competitions, Sagittarius siblings can be quiet, even shy, in their private interactions with family members and friends. They will rarely seek to draw attention to themselves, often being content to play on their own, particularly when creating a fantasy world for themselves. Allowing a favorite brother or sister (often of the same sex) to share their vivid, imaginative creations should be viewed as a compliment.

Past Issues and the Sagittarius Sibling

Sagittarius siblings can be very unforgiving and may never forget an insult delivered by one of their brothers or sisters. Extremely protective toward pets or animals encountered on the street, Sagittarius siblings will condemn acts of cruelty or neglect and not easily forgive them. Should they feel they are on the receiving end of cruelty or neglect by their parents, Sagittarian children will at times suffer in silence and even take the blame in order to protect their siblings from harm. Such past issues will be carried into their adult lives and periodically surface, resulting in disturbances of the family equilibrium.

Dealing with the Estranged Sagittarius Sibling

Engaging an estranged Sagittarius sibling in physical activity of any sort is usually the best way to bring them back into the fold. All the idle chatter, promises, reminders of past joys, and such will usually have no effect. But if estranged Sagittarius siblings agree to an invitation to a sporting event, a fashion or technology show, or an afternoon at the beach, this could be the first step toward reconciliation and, ultimately, forgiveness. Sagittarians do not enjoy having bad feelings. They are quite relieved to be rid of them while keeping their dignity without apologizing or admitting defeat.

Money Issues (Borrowing Money, Wills, Etc.) and the Sagittarius Sibling

Since fairness and honesty are so important to Sagittarius siblings, they will insist on ethical treatment for all concerned in the matter of wills and inheritances. They are just as likely to stand up for their siblings as they are for themselves, and they will condemn and oppose any unfairness. Unfortunately, their frequently moral attitudes can also be condemning, and in casting actions in black-and-white terms as either bad or good, they may close themselves off from meaningful contact with others. Their great lesson in life is to learn to be more accepting and understanding of the situations and viewpoints of others.

Holidays/Celebrations/Reunions and the Sagittarius Sibling

Sagittarius siblings enjoy a nice family celebration once or twice a year. They are also quite hospitable and will look forward to inviting everyone over to their place and going to some trouble to make sure guests have a good time. They will be wary, however, of committing themselves to being present more often—say, on a monthly basis—since they value their privacy and freedom so highly. Moreover, past issues are more likely to surface when get-togethers are held more frequently; also their irritation threshold is often quite low and easily reached.

Vacationing with the Sagittarius Sibling

Sagittarius siblings prefer to vacation alone, with their friends, or as the head of their own families. Thus it is better if siblings of Sagittarians refrain from trying to include them in their vacation plans. Instead of getting stuck far away from home with a suddenly cantankerous Sagittarian, it would be more prudent to invite them to a larger social gathering during the summer, like a cookout. If they are vegetarians (as many Sagittarians are), be sure to meet their special dietary requirements. Their love of animals and aversion to meat-eating usually go hand in hand.

The Sagittarius Child

The Sagittarius child can be difficult or even impossible to control. Freedom-loving to the extreme, Sagittarius children will break established rules and batter down barriers designed to contain them. These irresistible forces sweep all before them, except, of course, if they have a parent who is a true immovable object. In this case, knockdown, drag-out battles are likely to ensue, causing continual upsets within the family. The wise parent will not only give Sagittarius children their freedom, but also allow them to win such freedom and take it at the end of a long struggle. Sagittarius children thrive on impossible challenges and pride themselves on winning as underdogs in unequal combat.

Personality Development and the Sagittarius Child

Sagittarius children should be wisely guided through the various stages of their personality development. Should they be blocked at a crucial point in such development, they are likely to suffer severe psychological consequences that can inhibit their personality growth in adulthood. Sagittarius children demand a great amount of understanding and

STRENGTHS

Challenge-oriented

Striving

Overcoming

WEAKNESSES

Antagonistic

Rebellious

Unheeding

INTERACTIVE STYLE

Feisty

Combative

Insistent

patience if they are to develop properly, and all knee-jerk responses to their provocative actions should be avoided by good parents. Often their rebelliousness is simply a manifestation of hurt at not being understood, and a sagacious parent will understand such behavior and not impulsively react to it.

Hobbies/Interests/Career Paths for the Sagittarius Child

Sagittarius children have unusual ambitions that should not be derided, even if they are not taken entirely seriously. Aside from the standard childhood wishes of wanting to be a firefighter or sports or movie star, Sagittarius children can dream up the weirdest career aspirations, usually based on their hobby or principal childhood interest. Never laugh at or deride their choices, since they take such matters very seriously and may find it difficult to forget your mockery later in life. Sagittarius children will usually change or adjust their career aspirations in late adolescence and can wind up picking a quite practical career and becoming successful at it as well.

Discipline and the Sagittarius Child

Fight any tendency to get physical with Sagittarius children. Normally a word of warning or a threatening look will be more than enough to let them know how you feel. Disciplinary measures to counter their frequently wild tendencies are best applied in the form of structures and practical rules that make sense to them after being carefully explained. Once Sagittarius children agree with you, they will follow your rules with enthusiasm, and rebelliousness should not be a problem. If, however, you institute arbitrary restrictions to which they are flat-out opposed, expect the worst. Sagittarius children do not back down from confrontations with parents and frequently exult in them, so avoid giving them an excuse for this kind of expression to run out of hand.

Affection Level and the Sagittarius Child

Sagittarius children thrive on affection. Like flowers turning toward the light, they will open up and respond in kind. However, because they hate phoniness of all sorts, they will shrink from false displays of affection that parents make in public. Unless you want to be unmasked and embarrassed in a most unequivocal manner, refrain from any fake actions of this sort. As much as they thrive on affection, so Sagittarius children suffer from lack of it. A cold, critical, or overly demanding parent who withholds love or uses it as a weapon can do untold psychological damage to a sensitive Sagittarius child. Neglect can also prove to be an insidious form of abuse.

Dealing with the Sagittarius Child and Interactions with Siblings

Most Sagittarius children do not demand special treatment; they just want to be afforded the same opportunities as their siblings. If their brothers and sisters do not understand or accept the unusual qualities of their Sagittarius siblings, they should never be openly forced to get along with them. Children can be guided to coexist with Sagittarius siblings in a more subtle manner, one that will not further exacerbate the already volatile situation. Defusing conflicts between Sagittarians and their siblings can become a regular family activity, one that can yield great rewards and diminish the domestic stress level.

Interacting with the Adult Sagittarius Child

Being such strong-minded individuals, adult Sagittarius children should be approached with respect for their frequently unusual lifestyles and habits. Making assumptions about them can be a recipe for disaster. Rather, they should always be asked whether something agrees with them before it is implemented, not in a hesitant or demeaning way but just straight-out, without being defensive. Furthermore, when planning an activity, it is often best to drop a suggestion, plant a seed in their minds, and later let them take the lead. Their pride over successfully setting up a simple meeting, perhaps having a drink or going for a walk, is often one that adult Sagittarius children will cherish and can leave the door open for future interactions.

Capricorn

BIRTHDATE **DECEMBER 22–JANUARY 20**

Ruled by the fateful planet Saturn, Capricorns are serious, ambitious individuals, most certainly ones to be reckoned with. The cardinal earth nature of this sign makes Capricorns highly responsible people who can be dominant and demanding figures in any group of which they are a part. Capricorns need to lighten up periodically and not take themselves so seriously. Their capacity for enjoyment is great when they are finally able to relax. Those who know them well come to value their practical and pragmatic attitudes.

Work

The Capricorn Boss

Capricorns are dominant personalities, and therefore bosses born under this sign will want to be obeyed without question. Moreover, they will insist on maintaining their position as leaders of the department or company, and under no circumstances will they allow you or anyone else to undermine their authority. "Never outshine the master" is a good rule to follow when working for a Capricorn boss. Not necessarily hungry for advancement, Capricorn bosses are more likely to hang onto their rung of the corporate ladder having once reached that level and, in most cases, intending to remain there for as long as possible.

Asking the Capricorn Boss for a Raise

Capricorn bosses will expect you to back up your request for a raise with facts and figures that clearly show your indispensable qualities, your track record of hard work, and your history of taking initiative while remaining firmly within company guidelines. Avoid making startling pledges or promises about your future contributions; such statements will only be dismissed by Capricorn bosses as wishful thinking. Once these pragmatic individuals are convinced that your request for a raise is warranted, they will give it serious consideration and then get back to you promptly with their decision.

Breaking Bad News to the Capricorn Boss

If you are the person mainly responsible for the failure or breakdown you are reporting, you should be prepared for the average Capricorn boss to judge you severely and to turn a deaf ear to most of your excuses and explanations. On the other hand, should you be breaking bad news concerning a situation in which you played only a small role or were not involved at all, you can emphasize your loyalty to the company and your intentions to work hard to rectify things. If the failed project is worth saving, you could volunteer to head the cleanup or damage control or to brainstorm a new department to take the place of the old one.

STRENGTHS
Dominant
Determined
Self-assured

WEAKNESSES
Insensitive
Unheeding
Stubborn

INTERACTIVE STYLE
Authoritarian
Commanding
Firm

Arranging Travel and/or Entertainment for the Capricorn Boss

Although Capricorn bosses enjoy having a good time, they are thrifty individuals who tend to be tightfisted about cash outlays for entertainment, whether designed for others or themselves. Lovers of good food and drink, Capricorns have appetites that should be indulged by dinners that include large portions of delicious food and a good choice of wines. Picking chic or "in" restaurants is not important. In arranging travel accommodations, Capricorn bosses require only moderately priced or slightly above average hotels, and unless the company is flush with cash at the moment, there is no need to fly them first class.

Decision-Making and the Capricorn Boss

Capricorn bosses will insist on all important decisions being left to them and will expect you not to question their directives. On the other hand, they do value your taking initiative when called upon to do so, but ultimately they will expect you to make the same kinds of decisions they themselves would have, had they been present. This requires that you know your bosses' minds and methods thoroughly and that you always seek the most effective ways to follow them. Thus, Capricorn bosses demand unswerving allegiance but also a deep level of understanding of their outlooks.

Impressing and/or Motivating the Capricorn Boss

Being highly pragmatic and practical, Capricorn bosses are only impressed with results. Whether these are modest or spectacular is not most important in the long run, and they tend to value steady growth more than sudden windfalls, of which they are a bit suspicious anyway. Capricorn bosses will not really be motivated by your excitement and enthusiasm, instead demanding good, solid arguments to back up your ideas. Once they know they can trust your judgment, they will react positively to your thoughts and be motivated to throw their support fully behind them.

Making Proposals and/or Giving Presentations to the Capricorn Boss

In giving presentations to Capricorn bosses, be sure to take your time, don't hurry over details, and, above all, be thorough in clearly stating every aspect of your proposals. Capricorn bosses are thoughtful individuals who will take the time to listen to you once they have invited or ordered you to make such a presentation—in many ways, your success in impressing others will be seen as a shared achievement, one that demonstrates how well you and your boss work together. Capricorn bosses are happiest when they can reward their best employees by giving full approval to their proposals, either in private or group settings.

The Capricorn Employee

Classically, Capricorn employees are dedicated and hardworking but also highly ambitious souls. Heading up the ladder of success is usually their aim, one that is best accomplished by jumping from one rung on the first ladder to the next highest on the next, and so forth. Therefore, they will be loyal to the company only to a point, always looking out for their own interest and advancement. They usually jump ship at the right moment and handily shift gears to fit the new position. The quality of their work is high, and what they lack in inspiration they make up for with perspiration.

Interviewing and/or Hiring the Capricorn Employee

Extensive vetting of prospective Capricorn employees is not usually necessary. As a matter of fact, they may very well have vetted *you* beforehand to learn your likes and dislikes, character traits, and experiences. Their CV or résumé is usually adequate, and their technical background and work qualifications sufficient for the job. This is because Capricorns rarely apply for positions they just hope to get, instead focusing on ones they know objectively they have a good crack at. Realists, Capricorns are more aware than most of their competitors and also know how to make a good impression at the first interview.

Breaking Bad News to or Firing the Capricorn Employee

Try to avoid breaking bad news to Capricorn employees when they are depressed or in pain or discomfort. If you do, you may see their chins drop, their heads hang, and their shoulders slump. Firing them in such a situation could lead to extreme upset and a quiet nervous breakdown. However, when in a more content frame of mind, Capricorns tend to get emotional and can even lose control if they are told that they did a lousy job. After denying it, arguing vehemently, and finally yelling, they will be difficult to calm down. Storming out of the room and slamming the door usually is Capricorn's grand finale to this tempestuous scene.

Traveling with and Entertaining the Capricorn Employee

Sensualists, Capricorns are pleasure lovers who enjoy the comforts and luxuries of travel and entertaining. They are thrifty, however, and will not part with their money easily unless the meal and the wine are something special. However, on a low-budget trip, Capricorns are good at roughing it; even if they are not enjoying themselves, they will not complain. However, if cleanliness and hygiene are not adequate, they will want to leave immediately and find better, and only slightly more expensive, rooms. If the company travel budget is generous, Capricorns are not at all ashamed or shy about indulging themselves.

Assigning Tasks to the Capricorn Employee

Capricorn employees are good at taking instruction, noting what is required of them and how the rules of the job and the department are best followed. Before throwing themselves into a new task, Capricorns will want to be prepared and will insist on being extensively briefed and instructed, perhaps manually, in a series of training sessions. Failure is not a word found in the Capricorn lexicon, and they aren't interested in getting it right the second or fourth time either. Part of the problem may arise from their workaholic habits as well as their tendency to put themselves under tremendous stress.

(The Capricorn Employee)

STRENGTHS
Dedicated
Persistent
Hardworking

WEAKNESSES
Overambitious
Disloyal
Selfish

INTERACTIVE STYLE
Aspiring
Upwardly mobile
Unrelenting

Motivating or Impressing the Capricorn Employee

Capricorn employees are impressed by good, solid, down-to-earth, practical reasoning. When bosses show good sense in making an executive decision, they earn points from their Capricorn employees. The latter will respect bosses capable of working side by side with them, without fanfare, just rolling up their sleeves and diving in. If they can think of their bosses as not only colleagues but also friends, they will always go that extra mile for them. Often Capricorn employees' whole social life is tied up with their fellow workers, and so they make good committee members, party planners, and union members.

Managing, Directing, or Criticizing the Capricorn Employee

Managing and directing Capricorn employees should not be a problem, as long as two things are guaranteed and agreed upon: first, that everything is spelled out about their responsibilities from the outset; and second, that a realistic estimate of what is expected of them follows. Should the first be ambiguous or fuzzy and the second be only wishful thinking, Capricorns will usually bring the proceedings to an abrupt halt and ask that these two points be more fully discussed and ironed out before they will proceed with the job. Being patient with and listening noncritically to Capricorn employees at this stage will yield dividends later.

The Capricorn Coworker

Capricorn coworkers are steady and dependable. They form a solid part of any work team and can perform at an adequate or high level for years on end. Not at all humorless individuals, they enjoy their social contacts at work and love to tell an occasional joke or story that they hope can rivet the attention of their colleagues. Capricorns are particularly fond of office parties, celebrations, and special events that give them a chance to

revel in the good feelings that abound at such get-togethers. Infrequently, Capricorns will have a single best friend among their coworkers, one with whom they usually have lunch and sometimes go for a walk when there is time to do so.

Approaching the Capricorn Coworker for Advice

Capricorn coworkers take giving advice seriously. Consequently, if they do not think they can help, they will refrain from offering counsel. However, by this time, they may have achieved a reputation around the office for having given sage advice in the past; therefore, it is worth pursuing and also pushing them a bit to help in a difficult situation. Ultimately, Capricorn coworkers will regard your continued efforts as a form of flattery and will usually agree to lend their wisdom to help solve the problem. They are conservative in their approach. Their judgment can be trusted and their recommendations followed.

Approaching the Capricorn Coworker for Help

Capricorn coworkers are prepared to help with deeds as well as with words. However, they must be fully convinced that the individuals who ask for help truly need it and that helping will contribute to the well-being and success of the entire work group. In fact, Capricorn coworkers feel better about helping the professional situation rather than giving personal aid to an individual. Thus, Capricorn coworkers often put the good of the group before personal interests, either those of others or even their own.

Traveling with and Entertaining the Capricorn Coworker

Traveling and entertainment give the more serious and quiet Capricorn coworkers a chance to step out, express themselves, and indulge their social side. Consequently, taking part in these two areas often finds them in a good mood and ready to do their best to make the experience a success. Not ones to be picky or difficult, most Capricorn coworkers will not ask for special treatment but will be respectful of the company's budget allowances for travel and entertainment, and they will work within them in a thrifty and thoughtful manner. Usually Capricorn coworkers can be counted on to make the best of a difficult situation.

The Capricorn Coworker Cooperating with Others

Capricorn coworkers do not always find it easy to cooperate with others in work matters, particularly when they disagree with motives or methods that they feel are improper. Furthermore, they have strong likes and dislikes as far as people are concerned. They may in fact have positive feelings about the work group of which they are a part but find one or two members of that group highly irritating, causing occasional sharp confrontations. Not troublemakers themselves, Capricorn coworkers are particularly bothered by colorful individuals needy of attention who periodically cause turmoil by stirring the pot.

Impressing and Motivating the Capricorn Coworker

Capricorn coworkers are most impressed by bosses and fellow employees who produce steady, dependable results over time. Also impressed by the high degree of an individual's commitment, they particularly admire those who put the needs of the company and their work group before their own. Capricorn coworkers are strongly motivated when they see those around them lending dedicated service, pitching in, and pulling together. Motivating Capricorn coworkers can substantially help in producing results, since their steady and forceful energies are prodigious once fully aroused. Few obstacles will stand in their way when they are determined to win, and they rarely give up before goals are realized.

Persuading and/or Criticizing the Capricorn Coworker

It is best to use lighter forms of criticism and more subtle, persuasive approaches in dealing with Capricorn coworkers, since a direct approach may strike them as confrontational and just cause them to dig in their heels and stubbornly resist your efforts. Capricorn coworkers love to be charmed, seduced, and enchanted despite their often serious and pragmatic stance. The job of persuading them and of making critical

(The Capricorn Coworker)

STRENGTHS

Appreciative

Faithful

Social

WEAKNESSES

Boring

Unappreciated

Overlooked

INTERACTIVE STYLE

Steady

Dependable

Selfless

observations should be left to the one or two individuals in the group who are able to work their seductive magic on them. Such individuals usually know when to approach Capricorn coworkers and also how to get them to listen.

The Capricorn Client

Your first meeting with Capricorn clients will leave little doubt about what they want. Self-assured and well-directed, these solid individuals have a clear picture of what they desire you to accomplish for them. However, they may not understand what it is they really need, and here your analytical powers and intuition may serve to enlighten them, allowing you to help in their efforts far more than they ever realized possible. Capricorn clients will be open to your suggestions as long as you bring them to the table in an intriguing, inoffensive, and nonconfrontational manner.

Impressing the Capricorn Client

Capricorn clients will be impressed if you can give them a new slant on promoting and selling their product or service, one that they never considered. Very ambitious, Capricorns are always on the lookout for new approaches that will allow them to move ahead. That said, their innate conservatism must always be taken into account—you must be sure that your arguments are backed up with solid facts and that your approach is pragmatic enough to satisfy them. Capricorn clients will listen to very far-out ideas with interest, as long as they have a firm basis, particularly financially.

Selling to the Capricorn Client

Allow your ideas to speak for themselves, rather than dressing them up in fancy paper and ribbons. Capricorn clients are straight shooters who want you to deliver your information and concepts straight from the hip. They will let you know immediately if they agree or disagree, but characteristically will also probably tell you they need time to mull things over. Thoughtful to the extreme, Capricorns are not just talking when they say they will get back to you in a given amount of time. Nor will they be ambiguous in their decisions, which usually reflect a clear "yes" or "no" to your offer.

Your Appearance and the Capricorn Client

Your appearance is not overly important to Capricorn clients, since they are much more interested in what you say than how you look. In fact, they are most interested in what they have to say, and they expect you to listen carefully. Thus your attitude should be a highly receptive one—always attentive and manifesting such attention by silence and occasionally posing carefully worded questions. In such a meeting, you would best appear as a reporter would while conducting an interview. This does not imply putting yourself down but simply letting the Capricorn client take the lead, with you providing the gentle guidance to keep things on track and mutually rewarding.

Keeping the Capricorn Client's Interest

The Capricorn client's interest in you is usually directly proportional to the interest you show in them. Nothing displeases Capricorn clients more than being faced with someone who finds them boring and who nods off as they drone on and on. If you are attentive to them, they will be not only more likely to engage your services but also inspired to do their best thinking, making things ultimately more productive for any future project. Once you two have defined the task, waste no time in showing Capricorn clients that you are also able to implement plans in a prompt and efficient manner.

Breaking Bad News to the Capricorn Client

Matter-of-fact in most professional situations, Capricorn clients can handle bad news without being knocked off balance. Often, they have already anticipated such news, as they normally keep their ears close to the ground to monitor the progress of any business endeavor. They will probably already have thought up an alternate plan, and in immediately bringing up such a new approach they will relieve you of the responsibility of explaining your bad luck or making excuses for an outright failure. Rather than summarily dismissing you, they will make you feel accepted and even rewarded by giving you a second chance to prove yourself.

Entertaining the Capricorn Client

Because of their serious demeanor in business matters, Capricorn clients love to blow off steam in a pleasurable way. Working hard and playing hard are Capricorn characteristics, so be sure you provide forms of entertainment that will knock their socks off, rather than just mildly arousing them. Remember the innate Capricorn physicality by presenting an impressive menu of food, drink, music, dance, and funny, provocative activities. Pulling out all the stops in the entertainment area can yield tangible results, often in the form of a more intimate rapport in your next professional meeting together.

The Capricorn Business Partner

Capricorn business partners exhibit obvious positive and negative qualities, which should be taken into consideration when entering into a partnership with them. Capricorns are ambitious and hardworking folks who can be relied on to produce steady—albeit unspectacular—results over the years. Not always the most imaginative or colorful individuals, Capricorn business partners offer little flexibility and versatility, but they do well when ensconced in one or several restricted areas and job functions, being free to oversee and administer the more varied work of others. Excellent administrators and bookkeepers, Capricorn partners will see to it that all records are kept in perfect order.

Setting Up the Business Partnership with Capricorn

Most Capricorns will insist on sitting down with you and hammering out both the structure of the company and the roles the two of you will play in implementing it. Before becoming your business partner, Capricorns are also likely to engage in a thor-

STRENGTHS

Focused

Orderly

Administrative

WEAKNESSES

Bland

Unimaginative

Dull

INTERACTIVE STYLE

Capable

Dependable

Steady

ough vetting process in which your background and track record are closely scrutinized. Only when they are absolutely sure of your reliability will they agree to draw up a tight partnership contract that binds you two securely into one organic team. Because these contracts are likely to offer little or no wiggle room, you had best give them your full attention before signing.

Tasking with the Capricorn Business Partner

Capricorn business partners are usually aware of their strengths and weaknesses and have a good idea of which tasks are best left to them. You would do well to listen carefully to their ideas on the subject and then to assume the tasks left to you. This can create problems only if there are jobs to be done that neither of you feels comfortable with, and this can necessitate bringing in a third or even fourth party who is given important administrative duties without entering the company as a full partner. Tasks can also be shared with your Capricorn partner as long as the work protocol is carefully defined.

Traveling with and Entertaining the Capricorn Business Partner

It can be quite reassuring to travel with a Capricorn business partner at your side. Capricorns have a lot of practical know-how and are good at implementing, scheduling, and structuring business meetings and trips. On such a journey you can be sure that little will be left to chance. This has its good and bad sides, however, since at times you will prefer to follow your hunches and wing it, while Capricorn partners may try to hold you to their fixed plans. You may have to find a way to follow your own promptings, going off on your own to visit entertainment spots of your choice without insulting or alienating your Capricorn partner.

Managing and Directing the Capricorn Business Partner

It will be very difficult to manage and direct a Capricorn business partner if your plans are always changing and too highly imaginative. The best way to control Capricorn partners is to hold them to specific agreed-upon details (or at the very least ones discussed in an earlier stage of planning) and to keep to them yourself as much as possible. Strangely, Capricorn business partners have an erratic side, often brought out when they are emotionally engaged or upset, and here your application of rules and guidelines in a calm but firm manner will serve to calm them and get them back on track. In most situations, however, Capricorn partners do not need extensive managing or direction.

Relating to the Capricorn Business Partner in the Long Run

Once Capricorn partners know they can trust you and you have proved yourself capable while under fire, they will leave the day-to-day running of your departments up to you. From time to time, they will scrutinize your work, but usually only during the normal four to six times a year when the company undergoes a full review of its financial and business condition. Frictions can arise with Capricorn partners if you push them to make sudden decisions or urge them to change the basic direction or structure of the company's business activities. Otherwise, things should run smoothly over the long haul, given that steady and positive—albeit unspectacular—results are forthcoming.

Parting Ways with the Capricorn Business Partner

The dissolution of partnerships with Capricorns will probably be a foregone conclusion by the time you actually part ways. Realists first and foremost, Capricorns will be aware of difficulties as they arise and not kid themselves about how serious things have gotten between you two when on a downward spiral. The problem is that they may choose not to share their thoughts and can just proceed day-to-day as if nothing is wrong; one day they will drop the bomb that things are not working. Usually, by this time, they will already have figured out how the breakup can be most efficiently implemented.

The Capricorn Competitor

You can be sure Capricorn competitors will give you a run for your money. Persistent, they rarely give up in a struggle and can continue to compete for years on end. Do not make the mistake, however, of thinking that they are slow or that they will be unable to counter your quick and unexpected thrusts. Although they may be temporarily thrown off balance by such contact, they can mount formidable defenses once they see what you are up to. The analytic faculties of Capricorn competitors are high, and because of their abilities to painstakingly examine every detail of your campaign—as well as their willingness to counterattack when ready—they make formidable opponents.

Countering the Capricorn Competitor

The most effective way to counter Capricorn competitors is to set traps they can fall into. Because of their tendency to use reason rather than intuition, you should seek to throw out false clues and get them to make unsound assumptions about your campaigns. Once they think they have figured you out, they generally will adopt an attitude that can lead them far off the mark. Stubborn, they will hang on to their conclusions and refuse to change or adjust them, giving you the time and space you need to further your product or service without meeting resistance.

Out-Planning the Capricorn Competitor

It is difficult to out-plan these stubborn competitors, since thorough preparation is one of their fortes. Better to watch them carefully, figure out their direction, and throw them off balance with carefully considered tactics you know to be effective given the past histories of your Capricorn competitors. It is likely that they may adopt a waiting game, in which case your patience will be stretched to the limit. Remember that Capricorn competitors always think long-term, so you should seek to dominate them with constantly shifting and astute short-term decisions they may see as puzzling and therefore difficult to counter. As long as they do not understand you, you can win.

STRENGTHS
Persistent
Analytical
Watchful

WEAKNESSES
Plodding
Overly logical
Lacking insight

INTERACTIVE STYLE
Counterattacking
Competitive
Enduring

Impressing the Capricorn Competitor in Person

Keep Capricorn competitors off-balance by upsetting their expectations. Once you understand the assumptions they have made about you and your company, you can proceed to thwart these and therefore impress your competitor with your seeming know-how. In fact, while they are watching you, fascinated by your mysterious successes that have no explanation from their analytical point of view, you can confuse them further. Wearing provocative or bewildering color combinations, making non sequiturs, and laughing nervously or inappropriately can all prove effective. Like a snake, you will fascinate and flummox them, which will be evident in their loss of concentration and overall discomfort.

Undercutting and Outbidding the Capricorn Competitor

Play your cards close to your chest in bidding wars, and never let your Capricorn competitors see your true intentions. These solid individuals can be misled when you change tactics with puzzling regularity. If you study their plans carefully, certain defects in their reasoning will emerge that can allow you to disarm them and gain the upper hand. Also an effective tactic is to secure a client or property that has no seeming advantage to you, since Capricorn competitors will then agonize about why you made such a decision and lose precious time and energy in doing so.

Public Relations Wars with the Capricorn Competitor

Public relations are not usually the strongest suit of Capricorn competitors. They often make the mistake of thinking they are good in this area and choose to save money by implementing public relations campaigns themselves rather than hiring a well-known and expensive firm to do this specialized work. If you allot a significant amount of your budget to public relations (perhaps hiring the very firm that your Capricorn competitor should have but did not), you should be able to prevail in such struggles. Capricorn competitors frequently lack an understanding of human nature, which can alienate them from their customers.

The Capricorn Competitor and the Personal Approach

Because of their lack of sensitivity and one-track minds, Capricorn competitors are easy to read. Using an astute psychological approach, one that preys on Capricorn's vulnerability to personal attacks, you can effectively incapacitate these competitors. Do some research into their personal life, uncovering invariant habits they have and stubborn tactics they adopt, in order to know precisely how they are likely to react in certain situations. Once you can predict their behavior, you will have established a serious advantage over them in any competitive struggle that may arise. Psyching out and countering their moves can then cripple their efforts.

Love

The Capricorn First Date

Things are likely to develop quickly on the physical plane with Capricorn first dates. If the sexual chemistry is right for both of you, touching, kissing, and perhaps going further may be inevitable. For this reason, it is good to plan where you are going to meet and to decide whether you will go out on the town or have a more intimate evening at home. Capricorn first dates can be matter-of-fact, so even if you see each other for only one date, they are not likely to experience feelings of rejection but will take the course of things right in stride. Should further involvement be in the cards, Capricorn first dates will prove attentive and involved, but not overly so.

Wooing and Picking Up the Capricorn First Date

If you have had your eye on a Capricorn for a while, it is very important to approach them in the right way to ensure the relationship advances. An effective tactic may be using an excuse for a first meeting, putting it in another category than a date. Suggesting a brainstorming session, study or work project, or computer activity will usually work to bring you two into closer proximity. Actually, both of you will probably know what is really going on, but it often helps not to pose a romantic threat to Capricorn first dates too early on. Make sure the wooing takes places in a more relaxed or neutral surrounding, rather than an overly private or secluded one.

Suggested Activities for the Capricorn First Date

Often it works well to suggest a choice of possible activities to the Capricorn first date rather than trying to force your prearranged agenda on them. After an initial conversation (keep it short), you can begin your "Maybe we could . . . sometime" speech and leave it at that. Give Capricorn first dates enough time to think things over and get back to you, up to a couple of weeks or one month later. (If they have not responded by that time, they are probably not interested and better left alone.) The best way to proceed further is often if you "happen" to bump into them and then can revive the subject concerning the choice of initial activities.

STRENGTHS
Observant
Straightforward
Appreciative

WEAKNESSES
Unenthusiastic
Matter-of-fact
Reserved

INTERACTIVE STYLE
Physical
Responsive
Sensuous

Turn-Ons and Turn-Offs for the Capricorn First Date

Capricorn first dates are usually selective about times and places they want to be seen with you, should you decide to go out in public together. Once the venue is set, whether a study, work, or entertainment setting, it is best to keep things as casual as possible and give Capricorn first dates enough space. Listening to your chatter may be something they welcome, since it poses no serious threat. Capricorn first dates will be turned on by your charm and turned off by boring and predictable suggestions or advances.

Making "the Move" with the Capricorn First Date

The "move" is likely to be mutual rather than stemming from either one of you. Capricorn first dates have radar out for mutual sexual attraction. They are highly responsive when the mood hits them, and their feelings are further heightened when attractions are shared. Capricorns can be very uninhibited, and things can get pretty wild pretty quickly. If events are moving too fast for you, and you decide to pull back, you will have to keep an excuse handy to avoid hurting the feelings of Capricorn first dates, thus rousing their disappointment or anger.

Impressing the Capricorn First Date

Capricorn first dates will be impressed by a cool, sophisticated, yet appreciative demeanor on your part. They will show special interest in your appearance, which they will take as an indication of your true nature as well as how you feel about them. Your choice of hair style, clothing, fabric, shoes, and fragrance will all interest them and, if interested in you, raise their curiosity level enough to probe deeper. If you both decide to go out for a bite to eat or to a show, make sure that you do not spare expense and, by all means, offer to treat beforehand. Most often Capricorn first dates will want to split the bill to avoid any dependency or one-upmanship.

Brushing Off the Capricorn First Date

Capricorns are easy to get rid of early in a relationship, but it is much more difficult to do so as things progress and grow more serious. Simply showing a lack of interest in them may not work, however, since this attitude might actually turn them on and rouse their need to seduce you. It is best to have a good excuse handy or to lie outright. The best thing to say is that it is a busy time for you but you enjoyed yourself and will get back to them when you have time. Capricorn first dates will usually take the hint and back off.

The Capricorn Romantic Partner

Capricorns are likely to treat sex in a very matter-of-fact but also highly natural manner. A typical Capricorn attitude is, "I got into bed quickly with the other person to get that out of the way; then we could get to know each other better." Although Capricorns are physical beings, going beyond sex is important to them, and they usually prefer to develop a serious and deep relationship rather than a brief, superficial one. Capricorns are quite capable of holding back until the right person comes along. Thus their innate efficiency and selectivity keeps them from wasting time and energy on losers.

Having a Discussion with the Capricorn Romantic Partner

Capricorns are not at all averse to discussions. When in a relationship that is truly important to them, they will gladly give it the time and effort to work out problems. Not ones to leave important issues hanging, Capricorns will usually be the first to raise the subject that needs to be discussed and not rest until it is mutually addressed and talked out fully. Capricorns will, however, be very selective about where and when such discussions take place. They are likely to wait quite a while until the circumstances are just right, giving the appearance of stalling, which is not usually the case.

Arguments with the Capricorn Romantic Partner

Capricorns are extremely stubborn and will not back down in an argument. Should things remain up in the air after the first confrontation, others are sure to follow until things are worked out, a compromise reached, or a separation or split manifests. If you take time to explain your actions or point of view, Capricorns will at least consider your statements carefully, rather than dismissing them out of hand. That said, they also expect you to reciprocate, questioning you thoroughly and calmly about all the points they made to be sure you understood what they said.

Traveling with the Capricorn Romantic Partner

Because of their fixed ideas and opinions, Capricorns romantic partners are not the easiest people to travel with. Moreover, they would often prefer to stay home, unless there is a reason for them to travel or you can woo them with promises of untold pleasures in distant lands. To get them on your flying carpet, be sure to stress the educational and career opportunities that travel can present, and of course assure them of your undivided attention, particularly against a romantic backdrop that offers rich sexual rewards.

Sex with the Capricorn Romantic Partner

Capricorns like frequent sex, as long as it is with someone they care for and see future possibilities with. Accepting good sex and its deepening emotional benefits, Capricorns realize its importance in the development of a romantic relationship. Sex and love are the same thing for many Capricorns, and only a few of them will treat either one of these in a superficial or wantonly excessive fashion without the other. Capricorns expect equal commitment in romantic matters from their partners and will not continue for long in a relationship in which they are the only one who is giving.

Affection and the Capricorn Romantic Partner

Capricorns have a lot to contribute in sensual realms as well as sexual ones, and thus giving and receiving affection are an important part of the romantic equation for them. However, their manner of expressing affection is not always easily understood, a fact that often causes others to characterize Capricorns as distant and cold when they are not expressing full-blown passion. Capricorn romantic partners are more likely to show

STRENGTHS
Selective
Efficient
Deep

WEAKNESSES
Opportunistic
Snobbish
Picky

INTERACTIVE STYLE
Serious
Demanding
Direct

affection in a glance, a tone of voice, or a brief smile and touch of the arm than through a kiss or outright embrace. Likewise, they may shrink from overly enthusiastic expressions of affection on your part, particularly in public.

Humor and the Capricorn Romantic Partner

Traditionally, Capricorns are often accused of having absolutely no sense of humor. This is not true, but again their idea of what is funny and showing their appreciation of your humor are not always easily understood. Capricorns have a little smile they exhibit after a good joke, often accompanied by a sparkle in the eye and a low chuckle, as opposed to an outright laugh. When they tell a story or make a witty point they expect to see a gleam of comprehension in your face but not to hear a side-splitting guffaw or hysterical giggle. Thus, their approach to humor tends to be subtler and more nuanced than most.

The Capricorn Spouse

Dominant figures, Capricorn spouses must be the unquestioned rulers in the family. Their need to control everyone around them is legendary, and nowhere is this more evident than in their attitudes toward their partners. Capricorn spouses can be extremely ambitious for their loved ones, and not infrequently they put formidable expectations on their partners to succeed in life. This push toward success is not only present in the professional sphere but in domestic matters as well. Because of their overbearing natures, Capricorn spouses must learn to back off and occasionally give their better halves the chance to breathe.

Wedding and Honeymoon with the Capricorn Spouse

Capricorn spouses have it all figured out, down to the last detail, when it comes to planning weddings and honeymoons—not only their own, but occasionally for others, too. Dealing with payments of all sorts and keeping things affordable are Capricorn specialties and, in the case of honeymoons, literally assure more bang for their buck. Assuring themselves the maximum pleasure and the fewest disturbances are high on their list of priorities, but they always do so in a sensible, economic fashion. The unequivocal success of the wedding and honeymoon is essential to the start of any marriage with a Capricorn.

Home and Day-to-Day Married Life with the Capricorn Spouse

Carve out your own niche right at the outset of your married life with a Capricorn spouse, or you may find yourself just trailing along or even left out in the cold. Capricorns are dominant and naturally want to control almost every domestic activity. Showing that you are capable and aggressive enough to lay claim to what is yours and establishing your strengths and expertise will cause Capricorn spouses to truly respect you and accept the futility of intervening into your private space. A telltale phrase to alert them to this, such as "Back off" or "I've got it," is frequently sufficient warning at first; later, replace this with a single knowing glance.

Finances and the Capricorn Spouse

In most cases, it is best to leave family finances to Capricorn spouses because of their pragmatic and responsible approach. However, in the making of budgets you should be sure to insist on taking part in decisions concerning how the family income should be spent. Not that Capricorn spouses will seek to spend all available funds on themselves, but they do tend to think practically, and thus the more enjoyable aspects of life sometimes get short shrift. You may have to face recriminations for spontaneous outlays of cash, particularly for clothes, entertainment, and nonessentials in general, but stick up for yourself and even use veiled threats if necessary.

Infidelity and the Capricorn Spouse

Most Capricorn spouses are very faithful. Should they stray, the problem is not so much the relationship they have formed with another person but their inability to handle things emotionally. Agonized confessions, emotional outbursts, and nervous or depressive attacks may come to dot the landscape, even on a daily basis. If only Capricorn spouses could handle their problems without feeling extreme guilt, their actions might be easier to accept and forget. Withholding your forgiveness can often prove to be a powerful weapon in maintaining your position of power, even with an awareness of the greater importance of love to any relationship.

Children and the Capricorn Spouse

Being family oriented, most Capricorn spouses will want to have at least one or two children. Unfortunately, they come to view parenthood as something that is there to further their private agenda rather than that of their progeny. Like the Old Testament creator, they usually choose to make their children over in their own image. Being the spouse of such a Capricorn parent will certainly involve sticking up for and defending the interests of your children. Too often this can lead to deep rifts and polarizations within the family unit, with the Capricorn spouse becoming the odd one out.

Divorce and the Capricorn Spouse

Capricorn spouses do not handle divorce well. Their attachment to objects, money, children, and, above all, the security of the home and family makes any breakup difficult. While you may even be enjoying your new-found freedom or feel relieved at finally getting out from under their dominant attitudes, Capricorn spouses may be suffering terribly, making things much more difficult for you to handle. Thus, in many ways the divorce can become as highly problematic, or even more so, than the marriage was. Your approach can be sympathetic to a point, but should be mainly pragmatic.

The Capricorn Lover

Capricorn lovers are quite capable of guaranteeing sexual fulfillment to their partners. Not only sexually oriented but possessing the stamina for long sessions, Capricorn lovers can help maintain mutual sexual interest for many months or even years on end. They believe that what happens between two people is their business and no one else's, so they are also good at keeping secrets and not compromising the established relationships of their partners. Although attentive, Capricorn lovers sometimes fail to take their partners' feelings into account and can lack subtlety in addressing their true needs.

Meeting the Capricorn Lover

Capricorn lovers are most often introduced to you by mutual friends, rather than met by chance. This can happen at a party or other social event or in a deliberately set-up home dinner situation. Most often Capricorn lovers will not give away a whole lot about themselves and will be relatively quiet on first meeting, being careful to observe you in great detail. Although it may be difficult to penetrate their armor and sense what they are feeling (including their interest in you, of course) they will not hesitate to get back to you in some way or another within a week or two—at the most within one month.

Location and the Capricorn Lover

Capricorns will bring you home or to a neutral surrounding they have some familiarity with. The challenge of dealing with your personal surroundings during your first intimate social or sexual interaction is usually too much for them to handle. Not really curious about their partners and how they live, Capricorns prefer to meet their lovers in a completely straightforward and intense fashion, without distractions. As long as the setting is quiet and clean and no interruptions are guaranteed, Capricorn lovers will be content. Make sure you turn off your cell phone to avoid insulting them.

Sex and the Capricorn Lover

There can be a curiously impersonal feeling about sex with a Capricorn lover. Often after such a session you may really wonder whether they were interacting with you at all as a person. In some ways, they are magnificent in their physical approach to love but deficient in their understanding of trust, intimacy, and respect. Thus, after a session with them you may feel good, and perhaps worn out, but also empty and even somewhat disturbed about what occurred. Having a conversation about it at a later date may be necessary to put Capricorn lovers on a truer course.

Holding On to the Capricorn Lover

As long as you are able to please and satisfy Capricorn lovers sexually, you should have few problems holding on to them. Quite simply put, if they are not getting what they need from you, they will contact you less frequently, eventually dropping you altogether. Continued satisfaction is key to holding on to Capricorn lovers, not only in the physical realm but also if you can prove fun to be with and a good pal, keeping them from falling into depressive states that they may be prone to experience with great regularity.

Entertaining the Capricorn Lover

When Capricorn lovers want to go out they like frequenting films, clubs, and swank, cool, or trendy venues. Once in a while, and as often as once a week, Capricorn lovers like to forget their troubles and go out on the town, sometimes indulging in surprisingly extroverted behavior. Appreciating and sharing their zany, energetic whims and going along with their flamboyance without being shocked or upset will endear you to them and allow them to trust you more. Any emotional withdrawal or criticism of the way they are acting may spell doom for the relationship.

Breaking Up with the Capricorn Lover

Abruptly breaking off with Capricorn lovers is not recommended, although they are quite capable of dropping you like a hot potato. Should you write them off and curtly dismiss them from your life, you can expect a sharp response, one not only directed against you personally but also delivered to mutual friends and even business associates. The best way to break off with a Capricorn lover is slowly and gradually, with contact between you becoming less frequent over time. Capricorns have a lot of pride, and when it is injured these lovers may explode with indignation.

The Capricorn Ex

Capricorn exes will usually adopt a responsible attitude toward their former partners, which can last for years after the breakup. It is not at all unusual for them to take a continuing active interest in them that is caring and concerned without any awakening of romantic interest or passion. Capricorn exes are particularly sensitive to the criticism of family members and mutual friends and therefore will usually act in the proper way. Likewise, Capricorn exes will insist that their former partners treat them decently and with respect. They can be very unforgiving if insulted or ignored.

Establishing a Friendship with the Capricorn Ex

Normally this is not a problem. However, the friendship is best kept within strict limits, which the Capricorn ex will have no difficulty defining and laying down. As long as you keep within these guidelines and obey the rules, there should be no conflict. Capricorns can get quite upset about continual breaches of etiquette, particularly when their exes act in an unpredictable and irrational fashion. Ringing the bell of a Capricorn ex without notice or calling in the middle of the night is definitely not appreciated. Contacting Capricorn exes or having them contact you once every month or two is more than adequate.

Issues of Getting Back Together with the Capricorn Ex

Discussions of getting back together with Capricorn exes should not be taken lightly. Even raising the subject is highly significant. During such talks, remember that any promises you make or feelings you express will be taken seriously, and wriggling later to get out of them by claiming you were just kidding around will be to no avail. You can be

STRENGTHS

Attentive

Caring

Alert

WEAKNESSES

Overly sensitive

Aggressive

Unforgiving

INTERACTIVE STYLE

Conventional

Respectful

Responsible

LOVE

sure that no Capricorn will seriously agree to getting back together without well-defined commitments from you. These can include, but are not limited to, legal guarantees, property and financial readjustments, and redefinition of familial ties and commitments.

Discussing Past Issues with the Capricorn Ex

Discussing past issues with Capricorn exes without arousing their blame, judgment, or tendency to lay on guilt trips may be difficult or impossible. Capricorn exes are likely to be very severe in such confrontations, and you will surely not leave them with good feelings. Any attempts you make to blame them or argue can arouse volcanic anger, so be very careful in this regard. It can be helpful to conduct such discussions in a public place over a cup of coffee to provide some social control rather than risking a dangerous private confrontation. Such meetings should be limited in duration and could even include inviting a mutual friend to be present as a referee.

Expressing Affection to the Capricorn Ex

Any and all displays of affection should be avoided or kept strictly under control. Such expressions will be viewed with suspicion by Capricorn exes, who will be convinced that you are employing them as tactics to manipulate and control. Rather than expressing affection, it would be better to show your care and concern in other ways, notably by offering help if needed or just being ready to listen and take what Capricorn exes have to say seriously. Often the most considerate thing you can do, and the action that will earn you the highest points, is just to leave Capricorn exes alone.

Defining the Present Relationship with the Capricorn Ex

Capricorn exes have a good idea of the status of the relationship and do not need your input on the subject. Convinced that their opinion on such matters is correct, they will generally reject your viewpoint unless it coincides with theirs. Realists first and foremost, they will be quick to point out whenever your observations are just wishful thinking. Discussions with them about the relationship are best avoided, but if you cannot resist broaching the subject and expressing your views, be prepared for a less than sympathetic reception.

Sharing Custody with the Capricorn Ex

The dominant traits of Capricorn exes will emerge whenever children are involved. They may be difficult to deal with regarding such issues, insisting that they be the sole custodians and that your presence in the lives of the children will only be upsetting and disturbing. If, however, you can assure them this is false through your highly responsible, unselfish, and caring attitude—one that truly puts the needs of the children first—they will begin to be more open about sharing custody. Capricorn exes tend to be morally condemning and will not hesitate to point out all your deficiencies not only in private but in public and judicial settings as well.

Friends and Family

CAPRICORN
December 22–January 20

The Capricorn Friend

Even when involvements with Capricorns are not deep, these individuals will exhibit concern over their friends' difficulties and be there for them in times of need. Traditionally, Capricorns only give emotionally to their partners, a couple of family members, and one or two friends on a regular basis. Thus, if you are a friend to Capricorns, you may find yourself their "best" friend, with all the seriousness that can attend occupying such a position in their lives. Being the best friend of a Capricorn can be a heavy task, and not always a pleasant one. On the positive side, Capricorns treat their best friends very well and, in some cases, even prefer their company to that of anyone else.

Asking for Help from the Capricorn Friend

If Capricorns regard you as a true friend, they will help you without question. One of the few restrictions on such giving can emerge if you repeatedly ignore their advice or misuse their help, in which case they may refuse it in the future. No matter how busy Capricorns are with other matters, they will drop them in an instant and go to the aid of a friend in true need. It is best not to misuse their help by calling out for it unnecessarily, perhaps as a ploy to gain their attention, and to ask for help only in extreme cases, perhaps once or twice in the course of the relationship.

Communication and Keeping in Touch with the Capricorn Friend

Capricorns are not always the best communicators. They do not place a great value on frequent chats, preferring to contact you only sporadically when the spirit moves them. Maintaining regular contact may be left up to you, and you should keep in mind that Capricorns can be hard to pin down to fixed obligations and schedules in their friendships, unlike their attitudes toward business contacts. Once they do commit to a meeting, however, they are absolutely reliable in showing up and will rarely let down their friends. Although not overly facile with words, they are straight shooters whose opinions and judgments can be trusted in most cases.

STRENGTHS
Steady
Giving
Reliable

WEAKNESSES
Claiming
Heavy
Judgmental

INTERACTIVE STYLE
Caring
Responsible
Attentive

Borrowing Money from the Capricorn Friend

Capricorns will lend money to their best friends but also demand that it be paid back on a regular schedule. In certain cases, they will even take on extra work or dig into their savings to make such funds available. Should they see you throwing their money away (which for them could take the form of your engaging in unreliable business dealings or giving money to unreliable friends or family members), they will no doubt refuse to be as generous in the future. On the other hand, if you put their loan to good use and even make money on it, they may show serious interest in outright investments in your future endeavors.

Asking for Advice from the Capricorn Friend

Since Capricorn friends have fixed ideas on so many subjects, you may already know what their advice will be before asking for it. This may keep you from seeking their advice at all, although frequently Capricorn friends can give you a slant on things that may prove quite enlightening. At any rate, they will take your questions seriously and be generous with their time and thought. Rarely will Capricorns change their minds over a suggested course of action or admit that they were wrong in their initial assessment of your situation. They will usually find another reason for the failure of a given tactic.

Visiting the Capricorn Friend

Although you are welcome in the home of a Capricorn friend, and may even spend quite a bit of time there over the years, you should never presume that the door is always open or that your friend has the time and interest in seeing you often. Although Capricorns may put up with more frequent visits, they can build up resentment and irritation over time. Only later will their anger erupt, when things get to be just a little too much. Inviting them to your place more frequently is not always a viable option either, since they prefer to spend most of their time on their own turf.

Celebrations/Entertainment with the Capricorn Friend

Generally speaking, Capricorn friends prefer to give rather than to receive. In planning celebrations and parties, they are solid contributors both work- and money-wise but may back off when such events are for their benefit. This curious avoidance of being rewarded has to do with their reluctance to ever feel obligated to others and perhaps to be accused of ingratitude in the future. Capricorns tend to give unconditionally when it comes to festive occasions, rarely demanding anything in return. They gain great satisfaction in a job well done and secretly enjoy being congratulated for it.

The Capricorn Roommate

The sensible and steady energies of Capricorn roommates should keep most domestic activities on track on a day-to-day basis. Of course, Capricorn's demands for economy and efficiency can drive their roommates crazy. On top of every expenditure of energy and cash, thrifty Capricorn roommates guarantee that wastefulness is kept to a minimum.

Being questioned about seeing the lights burning in your room late at night can prove irritating enough, but when Capricorn roommates suggest that you pay more of the utility bills because of this, you may find yourself at the end of your rope. Your more carefree attitude may not garner a great deal of appreciation around the house.

Sharing Financial Responsibilities with the Capricorn Roommate

Although financial responsibilities will be shared, Capricorns may insist on making most of the executive decisions about making payments, shopping, and using utilities. They not only naturally assume command in these areas but also support such attitudes by pointing out their superior practical thinking. Unfortunately, this often casts you in the role of a dreamer who has little idea of pragmatic realities, in contrast to their own sensible approach. It is best not to engage in endless conflicts over such matters, but simply to leave it to them. In most cases, your financial responsibilities will be spelled out clearly and fairly by Capricorn roommates.

Cleaning and the Capricorn Roommate

Capricorn roommates can get pretty sloppy at times, but in between periods of chaos—particularly in their own rooms—they will draw up strict cleaning schedules for themselves and their roommates. Thus, the appearance of the dwelling is likely to fluctuate wildly between sloppy and orderly. Oddly, for all their boasting about practicality, Capricorn roommates can go way off track in pursuing their personal interests, being blind to how things look. You may have to do extra work in common living spaces to keep things in order, without getting any thanks from your Capricorn roommate, who may not even notice.

Houseguests and the Capricorn Roommate

Capricorn roommates are generally not fond of having houseguests—either yours or their own. Conservative for the most part, Capricorn roommates are creatures of habit who like things to stay the same without much upset. Should you invite a friend or family member to stay longer than a weekend, be prepared for trouble. After insisting on increased contributions from you because of the added needs involved, Capricorn roommates will ultimately begin to try to remove the offending party through not-so-subtle, outright suggestions that they leave. To avoid these embarrassments, it is best to minimize the frequency and duration of such visits.

Parties and the Capricorn Roommate

Although not party animals, Capricorn roommates can enjoy a fantastic blowout now and then. Such events give them a chance to reveal a flamboyant and extroverted side you perhaps never knew existed. Capricorns let it all hang out at parties and can provide a good deal of the entertainment themselves. However, once they start adding up the sobering costs, they may not wish to repeat the experience for some time. Accompanying them to parties with mutual friends outside the house can be a fun experience, as long as they are not expected to pay anything.

(The Capricorn Roommate)

STRENGTHS
Economical
Thrifty
Sensible

WEAKNESSES
Overly fussy
Irritating
Prying

INTERACTIVE STYLE
Forthright
Administrative
Controlling

FRIENDS AND FAMILY

Privacy and the Capricorn Roommate

Although Capricorn roommates will insist on having privacy, at the same time they are remarkably good about sharing common spaces. One thing they will be insistent about is having extended, uninterrupted time for their baths, showers, and cosmetic needs. The same goes for their use of the kitchen, where they simply will not be dislodged or rushed. Too often Capricorns treat sharing as if they were giving you some special gift, rather than simply acknowledging equality. Occasionally, you may be forced to remind them that the house or apartment is yours, too.

Discussing Problems with the Capricorn Roommate

Problems invariably arise with Capricorn roommates, but rarely will they acknowledge that they are of their own doing. Thus it is better to discuss difficulties as if they are mutual ones and to seek the support of Capricorn roommates to solve them objectively. Never attempt to fix blame or lay the guilt for a domestic fiasco at the feet of Capricorn roommates. Not only will you invariably arouse denial, but you may also unleash a fierce storm of accusations leveled against you. Such arguments can easily run out of hand and cast a pall over the domestic mood for days on end.

The Capricorn Parent

Theoretically, every child should be granted the opportunity to have one Capricorn parent, but not two. Capricorns are so authoritarian, protective, and controlling of their children on a daily and even hourly basis that unless the other parent is more permissive and easygoing, the child is likely to suffer greatly. Capricorn parents take their roles seriously. They will see to it that their children are well looked after and will never shirk their responsibilities toward them. Although capable of giving love, many, but not all, Capricorn parents choose to withhold love as a weapon in coercing their children to seek their approval and accede to their demands.

Discipline Style of the Capricorn Parent

Capricorn parents are usually strict taskmasters. What they expect from their children will usually be carefully spelled out to avoid possible misunderstandings. A Capricorn parent may imply or outright state: "If you are good, you will get everything. If you are bad, then you will get nothing." Only later will the child finally figure out that being "good" just meant following the Capricorn parent's rules. Rarely will Capricorn parents administer physical punishment of any sort, but the threat of it can be a powerful deterrent to disobedience. The serious demeanor of many Capricorn parents leaves little doubt as to their determination to be obeyed.

Affection Level and the Capricorn Parent

Despite their strict attitudes and serious demeanor, Capricorn parents also love to have fun with their kids. Outright tickling, wrestling, competing, joking, and teasing are not at all uncommon. As long as the child follows Capricorn rules and avoids any manifestation of criticism of or open rebellion against such edicts, things will go smoothly. Actually, Capricorn parents have a strong need to express affection to their children, and although appreciative of affection returned, they do not require it. Many Capricorn parents dislike receiving expensive presents from grown-up children, feeling they do not want them to waste their money on something they regard as only a luxury.

Money Issues and the Capricorn Parent

Capricorn parents will be forthcoming with a modest weekly allowance for their children, but usually one that covers necessities only. They teach their offspring to be thrifty and never foolish enough to throw money away. Money occupies an important place in the Capricorn hierarchy, particularly when it is the result of hard and dedicated work. Capricorn parents may deride a child for being impractical and a dreamer, only so that they can have undisputed control over this domain. Unfortunately, many children come to fit this role, if only to please the egos of their demanding Capricorn parents.

Crises and the Capricorn Parent

Although Capricorn parents can be counted on in times of crisis, they can also resent having to bail out their wayward children. Frequently, the punishments they administer induce suffering even greater than that engendered by the crisis itself. Capricorn parents often take the attitude that the trouble their children get into is largely of their own doing; thus they are basically unsympathetic, albeit there to play their roles as responsible parents. Unavoidably there are cases in which the children of Capricorn parents get into trouble in the first place only because they are bound by excessive, restrictive rules and need to express their individuality.

Holidays/Family Gatherings and the Capricorn Parent

Capricorn parents will take part in family gatherings, but they prefer to keep holidays to themselves and their spouse. They may even find a babysitter—a grandparent or other family member—so that they can go off and at last be free of parental responsibilities for a while. As far as travel is concerned, Capricorn parents prefer to take vacations with only their nuclear family and do not include aunts, uncles, and cousins. When on vacation, Capricorn parents are not overly stingy, but still they will never pass up an opportunity to cut corners and avoid unnecessary spending.

Caring for the Aging Capricorn Parent

Aging Capricorn parents usually make it clear that they do not want anyone looking after them. Although they will appreciate your offers to help, they will accept them only if absolutely necessary. Hiring full-time help to look after them or committing themselves to an old-age home is not their speed. Capricorn parents are very attached to their surroundings and would prefer to struggle and suffer alone than move to an unfamiliar location. This often results in increased immobility, so they rarely go out, and they even limit their movements at home to a bare minimum.

The Capricorn Sibling

STRENGTHS

Cooperative

Caring

Versatile

WEAKNESSES

Dependent

Fearful

Needy

INTERACTIVE STYLE

Stalwart

Respectful

Protective

Unless they are the eldest, Capricorn children normally take a backseat to their siblings and fit into the family hierarchy quite well. Oldest Capricorn children are the undisputed bosses, wielding their power in a highly responsible manner. Younger Capricorn siblings can be quite wild but rarely rebellious against order and authority, mostly showing respect for their brothers and sisters. Capricorns will quickly take the hint from siblings; they are stalwart in times of need and able to fill in for anyone at a moment's notice. They thrive on the good feelings engendered through close contact with siblings and are psychologically dependent on the security and protection a close-knit family guarantees.

Rivalry/Closeness with the Capricorn Sibling

Capricorn siblings will fight to maintain their power in the family while at the same time being cooperative with endeavors that guarantee its stability. Consequently, they can deal very severely with rebellious family members who either insist on going their own way or work to undermine the family authority. Capricorn siblings often adopt the attitude of a watchdog, and their bite can be formidable when they attack. Sibling rivalry with Capricorns is not at all uncommon in any family group, although Capricorns would prefer to get along whenever possible. It is only when they are pushed to their limit and alarm bells go off that they get extremely aggressive.

Past Issues and the Capricorn Sibling

Capricorn siblings are quite unforgiving. Past issues remain present to them for years on end. Dealing with the past can be a real problem for them since holding on to past issues so fiercely can impede their self-development. A kind, understanding, and sympathetic brother or sister can help them deal with such issues and, if patient enough, cure them of their maladies. Getting stuck in the past, usually concerning one particular traumatic event, can be expected at some point in the life of most Capricorns.

Dealing with the Estranged Capricorn Sibling

Capricorn siblings can be exceedingly stubborn and continue to reject the approach of their brothers and sisters for years on end. The only way they can be finally reached is through a combination of persistence and backing off for months or even years. Usually all attempts to bully or rush Capricorn siblings into establishing a cease-fire or rapprochement will fail miserably. Having a feeling for the right time to approach them is essential to success. If handled correctly, the estranged Capricorn sibling might be the one to take up contact after highly judicious promptings over time.

Money Issues (Borrowing Money, Wills, Etc.) and the Capricorn Sibling

Capricorn siblings usually adopt a dominant role regarding wills and inheritances. They stick up not only for their own interests but for those of their brothers and sisters as well. They will normally not seek special rewards, but ally themselves with the group. Generally, Capricorns do not borrow money either from their siblings or estates and trust funds, unless a one-time emergency forces them to do so as a last resort. All money borrowed will be scrupulously paid back, although this may take some time.

Holidays/Celebrations/Reunions and the Capricorn Sibling

Capricorn siblings are often sentimental and enjoy reunions and annual holiday gatherings with their favorite brothers and sisters and their spouses and children. Few things give them more pleasure than watching their children and cousins play with one another at such occasions. Capricorn siblings have a real feeling for the warmth and conviviality offered by family celebrations, and because of their devotional nature, they will spare neither energy nor expense in making them a success. After such an event has ended, Capricorns will be satisfied and may not be very interested in renewing contact until the following year.

Vacationing with the Capricorn Sibling

Although they are family-oriented, taking even one brother or sister along on a vacation with a couple of their kids is about all Capricorn siblings can handle. For Capricorns, vacations mean truly getting away from it all, and this includes even their families. That said, finding yourself on a vacation with your Capricorn sibling can be a most enjoyable experience. Once Capricorn siblings have made up their minds to adopt a course of action that includes you, they will make little distinction between their interests and yours, feeling responsible for you and everyone else having a good time.

The Capricorn Child

Capricorn children often appear to have grown old before their time. Little adults, they have a serious demeanor that can be regarded by their parents with humor, but laughing at these kids would be a big mistake. Capricorns demand to be respected, and attempts to deny them respect will be repulsed with astonishing force, despite their diminutive size. Children born under this astrological sign are self-assured; they know what they want and how to get it. Using emotional blackmail and laying on guilt trips are not out of the ordinary, since Capricorn kids know a fair bit about human psychology.

Personality Development and the Capricorn Child

Since Capricorns show maturity at an early age, one wonders how much personality development remains to manifest in the lives of Capricorn children. Difficulties may arise for them later, in early adulthood, when they begin to realize they have been deprived of a real childhood. This feeling—that their inner child was starved through premature emotional development—can be an overpowering realization that awakens all sorts of regret and resentment. Most often, the parents were not at fault, but they may very well be the ones who become the objects of blame for their Capricorn offspring.

Hobbies/Interests/Career Paths for the Capricorn Child

Many Capricorn children have a good idea early on what they want to do career-wise. However, they have a curious inability to carry through on such realizations and may take quite a long time in adulthood to settle on one profession. Usually the victims of several false starts, young Capricorn adults may finally hit on one profession that is

STRENGTHS
Canny
Mature
Impressive

WEAKNESSES
Egocentric
Overly demanding
Tense

INTERACTIVE STYLE
Confrontational
Unyielding
Insistent

related to a hobby or life interest that has been present for as long as they can remember. Once they make up their minds for good and move to implement their desires, they can remain true to their choice for the rest of their working days.

Discipline and the Capricorn Child

Capricorn children understand the need for discipline to curb wild energies, including their own. They can understand, even sympathize with, a parent who feels that discipline is necessary. Such understanding allows them to endure and rise above punishment meted out to them and their siblings. This is because they have a good idea what is right and wrong, and when they break such rules, they do so knowing that they risk reprisals. They see discipline as unnecessary, but accept punishment as an unavoidable consequence of their transgressions.

Affection Level and the Capricorn Child

The need of Capricorn children for affection is a complex matter. It would seem as if they do not seek or crave it and that they are perfectly content to live without it. However, they have a curious need to give affection that can be readily seen in their attitudes toward younger family members and pets. Once this essential fact is grasped by their parents, it will be equally evident that Capricorn children do need affection (as most kids do) but that they have a great deal of trouble admitting it to themselves or outright asking for it. Their pride and self-assurance is usually to blame for their feelings that a request to be hugged or cuddled—even an unspoken one—is an admission of weakness.

Dealing with the Capricorn Child and Interactions with Siblings

If the eldest sibling is a Capricorn, that child must be guided in interactions with brothers and sisters. Too often, an eldest child that belongs to this sign is a little parent, constantly usurping the prerogatives of the mother and father with the interests of the younger siblings in mind. The best way to handle these independent and often troubling interferences with parental authority is for the parents to give Capricorn children, regardless of their age or position in the pecking order, chores and responsibilities that make them feel important, needed, and wanted. However, these duties must be kept under control to avoid the deprivations described earlier.

Interacting with the Adult Capricorn Child

As stated, the adult Capricorn child can emerge long before adulthood. Therefore, when Capricorns are at any age over thirty, their family members may just continue to interact with them in a way very similar to how they did when they were much younger. Since many Capricorn children seem to have been born adults, at least psychologically, they will be very comfortable with their role throughout their lives, as long as any resentments they had of not having been granted a true childhood are resolved. Since adulthood is the natural state of most Capricorns, they wear advanced age well and are not uncomfortable about being entirely responsible for themselves and others. Overestimating their capabilities, however, can always emerge as a problem.

Aquarius

BIRTHDATE **JANUARY 21–FEBRUARY 19**

The fixed air sign Aquarius rules the new age in which we now live. Governed by the revolutionary planet Uranus, Aquarians tend to be modern, forward-looking individuals who are unusual and accepting of this quality in others. Often the joy and despair of their sweethearts, Aquarians can be maddeningly unstable and cool, neglecting human feelings and making enduring relationships with them difficult. Yet their fascinating qualities and quick minds attract people who seem willing to overlook or forgive their wayward tendencies.

AQUARIUS
January 21–February 19

Work

STRENGTHS
Quick
Bright
Open

WEAKNESSES
Impatient
Erratic
Elusive

INTERACTIVE STYLE
Immediate
Unpredictable
Ungovernable

The Aquarius Boss

Since Aquarians are not particularly suited to be bosses, they are, generally speaking, rather few and far between. There are several reasons for this, among them their erratic and impulsive behavior, need to act on their own, lightning-quick moves, and general disinterest in holding power over others or setting up a dynasty. That said, if you have an Aquarius boss, at least you have been forewarned. Actually, they are often fun to work with (when you can catch up to them) and treat their employees quite generously. Their impatience is legendary, so do not try their quick tempers or frustrate them with your absence or tardiness when they need you in the clutch.

Asking the Aquarius Boss for a Raise

Since Aquarian bosses move with the speed of light and have a bad habit of canceling appointments, your first problem will be catching up with them and pinning them down for a meeting. You may have to be content with trying to ambush them in a corridor or while exiting the lunchroom for a three-second chat. Physically taking them aside for a moment or two may have to do in lieu of a full-fledged appointment. Relying on their assistants to relay the whereabouts of the Aquarius boss will not work, since they may be just as frustrated as you with your leader's erratic peregrinations.

Breaking Bad News to the Aquarius Boss

If you are called in out of the clear blue sky to explain a recent loss or drop in sales, you will barely have time to collect your thoughts. Therefore, if you have an Aquarius boss, you had better be prepared to explain your most recent actions at a moment's notice. This can be accomplished by thoroughly documenting your work and keeping all important records within reach. Such thorough preparations will result in greater success, allowing you to grab a file on the way out the door and on the way to the boss's office. Make sure you regularly brush up on this material and organize it for easy reference.

Arranging Travel and/or Entertainment for the Aquarius Boss

The whirlwind energies and split-second decision-making of Aquarius bosses make it very difficult to arrange travel and entertainment reservations in advance. Yet Aquarius

AQUARIUS

290

bosses demand that everything run smoothly and that they are able to implement important business decisions without having to worry about schedules and logistics. It is best to keep as fluid and flexible as possible in making arrangements and to have backup plans, good cancelation insurance for plane flights, and an understanding maître d' who can roll with the punches. Using a regular, reliable, and sympathetic travel agent who knows what to expect is essential.

Decision-Making and the Aquarius Boss

Aquarius bosses make lightning-quick decisions and expect you to be able to follow them. If too slow to come about, your decisions will probably frustrate them, since waiting is not their forte. Decision-making comes easily to them, perhaps too easily for most of their employees to follow or even to understand. After such a decision comes down from on high, it frequently leaves a group of employees bowled over, staring at each other in bewilderment. Asking for further explanations may be difficult or impossible, so at least you know what to expect.

Impressing and/or Motivating the Aquarius Boss

Aquarius bosses are self-motivating and cannot be pushed in any direction they do not want to pursue. They can only be truly impressed by your ability to comprehend their quick minds and methods and to implement their plans immediately. Should they encounter you in a hallway or when they're entering or exiting the building, they will expect you to keep up with them as far as the elevator (and perhaps invite you to ride up or down with them), listening carefully to their succinct orders all the way. Make sure you write down what they have just said as soon as possible after your short journey.

Making Proposals and/or Giving Presentations to the Aquarius Boss

Aquarius bosses have no time for lengthy proposals and are particularly impatient with long documents or presentations that drag on interminably. Keep things short and sweet, preferably speaking without notes or audio-visual aids. Remember that you will have the undivided attention of Aquarius bosses for only a few minutes, so condense your thoughts and be economical with your words. Do not be surprised if Aquarius bosses cut you off right in the middle of your presentation or continually interject their thoughts, objections, and demands. Remain focused yet light enough on your feet to change direction and wing it at a moment's notice.

The Aquarius Employee

The unusual aspects of the personalities of Aquarius employees can remain an ever-more-interesting subject of study for their bosses. Aquarius employees have a peculiar way of doing things, and once they get into a groove, it is difficult to dislodge them or teach them other methods. Furthermore, Aquarians in general have a rebellious streak. Consequently, employees born under this sign do not always take orders well from higher authorities, resenting being told what to do since they usually have a better approach at

STRENGTHS
Interesting
Fun
Individualistic

WEAKNESSES
Peculiar
Strange
Ungovernable

INTERACTIVE STYLE
Lighthearted
Friendly
Accepting

hand. That said, Aquarius employees can bring fun and lightheartedness to any group, and they prefer things to go smoothly without hassles.

Interviewing and/or Hiring the Aquarius Employee

Prospective Aquarius employees can impress with their quick minds and a track record that shows their ability to carry through on their ideas as well. Normally, Aquarius interviewees will quickly absorb any information thrown at them and immediately demonstrate that they understand it. However, they may not agree with it, and they will in no uncertain terms suggest changes more in line with their likes and dislikes. Aquarians want to see prospective employers who are open to their suggestions and responsive to their needs before they can feel good about accepting an offer and signing contract.

Breaking Bad News to or Firing the Aquarius Employee

Aquarius employees usually belong to one of two extremes, with no middle ground: ones who are accepting of bad news and ones who are not. The accepting ones are likely to agree with their bosses that they would do better with another firm and are realistic enough to accept criticism and suggestions. The non-acceptors can get pretty wild over being fired, lashing out verbally and appearing ready to do so physically also. Their tempers and overreactions are probably already known in the company, and this sort of Aquarius employee should be handled with care and the blow softened and sweetened a bit, perhaps by generous severance pay or a golden handshake.

Traveling with and Entertaining the Aquarius Employee

Aquarius is a fun-loving sign. Aquarius employees hate formality, strict schedules, and other serious attitudes that take the joy out of travel and entertainment. Consequently, those who travel with them should be similarly light and friendly in their approach and certainly not depression-prone. Aquarius employees can sometimes be too bubbly, making it difficult to be with them on a daily basis. Thus trips with Aquarian employees are best kept short, and they may be cautioned beforehand to keep their enthusiasm under control without, of course, extinguishing it completely.

Assigning Tasks to the Aquarius Employee

Because Aquarius is a fixed sign, the Aquarius employee is quite capable of sticking to one task and performing it adequately over time. However, to develop amazing results (of which Aquarians are quite capable) they must have a lot of enthusiasm for their work. In order to engender such enthusiasm, it is usually a good idea to give them some say in picking their task from the outset or at least helping to give it definition and shape. Just loading any old job on an Aquarius will not work, because of their highly individualistic, even peculiar, approach to most tasks. Their particular task is best developed by an employer not in the abstract but with the Aquarian employee in mind.

Motivating or Impressing the Aquarius Employee

Motivating Aquarius employees is done simply by finding out more about their preferences and giving them what they like best. For example, if they like working with others, make them part of a group; if they prefer doing work alone, give them their own space and facilities. Aquarius employees will be most impressed by an employer who understands their unusual nature and is responsive to both their needs and wants. Any attempt to make light of Aquarius employees' comments or requests by refusing to take them seriously, or hinting that they are too kooky or erratic to trust, will rouse most Aquarians to fury, even if such observations are true.

Managing, Directing, or Criticizing the Aquarius Employee

In certain situations, Aquarius employees can be almost completely ungovernable. Easily irritated, upset, and moved to anger, many Aquarius employees will find it difficult or impossible to be directed or criticized if they are approached in the wrong way. If smart bosses want to manage Aquarius employees well, they will take the time to get to know them, maintain a light touch, and not throw too many inflexible rules at them at once. Blaming them constantly will drive most Aquarians crazy, as will insisting on peering over their shoulders at their work on a regular basis.

The Aquarius Coworker

Aquarius coworkers can be very accepting of their associates, and although they have a habit of keeping to themselves, they will also take part in group activities when asked to do so. Preferring to keep things light, Aquarius coworkers love to trade jokes and, in particular, witty ripostes or one-liners that show off their verbal abilities. The sparkle of an Aquarius coworker can come to be highly valued by all in the group, since it lifts spirits and raises morale. Although Aquarius coworkers can be counted on to do their fair share of tasks, they will not usually seek overtime work for extra pay, since they value their free time so highly.

STRENGTHS

Witty
Morale-building
Entertaining

WEAKNESSES

Superficial
Detached
Uncommitted

INTERACTIVE STYLE

Humorous
Ironic
Sparkling

Approaching the Aquarius Coworker for Advice

Aquarius coworkers have the ability to look at situations with a cold eye and render objective judgments. Although they are not always easy to pin down for a scheduled appointment, they are quite open to talking to you if you catch them at the right moment. Because of this, it is best to just peek into their office or give them a quick call to see if they are free. Usually a few of these efforts should succeed in establishing contact. Keep your questions short and to the point; you will find their answers also succinct and helpful. Ignore their more extreme suggestions and follow the moderate ones.

Approaching the Aquarius Coworker for Help

Aquarius coworkers believe that heaven helps those who help themselves. Thus as a matter of principle they may not go out of their way to help you, thinking that it will only erode your morale and personal initiative. However, if they see that you have already tried and are at your wit's end, they can be surprisingly helpful in resolving your problem. Aquarius coworkers are more likely to help in such a situation if it concerns personal rather than business matters. They often show a genuine concern for others in times of need, being rather idealistic by nature. But in professional matters they will guard their time zealously and expect remuneration for their services.

Traveling with and Entertaining the Aquarius Coworker

If Aquarius coworkers are not close friends or associates, you may be amazed at all of the little peculiarities and preferences that emerge on your trip together. Aquarius coworkers can be worriers and manifest their concern in the form of nervousness that could throw you off-balance. Once they have calmed down and are assured that things are going well, they are capable of being a lot of fun. Entertainment-wise they love to attend live performances, including music or dancing at clubs. They are less interested in long sit-down meals, often preferring to eat on the run and pop in and out of various venues so they don't risk missing anything.

The Aquarius Coworker Cooperating with Others

Aquarius coworkers do not respond well to being ordered to cooperate with others, particularly if they are busy with their work. If they believe, however, in the aims and principles of the group effort they are being asked to join, they will give unstintingly of their talents and energies. Generally speaking, Aquarians do not find it easy to work with others, since they have particular ideas about how things should be done. They do not do well when required to take part in social or group settings on a daily basis. A better way to put them to work with others is to link them up with just one other person, preferably a coworker they already know and like, and then fitting this duo as a unit into the endeavors of a larger group.

Impressing and Motivating the Aquarius Coworker

Aquarius coworkers can be motivated to take part in projects that promise them more free time and less concentrated hard work in the long run. Promises of higher salaries and greater prestige will not have a big effect on them, since they know that they will be required to put out more time and energy to earn them. Aquarius coworkers are impressed by clear and logical thinking, rather than by poorly defined aims and fuzzy, overly optimistic and vague plans that promise the moon. Although idealists, Aquarius coworkers also have a strongly scientific and pragmatic bent that demands an empirical approach when it comes to facts and figures.

Persuading and/or Criticizing the Aquarius Coworker

Aquarius coworkers can be open to constructive criticism. If you are careful enough to approach them in the right way, they will be particularly amenable to listening to plans that show them how to achieve the same results with less effort. Quick learners, Aquarians can pick up new methods and techniques very fast, usually after only a single explanation or demonstration. If Aquarius coworkers disagree sharply with your persuasive efforts, they may just be playing the devil's advocate, encouraging you to tell them more or go further in your explanations. Once you satisfy them fully, they will be open to going along with your plans, even becoming enthusiastic about them.

The Aquarius Client

Oddly enough, Aquarius clients do not always have a clear idea of what they want. So much depends on what your specialties are and what you are able to offer them that they will wait until they have heard you fully before making their choices. Open to many different approaches to any particular problem or need, Aquarius clients will enjoy discussing these matters with you and can ask for a second or even third meeting. Your interpersonal relationship may deepen slightly during this time, giving them a much better idea of what kind of person you are and whether they can trust you to further their best interests.

Impressing the Aquarius Client

Aquarius clients will be most impressed by the wide ranges of choices and approaches you can offer. They will also be wowed by your willingness to devote time to them, and to work with them to develop a common concept or approach. Since you are probably not charging anything for these initial meetings, they will be happy to gain the benefit of your knowledge for free. Be sure to allow an hour or two for your first meeting so that neither of you feels rushed. Aquarius clients love humor and wit, so also be sure that you have some amusing stories or jokes to tell. They will be particularly open to hearing juicy gossip about their competitors.

Selling to the Aquarius Client

Just your openness, innovations, and willingness to listen to their problems will be enough of a sell for most Aquarius clients. Of course, they will also be impressed with your background in the field and earlier successes, so be sure to have a printout of your business record handy. Also remember that they will be going back to tell their associates about your encounter, hopefully with a feeling of pride in having met and interested you. Performers themselves, Aquarius clients will show open admiration for your own performance in presenting yourself, your achievements, and your guarantees.

Your Appearance and the Aquarius Client

Aquarius clients are particularly impressed by the latest styles and fashions. Therefore, be sure that you do some shopping for eye-catching cuts, fabrics, patterns, and colors. They will not only find stylish touches interesting but will also be impressed that you took the trouble to select and don them for the occasion. Rarely will Aquarius clients feel competitive and inferior to you in such confrontations, since they are usually content with their appearance and do not make unfavorable comparisons with others. Should you choose to create a more relaxed or casual appearance, you may do so, but by all means avoid highly formal or overly conservative dress.

Keeping the Aquarius Client's Interest

At your meetings with Aquarius clients make sure to maintain a rapid-fire approach that keeps them from getting bored with you. Likewise, respond immediately to their many questions and comments, showing that you are on your toes. Holding their interest over the long run will depend on how much energy you choose to invest in their account.

STRENGTHS
Attentive
Accepting
Sympathetic

WEAKNESSES
Vague
Unfocused
Uncertain

INTERACTIVE STYLE
Responsive
Cooperative
Trusting

Sending them frequent updates on your progress and also copies of the public relations programs you have developed for them are both essential. Be sure that Aquarius clients will spread their praise of your abilities far and wide, and in the course of doing so, they will attract many more customers to you.

Breaking Bad News to the Aquarius Client

Because of their openness to the adoption of new methods, breaking bad news to Aquarius clients may just signal a change of tactics. Rarely will a single stroke of bad luck cause Aquarius clients to drop you outright. They enjoy analyzing what went wrong and, along with you, planning a whole new campaign that promises greater success. This is also true of temporary setbacks, since Aquarians are able to see the broader picture and are usually accepting enough to wait for change. There is, however, a decided limit to their patience, and they will insist on results within a few weeks or months.

Entertaining the Aquarius Client

Aquarians love having fun, and the Aquarius client is no exception. Setting up a dinner at a fashionable restaurant, a drink at a trendy watering hole, or a front-row seat to a new show will do a lot to further your cause. Aquarius clients do not expect friendship to emerge from a business relationship with you, although good feelings are important to them. Usually cool and detached in their approach, Aquarius clients are happy to share entertainment opportunities in a manner that offers objective enjoyment rather than emotional involvement. Expect them to respond in kind by inviting you out also, which is always a good indication that things are going well.

The Aquarius Business Partner

Aquarians can bring life and zest to any business partnership. However, they will have to be watched carefully since their prodigious and often erratic energies can easily spin out of control. Unpredictable, Aquarians will go their own way without consulting you or heeding your counsel if given. Keeping them on a tight leash will be impossible. The next best thing is to schedule weekly meetings that can let them know of your expectations and give you some advanced warning of their intentions. Both detailed and global discussions are recommended in the course of such meetings.

Setting Up the Business Partnership with Aquarius

The time to pin down Aquarius business partners is before rather than after signing the partnership agreement. Extensive discussions concerning the new company and their role in it should be engaged in, during which special attention should be paid to keeping them under control. Any clause that can be interpreted in the direction of giving them more freedom from your scrutiny or evaluation should be carefully edited. Aquarius business partners will be quite agreeable to acceding to your demands in drawing up such an agreement, thinking that they will proceed as they like later on anyway. Your job will be to hold them to their written word.

Tasking with the Aquarius Business Partner

Aquarians are generally agreeable to dividing tasks equally and fairly. The problem is getting them to follow the agreed-upon plan. Their more erratic and wayward energies can create real problems here, for they frequently will abandon their preordained responsibilities in favor of some new thing that comes along. This puts you in the uncomfortable position of dreaded taskmaster, always spoiling their good time. Putting a damper on the Aquarius business partner's enthusiasm is a thankless task, but certainly a necessary one if the company is to survive. Try to be as sensitive and understanding as possible, yet remain firm in your resolve.

Traveling with and Entertaining the Aquarius Business Partner

Aquarius business partners can be wonderful traveling companions. Alert and always ready to enjoy themselves, they have a witty repartee that can keep you amused for hours. Problems can arise when their spirits are dashed by an unexpected setback, since they are difficult to rouse from resulting depressions. Furthermore, you could tire of their general hilarity and pray for them to slow down a bit. Inevitably, you will have to figure out how to go off on your own for a respite without losing them.

Managing and Directing the Aquarius Business Partner

Because of Aquarians' ungovernable nature, you had better forget about managing them. Directing them is possible if you use psychological methods that work on their complex personalities. Here it is best to follow a preordained plan or proven course of action rather than simply reacting to each of their impulsive actions, which will drive you crazy eventually. Always be soothing, calming, and reassuring, avoiding issues that would upset them. Aquarians are good at objectively examining situations with a cold eye, so appeal to their sense of logic and their rational side for best results.

Relating to the Aquarius Business Partner in the Long Run

Try to be a companion and friend of Aquarius partners rather than their boss. They want to like you and will do so as long as they do not feel you are constantly on their back, endlessly nagging and quibbling. Get them to understand your concerns one time rather than hassling them constantly. Aquarius business partners are happiest when things are going well and they feel appreciated by you and valued for their efforts. Keep interactions light as much as possible since a serious or glum demeanor on your part will have negative effects on them over time, making them even harder to handle.

Parting Ways with the Aquarius Business Partner

A sudden break with Aquarius business partners is undoubtedly something they have experienced before. Either instituted by themselves or the other person, a parting of ways is something Aquarians are familiar with since they know that they can be difficult to get along with and are also highly demanding of their partners' patience. An abrupt parting of the ways is most often characteristic of such breakups, but there need not be bad feelings involved, at least not on their part. You may be hurt or resentful of their abrupt actions and left bewildered just when you thought things were going so well. Here

(The Aquarius
Business Partner)

STRENGTHS

Lively

Zestful

Individualistic

WEAKNESSES

Unpredictable

Impulsive

Erratic

INTERACTIVE STYLE

Friendly

Versatile

Energetic

the contract will play a key role, since it should carefully spell out the details of a breakup with an Aquarius partner before you sign on the dotted line.

The Aquarius Competitor

The best way to oppose Aquarius competitors is to encourage their recklessness and knock them off balance. Arousing doubts and insecurities is a very effective means of accomplishing this aim, along with proceeding along an established course, remaining calm and consistent in your behavior. Both strategies can be employed simultaneously: progressing steadily while jabbing and poking holes in Aquarius competitors' defenses and watching them overreact. These competitors can be powerful opponents, since they will not hesitate to throw everything they have at you. The game is to deflect or reroute their aim, hopefully creating a boomerang effect.

Countering the Aquarius Competitor
Encouraging your Aquarius competitors to mass all their forces in service of one big push and then to fall into your trap is one way of handling them. Once they get used to such tactics, however, they will be wary of falling for them in the future. This can also be used against them psychologically, and indeed the psychological approach, or simply psyching them out, is always a good tactic to employ. Aquarius competitors are overly hasty in their reactions and normally lack the patience to wait and think things out. Furthermore, they are unlikely to be planning a massive counterstroke since they want to make their own lightning strike first.

Out-Planning the Aquarius Competitor
Aquarius competitors are difficult to out-plan since they are unlikely to let you know how they are going to proceed. Rarely logical in their approach, they act on intuition and hunches that are difficult to divine. Your planning should be well thought out and thoroughly implemented regardless of your Aquarius competitor's counterstrokes, and your ability to wear them down through sheer persistence is likely to decide the struggle in your favor. That said, you must also be cognizant of their moves and, even if not directly reactive to them, at least aware of their intent. You will have to be fast on your feet to keep up with their rapid-fire approach.

Impressing the Aquarius Competitor in Person
Aquarius competitors are most impressed with your abilities to innovate. They will be disinterested in more conservative attitudes that stress the tried and true and will not respond to them, except with impatience. If your meeting is a nonconfrontational one and you truly wish to impress them, be able to stand toe-to-toe with the Aquarius competitor and trade truly original and thought-provoking ideas, of course not giving away your most important plans in the process. They can be competitive in such exchanges and will always seek to best you through their sharp criticism and speed of thought.

Undercutting and Outbidding the Aquarius Competitor

When Aquarius competitors see what they want, they go for it, leaving little doubt of their intentions. Thus, if they have sufficient capital at hand they tend to outbid their opponents in any straight bidding war for something they want. However, you will do well to exhaust both their funds and their energies in early smaller bidding struggles in order to gain an advantage in the big ones to follow. Undercutting the bids of Aquarius competitors for favored contracts is best accompanied by convincing arguments showing your ability to deliver the goods, based on a long and reliable track record. Having facts and figures at hand is the best way to combat the tendency of Aquarius competitors to make unfounded promises that they probably cannot keep.

Public Relations Wars with the Aquarius Competitor

Aquarius competitors tend to be masterful in their approach to media wars. They have a sixth sense for what will work and what will not, given the current condition of the market and the public's mood. Technically adept, Aquarians are very much at home in the world of public relations: their advertising, marketing, copywriting, and visual skills in presentations to professionals and the public alike are extraordinary. You should not seek to directly best them in an all-out war, but to allow them to deplete their reserves in glitzy campaigns while you concentrate on increasing the quality and long-term appeal of your own products and services.

The Aquarius Competitor and the Personal Approach

Aquarius competitors are cool customers who are uncomfortable dealing with personal matters, particularly when emotions are involved. Their refusal to adopt a personal approach and their vulnerability to your psychological tactics are their Achilles heel. That said, Aquarians can be extremely seductive in business matters, not out of real feeling, of course, but through their innate charm and abilities to convince others with persuasive arguments. By pretending to fall for their spiel while at the same time exhibiting wisdom and cunning, you can disable them with occasional personal barbs that throw them into confusion.

Love

AQUARIUS
January 21–February 19

STRENGTHS

Spontaneous
Natural
Enjoyable

WEAKNESSES

Flighty
Superficial
Unreliable

INTERACTIVE STYLE

Lively
Animated
Particular

The Aquarius First Date

Aquarius first dates are, for the most part, lively and fun-loving. Not interested in hassles or complications, these colorful personalities just want to have a good time. An opportunity to get to know you better and possible deep involvements lie somewhere way down the tracks. To stay on the rails with Aquarius first dates, you should offer a few choices of restaurants, bars, clubs, or concerts for them to pick from. Don't be surprised if they have already decided what they want to do, probably five or ten minutes before you see them. Thus it is not a good idea to make fixed plans before hearing what they have to say at the present moment.

Wooing and Picking Up the Aquarius First Date

Aquarius first dates move very quickly, both mentally and physically, and are hard to keep up with. Moreover, you had better take advantage of the first few seconds that you have their attention or have caught their eye, for they are apt to disappear rapidly in the crowd. Do not be surprised if, when trying to pick them up, they suddenly drop all interest in you and turn toward someone else at a party or other social gathering. These ephemeral creatures are hard to pin down, particularly on first meeting, unless they find you highly attractive.

Suggested Activities for the Aquarius First Date

With Aquarians, the first date is likely to be the last unless you come up with something unusual. Bored with the same old routines, Aquarius first dates expect a special experience; in particular, they want an activity tailored to their peculiar needs and wants. Listen carefully to what they say and make decisions accordingly if you want to survive the first fifteen minutes together. Activities involving media and music or dancing are good bets. Starting off with a quiet dinner by candlelight is not usually Aquarians' speed—your romantic intentions toward them will be too blatant, and the time required to sit opposite you in one place will be excessive.

Turn-Ons and Turn-Offs for the Aquarius First Date

Aquarius first dates are turned off by assumptions you make about them or any obviously practiced routines you fall into that demonstrate your inflexibility and unresponsiveness to their individuality. Aquarius first dates will be startled and impressed if you can manage to take the lead in whirlwind style and sweep them off their feet. Avoid penny-pinching attitudes such as patting yourself on the back for finding such a good deal for food or entertainment. While respectful of your Aquarius first date's privacy, be your liveliest self by flamboyantly leading the way to the next mutually pleasurable experience.

Making "the Move" with the Aquarius First Date

Although Aquarius first dates who are interested in you can be highly flirtatious and open to your advances, you are treading on thin ice should you decide to make the first move. If they are not interested, you may never get a second chance since Aquarius first dates can be quite unforgiving of a premature advance. It may work out much better for you to hang back and wait for them to make the first move or, at the very least, flash an unequivocal green light for you to do so.

Impressing the Aquarius First Date

Aquarius first dates will be impressed by the more unusual aspects of your personality and behavior. If they find you truly funny, this is a big step in the right direction. Most Aquarius first dates will show little if any interest in a depressed, unhappy, or troubled personality. Although keeping light and happy might appear to lead nowhere in particular during the first meetings with them, at least it will ensure that you will not be dumped early on. When Aquarius first dates are not amused or impressed, you will know it immediately, for they have little interest in hiding their true feelings.

Brushing Off the Aquarius First Date

Normally, a couple of bad looks or negative remarks are enough to send Aquarius first dates scurrying off in a flash. Thus if you are truly interested in them, avoid sending any negative signals that could be even remotely interpreted as a brush-off. Smiling, laughing, and above all responding to their light chatter are recommended. If you two don't get along, chances are the Aquarius first date will brush you off first anyway, before you even have a chance to decide one way or another. Avoid teasing them about their little idiosyncrasies and peculiarities.

The Aquarius Romantic Partner

The Aquarius romantic partner is faithful up to a point—that point usually being when something more interesting comes along. Thus if you can manage to keep Aquarians' faces turned toward you and can satisfy their prodigious and often kinky needs, you stand a chance for longevity in the relationship. Invariably you will have to be forgiving when they do inevitably stray and be able to laugh off some involvements as being trivial. Your

STRENGTHS

Fun

Interesting

Exciting

WEAKNESSES

Drifting

Noncommitted

Unfaithful

INTERACTIVE STYLE

Bright

Cheerful

Open

own self-assurance may be the most important anchor for the ever-drifting Aquarius ship. Needless to say, Aquarians can be more fun than a barrel of monkeys, albeit just as difficult to keep under control.

Having a Discussion with the Aquarius Romantic Partner

Having a talk about certain subjects is possible, whereas other subjects are off-limits. For example, when it comes to Aquarians' behavior, it is best not to arouse their sharp opposition, which will lead to an inevitable clash of wills. After a while, if you take them to task for their erratic and unpredictable behavior, and attempt to patch things up each time, it will be like trying to close the pores of a leaking sieve. It's best to simply make note of what they have done and not raise the subject for discussion. Working subtly behind the scenes without arousing their opposition is best in most areas.

Arguments with the Aquarius Romantic Partner

Aquarians fly off the handle very quickly. Easily irritated and aroused, their reactions can be severe and swift. After one or two clashes, you will wisely choose to keep knock-down, drag-out fights to a minimum. The problem with Aquarians is that discussions become arguments in a split second, and if you head down this path, severe damage is usually inflicted on both sides by the time you reach the end (if indeed you manage to do so). Therefore, arguments should be studiously avoided. Often it is effective to leave Aquarians a short comment or warning in written form on the kitchen table just before you go out or later send a short email or text message.

Traveling with the Aquarius Romantic Partner

In the right mood, Aquarians can accept any planned activities you throw at them; in the wrong one, nothing seems to be right. The best way to travel with them is to keep light on your feet and be ready to adjust to their ever-changing preferences and demands. The worst thing is to get fixed to one special desire that involves their cooperation. Above all, do not make assumptions about what you think they might like or dislike based on past experience. Aquarians are too likely to come up with a new surprise.

Sex with the Aquarius Romantic Partner

Aquarians may love doing it with you, but unfortunately they may equally well enjoy doing it with someone else. The best advice in this area is to have fun while you can and not pay too much attention to what they do in their time away from you. If Aquarians feel free and not judged by you, they will definitely stick around longer. But when they feel the noose tighten around their necks or sense that the tender trap of marriage is about to be sprung, they are likely to disappear with the speed of light.

Affection and the Aquarius Romantic Partner

Aquarians are more into superficial shows of affection than deep or emotional ones. Once you get into the rhythm of their cool and detached manner, you will understand the true significance of a passing smile or touch of the hand. Do not be surprised if such a demonstration of affection is accompanied by a wry laugh, smile, or even a mocking consolation such as: "Oh, poor baby!" Most Aquarian displays of emotion and affection are expressed with a twinkle in the eye that frequently precedes a tauntingly provocative statement tinged with irony or outright sarcasm. Remember that such expressions are not usually delivered with malicious intent.

Humor and the Aquarius Romantic Partner

Humor is quickly expressed by Aquarians, but unfortunately you may soon become the butt of the jokes. Being made fun of can wax highly irritating over time, wearing you down and ultimately making you unhappy. Therefore, it is good to set limits on such behavior from the outset and not let things fall into a mocking pattern or spin out of control. Finding objects of common derision is often a good alternative to your always being the goat. Do not try to turn the tables and laugh at your Aquarius romantic partner, since their sense of humor is definitely limited when it comes to themselves.

The Aquarius Spouse

Aquarius spouses can be quite devoted to their families. Once they decide that marriage is the best course, they will commit fully and without reservation. Their being faithful requires that they feel needed by their spouses and children. Although Aquarians will spend lots of time away from home, principally when engaged in professional activities, they enjoy domestic interactions tremendously, particularly when celebrating during vacations and holidays. Aquarian spouses bring excitement and sparkle to even the most mundane day-to-day events. Their good moods elevate the spirits of those around them.

Wedding and Honeymoon with the Aquarius Spouse

Aquarius spouses are not overly interested in the extravagances of overblown social events, and their own weddings are no exception. However, although they would be quite content with a simple ceremony, they will be accepting of your need to proceed in a more flamboyant fashion and will enter into expensive celebrations fully and without reservation. They do not generally bring great expectations with them to the honeymoon suite, preferring just to take things as they come. Thus disappointment or letdown is generally avoided. Count on them to do their best to make weddings and honeymoons very special, but don't be surprised when they ask, "How was I?"

Home and Day-to-Day Married Life with the Aquarius Spouse

Many Aquarians have trouble adjusting to the mundane demands of everyday life, even when they are livening things up. They bore easily, and the constant strain of providing all the interest and excitement can wear them down over time. Make sure that you contribute sufficient energy and interest to keep them entertained so that you don't lose their attention. Also, allow them the freedom they need away from home, and never question them closely about where they have been and what they have done. They will tell you what they want you to know. Sharing comes naturally to most Aquarians.

STRENGTHS
Enjoyable
Faithful
Committed

WEAKNESSES
Busy
Hassled
Egotistical

INTERACTIVE STYLE
Positive
Sparkling
Interesting

Finances and the Aquarius Spouse

Aquarians in general have to feel free to spend money as they wish. This can create acute problems for their family if they are on a strict budget. Unpredictable in their actions, Aquarians are often faced with the difficulty of owning up to cash outlays after a bank statement arrives showing that your mutual account is heavily in the red or credit cards are maxed out. It is best to avoid having entirely separate bank accounts; otherwise your ability to put some limits on their spending will be eliminated. Aquarius spouses have a special weakness for flashy gadgets, vehicles, and appliances.

Infidelity and the Aquarius Spouse

Although Aquarius lovers can be notoriously unfaithful, Aquarius spouses are generally not. They take great pride in their families and are quite concentrated in their efforts to support and encourage their growth. However, it is inevitable that once or twice in any marriage, Aquarius spouses will be sorely tempted to stray when an especially attractive individual comes along or when unhappiness and pain in their marital relationship becomes too much to bear. Such infidelities can cause them emotional suffering, which most Aquarians are not built to handle. Encourage them to talk, and be forgiving if you want to hold on to them.

Children and the Aquarius Spouse

Aquarians can make wonderful parents. Their childlike side prompts them to indulge in mutually enjoyable activities with their offspring, including but not limited to sports (both as participants and as spectators), games, solving puzzles, creating art, taking trips, and many sorts of social gatherings. Getting down in the sandbox with their kids is characteristic of Aquarius parents, who are not at all self-conscious about fully expressing their inner child for all to see. Aquarius parents are likely to fall into deep depressions if their marriages are not fruitful or if their mates become unwilling to have or raise children.

Divorce and the Aquarius Spouse

Particularly when kids are involved, Aquarius spouses can suffer more from a broken marriage and a resulting dysfunctional family than almost any other area in life. Accepting in so many other ways, Aquarius spouses may refuse to accept a breakup and be wracked with emotional pain that can continue for years and seriously affect the lives of their exes and offspring. Divorcing an Aquarius spouse should thus be avoided whenever possible, and even if they are primarily the ones at fault, you should always give them a second, or even a third, chance. They will sincerely do their best to live up to your future expectations once they fully realize what they are at risk of losing.

The Aquarius Lover

When involved with Aquarius lovers you will have to resign yourself to the fact that you are not the first, nor the last. Moreover, it is quite likely that you are also not the only lover they have at present. When it comes to matters of love, Aquarians figure they have enough to go around without neglecting anyone they care for. Consequently, the amount of love they share with any one person is limited in quantity, although the quality may be high, at least for the moment. Those looking for depth and meaning in a relationship may be dissatisfied with what Aquarius lovers dish up, finding it too superficial (albeit exciting) and ephemeral to last.

Meeting the Aquarius Lover

Aquarius lovers are generally up for meeting any time, any place. Not at all particular, they will take what they can get whenever possible. Reaching them by email or cell phone is not usually a problem, since they check in regularly and will usually get back to you within twenty-four hours. They are particularly vulnerable to spontaneous actions on your part, since the unexpected and the exciting are two areas that attract them like a magnet. You also will need to get used to sudden communications that summon you to be at a certain place at a certain time—sometimes even within fifteen or twenty minutes! They usually consider an hour more than adequate notice.

Location and the Aquarius Lover

Location is not a big issue for most Aquarians. Sometimes the risk or danger of being discovered can act as an aphrodisiac, prompting Aquarian lovers to actually prefer the more sensitive location. Breaking rules and causing uproars is usually part and parcel of an involvement with an Aquarius lover, so you had better get used to it. These spontaneous individuals will just not be controlled in any way, often resulting in the most bizarre behavior. They find the excitement well worth the risk and expect that you will come to appreciate it as well.

Sex and the Aquarius Lover

The Aquarius lover has an instinctive feeling for variety, but also has probably thrown a glance or three at the *Kama Sutra*, Henry Miller, or *The Story of O* at one time or another. In matters of sex, Aquarius lovers bore easily, so you had better read up on the subject or be willing to follow their wildest promptings if you wish to remain an object of continued interest. Uptight or overly conservative and prudish attitudes are a sure turnoff, but in certain cases they may stimulate the outrageous Aquarian lover to new heights of shocking behavior, which can be quite enjoyable and stimulating.

Holding On to the Aquarius Lover

It is not really possible to hold on to these fleeting characters for very long. Aquarius lovers specialize in short-term relationships. Should you desire to hold on to them for longer periods, you will have to be a wizard to keep their interest and keep their roving eyes in check. Like Scheherazade who wove a never-ending tale for *One Thousand and One Nights*, you will have to be enchanting in your approach and probably wind up sealing the

STRENGTHS

Exciting

Creative

Nonclaiming

WEAKNESSES

Fleeting

Superficial

Scattered

INTERACTIVE STYLE

Giving

Active

Quality-oriented

deal with the act of marriage, eventually. The more you try to hold on to Aquarius lovers, the more you will feel them slipping like water through your fingers.

Entertaining the Aquarius Lover

Aquarius lovers enjoy being entertained in private but are usually more at home when they do the entertaining. They feed on appreciation and recognition, and you may be called upon again and again to stroke their egos and allay their insecurities by telling them how terrific they were, or are, during lovemaking. Should you want some relief from their frenetic advances, you might suggest going out on the town, since they are usually open to suggestions that involve a quick and spontaneous change of location. Aquarius lovers are fond of being seen in public with their companions and of being at the center of controversy of all sorts.

Breaking Up with the Aquarius Lover

This is not usually a problem since Aquarius lovers have probably already broken up without your having realized it, or perhaps they were never really involved with you in the first place! It is rare that Aquarius lovers will lay a strict claim to you and force you to remain with them. To them, the world is full of new interests, and the latest one is probably waiting just around the corner. It is not their self-assurance that spurs them on—they are often insecure about their abilities to love and make love—but rather their faith in the universe that they will be provided with a new involvement whenever they lack one.

The Aquarius Ex

Do not be surprised if Aquarius exes do not show a great interest in you. Chances are that they have moved on to someone else, causing you to either sigh with relief or suffer extreme pain, depending on your feelings. A short while after the breakup you may not recognize these people, so changed will they be, and they may not show much recognition of you either. Aquarius exes are sometimes prone to treat you as though you never existed, thus making any sort of relationship with them difficult or impossible. Thus with most Aquarius exes, once it is over it is over, and you cannot expect too much more.

Establishing a Friendship with the Aquarius Ex

Aquarius exes are not usually interested in having friendships with you after a breakup, but it is possible to make contact as long as encounters are kept sporadic and superficial. Making pro-forma matters covering practical matters and decisions are the best you can hope for. Above all, do not expect displays of emotion from them; you will save yourself a lot of frustration and hurt. Should they show interest in you, it may only be a gambit to gain something that they want, and you should refuse to play their game.

Issues of Getting Back Together with the Aquarius Ex

In the rare cases that Aquarius exes show a bona fide interest in rekindling the relationship, they could be willing to commit on a permanent basis. However, they are equally capable of discussing getting back together as a ploy to exercise control over you—in effect, using you for selfish purposes. Tread lightly in any discussions of this subject, forcing them to provide definite guarantees of their intent, even legally binding ones in writing. If you are interested in getting back together and they are not, you can only look forward to a future filled with pain and suffering.

Discussing Past Issues with the Aquarius Ex

Most Aquarius exes are definitely not interested in discussing the past at all, let alone going over past issues. They may not even remember what happened, good or bad, and they may in fact be in permanent denial over most past subjects. Should you try to confront them with photos or written material that demonstrates their devotion to you or the family, they will probably refuse to look at them, claiming you are just trying to manipulate their feelings. ("What feelings?" you may very well ask.) They are also quite capable of refusing to talk to you about the past on the grounds that their present partner would not like it and that it could damage your relationship with their new partner.

Expressing Affection to the Aquarius Ex

This is usually out of the question. Again, if Aquarius exes wax affectionate it is usually because they want something, either physical or financial. This expression of affection may have a sexual overtone and be a direct lead-in to stirring up old emotions that could quickly find you in bed together. What could appear to be the rekindling of love's flame unfortunately, in most cases, will prove to be just an isolated incident, and it is certainly advised that you keep it just that, no matter how enjoyable the encounter was.

Defining the Present Relationship with the Aquarius Ex

What relationship? The entire thing could probably be summed up in just a few words, not leaving much to the imagination, either. Aquarius exes will tend to define the present relationship by simply limiting it to a few essential areas, such as children, taxes, or property, that must be addressed. Any discussions that attempt to further describe or define the relationship are usually out of the question because of the disinterest or outright hostility of Aquarius exes. Your ideas on the subject can be put into a letter or email to them, but do not expect much of a response.

Sharing Custody with the Aquarius Ex

Sharing custody is the single area in which contact with Aquarius exes can be expected and maintained. Because of their love for their children and wish to continue to be in their lives, they are likely to make some concessions to seeing you and even discussing certain matters. Children will often demand equal time with Aquarius parents, who provide a lot of fun and special treatment. This expectation can put you in the uncomfortable position of being the taskmaster or ogre.

(The Aquarius Ex)

STRENGTHS
Nondependent
Controlled
Objective

WEAKNESSES
Cold
Detached
Unconcerned

INTERACTIVE STYLE
Matter-of-fact
Unresponsive
Disinterested

Friends and Family

STRENGTHS

Idealistic

Universal

Spontaneous

WEAKNESSES

Bizarre

Unreliable

Uncertain

INTERACTIVE STYLE

Abstract

Objective

Cool

The Aquarius Friend

Friendship is extremely important to most Aquarians. For them, it often assumes an idealistic, global, and universal significance more than a personal one. Consequently, most of their friendships are tinged with a highly abstract and objective quality—cool rather than passionate. Rarely interested in committing themselves to daily or even weekly contact, Aquarians will contact you while they are on the run or when one of their latest active exploits has simmered down or momentarily come to rest. Thus you should not count on them as a pillar of stability but rather as an interesting sidelight in your life—one that can be both entertaining and a bit special.

Asking for Help from the Aquarius Friend

It's best to have just one or two questions for your speedy Aquarius friend—especially ones that can be posed and answered in a rapid-fire interchange. As far as help with moving, planning, arranging functions, making lists for work and future plans, and shopping for hard-to-find items, you had better not count on it. To Aquarius friends, help is something they can offer only in their spare time, which is already probably extremely limited or nonexistent. Then there is the problem of contacting them, which is also difficult. It's best to leave a voicemail or give a heads-up email several days or even a couple of weeks before you need assistance.

Communication and Keeping in Touch with the Aquarius Friend

Although they are generally good communicators, Aquarians are probably the ones who will contact you rather than the other way around. Not only are they difficult to reach, but they also prefer being the ones who initiate contact, depending on when, where, and how it suits them. Too often this will come smack in the middle of something you are presently busy with, and once you find it impossible to respond to their spontaneous gestures, they may prove even more difficult to contact in the future. Aquarians have to feel that you truly need them urgently, first of all, and, secondly, your attempt to communicate has to strike them in exactly the right way and at the right moment.

Borrowing Money from the Aquarius Friend

Don't depend on Aquarius friends for loans, even those that have been agreed to or promised. Chances are that just before they are about to deliver, with all the best intentions, they spent the money elsewhere. So spontaneous are they with outlays of cash that they absolutely cannot be counted on to fulfill fixed financial obligations. If you can interest them in what you will do with the money, however, they may look on the loan as an interesting investment and come through with even more than you asked for. This awakening of their interest is worth developing over time, since it is likely to pay off in a generous outlay of cash.

Asking for Advice from the Aquarius Friend

Aquarians are not ones to give lengthy advice. Normally they can tell you what they think in a few words and do not need time to mull things over. Usually they are perceptive when it comes to objective issues, but they are not particularly talented in the areas of psychological observation, human emotions, and the darker side of life. Sometimes they outright refuse to get involved in discussions of depressing or unhealthy matters, not only out of dislike but also out of principle. It's best to limit your requests for advice to areas that they have shown adeptness for dealing with, particularly in technical matters.

Visiting the Aquarius Friend

It is difficult to visit an Aquarius friend since they are often not at home. Furthermore, if they are there but are fully engaged in a professional or private matter, they may not answer the bell or a knock at their door. Aquarians' full engagement with the matter at hand, which of course can change from minute to minute, frequently precludes even visits that have been scheduled well in advance, so be forewarned not to make assumptions or get your expectations up. You may find it better to suggest that they visit you, giving them a wide range of choices and allowing each of these to span a period of several hours or even days when they might drop in.

Celebrations/Entertainment with the Aquarius Friend

Fun-loving Aquarians enjoy celebrating special occasions and going out on the town for a good time. However, because of their rapidly changing schedules, it usually works best to make the decision to celebrate or go out on the spur of the moment. Following such impulses, you are both likely to have a great time in a wide range of activities, from a simple meal or drink to a full-blown binge of entertainment possibilities. You will find Aquarians inexhaustible in their ability to have a great time, only posing a problem when you try to put on the brakes and bring things to a halt.

The Aquarius Roommate

STRENGTHS

Tolerant

Accepting

Open

WEAKNESSES

Evasive

Forgetful

Uninvolved

INTERACTIVE STYLE

Detached

Capricious

Individualistic

Aquarius roommates tend to come and go at a furious pace, refusing to stay in one location or even position for very long. Keeping up with or even adjusting to them can be difficult or impossible, so it is best that you just do your own thing and ignore them as much as you can. They will not seek to irritate you intentionally or interfere with what you are doing, so things will work out best when you are mutually tolerant. The detachment of most Aquarians precludes any real deep involvement. You should avoid loading them down with extensive domestic responsibilities. They are likely to quickly agree to them in order to get you off their back and then just as quickly ignore them.

Sharing Financial Responsibilities with the Aquarius Roommate

Unfortunately, Aquarius roommates are often hopeless with money. They spend it so quickly that they are invariably caught short at the end of the month. Owing you for rent unfortunately can become a pattern, although when they are flush with cash they are likely to throw a whole bunch of it your way. When it comes to making payments in general, Aquarius roommates simply cannot be counted on unless you pin them down and risk an outburst of temper followed by a quick exit.

Cleaning and the Aquarius Roommate

Do not go down the road of cleaning up after them—your task of dealing with the results of a perpetual whirlwind will be exhausting and endless and will only arouse your resentment. It is best to let them drown in their mess while keeping your room neat as a pin, hopefully as a good example. The problem is keeping common rooms in order, such as the kitchen, bathroom, or living room. You will invariably have to do most of the work. But when things get disorderly, you will have to pin down your Aquarius roommate to get the work done and firmly refuse to accept any excuses or assurances of future involvement.

Houseguests and the Aquarius Roommate

Most Aquarius roommates will be remarkably tolerant and accepting of your houseguests, even ones who drop in at unexpected moments and decide to stay a bit longer than expected. Aquarians are fun-loving and rarely miss an opportunity to share in having a good time with others. Should your houseguests be unusually conservative or uptight, however, they may have quite a shock viewing the cavortings and shenanigans of your highly unusual Aquarius roommate. Sharp interactions between these contrasting personalities may bring such visits to an abrupt end.

Parties and the Aquarius Roommate

Having a party is often a good way to get your Aquarius roommate to clean up, both before and after the event. Aquarians love to party and are likely to contribute both time and energy to ensure that everyone has a good time. Keeping them under control can be a bit of a problem, although they usually dance 'til they drop and may suddenly remove themselves from the picture. Sometimes, however, they may have to be literally carried to their room and dumped on their bed. Aquarius roommates will not usually impose limits on how far things go during even the wildest of events.

Privacy and the Aquarius Roommate

Aquarius roommates will not be particularly respectful of your privacy, since they think in group, rather than individual, terms when it comes to living together. They are also tolerant of your intrusions into their private space, although they will often draw a strict line when they are deeply involved in professional or intimate activities. Usually up for sharing, Aquarius roommates will be open to sharing their food, their space, and their money (when they have it, that is). The doors to their rooms are more likely to be left open than closed, thus inviting occasional remarks and visits without the need to knock first.

Discussing Problems with the Aquarius Roommate

Aquarius roommates are open to discussing problems on a spontaneous basis but are likely to balk at prearranged and more formal conferences. However, particularly when they agree quickly with a demand you make, you can expect them to totally ignore what they seem to have so easily agreed to. Extremely hard to pin down to fixed obligations, Aquarius roommates are understanding but not practical in implementing your wishes. They have a blind spot in recognizing that they are part of the problem under discussion and are more likely to level criticism at others or just to blame the times as having been inauspicious or unlucky.

The Aquarius Parent

Many Aquarians, being free spirits, do not choose to marry or to have children at all. Those who do are likely to maintain their independent stances or to encourage their children to fly the nest once they have reached young adulthood. Not ones to be overly commanding or possessive, Aquarian parents love to see their children develop independent attitudes but can be quite intolerant when their children break certain ironclad safety rules they have set for them. Thus, Aquarian parents draw the line on freedom when they feel their children are putting themselves in harm's way. Aquarian parents usually take as much or more interest in after-school activities than in academics, being particularly encouraging of their children's involvements in sports, social activities, friendships, and creative projects.

Discipline Style of the Aquarius Parent

Most Aquarian parents prefer not to discipline their children at all, except when it comes to safety. Should a child break the rules and court danger, Aquarius parents will come down hard on them and probably ground them for a period of time. Otherwise, Aquarius parents try to teach their children to be accountable for their own behavior, giving them liberty with the proviso that they know that although free, they are responsible for their actions as well. For example, if they are allowed to go out on a weeknight, getting up on time and having their homework done is their responsibility. Aquarius parents hate to nag.

STRENGTHS

Encouraging

Interested

Liberating

WEAKNESSES

Intolerant

Fearful

Selfish

INTERACTIVE STYLE

Active

Enthusiastic

Nonacademic

Affection Level and the Aquarius Parent

Aquarius parents can be affectionate to their children without a lot of fuss or to-do. Daily hugs and little kisses are normal for them, both given and received. However, the affection level for most Aquarius parents does not go deep; in many cases these individuals can be quite cool, often oblivious to the emotional needs of their children. Being a bit quirky, most Aquarius parents have funny ways of showing affection that can go so far as teasing or even ridiculing their offspring. Many children will not recognize such actions as being affectionate, and even when they do, their friends may not be so understanding and may remain confused.

Money Issues and the Aquarius Parent

Aquarius parents can be quite generous with cash outlays. They will usually provide their children with an ample weekly allowance, and they love to see them spend it on pleasurable (but harmless) pursuits. Even when they realize that a little bit of chocolate consumption can lead to cavities, they may feel that its mood-enhancing qualities outweigh such risks. Aquarius parents will also give generously when it comes to major items needed by their children, the only problem being that the money may have already been spent on the Aquarius parent's latest passion or fad. They will most often have the good sense to avoid putting the family in serious debt over expensive items desired or demanded by their offspring.

Crises and the Aquarius Parent

Being high-strung, many Aquarius parents are liable to overreact when it comes to their children being in danger, at least as they perceive it. Registering extreme alarm and coming to the rescue prematurely are typical Aquarius traits that can frequently enhance rather than diminish the danger. For example, an alarmed Aquarius parent seeking to warn children may actually distract them, like when a car is bearing down and their awareness is diverted by the parent's voice. Aquarius parents must learn to have more faith in their children's perceptions.

Holidays/Family Gatherings and the Aquarius Parent

Aquarius parents are not that fond of family gatherings, but they love to take vacations with their children, and they will even bring a couple of their kids' friends along. The key here is the difference between what they like to do (vacations) and what they are required to do (family gatherings). Aquarians hate doing things over and over in a repetitive and predictable fashion, and therefore, the same old family stuff every year bores them totally. For an Aquarius, boredom leads to irritation, irritation to resentment, and resentment to a stubborn refusal to participate, eventually. On vacations, however, they can fully indulge their spontaneous impulses and their hankering for adventure. Aquarius parents will often act like big kids themselves.

Caring for the Aging Aquarius Parent

Aging Aquarius parents usually demand to be left on their own and stubbornly refuse to accept help from their children, either physical or financial. They have a marked tendency toward stinginess as they get older and so are well suited to surviving on very little, whether or not they need to. The pittances they are able to exist on would not be possible for most others their age, and certainly not desirable. Since the peculiarities of Aquarius parents also increase with age, their children often show great concern for their incomprehensible antics and even begin to assume that some form of dementia may be present. It is best to just keep an eye on aging Aquarius parents and not to cramp their often bizarre lifestyles.

The Aquarius Sibling

Aquarius siblings inevitably light up the fun side of life for their brothers and sisters through their wit and sparkle. They can be counted on for having a good time, but also for just quietly lending a relaxed and nonserious note to family life. Their mood can shift abruptly from low-key to frenetic, often sending shock waves through the sibling community. However, after some years of such behavior, the unexpected becomes expected, and reactions to them are muted. Coming up with new plans and unusual thoughts—which is their special province—is an ability that comes to be highly valued by their brothers and sisters, and when things become too boring or predictable, they will often turn to their Aquarius sibling(s) for inspiration.

Rivalry/Closeness with the Aquarius Sibling

As a rule, Aquarians are not overly competitive with siblings, even when they show aggressive characteristics outside the house. They would choose to be close to their siblings, but this is not always possible since they have traits that can be found annoying and upsetting. They have a way of winning hearts, however, and are frequently forgiven for their distressing and noisy transgressions. Rather than compete, Aquarius siblings are usually content to do their own thing; their competitive drives are often transmuted into a search for excellence and surpassing their personal best.

Past Issues and the Aquarius Sibling

Not only are Aquarius siblings forgetful, they are also able to forgive and forget when it comes to past issues. Their forgetfulness usually is indicative of their tendency to move on, live very much in the present moment, and anticipate the future. The past has little significance for most Aquarius siblings. However, this tendency may not be shared by one particular brother or sister who feels wronged, in which case the forgetfulness or accepting qualities of their Aquarius sibling will only infuriate the wronged one even further. Aquarius siblings must learn to recognize how important past issues can be to others.

Dealing with the Estranged Aquarius Sibling

Because of their wish for things to work out and their intense need to express friendly feelings to their siblings, Aquarians are usually open to reconciliation. Chances are, they were ostracized from the group rather than estranged by choice. Therefore, it is

STRENGTHS

Inspiring

Imaginative

Innovative

WEAKNESSES

Disturbing

Shocking

Alarming

INTERACTIVE STYLE

Abrupt

Spontaneous

Nonserious

up to the family to talk things over amongst themselves, make a decision to take the errant Aquarian sibling back into the fold, and finally move toward reconciliation. In most cases, the estranged Aquarius sibling will agree to return and even consent to meet certain demands in doing so. Still, Aquarian siblings may never fully understand why they were cut out in the first place.

Money Issues (Borrowing Money, Wills, Etc.) and the Aquarius Sibling

Generally speaking, money is not the most important thing to Aquarians, and therefore lending it is no big deal for them. Also, they will not suffer overly by having been neglected financially in a will, unless of course the deceased is a parent or relative they were very close to emotionally. Aquarius siblings are most happy when all the brothers and sisters, including themselves, are given an equal share. They hate fighting over money and may simply refuse to do so, even to their financial detriment. More idealistic than others, they will rarely forsake their principles in money matters.

Holidays/Celebrations/Reunions and the Aquarius Sibling

Aquarius siblings are very happy playing a modest role in all family holidays, celebrations, and reunions. They immediately respond to the good feelings shared by all family members, never seeking any special attention or power position for themselves in such activities. Keeping them happy and avoiding arguments will pay dividends in freeing the company from Aquarian irritations and sudden emotional outbursts. The presence of a joyful, beaming Aquarius will lend good cheer to almost any family gathering. Make sure to include them in skits, stories, games, or outdoor recreational activities to put their abundant energies to good use.

Vacationing with the Aquarius Sibling

Being left out of any vacation activity can be torture for most Aquarius siblings. They must be included in what goes on, and if they are not, be prepared for a sulky, resentful, even tearful reaction on your return. Aquarius siblings favor the more challenging and exciting endeavors on vacation, rarely shrinking from danger and in fact being spurred on by it. The siblings of Aquarians must therefore keep an eye out for them, since the abrupt end to an otherwise enjoyable vacation could be signaled by an unforeseen accident or illness. Aquarius siblings must be reminded of their limitations from time to time and put under some restrictions, although they will usually balk at severe ones.

The Aquarius Child

Aquarius children can pose acute problems to their parents, but because of their joyful natures, they respond immediately to the attention, understanding, and acceptance of their mother or father. Problem areas usually involve their unusual manner of doing things and their absolute refusal to do them your way, or any other way for that matter. If shoes do not feel comfortable on their feet, they will walk barefoot in the snow; if food that is good for them but is disliked is forced on them, they will refuse to even look at it; whining, crying, writhing, and screaming are frequently manifested in their younger years as reactions to attempts to control them.

Personality Development and the Aquarius Child

Aquarius children should be allowed to work their way through the various stages of childhood in their unusual fashion. Should you, as the parent, oppose them at crucial points in their development, they are likely to get stuck there, producing huge psychological problems in adolescence and adult life. Remember that Aquarius children are not like others and that their highly individualistic approach to most matters must be acknowledged and even honored. Thus they demand and should get special treatment, particularly if you want to avoid big-time troubles. If childhood development is likened to a tree's growth, try to avoid too much pruning or clipping of the Aquarian's branches.

Hobbies/Interests/Career Paths for the Aquarius Child

Aquarius children should be presented with a broad palette of activities to choose from. This is not only necessary because of the abundant energies that must be used up, but also because Aquarian children will not be interested in most things that are offered to them. Watching their hobby preferences may often yield real clues to a possible profession in adult life. Never try to thrust Aquarius children into premature molds or force them to follow a path preferred by you. Their highly rebellious nature will explode sooner or later and break out of it, causing you more intense disappointment and unhappiness in the long run than simply accepting their personal choices, however difficult that may be.

Discipline and the Aquarius Child

Aquarius children are difficult or impossible to discipline. Moreover, since their severe reactions to such treatment can quickly lead to all-out conflict, even war, they are best left alone whenever possible. The firm application of certain basic rules and understanding, gentle, loving attitudes are usually the best ways to keep their wayward energies under control. Should you administer physical punishment, do not be surprised if the Aquarius child lashes out in return, since they simply will not tolerate being abused. They are likely to stand up for other creatures in their vicinity that also receive unfair treatment.

Affection Level and the Aquarius Child

Aquarius kids need hugs more than most. When younger, cuddling, soothing tones of voice, loving glances, and reassuring pats are essential to calm their excitable natures. Aquarius children feed on affection and are also capable of returning such investments

STRENGTHS
Joyful
Appreciative
Responsive

WEAKNESSES
Irritable
Rebellious
Uncontrollable

INTERACTIVE STYLE
Demanding
Particular
Individualistic

with dividends in their early adult years to an understanding and supportive parent. Because of Aquarians' energetic and frenetic natures, their parents may make the mistake of thinking they do not need much encouragement and affection, but withholding it from them would be a big mistake. Aquarius children should be given small pets to take care of so that they can learn to be gentle and nurturing rather than wild and uncontrollable.

Dealing with the Aquarius Child and Interactions with Siblings

Aquarius children will require especially understanding parents to monitor their interactions with siblings. Too often they fall afoul of their brothers and sisters, who can be less than understanding of their unusual and frequently disturbing habits. Parents will be challenged to the fullest to maintain harmony in a family harboring a particularly tempestuous Aquarius child. On the other hand, if they are truly accepted and fully satisfied with their treatment, Aquarius children will rarely, if ever, intentionally stir up trouble or seek to disrupt the peace of a family's daily life just to gain attention.

Interacting with the Adult Aquarius Child

Strangely enough, even the most upsetting Aquarius child can become the model of tranquility in adult life. Once they get a lot out of their system in childhood and adolescence, they frequently settle down to a remarkably harmonious adulthood, showing a spirit of cooperation and understanding that they lacked in their early years. Thus the adult Aquarius child can become a force for stability in a family they may have terrorized for years. Those who only knew them as children are frequently amazed by the transformation when meeting them years later.

Pisces

BIRTHDATE **FEBRUARY 20–MARCH 20**

Pisces, the sign of the fish, is the mutable water sign ruled by Neptune. The deeply feeling individuals belonging to this sign value emotional matters more than most and demand profound involvement in their more serious relationships. Extremely sensitive, Pisces is easily wounded emotionally and particularly vulnerable to rejection. Their spirituality or belief in a divinity is often strong, as is their involvement with the arts, principally music. Although sensuous, a Pisces knows there is more to life than what they can see and touch.

Work

PISCES
February 20–March 20

STRENGTHS
Affluent
Fluid
Empathic

WEAKNESSES
Easily manipulated
Oversensitive
Overprotective

INTERACTIVE STYLE
Relaxed
Adaptable
Influential

The Pisces Boss

For some strange reason Pisces are thought of as being bad with money. Yet in history, and also in one's own circle of friends, money seems to come easiest to those born under this sign. In the same way, a Pisces boss too frequently invokes the mistaken picture of an ultra-relaxed and indecisive fish flopping out of its depth, but in fact those born under this sign frequently make excellent bosses, even dynasty builders. Making money comes naturally to them, as it is a fluid medium that they totally understand, and nurturing Pisces bosses are more than capable of guarding the interests of their businesses and employees, bringing profit to all concerned.

Asking the Pisces Boss for a Raise

Pisces bosses like to see their money put to good use. Consequently, if they recognize that you have a good track record with the company, they will want to reward you in order to motivate you even further to produce high-quality work and to increase profits. Your request for a raise should be stated forthrightly, along with the reasons you feel such an increase in salary is justified. Promises about future work will be taken with a grain of salt by most Pisces bosses, but by granting you a higher position they can cleverly give you the tools you need to succeed.

Breaking Bad News to the Pisces Boss

Pisces bosses are always willing to give things another try or even two when they do not work out. Therefore, bringing bad news is usually just a prelude to a bit of a shakeup in the organization and a few changes of plans before the start of a second attempt. It is usually best to let Pisces bosses come up with the new agenda, since they are very good at thinking on their feet in times of disadvantage or outright disaster. Indeed they are often at their best when their backs are to the wall. Remember that pain, suffering, and misfortune are well-known quantities to most born under this sign—they know how to hang in there despite major setbacks.

Arranging Travel and/or Entertainment for the Pisces Boss

Pisces bosses are heavily into quality, and some of them even occupy positions of power in order to be able to fully enjoy the fringe benefits. Normally their travel, lodging, and dining budgets are high, allowing them to indulge their well-developed tastes. Pisces love sophistication and therefore are extremely comfortable, one might even say at home, in the luxurious settings of high-class restaurants and hotels. Pisces are unlikely to hold back on lavish spending, knowing that where you are seen can often be a potent business tool in impressing clients and competitors alike. Pisces will want to wear fine clothes when going out, and they are particularly fond of beautiful footwear.

Decision-Making and the Pisces Boss

Known to be indecisive, Pisces bosses have the great advantage of being flexible in most business settings. They are not indecisive at all but like to have time to contemplate many factors before coming to a decision, which is usually rendered at the right moment. Because of this sensitivity for *kairos* (the right time for performing an action) they are likely to succeed in most of their endeavors. Once Pisces bosses have made up their minds, they are immediately ready to implement their ideas and to bring their projects to fruition.

Impressing and/or Motivating the Pisces Boss

Pisces bosses know that a successful company means increased rewards for everyone, so the best way to impress them is to show how well you work as a team player. Likewise, when the group is meshing well in its endeavors, Pisces bosses will be more motivated to sell products and render services at the highest level of professionalism. When Pisces bosses wander from desk to desk, looking over the shoulders of their employees, they will often begin by inquiring about matters seemingly unrelated to their job in order to put workers at ease. To impress your Pisces boss you should also adopt the same relaxed, informal tone.

Making Proposals and/or Giving Presentations to the Pisces Boss

Pisces bosses need convincing. They always want to know why they should believe what you have to say, and they usually come to the conference table to be confronted with convincing evidence that supports your claims. Although it is not necessary to adorn your presentations with attractive technical bells and whistles, Pisces bosses are very aesthetically oriented and will fully enjoy an elegant, pleasing presentation as much as they will find a sloppy, careless one highly distasteful. Pisces bosses will usually indicate their approval and appreciation with a simple nod of the head rather than engaging in flowery praise.

The Pisces Employee

Because of their extreme adaptability, Pisces employees are frequently highly prized. Able to pinch-hit in almost any situation, they are used as reliable stopgaps that can kick in at a moment's notice. Pisces employees tend to be selfless, and as such will sacrifice their interests for those of the common good. This sacrificial quality can work to their detriment, however, since self-effacement can lead to lowered self-esteem and ultimately to a buildup of resentments. Things work out best when Pisces employees are fully rewarded for their efforts financially and allowed to slowly climb the corporate ladder.

Interviewing and/or Hiring the Pisces Employee

Successful interviewees can offer flexibility to their new employers and back up their claims to diversity with a CV that shows the wide variety of tasks they can perform. Prospective Pisces employees are generally modest although quietly confident, and they rarely if ever blow their own trumpet. They know how to make a good appearance, keenly aware of how they look and of current styles and tastes in fashion. They will be quite honest about whether they think they are suited for the job after hearing more about it. Should the interview go smoothly, they are usually agreeable to start work immediately if needed.

Breaking Bad News to or Firing the Pisces Employee

Pisces employees are able to handle bad news, and they may already have anticipated it by the time you break it to them. Usually they will not try to deny their responsibility for what happened; in fact they may even blame themselves more than is necessary, often out of a desire to protect others. In serious cases they are more likely to offer their resignation than wait for the ax to fall. When it comes to things not working out, these realists have sufficient awareness to know when enough is enough and that a parting of the ways is mandatory.

Traveling with and Entertaining the Pisces Employee

Pisces employees travel well, but not often. On such occasional business trips they can be reserved and highly appreciative of all comforts that are provided for them. Not overly demanding of entertainment, they have a weakness for good food and prefer to spend a free evening sitting with you in a quiet restaurant that serves quality cuisine. Pisces employees are also extremely helpful in making plans and reservations beforehand, particularly in cities that they have visited before. Prone to having favorite haunts, they are happy to share them and show their traveling companions special places they would not necessarily see otherwise.

Assigning Tasks to the Pisces Employee

This is where Pisces employees really shine. Not only will they listen carefully to instructions and devote themselves selflessly to their tasks, but they will be flexible enough to apply their skills to a wide variety of endeavors. Pisces employees are good at fitting in with an existing team and playing their new role without hesitation or complaint. They are extremely sensitive, however, and usually do not take well to rough treatment. That said, they can usually give as good as they get and will not back down when treated unfairly, although they always prefer not to fight.

Motivating or Impressing the Pisces Employee

Pisces employees are most impressed by employers and coworkers who do their work with modesty and consideration. They are also impressed by expertise in technical matters and are frequently in awe of those miracle workers who have a profound insight into the material at hand. Working alongside such an inspirational figure can be a highly motivating factor in bringing out the best in Pisces employees. In the future they dream of being such a person, and frequently they are able to grow naturally into this type of role over an extended period.

Managing, Directing, or Criticizing the Pisces Employee

Pisces employees are not afraid of criticism and in fact welcome it when it is given freely by someone they respect. Looking on constructive comments and corrections as an important part of the educational process, Pisces employees will thank you for your advice and mean it. Another strong point is the degree to which Pisces workers can be managed and directed. At ease in a subordinate role, they are able to keep their egos out of the work, therefore dealing more effectively with what needs to be done.

The Pisces Coworker

Pisces coworkers like working in a relaxed environment in which their colleagues have a free and easy attitude toward one another. Because of their extremely sensitive natures, Pisces are vulnerable to negative feelings engendered in others and therefore are happiest when their coworkers get along. Goodwill is as important to Pisces coworkers as anything else, for they know that if this quality is present, things will flow smoothly. Sometimes Pisces coworkers do not push themselves hard enough, preferring to do just their job and submit their work on time whenever possible.

Approaching the Pisces Coworker for Advice

Pisces are naturally sympathetic people and will always lend their coworkers a shoulder to cry on. Because of their emotional orientation and empathic abilities, Pisces are able to feel the reasons behind problems and to divine the deeper motives and desires involved. They also are able to bring these realizations in a sympathetic manner that does not subject others to being upset or shocked by them. However, since Pisces coworkers have trouble distancing themselves from the pain of others, you should be careful not to upset their sensitive nature or cause them to adopt your sorrows as their own.

Approaching the Pisces Coworker for Help

Although sympathetic to your plight, Pisces coworkers do not always have enough confidence in their abilities to help you. And even if they feel they offer assistance, they may

Good-natured
Sensitive
Empathic

Vulnerable
Easily upset
Recalcitrant

Relaxed
Appreciative
Subdued

still hold back either out of a desire to remain less visible or a need to attend to their own problems first. Self-involved, Pisces tend to put themselves first. If they are able to get through their work in time, they will get back to you as soon as they can. Therefore they are of more potential help over the long term than in a pressing situation that demands immediate attention.

Traveling with and Entertaining the Pisces Coworker

Pisces's receptive nature makes them ideal companions to travel with and entertain. Highly appreciative, they will be grateful for any attention you pay to them and to efforts expended on their behalf. Do not expect them to take an active role in setting up travel arrangements or appointments, and get used to the notorious Pisces characteristic of not showing up on time. Furthermore, they need a long time to wake up in the morning. Usually only after their second cup of coffee or glass of orange juice are they conscious enough to converse with.

The Pisces Coworker Cooperating with Others

Pisces coworkers are open to cooperating with others, but they are not always able to do so, usually for personal reasons. Their problems with group endeavors usually center around their self-consciousness and lack of confidence; in more private situations they find it hard to open up, tending to be shy and reclusive. Thus with all the best intentions they will be open and even eager to help but can be impeded in these efforts by their own personalities. It is often best to let them volunteer for a project when they feel ready to start, rather than putting pressure on them to do so.

Impressing and Motivating the Pisces Coworker

Pisces coworkers are most impressed by those who treat them in a sympathetic fashion, being sensitive to their many moods and complex emotional states. Only very few of their colleagues know how to treat them, and consequently Pisces coworkers may feel alienated from the group, even to the point of manifesting paranoid tendencies. Having one good friend or associate among their coworkers who understands them and knows when and how to approach is usually key to motivating them to work. Such an individual whom they can trust may be relied on to function as an effective bridge between Pisces coworkers and their colleagues.

Persuading and/or Criticizing the Pisces Coworker

It is difficult to persuade Pisces coworkers against their will. In their stubbornness and strong likes and dislikes they may resemble the horse that can be led to water but not made to drink. Also, since they are exceedingly sensitive, they do not take well to direct criticism. When they do not feel appreciated they inevitably withdraw, grow quiet, and prove difficult to be roused from this internalized posture. Unable to express their anger and resentment, they too often fall prey to depression when unduly criticized, and thus if you want them to function effectively, you must be gentle and understanding in your approach.

The Pisces Client

Good with money, Pisces clients are not likely to waste it on fruitless endeavors. On the other hand, when they see the value in your goods or services, they will not hesitate to invest lavishly in what you have to offer. Pisces clients are highly astute in business matters and will question you thoroughly before making up their minds. It is quite likely you have already undergone an extensive vetting process before they meet with you, and they have also done a thorough investigation of your firm or department as well. Thus do not be surprised at what they already know about you.

Impressing the Pisces Client

Pisces clients are interested not only in your track record but also in your vision, in particular your ability to dream along with them in developing imaginative projects. They are most concerned with the possibility of building a personal bond that will guarantee your complete understanding of their desires and your ability to bring them into being effectively but also with sensitivity. Your capacity to anticipate their wishes is very important to them. If they feel that you are responsive enough to their desires, they will invest their money without hesitation and then leave you alone to do your work.

Selling to the Pisces Client

The Pisces client will not respond to aggressive gestures or glitzy presentations that attempt to convince them, no matter how compelling your efforts are. Sitting quietly, they will usually pose a few questions, and the success of your sale will rest almost entirely on how you answer. Thus, when such inquiries surface, take the time to respond thoughtfully, even if it requires some time. On the other hand, answers to questions that can be dealt with briefly should never ramble on. Pisces clients will be very observant of your emotional reactions and attentive to the logic of your responses.

Your Appearance and the Pisces Client

Your appearance will be important to the Pisces client, as will the condition of all written and visual materials you present. If you are lacking in any of these areas or outright sloppy, they will find it difficult to believe any of your claims or plans. Thus they are likely to judge you even more on your appearance and presentation performance than on the materials themselves. Normally they will be well groomed and dressed as a sign of respect to you but also as an indication of their quality. Pisces clients want to be proud of working with you. Do not let them down in this sense if you want to gain their respect.

Keeping the Pisces Client's Interest

Once you have impressed Pisces clients and landed the deal, they will wait to see what you can produce. However, as already indicated, they will not breathe down your neck, usually granting ample time for you to come up with results. Pisces clients do not necessarily demand anything spectacular in the first month, but if after a few months you have not shown substantial progress, they will grow increasingly nervous. Aim to produce one major success within three or four months that will really knock their socks off, and then you will be sitting pretty in their eyes for the remainder of the year.

STRENGTHS
Investigative
Astute
Generous

WEAKNESSES
Spendthrift
Insecure
Suspicious

INTERACTIVE STYLE
Thorough
Informed
Canny

Breaking Bad News to the Pisces Client

It is recommended that you adopt a somewhat devious approach here, since hitting them with the full force of negative shock may be too much for them to handle. Spread out your bad news over at least a week, and refuse, deliberately but in a subtle fashion, to release it all at once. This will also give you a wee bit of extra time to begin to recoup some of your losses or at least figure out a way to do so. Chances are that your Pisces client will allow you to proceed further once they see you were good at quickly controlling the damage and flexible enough to change course for the better.

Entertaining the Pisces Client

Pisces clients want to have a good time and will expect you to pull out all the stops in entertaining them. Any sign of stinginess will turn them off, although they will also think you foolish for wasting money or throwing it around just to impress them. Remember their love of luxury and quality and also their attraction to renowned brands. True aficionados of the good things in life, Pisces clients will enjoy sharing the enjoyment of their expensive tastes with you. Although they would not hesitate to pick up the check, they will expect you to pay and also to tip generously.

The Pisces Business Partner

Although Pisces business partners will try to be fair, at least in their minds, you must keep one eye on them at all times. Very subtle, even devious in their methods, Pisces fish are slippery customers and not easy to hold on to or control. They are quite capable of playing stupid or uttering vague statements or replies that either give you no real idea where they stand or are outright misleading. Their motives will probably remain unknown to you since they reveal little about themselves and firmly resist attempts to probe their psyches. On the other hand, they can be excellent allies against a common foe, employing their tactics effectively for your mutual benefit.

Setting Up the Business Partnership with Pisces

Make sure that the partnership is set up in a careful, orderly fashion. An excellent lawyer agreeable to both of you is essential in drawing up the initial contract. Should this not be possible, each of you will have to have separate legal representation. Make sure the contract is tight—leave little if any wiggle room, since Pisces are notorious for wriggling out of agreements previously thought to be airtight. Ruthlessly correct and eliminate all contractual ambiguities. What is not stated is often as important as what is, in this respect.

Tasking with the Pisces Business Partner

It is not a bad idea to set up tasking guidelines in the initial partnership agreement. Hold your Pisces partner to these in the early months and years of your partnership whenever possible—out of principle as well as necessity. If you allow a more fluid arrangement, you may find Pisces partners swimming away in another direction before you can stop them. Generally speaking, Pisces partners will covet the more imaginative projects and the financial decision-making, leaving more mundane matters of maintenance and sales to you. Do not leave the vision of the company entirely to your Pisces partner. They are good at it, but also capable of going completely off the rails on the wrong track.

Traveling with and Entertaining the Pisces Business Partner

You will have to watch the spending of your Pisces partner carefully; otherwise budgets will be exceeded, and before you know it you will have major credit card bills to pay. Furthermore, if they use up the budget, this will leave little opportunity for you to spend any of the money, unless you dig into your own private funds. Pisces partners have the most fun when both of you are having a good time. However, if you decide to quit early and go to bed, they have no problems partying until the wee hours without you. Travel accommodations and dining should be first-rate if you want to keep your Pisces partner in a good mood while on the road.

Managing and Directing the Pisces Business Partner

Managing and directing the Pisces business partner may seem to be going very well until one day you wake up to discover what they have really been up to. In fact, managing and directing a Pisces is not as easy as it may seem. Although they will agree to everything you say, once they are off on their own they are likely to forget everything they promised initially, and without qualms. They may not even be aware that they are breaking your trust, so distracted are they by the latest thought or opportunity that comes along.

Relating to the Pisces Business Partner in the Long Run

Once you get used to the way Pisces business partners operate and accept their unusual methods of working, things will become much easier. However, you better devote some time and trouble to the majority of the text of any good partnership contract, covering how things will be handled when they go wrong or if either of you wants to quit. You may very well be facing such a possibility with a Pisces partner who is just too difficult to control or one that has a true penchant for disaster.

Parting Ways with the Pisces Business Partner

If things are contractually sound, you can just follow the partnership agreement to the letter. Do not get in the position of having to meet your Pisces partners' ever-changing demands, or they will drive you crazy. Once the two of you agree that it is time to part ways, proceed point by point in a highly methodical fashion. Above all, watch your Pisces partner carefully during this difficult period, since their spending of the partnership's money may spin out of control and their desires to finally implement their dream projects before the company goes bust may balloon and, unfortunately, also burst, leaving you to clean up the mess.

The Pisces Competitor

Pisces competitors are tricky customers. The favorite ploy of Pisces competitors is to let you think that you are catching them, like a fish, when in fact they are catching you! They will often pretend that they have succumbed, fallen for your line and been hooked, or simply been outwitted, all the time fully aware that they fooled you and gained the advantage. While you are busy congratulating yourself or even crowing, they are already planning or executing your downfall. Therefore, do not ever take their actions at face value but look deep below the surface to divine their true tactics.

Countering the Pisces Competitor

Pisces are master tacticians, so to counter them you have to understand what they are intending to do and figure out a way to stop them. Because they are superb at luring you in, you must develop the patience to outwit them through waiting and not reacting. Once you have a chance to truly gain the advantage (and not be tricked into thinking you have, which can be fatal), you must strike and destroy their campaign without mercy. Otherwise, Pisces competitors will resume it and take their revenge months or even years later, when you least expect it.

Out-Planning the Pisces Competitor

Do not try to out-plan Pisces competitors, but force them to show their hands, thus revealing their plans. Two possibilities then exist: one, that they have designed a feint to pull you off balance and overreact to their deception; or two, that they have launched a serious, direct attack that must be responded to immediately. You will have little luck trying to out-plan the Pisces competitor before the first move is made, since they are so devious and clever, unless you have sequestered a mole or listening device within the heart of their organization. Give them a dose of their own medicine by allowing phony plans to fall into their hands and completely throw them off the track.

Impressing the Pisces Competitor in Person

Pisces competitors will be impressed by those who refuse to fall for their many ruses. They will only laugh at those who are foolish enough to believe them. Likewise, they will be impressed by opponents who look better, talk better, and are more convincing than they. Remember that Pisces opponents are among the best con artists there are; if you don't, they will remind you. For example, should you try to fool them, they very well might seem to be convinced, but just at the moment you think you have fully deceived them they may fix you with an intense stare and a firm arm grip while saying or implying: "Never con a con."

Undercutting and Outbidding the Pisces Competitor

Pisces are so fluid in their responses and light on their feet that they are difficult to undercut or outbid. Excellent bluffers, they will often sit behind quite a weak hand and force you to throw in your chips and give up before what seems a determined onslaught, but this is only a ploy. Driving up your bids for items or properties you desire as well as driving down your bids when competing for contracts with prospective clients are their specialties. It is so difficult to outpsych or even outguess a Pisces opponent that you might as well give up doing so from the start. Just stick to your guns and try not to change your mind when provoked.

Public Relations Wars with the Pisces Competitor

Most often Pisces competitors work behind the scenes. They will usually not attack your advertising and public relations campaigns directly but will subvert and sabotage them using all kinds of devious and underhanded means. Rather than mounting their own campaigns first, they are more likely to wait for you to do so and then undermine your efforts. They will try to turn your words against you, show your weaknesses and contradictions, lure you into spending money in futile attempts to match them, and gradually wear down your energy to attack and your will to resist. Well-timed, lightning thrusts can often stop them in their tracks, at least temporarily.

The Pisces Competitor and the Personal Approach

Pisces competitors can be very smooth operators, highly seductive in their abilities to hypnotize and take control of you. Even their worst enemies can be charmed by them and find themselves liking them. The best way to counter their highly manipulative approach is to greet all such overtures with stony silence and a firm refusal to believe anything you see or hear. Above all, do not try to play their game or outwit them, since you have little chance of success. You should of course be cordial, but at the same time send them an unambiguous and direct signal that you are not taken in by their line.

Love

STRENGTHS

Well-dressed

Beauty-loving

Special

WEAKNESSES

Strange

Peculiar

Manipulative

INTERACTIVE STYLE

Intriguing

Seductive

Responsive

The Pisces First Date

Pisces first dates are often immediately responsive to your advances, that is, if they find you attractive. For many Pisces, physical beauty is valued but not the most important thing. Thus your Pisces first date will be appreciative of your personality, in particular of your unusual qualities. Pisces first dates are usually searching for something special— something out of the ordinary—and you may very well fit the bill. Because clothes are important to them, they are likely to be well dressed and will expect the same from you, although overly ostentatious and expensive clothing is not a strict requirement.

Wooing and Picking Up the Pisces First Date

Meeting Pisces first dates under strange or unusual circumstances is par for the course. Usually Pisces first dates will not go out of their way to meet you, but will just kind of drift into your life, often more by chance than by plan. However, Pisces are also capable of preparing a subtle trap that reflects a bit of planning but gives the impression of being casual. Once they have attached to you, Pisces first dates are unlikely to let go until they have gotten what they want. These desires could range from just a one-time casual meeting to a prolonged love affair.

Suggested Activities for the Pisces First Date

Pisces first dates are unlikely to hold back if feelings are strong and mutual. Thus spending intimate time in a highly private setting may be more appropriate than going out on the town. Pisces are emotional people and not at all afraid of expressing their feelings, which can be decidedly romantic and sexual. Winding up in bed with a Pisces first date should not be viewed as surprising, certainly not from the Pisces point of view. Going out for a quick drink either before or after sex is also a possibility.

Turn-Ons and Turn-Offs for the Pisces First Date

The biggest turn-off for the Pisces first date will be if you do not find them attractive or if you ignore their seductive come-ons and rebuff their advances. Pisces first dates would not be with you if they did not have desires in your direction. They are easily turned on to many different kinds of people but are quite discriminating when it comes to whom they choose as their true romantic interests. Turn ons for Pisces first dates will include your being sensitive enough to immediately determine their likes and dislikes without them having to recite a checklist.

Making "the Move" with the Pisces First Date

Making the move with a Pisces first date is likely to be a mutual activity. Once certain silent signals are sent and then reinforced by the eyes and hands, everything else follows naturally, usually without interruption, except for the shedding of excess garments. Characteristic of this spontaneously unfolding process is a fluidity of movement that, once started, will rarely stop until both of you have achieved sexual satisfaction. If you have any doubts or misgivings about going so far so fast with Pisces first dates, you had better not get involved with them in the first place.

Impressing the Pisces First Date

Pisces first dates are impressed with emotional honesty and hate all forms of superficiality and phoniness. If your feelings are fake and your actions dishonest, they will know it immediately and choose not to see you again. It is the immediacy and depth of their emotional awareness that is so surprising and often gratifying, should you choose to accompany them on their exciting romantic adventure. They will be further impressed by your fearlessness and your ability to disregard conventionalities and social mores. For them, everything done out of love takes place beyond good and evil.

Brushing Off the Pisces First Date

Since Pisces first dates are not at all interested in superficialities and conventions, your critical, uptight, or condemning attitudes are enough to send them scurrying away. Pisces first dates are so sensitive to disapproval that they may even choose to confront you with the fact that things are not going well and quite candidly suggest that they not go any further at all. At any rate, the first date is likely to continue only if you and your Pisces get along and share a mutual appetite for each other. If things do not go well, termination can be abrupt and occur right in the middle of almost any activity.

The Pisces Romantic Partner

Pisces romantic partners give their all in any full-blown relationship. Even the most ordinary or prosaic pairings are given new life and suffused with the profound emotions of such a partner. Those involved with them will attest to their demanding, possessive, seductive, controlling, and passionate natures. Even the most fickle or independent romantic partner will find it difficult or impossible to carry on other relationships at the same time. Long after their Pisces mate is gone, they may well remain in an exhausted state of shock for some time to come.

STRENGTHS
Passionate
Seductive
Romantic

WEAKNESSES
Possessive
Controlling
Fearful

INTERACTIVE STYLE
All-involving
Uncompromising
Committed

Having a Discussion with the Pisces Romantic Partner

Pisces romantic partners are not at all reticent about airing grievances. Thus discussions with them are likely to consist mostly of their telling you what you are doing wrong. Born complainers, Pisces feel they have good reason to voice their dissatisfactions fully and without reserve. It is their way of processing what they feel has happened to them. There is no need for you to talk in such "discussions," only to listen and, when required, to answer their questions. Do not say too much, otherwise you will often be digging your own grave a bit deeper.

Arguments with the Pisces Romantic Partner

Forget about having arguments with Pisces, particularly if winning is what you have in mind. Tenacious in the extreme, Pisces will not give up arguing until they have fully exhausted each of you and put you both in a very bad mood, one that is likely to hang around for days or even weeks on end. Therefore, picking a fight with them is not a good idea. Better to refrain from outright arguments in favor of short remarks delivered off-the-cuff; should Pisces begin to argue, refuse to join in battle and quickly put out the fire before it becomes a raging inferno, perhaps by walking out.

Traveling with the Pisces Romantic Partner

Pisces enjoys occasional trips as well as long, extended ones. They have a knack for quick adaptation and are usually at home wherever they are. Preferring a quick change of scene to a boring permanent location (quite likely to manifest, since they bore easily), Pisces are always up for a new exciting place to fix their sights on. They prefer romantic locations; if you cannot or will not appreciate the allure of such spots, then you will eventually be unceremoniously dumped. If able to share these journeys and participate in them fully, you will have a real treat in store.

Sex with the Pisces Romantic Partner

Sex with a Pisces is usually never-ending and frequent. When Pisces is sexually attracted to a person, they may remain in a high state of arousal for weeks, months, even years. Although they can be accused of being easily excited and turned on, in fact they will give themselves fully on a deep emotional level to only a few romantic partners. With Pisces, love is exalted to a high position, and in its absence sex may assume the proportions of a prosaic, uninspired act.

Affection and the Pisces Romantic Partner

Pisces can be extremely affectionate. They are happiest when sex, romance, and affection blend naturally into a pleasing medium that they can swim around in all day and all night. Happy to share their watery medium with you, it is not absolutely necessary that you always share their feelings completely, since they can usually express and enjoy love enough for both of you. In fact, Pisces has a knack for getting involved with others who find it difficult or impossible to share such feelings, and they are then put in the position of becoming their mentors in such matters.

Humor and the Pisces Romantic Partner

Despite their seemingly serious demeanor, Pisces like nothing more than to joke, laugh, banter, and indulge in witty repartee with their romantic partners. Those who bring out this side of them are very dear to their hearts. Therefore it is not that Pisces prefers being suffering, pain-wracked individuals, but rather that they accept it as their lot in life, feeling condemned to it. When they feel they are drowning emotionally, the good humor and outright comedy generated by their partners can function as a life preserver they can hang on to until their mood clears.

The Pisces Spouse

The Pisces spouse is family-oriented and enjoys time spent at home. Pisces spouses are dedicated to raising a family, but a marriage without children makes little sense to them. Therefore if adoption is not desired by their spouses, they often seek to transfer their parental urges onto a nephew, niece, or other close family member or friend's child. So strong are the parental urges in many Pisces that their pets also become their children. The Pisces spouse can be overprotective toward their mates and overly fearful for their well-being. Although normally appreciative of attention, they do not seek such protection for themselves.

Wedding and Honeymoon with the Pisces Spouse

Although Pisces have been described as not terribly interested in sex, particularly Pisces women, this is not true when it comes to the honeymoon. A Pisces will spend lavishly on the ceremony and expect rich rewards on their wedding night, as well as those immediately following it. However, their partners are frequently the beneficiaries of such rewards. Pisces spouses love to share, and they find their most fulfilling satisfactions in the give-and-take of romance. Arranging the details of the wedding, invitations, ceremony, and the honeymoon destination, hotel, and restaurant reservations are a source of great joy for them.

Home and Day-to-Day Married Life with the Pisces Spouse

Pisces spouses are not always easy to live with on a day-to-day basis. Their biggest problem is usually depression, frequently brought on not by the marriage but by the low self-esteem that makes them feel less than useful and often inhibits their professional aspirations. Indeed, many Pisces spouses have little ambition, being content with a comfortable family life and an ordinary job. Certainly, the more unusual Pisces may lead quite an extraordinary life, but they mostly do not opt for marriage or, if they do, eventually leave the partnership out of boredom or because they feel neglected.

Finances and the Pisces Spouse

Pisces spouses are responsible enough to stick with their jobs over time and be adequate or, in some cases, outstanding breadwinners. In their managing of household accounts and budgets they can be extremely effective, appreciating the fluid nature of money and

STRENGTHS
Protective
Nurturing
Family-oriented

WEAKNESSES
Nervous
Overprotective
Closed

INTERACTIVE STYLE
Participatory
Responsible
Devoted

knowing how to spend it. Overspending is one of their biggest problems, frequently landing their families in debt, but somehow they always seem to work their way out of it. Even poverty and bankruptcy can be taken in stride, endured, and ultimately surmounted.

Infidelity and the Pisces Spouse

Pisces are unfaithful only when they are misused, abused, or neglected by their spouses. Even then, they may remain faithful, suffering painful encounters with their mates and falling into deep depressions but refusing to give up. There is an undeniable masochistic streak in many Pisces that makes one sometimes suspect that they enjoy their suffering, and certainly being able to talk about it. Their constant complaining, even in fairly happy periods, can wear down their partners and strain their marriages. Some family members sometimes wonder why they ever got married in the first place.

Children and the Pisces Spouse

Pisces spouses are usually completely devoted to their children, sometimes too much so. Their claiming and overprotective attitudes toward their progeny can severely cripple their development and produce young adults who are overly dependent on their Pisces parent. Part of the problem is the Pisces penchant for fearfulness and suffering that can make their children feel terribly guilty and insecure about their actions. Thus their kids' confidence is undermined, frequently leading to neurotic behavior in adulthood. It is essential, therefore, that Pisces parents learn to let go and to encourage their children to be more responsible and independent.

Divorce and the Pisces Spouse

The divorced Pisces spouse often appears to the world as a truly lost soul. Once Pisces are deprived of daily family interactions, they tend to flounder and sink into the depths of despair. One exception is a Pisces spouse who has the courage to divorce after suffering years of unhappiness; these souls may experience the exhilaration of being set free. Other divorced Pisces spouses of a healthy type will remarry after a few years, frequently to someone very different from their first mate, a person who is more deeply appreciative of them. However, a more emotionally damaged Pisces may remarry a person remarkably like their ex and start the same cycle of suffering and abuse all over again.

The Pisces Lover

Pisces lovers can frequently be found falling in love with love again and again, rather than with a real person. Deluding themselves into thinking they truly love another being, they are in fact indulging their narcissistic and highly idealistic urges. Repeating the same patterns of enthrallment quickly followed by passionate and jealously possessive behavior in which they torment themselves and their lovers, they run the gamut of the pleasures and pains that high romance can offer. Perhaps no better description of a Pisces love affair has been given than these lyrics from the theme song of the film *Casablanca*: "Moonlight and love songs never out of date / Hearts full of passion, jealousy, and hate."

Meeting the Pisces Lover

Pisces lovers are extremely sensitive to the needs of others, particularly when they feel they can cure the unhappiness or neglect that another person is suffering. They will give of themselves selflessly and lavish their energies on a relationship in which they feel needed. Many Pisces lovers are fulfilling secret fantasies in which they appear as the savior of creatures even more helpless than themselves, and in giving love they feel elevated in their own eyes. Too often the results are two people rather than just one drowning in a sea of emotion. Building true self-esteem invariably necessitates Pisces lovers dropping such hurtful attitudes.

Location and the Pisces Lover

Either of your homes will do as long as total privacy is guaranteed. Often their place functions better, particularly when they are single and when you are seeking refuge from an abusive spouse or live-in lover. For Pisces, their places carry feelings of protection, at times resembling a kind of comfortable cocoon or grotto in which they can effectively retreat from the world. Frequent visits to such a location will soon raise the idea of your moving in permanently, but such a situation is unlikely to work out. Once you are caught in the net of a Pisces lover, a whole new set of problems may begin to emerge that make your original relationship look not so difficult in comparison.

Sex and the Pisces Lover

Sex with your Pisces lover can be extremely satisfying, particularly if they are lonely and you are unhappy enough. These negative feelings somehow mesh and produce ecstatic sexual highs, punctuated of course by further loneliness and cravings that simply must once more be allayed and satisfied. Once caught on the old roller-coaster of sex and love addiction, it is extremely difficult to get off, particularly when sharing the ride with a Pisces lover. When things become frantic, family members and friends may also get involved emotionally or, if they remain objective, just sit and gape in amazement over such cavortings.

Holding On to the Pisces Lover

Holding on to a Pisces lover can be as impossible as trying to grapple with a slippery fish in its element, water. Quite quickly you will see that the one thing that really turns them on is your suffering, and consequently the continuity of your relationship with them will directly depend on the abuse you are supposedly suffering at the hands of another. Sympathy leads to comforting, comforting to desire, desire to passion, and the whole crazy roller-coaster ride starts all over again. Consequently, holding on to your Pisces lover may entail your holding on to your own unhappiness.

(The Pisces Lover)

STRENGTHS
Giving
Appreciative
Responsive

WEAKNESSES
Suffering
Narcissistic
Deluded

INTERACTIVE STYLE
Enthralled
Tormented
Intense

Entertaining the Pisces Lover

Pisces lovers relish being told how wonderful they are, particularly when compared with that evil person who is causing you such grief. It is not at all uncommon for Pisces lovers to tell jokes about such an individual and gloat over having outwitted them, all the while oblivious that your relationship is built around the common hatred of a third person. Healthier activities with a Pisces lover would include going out for a meal, a film, or a party with friends, but generally the paranoia over being seen together in public will force you both to hide out at home.

Breaking Up with the Pisces Lover

Since breaking up with a Pisces lover can signal your finally being ready to drop the pain and suffering involved, you will frequently find yourself in a less passionate but healthier state. Your Pisces lover need not be pitied, for surely enough they will find another suffering soul to attach to, and hopefully you will find a well-balanced and less needy individual as well.

The Pisces Ex

STRENGTHS
Honest
Natural
Forgiving

WEAKNESSES
Difficult
Destabilizing
Unhappy

INTERACTIVE STYLE
Vague
Uncertain
Timid

It may take a while, but once Pisces exes have truly finished with you they will generally not return or even attempt to make contact. It is the period between the initial breakup and this point of no return that can be uncertain and trying. Like two fish swimming around in different directions (the Pisces symbol), these people have a great deal of difficulty making up their minds, often changing course from day to day. Your Pisces ex can thus have a very destabilizing effect on your life and that of the family. They are generally not vindictive, though their uncertainty is real and not usually a tactic they employ.

Establishing a Friendship with the Pisces Ex

Pisces exes do not object to forming friendships, but because they no longer trust you after a breakup, they can never enter into one wholeheartedly. Extremely suspicious of all overtures and statements of intent concerning the formation of such a friendship, it is best to avoid the subject altogether and allow your actions to speak for themselves. Do not expect your Pisces ex to make overtures, since they usually retreat into their own little world and do not seek to initiate contact. Normally an absence or lack of arguments and strife is about the best you can hope for.

Issues of Getting Back Together with the Pisces Ex

Although watery, weak, and vague in many ways, Pisces exes are quite adamant about getting back together: the answer is invariably *no*. They will point out that they are upset and not in an emotional state to discuss such a possibility, pointing out that you have hurt them so much they are not about to come back for a second helping, at least not quickly. Pisces exes take a long time before their feelings are settled enough to speak objectively about most matters, including this one.

Discussing Past Issues with the Pisces Ex

Pisces exes really pile it on you, laying on all kinds of trips. When their aggressive negativity gets to be too much, you may do well to repeat the mantra, "Blame, blame, guilt and shame," until they finally understand what they are doing. Coming to such a realization concerning their endlessly repetitive statements is difficult for them, so intent are they on raising every last example of your inexcusable and atrocious behavior. Attempts on your part to excuse yourself or apologize for such deeds will fall on deaf ears.

Expressing Affection to the Pisces Ex

Pisces generally respond to affection, but in the case of Pisces exes they are so suspicious of your motives that they will find it difficult or impossible to accept. The best you can hope for is to build trust with them over years until they finally reach a point where they can allow you to make overtures of this sort. Likewise, do not expect them to express affection to you, and if they do, you can be sure there is some wayward feeling, probably one of which they are unaware, that is prompting them to do so.

Defining the Present Relationship with the Pisces Ex

The present relationship with the Pisces ex is liable to fluctuate so much—particularly to oscillate between extremes—that it will be impossible to define. This means that from day to day and week to week you will be able to be sure of only one certainty—its uncertainty. Making predictions and coming to fixed agreements will be extremely difficult, and you may have to rely on the constancy of the original divorce papers as the only fixed reference point, as changes of feelings on both sides will destabilize any ability to keep to agreed-upon decisions.

Sharing Custody with the Pisces Ex

The Pisces ex usually has a strong emotional bond with their children and will suffer terribly in their absence. If a fair agreement can be worked out for both parents to share custody equally, you should propose this option to your Pisces ex, rather than attempting to gain full custody. Even if such custody distribution is fair, you must expect constant upset in matters concerning the children, which will be directly proportional to the degree of emotional upset that your Pisces ex is undergoing at the time. Often the children can be relied upon more than any other factor to help keep the extreme emotionality of their Pisces parent under control.

Friends and Family

STRENGTHS
Giving
Sharing
Generous

WEAKNESSES
Time-consuming
Overemotional
Spendthrift

INTERACTIVE STYLE
Interesting
Selective
Devoted

The Pisces Friend

Pisces are a never-ending fascination to those who are lucky enough to become their fast friends. Moreover, their sensitivity and responsiveness guarantee that they will be well aware of your emotional state and highly respectful of your feelings. Pisces friends can be particularly counted on in times of need. Although their own friends are usually limited in number, they value friendship highly and, as with most other areas of their lives, value quality more than quantity. The door to a Pisces house is always open to you as their dear friend, and they are very giving and generous when it comes to helping out in times of need.

Asking for Help from the Pisces Friend

Normally you do not even have to ask for help from Pisces friends, since they will have already assessed your circumstances and volunteered their assistance before you know it. Pisces friends know what it is to be down and out, or to suffer, and because of their extreme empathy are likely to put themselves immediately in your place. In many ways, your pain is their pain; this grants instant sympathy with your plight and awakens a desire to help. When Pisces friends make promises of aid, they can be counted to go through with them.

Communication and Keeping in Touch with the Pisces Friend

Pisces often lead low-key, private lives, and even those in the public eye are extremely protective of their personal affairs. Therefore, whether they are the more withdrawn or the public type, they do not always have the time or inclination to keep or initiate contact with you on a regular basis. However, they will almost always respond to your contacting them, and it is this approach that is recommended in most instances. Rarely will they reject your advances once they have admitted you to the hallowed circle of their friends. If they take a while to get back in touch, do not be surprised: Pisces can be slow movers.

Borrowing Money from the Pisces Friend

Pisces friends will share whatever they have with those closest to them, including money. For them money is like anything else they own, there to be shared, and requesting it from them will not set off alarm bells. Since Pisces spend money freely, it may take some time before they are flush enough to help you out, but help you they will. Rarely will they ask for money back or request a formal loan, but should they need it they will take for granted that you will reciprocate in kind. Generosity is a true characteristic of Pisces friends.

Asking for Advice from the Pisces Friend

Pisces friends are often reluctant to give advice because they are so respectful of the points of view of others and so modest about their own abilities in this area. However, if you insist, they will respond with counsel. Remember that such opinions will usually be highly subjective, since everything a Pisces does, thinks, and says is colored by emotion. You may, therefore, refuse to follow their advice literally, but rather pick and choose certain helpful tidbits and take them under serious consideration. Pisces friends will not object to this selective procedure, being happy to help in any way they can.

Visiting the Pisces Friend

Although they value their privacy highly, Pisces friends do not require that you make an appointment to see them beforehand. They like to have their close friends drop in unannounced, frequently welcoming such interruptions as pleasant distractions from their many moods and often as just the right antidote to lift them out of melancholy or depression. Pisces friends take your desire to visit with them as a true compliment, perhaps the highest one of all. They are also open to meeting for a drink or meal but will rarely knock on your door, preferring to meet you on the street or on the way out of your dwelling or workplace.

Celebrations/Entertainment with the Pisces Friend

As an occasional relief from their inward and private existence, Pisces friends love entertainment and celebrations from time to time, but they cannot usually handle large groups of people, preferring quieter evenings at home or out with a few intimate friends. That said, once a year or so they are capable of throwing big, loud, noisy bashes, for which they pull out all the stops and let it all hang out. Their extravagance in hosting such shindigs is legendary. They will cook, provide all the drinks, do the decorations, and treat each individual friend in a special way that shows their true affection and love.

The Pisces Roommate

Pisces roommates are not difficult to deal with as long as they have their own guaranteed, inviolable, private space. Once this is established and you know not to intrude upon it, things can work out well. Should you need them, simply knocking on the door or calling their name will be sufficient. However, there are times when they will ignore

STRENGTHS

Helpful

Domestic

Private

WEAKNESSES

Reclusive

Unresponsive

Self-absorbed

INTERACTIVE STYLE

Adaptable

Moneywise

Contributing

such a summons, treating it is an untimely interruption. Normally Pisces roommates, no matter how far-out they are (and they can get pretty far out there, in a cosmic sense), are available to help with daily domestic chores and to come up with rent and food money, although they tend to be late in most things.

Sharing Financial Responsibilities with the Pisces Roommate

As long as Pisces roommates know what their responsibilities are, they will fulfill them to the best of their ability. However, all responsibilities should be carefully spelled out, since sometimes Pisces hear only what they want to hear; consequently, things can get pretty vague and ambiguous unless you are clear. Even when they acknowledge having heard what you said, they can be off on cloud nine again in a few minutes, leaving all responsible thoughts behind. It is best to write down all of their financial responsibilities on paper and even get them to sign it.

Cleaning and the Pisces Roommate

Pisces roommates get a lot of satisfaction through cleaning and keeping things tidy. Yet with even the best intentions, they are capable of accumulating and generating messes that must be seen to be believed. Their particular form of chaos usually involves simply dropping whatever is in their hands on the floor when finished with it. Consequently, you will not have much trouble finding them—you only need to follow their trail. Once Pisces roommates are rounded up and enlisted for a cleaning team, you will find them to be excellent cleaners, with a real eye toward making things look beautiful.

Houseguests and the Pisces Roommate

Pisces roommates usually have only a very few close friends, but they like to feel that these individuals are welcome to stay with them at all times. This could mean one of them walking through the door at almost any hour or, even worse, ringing the bell and awakening you in the middle of the night. Furthermore, Pisces roommates believe in sharing everything with their friends, inevitably including things that either are shared domestically or belong to you outright. This fact can create real difficulties, for you have to watch Pisces roommates being overly generous with your personal property.

Parties and the Pisces Roommate

Usually when you throw a big bash for your friends, your Pisces roommates will arrange not to be at home at all. If they must stay, they will probably barricade themselves into their room and refuse to emerge. On the other hand, when you and your roommate(s) decide to throw a party together, Pisces roommates will take part avidly, albeit in a subdued manner, until the tempo of the gathering reaches its climax, at which point they may exhibit extremely extroverted behavior. Pisces roommates like letting it all hang out from time to time, and what better occasion than a party at home to do so.

Privacy and the Pisces Roommate

Extremely private people, Pisces will insist that you exercise discretion in guaranteeing domestic peace and quiet, curbing your enthusiastic impulses most of the time. Pisces regard loud noises and sounds as forms of pollution, so you will have to keep the volume level of your stereo cranked down most of the time. Furthermore, Pisces roommates have a thing about bathrooms. They will want to be guaranteed long periods of time in there without interruption, so they can attend fully and completely to bathing or showering, personal hygiene, styling, and all other bodily functions.

Discussing Problems with the Pisces Roommate

Pisces roommates usually have enough personal problems on their mind that they won't want to indulge in much conversation about domestic difficulties, particularly ones you might be having with them. Most often Pisces roommates look on you and the domestic space as providing relief from their inner turmoil. Thus they do not want to discuss problems with you, but at certain times they may need to unburden their tortured souls and even ask you for advice or help. You will make it easier for them to do so by simply remarking that they look unhappy and perhaps need to talk about it.

The Pisces Parent

Pisces parents are extremely dedicated to the welfare and personal growth of their children. Such parents not only have a tremendous need to have children but also to invest substantial energies in the years required to raise them to young adulthood. Pisces parents are proud of their children and anxious to give them the best opportunities. They also enjoy having fun with their kids and will schedule activities in which the whole family can take part. At times overly fearful and claiming, Pisces parents must show that they have confidence in their children by encouraging them to be independent. Only then can their children grow up to be individuals capable of standing on their own two feet.

Discipline Style of the Pisces Parent

Generally speaking, Pisces parents find most forms of discipline highly distasteful. Even when they feel it is necessary to punish their children, they find it difficult or even impossible to enforce discipline. Physical punishment is usually out of the question, running counter to their empathic feelings and their inability to inflict pain on loved ones. Grounding is a distinct possibility to try to set limits on teenagers, as well as a range of warnings, from sharp reprimands to a hand signal. Too often the children of Pisces parents are simply allowed to run wild, unfortunately.

Affection Level and the Pisces Parent

Pisces parents love to spoil their children, and part of that process is lavishing affection on them. The children of Pisces parents feel especially blessed to receive so much attention, but at the same time a spoiled child can develop huge problems that could possibly have been averted with less permissive and rewarding parental attitudes. Thus Pisces parents mean well but too often produce flawed results through being overly generous and understanding. The children of Pisces parents are not always adequately prepared for the realities of a hard, hard world.

STRENGTHS
Nurturing
Caring
Loving

WEAKNESSES
Fearful
Claiming
Possessive

INTERACTIVE STYLE
Protective
Enthusiastic
Proud

Money Issues and the Pisces Parent

Pisces parents are all too prone to lavish gifts on their children, including generous allowances that can be spent as the young ones see fit. In order to balance such generosity, they should also spend the necessary time teaching their children the value of money and some lessons on thrift and savings. Also, Pisces parents should encourage their children to earn money, particularly by performing difficult or demanding household chores. That way their progeny will not be on the receiving end of a silver platter.

Crises and the Pisces Parent

Pisces parents tend to be nervous worriers. Unaware that they are putting their fears into the minds of their offspring, they may in fact be causing crises rather than preventing them. Furthermore, the danger here is of repetitive behavior patterns being instilled in their children, often resulting from a poor self-image and lack of confidence. In crisis situations, Pisces parents can keep their more frantic and sensitive side under control and act swiftly and decisively to protect their own. This holds true for their children's friends and for family pets as well.

Holidays/Family Gatherings and the Pisces Parent

Pisces parents are able to throw marvelous parties for their children and to make substantial contributions to the success of family gatherings. When it comes to holidays, however, they enjoy spending them with their kids or with their spouse alone. When going off with spouses, or completely alone, they will normally find the best person available to help with the children in their absence. Pisces parents will also take cousins under their wings and treat them with the same tender loving care as their own children. Aunts and uncles are, generally speaking, trusting of their judgment.

Caring for the Aging Pisces Parent

Aging Pisces parents are thankful for all the help they can get. Since their lives invariably become more internalized and their needs more fixed and evident, the responsibility of taking care of them inevitably falls to their children. The greatest need of most aging Pisces parents is to be taken out for walks, occasional social events, and entertainment or special dinners, so they do not feel like shut-ins who are locked away. Often by keeping their spirits up and furnishing short periods of daily nursing care, the children can find their elderly Pisces parents doing surprisingly well. Being forgotten and neglected by their family is the worst-case scenario for the aging Pisces parent.

The Pisces Sibling

An atypical situation can arise when a Pisces sibling is the oldest child. Frequently such children are extremely protective toward their siblings and sweet and loving to them in the bargain. Living contradictions of the usually repressive and dominant older child prototype, an eldest Pisces sibling usually reflects the more passive and caring qualities of the Pisces personality. However, such a child can leave a gap in the leadership role of the sibling group that will have to be assumed by a younger child. Younger Pisces siblings are usually gently tucked into the bosom of the family and have comfortable, albeit highly sheltered, childhoods.

Rivalry/Closeness with the Pisces Sibling

Rivalries with Pisces siblings are usually only low-level conflicts. Although a more passive Pisces will occasionally be forced to fight for recognition, for the most part they are satisfied with their position in the family hierarchy and not overly competitive with their brothers and sisters. They tend to be close to all of their siblings but particularly close to one, often of the opposite sex in larger families. It is precisely with the close sibling that a Pisces will have the most competitive confrontations, usually in good fun and the right spirit.

Past Issues and the Pisces Sibling

Pisces siblings feel childhood hurts very strongly and do not let go of such feelings easily. Thus a Pisces sibling is likely to carry scars or even open wounds into adulthood that they cannot and will not allow to heal. Learning to be mature and able to accept past pain and put it behind them is one of the chief challenges in the development of any Pisces sibling, particularly when the infractions involve the actions or words of a brother or sister. Pisces siblings have a great need for harmony in their family group and are quite likely to suffer deeply when their brothers and sisters are not getting along, even to the point of becoming ill.

Dealing with the Estranged Pisces Sibling

Pisces in general have a tendency to feel overlooked, neglected, and ignored. They also tend to fall into patterns of hurt and feeling sorry for themselves. Because of these characteristics it may be difficult to deal with an estranged Pisces sibling who feels wronged or rejected. Sending sensitive feelers out to such Pisces siblings and persisting with honest and wise approaches are challenges that must be met if the Pisces family member is to be brought back into the fold. Pisces will respond to apologies that they feel are meant sincerely, and that the attempts at reconciliation with them are heartfelt and genuine, rather than pro forma.

Money Issues (Borrowing Money, Wills, Etc.) and the Pisces Sibling

Pisces siblings expect to be prominently mentioned in wills, and when they are not they may feel extreme anguish. More important than money or objects is the appreciation and love expressed to them by the departed one. Just a kind word in a will or testament can be enough emotional food for them. Money that is left to Pisces will usually be spent with consideration for what the deceased would have wanted or approved of. As far as borrowing money from a Pisces sibling is concerned, they are happy to share what they have with their brothers and sisters if they have it and rarely demand repayment, certainly not for smaller sums.

(The Pisces Sibling)

STRENGTHS
Protective
Nurturing
Caring

WEAKNESSES
Passive
Undirected
Uninspiring

INTERACTIVE STYLE
Low-key
Watchful
Considerate

Holidays/Celebrations/Reunions
and the Pisces Sibling

Pisces siblings can take an active role in these activities. They are nostalgic and sentimental creatures who have a soft spot for their brothers and sisters when it comes to reminiscing about the old days as children together. Taking photos is often a favorite hobby of Pisces siblings, who act as informal chroniclers of the family's past. Creating scrapbooks to pass around at family gatherings is one of their favorite ways of sharing with siblings, parents, and their own children. They are never happier than when good feelings reign.

Vacationing with the Pisces Sibling

Pisces siblings love to be part of what is going on. Unfortunately, their negative side often makes them feel left out, even when that is not really the case. Therefore wise parents will give them that extra-special bit of attention to guarantee they do not feel excluded by their brothers and sisters. Often the success or failure of a vacation rests in the hands of the Pisces child. After one negative experience, their siblings will either want to leave them at home with other family members or attend to their needs more studiously, at least as insurance against another bad experience. Pisces siblings invariably react positively to such special treatment.

The Pisces Child

Pisces children can be soft and sweet, bringing out the love of their parents. But they can also be very difficult, for their moods are frequently out of sync with the feelings of those around them. Capable of dropping emotional bombshells and freaking out when they are misunderstood, Pisces children have "handle with care" written all over them. Extreme sensitivity is their hallmark, but when they are happy and feel accepted and understood they light up their space and fill others with joy. Nothing is sadder than watching a Pisces child suffer; however, when they are making life miserable for you at the same time, it can be difficult to sympathize.

Personality Development and the Pisces Child

If Pisces children are treated in a wise and sensitive manner by an understanding parent, they will traverse the stages of personality development with ease. If, however, they are deprived and feel frustrated and misunderstood, they are likely to battle with their parents and the world at almost every stage. Somehow even the most difficult Pisces children make it through, but not without scars on both sides, their own and their parents'. Happy Pisces children respond to love and warmth as naturally as a flower turns toward the light, but when upset they find affection difficult to accept and will even reject it.

Hobbies/Interests/Career Paths for the Pisces Child

Pisces children often have a variety of hobbies and interests. These are usually confined to childhood, and they grow out of most of them. Rarely will their adult career be presaged in their childhood leisure-time pursuits and play. For most Pisces there is a strict separation between childhood and young adulthood. They seem to be two totally different worlds, and some do not even recognize Pisces children when they are grown up. Learning to be playful again in adult life is a major challenge for most Pisces.

Discipline and the Pisces Child

Pisces children react very badly to severe disciplinary methods and punishment. They may send them into a tailspin and a pattern of breaking rules, thus bringing on more punishment with accompanying suffering. The problem with Pisces children running afoul of rules and being disciplined is that, once they have fallen into this pattern, it will be almost as if they accept it as normal, forcing them to repeat their mistakes in a never-ending cycle. Therefore Pisces children should not be disciplined as other kids would be, but treated with special consideration of their highly sensitive natures.

Affection Level and the Pisces Child

Pisces children need more affection than most. Cuddles, hugs, kisses, and smiles are all healthy and essential ingredients in their daily diets. A Pisces child deprived of affection is a sorry sight—a bit like a bedraggled chicken. The withdrawal of affection can cause them to fall ill, both psychologically and physically. It is one of the cruelest things parents can do to Pisces offspring. A lifesaver would be a favorite dog or cat the Pisces child can turn to for affection. A little friend or close sibling may also help make up for the deficit, but normally Pisces children need to receive love directly from their parents.

Dealing with the Pisces Child and Interactions with Siblings

It is hard for parents not to be protective of their Pisces children, and they sometimes try too hard to get the siblings to accept them. Furthermore, once branded with the stigma of favored child, they are likely to evoke envy and jealousy, worsening the situation. Parents must draw a fine line between being just protective enough of the Pisces child while not evoking antagonism and hurting the feelings of their other children. Sometimes it is better to let all the children work things out without parental intervention. Once the storms clear, they may well have solved the problem by themselves.

Interacting with the Adult Pisces Child

Many Pisces leave their childhood behind them, metamorphosing into a different creature when reaching adulthood. The biggest problem for adult Pisces children is getting back in touch with their youth through a reawakening of their inner child. Frequently they must wait until they become parents. Only when they have their own children can they come back into true contact with the essential magic of childhood, adding an objective understanding of this period that they lacked when young. True for Pisces perhaps more than most is the thought: "Adults grow up to be children."

(The Pisces Child)

STRENGTHS

Joyful

Happy

Glowing

WEAKNESSES

Despairing

Misunderstood

Rejected

INTERACTIVE STYLE

Sensitive

Reactive

Demanding